From Graven Images

FROM GRAVEN IMAGES

Patterns of
Modern Materialism

Chandra Mukerji

Columbia University Press
New York 1983

Library of Congress Cataloging in Publication Data

Mukerji, Chandra.
    From graven images.

    Bibliography: p.
    Includes index.
    1. Consumption (Economics)—History.   2. Popular
culture—History.   3. Materialism—History.
4. Printing—History.   5. Europe—Manufactures—
History.   I. Title.
HC51.M77   1983   338.4'76862'09   83-10148
ISBN 0-231-05266-2
ISBN 0-231-05167-0 (pbk.)

Columbia University Press
New York   Guildford, Surrey

To Bennett, Kenneth, and Kristin

Contents

Preface

WE LIVE in a primarily artificial world, in an environment we once would have called "man-made." Although we may recognize from time to time our dependence on cars, computers, televisions, and supermarkets, and although we may realize that not all human beings have had these things, we know relatively little about how our world came to be filled with these objects or to what extent their proliferation has shaped our social life.

In the affluent 1950s and 1960s it was chic for sociologists to ridicule the "plastic bubbles" we lived in and to shake our heads at the number of plastic forks and paper wrappers that we threw away. But this joke grew less funny in the 1970s as plastics factories closed for lack of oil and increasing inflation began to diminish our affluence. It became hard to sneer at three-car families when so many families were humiliated by their inability to keep one car running.

Suddenly the newspapers were filled with stories about the sagging economy that told of young couples unable to buy their own houses and old people freezing to death in the winter because they could not afford the insulation or fuel they needed. These stories began to reveal how much we depended for both our sense of social legitimacy and our physical well-being on our material environment.

The seventies also seemed to bring a rash of lessons about the potential dangers of this artificial world. Information about the hazards of asbestos factories, nuclear reactors, and chemical dumps began to suggest that this environment that had been built to protect us from the vagaries of nature had its own dangers, including threats to our emotional and physical well-being.

In all these ways, the news of the 1970s began to make our artificial environment seem an important issue for precisely the opposite reasons that it had attracted attention in the 1950s, i.e., by revealing some of the effects of its disintegration. But the news did not provide the theoretical basis for understanding how this environment affected social process because these stories were written as statements on the *economy*, as indications that Americans were caught in a maze of financial and technological problems, stemming both from international trade and the nature of the domestic economy. But these news items were not simply records of economic woes; they were also statements about a culture that identifies cars with freedom, houses with adulthood, and patterns of consumption with social status. They were indicators of a materialism that pervades modern society, that makes objects and objective measures essential for providing the meanings we take for granted in our daily lives.

This book examines the origins of this culture. It begins in the fifteenth and sixteenth centuries, during what historians call the commercial revolution or the beginning of the early modern period, a time when expanding trade changed the European economy and the kinds of goods that Europeans used in their daily lives. It tries to find there some of the long-standing patterns by which Westerners have become attached to their objects—their homes, their clothing, and their books.

There is some reason to look to this period to begin to locate these patterns. The construction of the "man-made" environment has not been a gradual and continuous process spanning all of human history; the manipulation of the fabricated world to solve human problems has grown in fits and starts. Only in the last four hundred years has it been rapid enough to stimulate a complete reorganization of social process as the growth of capitalist forms of trade and manufacture has provided the means for creating a material revolution, and the development of materialist values has provided the reasons for continuing it. Together capitalism and materialism have given birth to a new type of social order, one centrally organized around the domination of nature for the manufacture and use of material culture.

Anthropologists know a great deal about the ways in which the patterned uses of material culture (like ritual exchanges during rites of passage) can permeate social process. And some of the best of them, like Marshall Sahlins and Mary Douglas, have even studied the complex uses of goods in the materialist culture of the West. But they have not clearly delineated the connections between the historical development of capitalism in the West and the growth of this culture, and therefore they are limited in their abilities to explain contemporary crises in Western materialism.

Most sociological theories of culture are similarly deficient because they have not followed Georg Simmel's lead in examining the cultural bases for economic behavior. Sociological theorists still cling to the traditional Weberian view of the relationship between culture and capitalism, which takes religion as the cultural prime mover. The value of extending and revising these theories (as I try to do in this book) is to understand those facets of contemporary society tied to the materialist culture born in the West some centuries ago.

Acknowledgments

HOW DO you begin to thank people who have made it possible for you to write a book that turned out better than you expected? The answer, by convention, is that you put them in your acknowledgments. It does not seem like very much. But there seem to be no alternatives. No publisher would pay to print an exhaustive account of all the good advice and warnings provided to an author. So it must suffice to be brief and conventional.

I am particularly grateful for the generous and patient help of my husband, Bennett Berger, who saw more of the painful beginnings of this project than anyone should be expected to see but who has continued to support my work with concern and detachment. His critic's eye has been unfailing and always useful. His patience has been a blessing.

Joseph Gusfield has also given his time and deep knowledge of both sociology and history to protect me from my ignorance and help me find a theory worth presenting. Robert Ritchie has given me the pleasure of both his encouragement and the keys to new literature. Murray Davis has prodded me with his fine wit when I was getting bored and boring, stimulating my mind with his knowledge of and insights into social process. David Phillips has continued to help me discipline my ideas and find ways to show them to best advantage, even though I have no way to repay him for my accumulating debt. Kristin Luker has given me numerous readings of this manuscript to help me sharpen my prose and thought. Her continued encouragement has helped to ward off bouts of writer's despair and her criticisms have made me a better writer. Tim McDaniel and Rae Blumberg have also been generous with their time and minds, reading and commenting on this work in ways that proved particularly beneficial. And Gerald Holton, Alvin Gouldner, and Howard Becker have all read chapters of this manuscript and provided both editorial and substantive criticisms that have tightened this piece and corrected some of its inaccuracies.

I am also thankful to the Southern California Early Modernists for their stern critiques of my efforts at historical analysis as well as the kind support of some of its members, namely, Robert Ritchie and Hillel Schwartz.

I am indebted to the typists, Andrea Dougherty and Beverly Strong, who patiently accepted my never-ending changes and carefully read the scratches that I took to be the text of this book. And I am even more deeply indebted to the CATT consultants, Rick Accurso and Mike O'Hagan, who enabled me to learn word-processing and saved my book from my inadvertent attempts to erase it.

Finally, I must thank the University of Chicago Press for allowing me to reproduce the table from Smelser's *Social Change in the Industrial Revolution*, Cambridge University Press for giving me permission to use the figure from Deane and Cole's *British Economic Growth*, and both the Kenyon Review and Countryman Press for allowing me to quote from Frederick Turner's "The Return." I am equally indebted to the Metropolitan Museum of Art, the Pierpont Morgan Library, the Huntington Library, the British Library, the Victoria and Albert Museum, the New York Public Library, the Research Library at UCLA, the Art Museums of San Francisco, the Los Angeles County Museum of Art, the National Gallery of Art, the Frick Collection, the Houghton Library at Harvard University, the Rhode Island Historical Society and the libraries at the University of California, San Diego for facilitating this research and/or providing photographs for illustrating the text.

None of these kind people or institutions are responsible for the content of this book. The faults that remain are mine. But none of this work would have been possible without the gracious aid given by my friends and colleagues.

What we miss [in Vietnam]
are the bourgeois trivia of capitalism:
the smell of a new house, fresh drywall, resin
adhesive, vinyl, new hammered studs; ground coffee
in a friend's apartment in San Francisco, the
first day of the trip; the crisp upholstery
of a new car, its anodized aluminum
dials, the flick of the synchromesh gearshift
white metal gears in their bath of light oil, the glass
tinting the dullest day at the zenith to a
fantastic halcyon glow, the snaking response
of four hundred twenty-eight cubes (yes we know
they wanted the offshore oil); the sound of a fridge
coming on at two in the morning, quiet suburban
night; there was a tenderness, life, a wild hope in all
that technology, there *is* an undeserved good;
the open channel beam of a powerful stereo
system before the record begins, a subliminal
boom like the sound of a disused cello, dust
in the air drones. . . . It is the things
money *can* buy we remember, the innocence
of our unfallen materialism. . . .

— From Frederick Turner's "The Return"

CHAPTER ONE

Patterns of Modern Materialism

Asia refreshes us with Spices, Recreates us with Perfumes, Cures us with Drougs, and Adorns us with Jewels; *Africa* Sends us Ivory and Gold; *America*, Silver, Sugar and Cotton; *France, Spain* and *Italy*, give us Wine, Oyl and Silk: *Russia* Warms us in Furs; *Swethen*, supplies us with Copper; *Denmark*, and the Northern Tracts, with Masts, and Materials for Shipping, without which, all this were nothing. It is Commerce, and Navigation that Breeds, and Accomplishes that most honourable and useful Race of Men (the Pillars of all Magnificence) to skill in the Exportation of Superfluities, Importation of Necessaries. —John Evelyn, *Navigation and Commerce*, 1674[1]

IN THE fifteenth and sixteenth centuries the markets of Western Europe were filled with silks, pottery, woolens, spices, potatoes and other foodstuffs, and woods, both exotic ones for inlays in fine furniture and lumber for building the ships that would move other goods into and around this flourishing continent. Homes of wealthy merchants and aristocrats began to fill with painted portraits, oriental rugs, tea services, and upholstered chairs; their grounds sprouted gardens set out in intricate knot patterns, terraces filled with fruit trees, and (increasingly) flowerbeds set with bulbs that were being discovered elsewhere and imported into Europe. Consumer goods spread quickly, becoming so common that even before the seventeenth century they were already found in the homes of peasants and laborers; these poor people indulged in such "frivolities" as pins, lace, and printed pictures.[2]

The number and variety of goods available for consumption by people from a variety of social stations in early modern Europe may come as a surprise to those who do not haunt museums or who have not noticed the dates on the European artifacts displayed there. The Renaissance is noticed because it gave birth to such nice paintings and lovely cities to visit in Italy. And, after all, it did see an intellectual revolution of some sort. But mass consumption? That, by most accounts, is a more modern evil, born in the nineteenth century and corrupting the twentieth.[3]

The role played by Europe's hedonistic culture of mass consumption in the social changes of the early modern period is neglected in most sociological writings, but it is too important to

forget—not only because it challenges the view that mass consumption was the product of industrial capitalism, but also because it contradicts the usual image of the sixteenth century as the
birthplace of that ascetic rationality (the "Protestant Ethic") that
Max Weber describes as the source for the spirit of capitalism.[4]
By the Weberian model, Protestants of the early modern era were
the cultural innovators of their day because they advocated economic rationality through methods of careful calculation to maximize profits and make the most of "God's goods." To do this,
Protestants were supposed to live modestly, save their money, and
make wise investment of profits. They were, by this account, pro-
totypical capitalists who articulated an ideology that supported
economic development; they were also meant to be precisely the
opposite of the hedonist consumers associated with industrial capitalism, people looking for happiness in a second car and a
Cuisinart.

The very existence of a hedonistic consumerism in the early
modern period raises questions about the traditional association of
early capitalism with asceticism and late capitalism with hedonism, and therefore challenges established sociological explanations of the relationship between culture and capitalism. It
suggests that so-called Capitalist Man was not transformed over-
night with the industrial revolution, suddenly losing self-control
and developing a voracious appetite for goods, but rather has always displayed some mixture of asceticism and hedonism.

The hedonistic culture of mass consumption was probably as
crucial in shaping early patterns of capitalist development in Europe as the asceticism usually associated with this era. Hedonism
was to consumers what asceticism was to entrepreneurs: it provided the cultural rationale for increased interest and participation in
economic activities. I am emphasizing hedonism over asceticism to
compensate for the tendency in cultural studies of capitalist development to overemphasize the cultural bases for entrepreneurialism, and consequently to underestimate the cultural reasons for
the increased aggregate demand for consumer goods that was also
essential to the spread of capitalism in early modern Europe.

It would be tempting to dismiss this idea by reducing the consumerism of the early modern era to a reactionary response to

economic change, to see it as hoarding and reluctance to embrace capitalist development. But, as Joan Thirsk points out, much of the consumption of this period involved items newly available on the market, in other words, precisely those goods that would stimulate economic activity rather than dampen it by removing wealth from circulation.[5]

It would also be tempting to consider conspicuous consumption in this period as a Catholic ethic, or part of the Counterreformation, and therefore another kind of reactionary response. Certainly, there was significant building in Rome and other Catholic areas. But descriptions of a consumer society in sixteenth-century England by Lawrence Stone and Joan Thirsk belie this perspective. Consumerism in the early modern period was not a Catholic defensive culture; on the contrary, it was, even before the Reformation, both parent and child to the Renaissance. The lively trade in books, paintings, and other artworks in Italy fed off a consumerist demand for such goods, even while their content expressed a kind of rational calculation (in the careful articulation of arguments and in attempts to reproduce bodily proportions and perspective exactly). Renaissance collections in museums display the simultaneous rationality and hedonism of the period, and show the complementarity of these factors in producing a cultural flowering.[6]

Received wisdom, at least in the social sciences, would have it that the Reformation suppressed whatever consumerist impulses had arisen earlier in Europe, at least among the converts to this new faith. By this account, ideology favoring capital accumulation over accumulation of consumer goods gave birth to entrepreneurs who bought only what they needed and invested most of their wealth, seeking further profits. The historical evidence tells a different story. Many of the seventeenth- and eighteenth-century English businessmen of Protestant faith who built up their enterprises by careful reinvestment eventually used large portions of their wealth to become the new gentry, building great country houses on their newly acquired estates and filling them with lovely artifacts (portraits, chairs, murals, and chinaware) that testified to their high social station.[7] These entrepreneurs are easy to type as Protestant businessmen in the Weberian sense if one simply ignores the way they lived at home. But such ignorance is costly. It masks the fact that pure ascetics or pure hedonists were rare in early modern Europe; most people, whether Protestant or Catholic, combined the two tendencies.

Hedonism and asceticism seem, on the surface, contradictory, but they share one feature: an interest in material accumulation. The pure ascetic rationalist of Weberian theory accumulates capital goods, while the hedonist consumer revels in amassing consumer goods. The two types can be envisioned as extremes on a continuum of materialist tendencies, using opposite systems of values to organize and make sense of material accumulation. While common sense might suggest that they have little in common, hedonistic consumers and ascetic investors have been, in fact, quite difficult to distinguish. Both acted as economic innovators in the early modern period replacing a traditional pattern of hoarding wealth with new ways to use it, to make it a more active part of social and economic life. In addition, their ways of using wealth (for mass consumption or for investment) were not so distinct as they might seem. If the line between capital and consumer goods were clear, the two forms of accumulation would be distinguishable and the ways of using wealth independent enough to act as opposites. The fact that this line is not clear suggests that a continuum is an appropriate model for describing their relationship.

The ambiguousness of the dividing line is readily apparent in the number of consumer goods that can also be used as investments. In the seventeenth century, Dutch merchants, for instance, frequently bought paintings, not only to decorate their homes, but also because they were good investments in a country where land was scarce and other forms of property had to be used more frequently for investment.[8] Is this kind of consumption hedonistic or calculating? It seems more like a form of calculated investment if we remember that in the sixteenth and seventeenth centuries inflation was increasing the value of such goods quite rapidly. Land, or in its absence, other forms of property would be good investments.[9]

The rational calculation guiding this type of consumption might be taken as evidence that conspicuous consumption, defined as wasting wealth in order to display it, did not exist in the early modern period. But rational calculation alone cannot explain all the proliferation in uses of material culture. With increasing wealth, many aristocrats and merchants provided themselves with greater comfort through consumption. They bought more and new kinds of furniture: chairs with backs to replace traditional stools, and, later, furniture that was stuffed and upholstered. They also had great houses built, and surrounded them with elaborate gardens filled with grottoes and other artifices to please the eye and entertain their visitors. At the same time, poorer consumers used their minimal new spending money on such things as ribbons and copper pots, goods that were certainly not intended to be investments.[10] In short, both rich and poor in the sixteenth and seventeenth centuries gave themselves luxuries that went beyond either need or investment.

The combination of rational calculation and ostentatious accumulation became manifest in many business establishments as well as homes during these times. We tend not to think of factories as

Embroidery of a seventeenth-century English garden with fountain and manor in the background. ALL RIGHTS RESERVED (64.101.1314). THE METROPOLITAN MUSEUM OF ART; GIFT OF IRWIN UNTERMEYER, 1964.

sites for conspicuous display, but there are too many similarities between, for instance, the mechanized fountains and grottoes of the seventeenth-century garden and the elaborate water and rail systems built in eighteenth-century factories like the Coalbrookdale ironworks, to dismiss this idea altogether. It is impossible to say authoritatively what the intentions were behind this elaborate industrial complex; certainly its creators, Abraham Darby and his successors, were interested in developing efficient manufacturing techniques. But it is also possible that they were playing with technological possibilities in much the same way that garden designers were, combining practical motives with more aesthetic ones.[11]

Conspicuous displays in industrial complexes such as Coalbrookdale could also have had practical import. When the Darbys were experimenting with the organization of their plant, they were also investigating ways to use their iron. To the extent that they found exotic new uses for iron, they were also suggesting new types of markets for it. As conspicuous consumers of their own goods, they were advertising uses of their products to potential consumers.

While establishing a dividing line between consumer and capital goods may be difficult (or even impossible), we assume, by convention, that one exists and identify objects as either one or the other. That is why most people identify a great house or estate as a display of wealth and power rather than as an investment, even though it may well be both. For analytic purposes, it is equally important to recognize the possible dual significance of objects and to remember that most of them are treated as *primarily* consumer or capital goods. The easiest way to do this is to think of them as lying closer to one extreme or the other of a continuum of indulgence and calculation in relationship to objects.

The extent to which scholars find it difficult to reconcile excess consumption and asceticism as complementary parts of the same social pattern is most dramatically illustrated by the famous Merton/Feuer debate about seventeenth-century scientists. While Robert Merton found these scientists to be ascetics, Lewis Feuer found them hedonistic. The traditional assumption that hedonism and asceticism are opposites suggests that only one theory was right. But it is now clear that Merton and Feuer could have been tapping different extremes of the same cultural system. Scientists, like most other elites in early modern Europe, enjoyed a combination of asceticism and hedonism. The Merton/Feuer findings only testify to the potency of a materialist culture that could appear in both guises at the same time.[12]

By arguing that both Catholics and Protestants were engaged in patterns of conspicuous consumption, I might also seem to be arguing either that there was no Protestant ethic or that it had little effect on the culture of early modern Europe. That is not my intention. Whether or not Protestantism succeeded in encouraging greater entrepreneurialism (and here the evidence is not clear), it did transform a diffuse impulse for accumulation into a tendency to amass capital by advocating a modest life-style rather than flamboyant displays of wealth and power. The result was not a lack of materialism among Protestants but rather greater design simplicity in the goods they produced and consumed. Some scholars argue that the English passion for classical design during the Baroque period and the proliferation of Dutch genre paintings in the same general time frame show the relative modesty of the material culture produced by Protestants in contrast to the elaborate and showy culture of Catholic areas. But the amount of material culture enjoyed in Catholic and Protestant areas did not seem to reflect ideological differences or indicate a lack of materialism in Protestant culture.[13]

There may have been some extreme Protestants who did not approve of any kind of material display, be it modest or extravagant, but they did not predominate; this is apparent in Quentin Bell's work on fashion. After writing about the lack of concern for fashion in Puritan England, he found he had to revise his ideas because he discovered too much evidence of elaborate dress in England to sustain his earlier hypothesis. Bell's experience is testimony to the surprising amount of sumptuousness in which many Protestants indulged.[14]

The legacy of Weber's theory in the sociology of culture has remained, in spite of major criticisms of the historical accuracy of his theory and major changes in sociology of culture. One reason why his work has survived so well is that many of the more recent theorists, in discussing the relationship between culture and capitalism, have focused on *industrial* rather than commercial capitalism. Members of the Frankfurt school, such as Herbert Marcuse and Leo Lowenthal, although they have contributed important ideas about the character of mass culture and capitalism, have not used the existence of mass culture in early modern Europe to dispute Weber's thesis. They have continued to associate materialism with late capitalism and encouraged others to assume the relationship. Thus, in spite of growing historical evidence demonstrating both the scope and power of early materialism in modern Europe, the implications of this evidence for social theories concerning the relationship of culture to capitalism have not yet been explored.[15]

The Character of Modern Materialism

One problem with referring to the culture of early modern Europe as a form of "materialism" is that the term is frequently used to mean a general lust for goods, a desire probably present in one form or another in most cultures. As the term is used here, materialism is the peculiar Western culture that anthropologists Karl Polanyi and Marshall Sahlins describe: a cultural system in which material interests are not made subservient to other social goals. Polanyi and Sahlins both argue that in most societies material accumulation or exchange is subjugated to social or spiritual goals; exchanges are used more for solidarity than for profit, and production of goods is integrated into religious or social ceremonies. These two argue, in slightly different ways, that Western society broke this pattern and loosed material concerns from other constraints, producing the first truly materialistic culture. Although the political scientist Samuel Popkin has recently taken issue with this thesis, arguing that rational economic calculation can be found in peasant villages where Polanyi and others would expect social values to play a stronger role, his work only suggests that the degree of economic calculation in social life is more *variable* than Polanyi's work would indicate. But because the level of concern about economic calculation and investment is necessarily dependent on the amount of surplus available for these activities, there is some reason to think that the existence of such interests is not necessarily evidence of their dominance in determining social relations.[16]

Even with this narrower definition, one might argue that materialism is the product of any high civilization where people have developed enough surplus to support an elite in rich material circumstances. But the materialist elites of most civilizations have been rather small, isolated groups whose values have not challenged more widely held beliefs. Only in early modern Europe did materialism begin to spread through a large section of the population as the international economy (and, increasingly, capitalist production) brought a vast array and quantity of objects to the marketplace. Even those people outside the ruling elite were increasingly able to buy objects and value their accumulation and use. As the new system of trade grew to the extent that it overshadowed other social institutions and became the central organizing force in social life, the value placed on accumulation began to gain priority over other cultural values.[17]

With the growth of the international capitalist economy, the proliferation of new kinds of material culture and the appearance of a variety of goods from faraway places initiated enormous social changes. In England, for example, they stimulated the development of a wide range of domestic industries that supplied local equivalents of foreign goods and provided new employment at home. More generally, as the content of European material culture began to change, traditional patterns for using objects broke down and were replaced by new social forms. For the first time, people faced choices in their purchases and had to develop some norms to limit and guide accumulation. The rise of fashionable change in the sixteenth and seventeenth centuries is the most notable manifestation of this development. Fashion rather than tradition began to be used to regulate patterns of dress as variety in the kinds of fabrics available and the diffusion of new styles in clothing started to make what one wore problematic. Concurrently, systems of table etiquette were invented as the variety of utensils and contacts at table increased. The new scale and variety of objects offered opportunities for new uses of goods and new cultural values for regulating their use.[18]

The sheer number of objects available to people and the increasing manufacture of goods for practical use—such as clocks, books, maps, and guns—also began to affect practical activities.

Abraham van Beyeren, *Still Life*, 1666. BY PERMISSION OF THE ART MUSEUMS OF SAN FRANCISCO. GIFT OF DE YOUNG MUSEUM SOCIETY.

Those who had clocks no longer needed to tell the time from the sun, and those who had books did not have to learn so much from others. Once they could use guns, soldiers did not rely so extensively on hand-to-hand combat to wage wars, and once they could rely on maps, sailors could travel to unfamiliar places without advice from those who had been there before. As Europeans could turn more frequently to things to solve problems and support activities, they became less dependent either on other persons or on nature.[19]

It is easy to see how this new system of international trade was important to the economic development of capitalist production; it allowed for raw materials to be brought to the manufacturing centers of Europe, and it established markets for the growing volume of goods produced there. But it also created a vast system of *cultural* innovation, diffusion, and exchange. Artisans were suddenly able to manufacture for the marketplace rather than solely for local customers; this gave them opportunities to produce novel goods that might not have appealed to their former clients. And as the goods placed in this trading system began to circulate among divergent regions of the world, new international patterns of culture began to appear.

Anthropologists routinely (if not frequently) treat production techniques and trading practices as cultural forms. Capitalist exchange and production practices with their emphasis on efficiency and profit may not seem, at first glance, to have the iconographic significance of, let us say, the potlatch ceremony, or traditional teapots for the Japanese tea ceremony. But concern for efficiency and profit, as Marshall Sahlins points out, is a cultural value. And, as Mary Douglas argues, exchanges of objects are cultural events—acts of communication.[20]

Cultural analysis of economic behavior can unveil patterns of culture that one might not otherwise see. It suggests, for instance, that the expansion of trade in early modern Europe constituted a revolution in communications as well as a commercial revolution. Economists who define transportation systems as communications and point to the growth of road and canal systems in this period unwittingly provide some support for this idea. They imply that these innovations in material culture necessarily created a new basis for human exchange. The authors who have studied the growth of printing in the same period have made similar assumptions about changes in the manufacture of books. They have uncovered a communications revolution in a form of manufacturing.

Marshall McLuhan and Elizabeth Eisenstein, for instance, explain many social changes of the early modern period as results of the development of printing.[21] But they do not associate this innovation with other changes in manufacture and trade in the same period; they do not pay attention to precisely those patterns that anthropologists have called to our attention, the symbolic and communicative character of all objects. Printing certainly enjoyed a unique and important role in the communications revolution of the period. As a mass production technology, it could help disseminate identical pieces of information. But print's importance was not limited to its role as a carrier of intellectual ideas or cognitive styles; it was part of the new material culture, an element in the growth of manufacture and trade itself. Printed work spread through the trading system as commodities, bringing with it ideas and tastes that created bonds among Europeans from a variety of geographical regions and social strata. In this way, printing helped to fashion cultural ties that paralleled the new economic ones, making, for instance, the material culture throughout Europe in the sixteenth and seventeenth centuries more cosmopolitan at the same time that the economic system was becoming more international (and also linking this culture more closely to social class as the economy became more capitalistic). Printing, then, contributed in a unique way to, but did not in itself create, the communications revolution that the commercial revolution engendered.

While Sahlins' reduction of economics to culture and Douglas' treatment of commodities as information carriers help unveil the cultural character of economic patterns, they do not provide an adequate basis for understanding economic value. After all, people would not exchange the same objects or complete exchanges in the same fashion if they were interested only in movements of meaning. The ideas presented by these authors are valuable in encouraging study of *how* economic value depends on cultural value, drawing attention to the mutual embeddedness of cultural and economic meanings.[22]

Clearly, one cannot sell objects that do not have meaning to other people. A wad of paper or ball of fluff does not have economic value, unless adopted by an artist for an artwork or otherwise used as a raw material. That is why the British had difficulty selling large quantities of their woolens in the hot areas of Africa and India. But objects do not have to have absolute cultural meanings in order to sell. A Mexican blanket may be bought in Mexico to be used on a bed for warmth while it will sell in the United States as a wall hanging. People need only find ways to make objects meaningful to make them economically valuable (without necessarily depending on the meanings of their creators).

This feature of economic value is crucial for understanding the international economy in early modern Europe because during this period numerous goods were brought to markets that had not been there before. The growth of the trading system depended on cultural innovation: the development of social meanings for the new consumer goods. A similar pattern held for capital goods. A variety of technological innovations were made to improve both trade and manufacture in the sixteenth to eighteenth centuries. These innovations were useful only because their designers envisioned manufacturing and trading practices based on their use. Innovations in both capital and consumer goods were accomplished when people made them meaningful and were able to convince others of their meanings, i.e., when they developed the cultural basis for assessing their economic value.

Developing these new meanings was not a simple task and did not go unnoticed by contemporaries. In fact, the great debate about the location and nature of economic value that appeared in the economics literature written in this period demonstrates the level of social strain and conceptual discomfort that accompanied changes in the meanings of goods. It is one part of the evidence that the proliferation of goods and their exchange in the early modern period was an important source of cultural confusion and innovation.[23]

As discussions of the Protestant ethic suggest, there was a complementary innovation in the practice of business—the growth of a new entrepreneurialism based on the adoption of what has become known as rational economic calculation. The proliferation of new strategies for conducting business and new ways to think about developing such strategies testify to the problems that Europeans had in making sense (as well as money) out of the economic environment that they were creating.[24] Business practices as well as products, then, were systems whose meanings directly affected the economic life of early modern Europe.

Three aspects of materialist culture—capital goods, consumer goods, and rational calculation—were discussed at the beginning of this chapter strictly as cultural forms; I have reintroduced them here as *economic variables* whose effects depend on cultural meanings. In the intersections of their economic and cultural meanings, one can begin to see more clearly the relationship between materialism and capitalism. For instance, one can see how the growth of fashion and other cultural systems for establishing tastes also increased the demand for new goods. Through these systems of taste, objects were given the cultural significance that made them attractive consumer goods. These cultural systems also shaped production by placing constraints on what manufacturers could profitably produce. One startling example, that will be elaborated in chapters 5 and 6 is the English fashion for calicoes, which acted as a stimulant for the invention of spinning machinery to manufacture cloth that fashion favored.

By investigating how technological innovations and other innovations in *capital goods* were designed to improve business practices, one can also see how cultural models were developed to anticipate and create business changes. The equipment used to improve ocean travel, for instance, acted as a resource for the expansion of European hegemony. It helped to give Europeans an edge over peoples from other cultures, paving the way for further European economic growth and augmentation of the international economy. Carlo Cipolla makes this point when he argues that the armed ships invented in the early modern period were essential to Europe's domination of the world's oceans. Since they were designed to serve this function, the ships embody in their designs ideas about how to approach this project. They document both Europe's technological capacity for economic expansion in this period and the ways that Europeans envisioned oceanic trade.[25]

To the extent that objects and trade permeated vast areas of European social life, they also invaded people's imaginations and perceptions, influencing their writings and pictorial designs. Increasingly, the books of the period were filled with mechanistic imagery, used particularly to describe nature but also political and economic processes. Paintings too showed some iconographic signs of the new economic system, among them a concern for the physical volume of things that some art historians take as a reflection of merchants' needs to estimate the quantity of bulk goods by volume. In these ways and others the expansion of trade and increased appearance of objects on the market were the occasion for the establishment of new and elaborate systems of thought, ones that advocated careful measurement and study of relationships among variables, conceived of as material forces. This way of thinking, I will argue in more detail later, enhanced rational calculation.[26]

Modern materialism, then, during its earliest phases of development shaped the environment in which capitalism could develop, acting as both a resource and a guide. In theoretical terms, it was becoming a semiautonomous force.

This idea contrasts with Weber and his followers' conceptions of the semiautonomy of culture that equate culture with ideas and treat ideas as social forces. They see ideology as a powerful tool shaping patterns of behavior. But here the point is that *objects* are carriers of ideas and, as such, often act as the social forces that analysts have identified with ideology-as-words. Objects can help to make autonomous forces out of ideas by remaining in the physical environment long after their production. They can create a setting for behavior (including intellectual activity) that simultaneously encourages people to behave in ways that take advantage of that environment and restrains them from acting in ways that the environment frustrates. Material culture is not located in the human mind, although it shows the stamp of its creators and is known to people through their senses; it does not gain its autonomy through free will or the spontaneity of subjectives process. Once it is produced, it is part of the world in which people must function (at least until it is destroyed or replaced with other goods) and to which they must adapt their behavior. That it can be *both* a physical and symbolic constraint gives material culture a particular power over human action.

It may seem like a small power if one takes the use of forks and knives as the ideal-typical case of material culture acting as social control. Perhaps a better image is of the transportation systems that human beings have constructed; road, rail, and water systems can clearly stimulate economic and other social activity while also determining or restricting the movement of people and goods. Such changes in material culture are often accompanied by and help to foster novel ideas about how to use them, which make them particularly powerful sources of social change. The history of transportation systems in Europe supports this idea. The great European road and canal systems built in this period seem to have affected capitalist development. And at least one historian has suggested that England's edge in transportation systems may account in large part for the appearance of the first industrial revolution in that country.[27] But the analysis sketched in this chapter was suggested not by transportation but by the history of printing, and will be elaborated here with studies from this history.

Printing and Modern Materialism

Printing, as heir to the stamping techniques used to print coins in the Middle Ages, was the first mass production technology, the first technology that would allow the mass production of exactly identical objects. Because we tend to think of printing as a medium for spreading ideas, its importance for the proliferation of objects in the early modern period, and thus its role in the growth of materialism in Europe, is easy to overlook. But once we acknowledge that printing was used to mass produce a variety of consumer goods (particularly popular prints, but also chapbooks and the like) and to reproduce capital goods (particularly items containing information useful for economic expansion, such as maps), then it is clear why the development of printing is an important indicator of a cultural shift occurring in early modern Europe, of an increased preoccupation with objects and their use to improve life-styles and business practices.

Studying printing is an interesting way to trace this shift because it was used to produce a wide array of objects whose symbolic content is relatively easy to recognize. The books, broadsides, and even wallpapers and fabrics manufactured with the press seem patently to be carriers of meanings and thus easily fitted into the traditional sociological conception of culture.

The remainder of this book will present four case studies from the history of printing in the early modern period which shed light on the role of materialist culture in the growth of capitalism and its child, the eighteenth-century industrial revolution in Britain. The first three focus separately on (1) innovations in consumer goods, (2) the development and spread of new capital goods, and (3) the growth of rational calculation as a pattern of thought. The last study (chapters 5 and 6) looks at the role of these three types of materialism in the growth of the eighteenth-century British cotton industry. Together these studies indicate how the economic changes of early capitalism were embedded in a materialist culture.

Chapter 2 examines the first form of mass culture: popular pictorial prints. Their appearance demonstrates how expansion of the international economy provided the economic opportunities for culture producers to innovate in the production and design of consumer goods. This moment of cultural innovation marked a deep cultural shift: the differentiation of elite from mass culture. It raised for the first time questions about how to fashion commodities that would appeal to a mass audience; it also suggested that the different life-styles and tastes of elites and the masses were issues of cultural and economic significance. Printed goods were dually involved in these problems, in some cases as mass cultural items and in other cases as carriers of designs for elite culture, i.e., as media for diffusing classical forms and contemporary innovations on them. In this way, printing contributed to the production of two new types of consumer goods—art and mass culture—designed for newly differentiated markets: elite and mass markets.

The differentiation of these new forms of material culture was crucial to the development of consumer societies in Europe; by helping to tailor consumer goods to different income groups, it encouraged new levels of consumption among diverse social groups. The new movement of consumer goods created by this increased consumption, in turn, constituted a new pattern of cultural diffusion, a spread of designs around different cultural regions in Europe that began to create international patterns of taste. These too changed the significance of consumption to European social life; they joined consumers throughout Europe in a common cultural web, one that created the broad patterns of demand to support increased mass production.

Chapter 3 examines printed writing and pictorial prints designed as capital goods which contributed to the establishment of the international economy in early modern Europe. New printed maps and printed writing about geography became important to (1) the decline of the Habsburg empire in Europe, (2) the participation of northern Europeans in overseas expansion (to compete with the Iberians), and (3) the definition of European states as geopolitical units. These disparate events in European political and economic history are connected in Immanuel Wallerstein's account of the development of the international economy, or what he calls the modern world system. According to Wallerstein all three were crucial to the development of a system of competing core states in Europe that gave the new world economy relative autonomy from the political fate of any one state. This system was particularly well suited for long-term economic growth because of its stability; it avoided the vulnerability of past large-scale economies to the political lives of individual empires.[28]

Wallerstein describes the establishment of this system entirely in economic terms, but the emergence of the modern world system in fact depended on the availability and use of material records of geographical information. Such information was a vital resource to the system of expanding trade itself and to the formation of states within the system. As printed maps and geographical writings about the world's oceans became widely available, they undermined the Iberian monopoly of information and facilitated competition for sea trade among a variety of European states. At the same time, the production of maps and geographical writings about Europe itself aided state formation there, helping to define the political units that could compete for control over world trade. This use of print, then, was more than a source of intellectual change; it helped to break down the traditional political and economic organization of Europe and to establish a new international economy dominated by competing European states.

Chapter 4 focuses on the relationship between the proliferation of material culture in this period and the growth of *materialist thought*, specifically rational calculation or philosophical materialism. It indicates how patterns for using printed goods became a model for study, which was used as a guide to both scientific and economic thinking. More concretely, it shows how Protestants used the opportunities for mass producing and distributing books to forge a new religious doctrine that emphasized independent study of the Bible. "The book" gained symbolic significance as a piece of finite culture capable of making the infinite accessible to the world.

The new significance given books by Protestants not only shaped a new general attitude toward the study of printed texts but also affected other intellectual pursuits when seventeenth-century scientists began to conceive of nature as a revelation like the Bible, as the "book of nature" or "text of creation." In applying to nature the symbolic meaning of the book, scientists began to see the natural world in new ways that contributed to the development of scientific materialism. Economic theories developed at the same time, while describing social patterns, were similar in structure, suggesting that rational calculation in both the natural and social sciences was tied to the materialist culture of the period.

The last study, presented here in two chapters, shows how the three types of materialism described above interacted in one of the major changes of the industrial revolution: the development of the British cotton industry. The fashion for one kind of printed object, cotton calicoes, seemed to affect the British balance of trade, providing an impetus for innovation in British textile manufacture.

Calicoes imported from India into Britain in the seventeenth century became a fashionable fabric for both clothing and home decoration. Because their light weight and colorful printed patterns gave them some of the look and feel of the traditional silks and embroideries, but at low cost, calicoes appealed to people from a broad range of social classes. Also because they were imported, they carried the air of cosmopolitanism appropriate for fashionable cloth in the period. But precisely because calicoes were not traditional British fabrics, their popularity seemed to threaten the local textile trades. According to mercantilist patterns of economic calculation, the fashion (and hence demand) for these goods was disturbing the British balance of trade, and undermining the British economy. For this reason, the British tried to reduce consumer interest in the cloth by banning calico imports and use, but the fashion for calicoes persisted. When British artisans found that they could not replicate Indian calicoes until they could manufacture inexpensive cotton cloth and learn to print on it with washable colors, they turned toward inventing machines that would spin and weave cotton, and developing dyeing techniques that they could use with the printing press. Thus, the search for a solution to the calico crisis led directly to the particular innovations in capital goods that many scholars take as the beginning of the industrial revolution.

Materialism and Historical Change

The growth of materialism in early modern Europe is evidenced by Europeans' increased preoccupation with objects, a bias of attention stimulated by increased exposure to the novel artifacts brought to Europe through trade. Europeans in this period were not only discovering that the natural world was filled with novelties, such as new continents, but also learning more about the fine fabrics and other goods made in Asia, Africa, and less distant parts of the world, from gold coins to sewing needles and from dyestuffs to fine furs. The material world was filled with wonders that had either evaded European attention or had been beyond the bounds of their knowledge before. Some of these delights were from other parts of Europe; the pins and pots from Holland that the English liked, for instance, were not exotic novelties from a distant continent, but they were new to English farmers, who had not seen, much less bought, many imported goods before. Other items were simply astounding; J. H. Elliot has suggested that many of the plants as well as the artifacts brought back from the New World were almost terrifyingly new to those who saw them. They were part of the information expansion that Elliot says was too great for Europeans to absorb immediately.[29]

Elliot describes the discovery of the New World as a revolutionary encounter with new *physical* realities. Although he wrote about cognitive resistance to novel information from the New World, he does not attribute the intellectual crisis to ideological problems. The discovery of a new continent did not challenge Europeans' ideas by introducing them to new philosophical systems; Europeans writing early chronicles about the Americas did not report on the beliefs of those they met there but rather about the physical wonders and material wealth that they saw. Material novelties, both natural and manufactured, were so varied and so new to European travelers and traders that they created a crisis of meaning only solved by new attention to the material world, i.e., by envisioning ways to explain and use it.[30]

This bias of attention and proliferation of new meanings is what is discussed here as "materialism." Its growth in early modern Europe can be seen as bred by the problems of meaning that the commercial revolution and European expansion brought to light. It was itself the system of meanings developed to make sense of the plethora of objects.

Because these problems of meaning were so closely tied to European economic expansion, they provide evidence of the relationship between materialism and capitalism. Expansion of capitalist trade, for instance, increased the amount of imported material culture that required explanation. At the same time, when capitalist manufacturers learned to make novel artifacts to increase sales of their products, they had to encourage customers to attribute some meaning to these goods. To the extent that buyers of the new objects imputed values to them that were not the same as those seen by the manufacturers or importers, consumers put pressure on merchants and manufacturers to accept different definitions of value; they even forced them to accept some new ideas about what to manufacture or sell. In all these ways, increased manufacture and trade fostered or was stimulated and shaped by patterns of materialism. Because the resulting materialist culture found expression in patterns of both production and consumption, it was as important to manufacturers as it was to those choosing what to buy.

Materialism, then, was a crucial link in the economic changes of the early modern period, giving new objects and their movements meaning. The sub-types of materialism discussed in this book represent different ways in which these meanings were generated.

Consumerism, for instance, made sense out of increased production and trade by tying patterns of consumption to new systems of self-presentation, new ways to make claims about social station. The merchant dressed in princely clothes could feel pleased with his dress once this kind of display was part of a system of fashionable change rather than a breach of etiquette. Similarly, manufacturers of consumer goods could make items for particular markets once they could understand and manipulate the meanings of different designs for consumers.

Innovations in capital goods were part of this new materialism in that they were attempts to think about problems of manufacture and trade as material difficulties and to fashion and disseminate material solutions to them. Innovations in ship-building, for instance, were attempts both to think about and to reduce problems in ocean trading by material means.

And, finally, materialist thought, including both the kind of rational calculation that Weber describes and the new science of the period, was another way to make sense of a bias of attention toward the material. It was an experiment in using material measures to the exclusion of others as the guide to human thought.

Here these three aspects of materialism function together as a kind of working definition. Since they represent aspects of materialism that were particularly salient to the early modern period, when expansion was giving birth to the new materialist culture, an analysis of their development should be sufficient to point to major patterns of interaction between materialist culture and capitalist development.

Materialism as a Problem in Social Research

The materialist culture under study here affected the design of objects as well as patterns of their exchange and use; hence much data for this analysis comes from the shape of the objects made or found in Europe during the period. These items are *documents* of the culture, one form in which the new cultural values found expression. Some are familiar sources of historical data, i.e., books. Some others are standard but not universally used items such as

paintings, buildings, gardens, and other elements of elite culture—
the kinds of documents studied more frequently by art historians
than social scientists, but also occasionally used brilliantly by historians, such as Lawrence Stone and Lynn White, Jr.[31] The other
documents used here—more common items of European material
culture like fabrics, cooking pots, and cutlery—are precisely the
type of goods that the *Annales* school has identified as major data
sources for the analysis of ordinary people and everyday life in
early periods of history.[32] Such items constituted the bulk of
goods traded in the early modern period, so their designs and
meanings were particularly important to the economic development of this period. Thus they are vital to this analysis.

Since crucial evidence for my argument lies in the design of
goods, and particularly the ways that goods are given the cultural
meanings underlying their economic value, my major methodological problem was determining how to examine their designs to locate this value. Practically, what I do here is to study the social
organization of the production of goods and the social uses of
these goods to see how the two factors affect design; conceptually,
I parallel here what art historians do to analyze artworks. When
Irwin Panofsky discusses iconological analysis, he identifies it as
search for the meanings of artworks in the deepest currents of the
culture.[33] What he means by this is drawing parallels between artworks and literature or other forms of elite culture—in other
words, investigating the cross-currents in the Great Tradition.
What I do here is similar in general design; I also look at the content of objects ("content" in Panofsky's sense of taken-for-granted
aspects) as expression of the cultural environment. But in this
case, I include the cultural meanings and uses of objects that stem
from or help to define economic value. This leads me to compare
printed pictures, for example, with cast iron pots, since both were
mass produced for a mass market. While this approach emphasizes parallels among forms of material culture that have similar
economic significance, it does not exclude comparisons of objects
to the Great Tradition, precisely because the iconological significance of an object can be important to its social or economic value. Instead, my approach takes patterns of consumption or
business practices as cultural currents that, like patterns in the

Great Tradition, affect ideas about what objects are and what they are good for. The virtue of this approach is that it invites attention to the ways in which objects are designed to display economic significance through manipulation of cultural meanings.

This type of analysis does not take the Great Tradition as independent of economic activity or any cultural development as a hermetic process. The Weberian model, by defining culture as a realm of formal ideas, has tried to show how belief systems affect behavior, but it has run into difficulties because so many studies show that formal beliefs, in fact, only inconsistently influence behavior. These results have encouraged at least some sociologists to view culture as detached from other social processes, a world of "mind" that exists apart from the world of "matter." This, in turn, has helped to produce in some parts of sociology an image of culture as impotent, insignificant in patterns of political and economic change. The perspective used in this book risks offending some as it expands the realm of culture into the world of matter and looks for forms in the taken-for-granted meanings of everyday life; but in doing so, it also permits another kind of argument about how culture can act as a powerful social force.

There are, of course, a number of studies by historians that document the existence of what I am calling "materialism" in early modern Europe, and also link it to important economic and political changes. Lawrence Stone's analysis of the English aristocracy describes quite well the importance of entrepreneurialism and conspicuous consumption to the disestablishment of the aristocracy and stimulation of the economy in the sixteenth and seventeenth centuries. But it attributes the social changes of this period to the weaknesses of the old social system rather than to the development of capitalism; hence, it does not thoroughly examine the relationship of consumerism to the growth of capitalism. Joan Thirsk's analysis is more directly pertinent to the problem, since it documents how innovations in manufacturing in this period both created consumerism among the lower social strata and increased levels of production and employment. But her study does not attempt to use this information to outline a theory relating culture to capitalism. Of course, Fernand Braudel has been directly concerned with the theoretical problem, carefully delineating how the culture of capitalism along with the capitalist market system spread slowly through the social ranks in early modern Europe. But Braudel is more concerned with using this relationship to produce a general model of historical change than with explaining capitalist development to challenge Weber's thesis.[34]

Art historians have analyzed large numbers of luxury goods from this period, inadvertently tracing the stylistic changes that helped to drive consumption by making old goods relatively undesirable. But their work is somewhat limited in its application to this project, since they have not addressed the character of consumption itself and since their concern for aesthetic standards has turned their attention away from the most ordinary consumer commodities, precisely the ones with the greatest social significance. But the literature analyzes material culture in European history with attention to detail and concern for methodological problems in identifying and analyzing European artifacts that is unsurpassed.[35]

There are, in addition, numerous studies of the early history of printing, including noteworthy analyses by Marshall McLuhan, Lucien Febvre and Henri-Jean Martin, Walter Ong, Alvin Gouldner, and Elizabeth Eisenstein. All address the subject of this book, but these works concern themselves primarily with the cognitive or intellectual effects of printing without considering in any depth the relationship between printing and economic changes. They do something equally important but different.[36]

The books by Karl Polanyi, Marshall Sahlins, and Marshall Hodgson provide something closer to a precedent for the argument to be made here.[37] They all examine particular European cultural tendencies to explain the peculiar patterns of economic growth in the West, and thus help to explain why other cultures did not undergo this transformation. Yet none, for its own reasons, directly addresses the problems raised here.

Polanyi, for example, traces a decline in paternalist values in the modern West that accompanied the rise of industrial capitalism. He does not note that new cultural forms were replacing paternalism, and as a result, treats modern European economic life as increasingly disengaged from paternalistic values rather than embedded in modern materialism. Yet, because he draws attention to the cultural constraints that regulate economic activities, his work paves the way for studying the cultural face of the modern economy.[38]

Sahlins studies the rise of modern materialism but writes not to explain its historical roots or consequences but to contrast the culture of the contemporary West with the cultures studied by most anthropologists. His purpose is to criticize materialist analyses by Western anthropologists of peoples that do not share this materialism, so he does not concern himself with locating it precisely in time or tracing its connections to capitalism.[39]

Hodgson, although he sees the economic transformation of the West in the early modern period as a historical problem, attributes this peculiar economic development to what he calls "technicalism," the propensity to experiment with technological solutions to practical problems. He draws attention to innovations in capital goods as a cultural strain in Europe, but he uses the term, technicalism, in a way that does not distinguish between technological innovation in the medieval period and the innovations in capital goods made in early modern Europe, after these innovations were understood as means for pursuing profits.[40]

The literature that discusses consumerism as a form of materialism is equally salient to this analysis, yet equally difficult to use. Most of it locates the rise of consumerism in the industrial revolution. One great writer on consumerism who does not, Thorstein Veblen, is also problematically useful for this analysis because he treats conspicuous consumption as a universal social form, one perhaps aggravated by the growth of cities and the industrial revolution but apparent in all periods of human history.[41] Such writers, then, either ignore or underestimate the burgeoning of materialism in early modern Europe. Their virtue is in condoning the treatment of consumerism as a form of materialism with social potency and close ties to economic forces.

Werner Sombart and John Nef are exceptions, since both identify conspicuous consumption in the taste for luxuries that developed in Europe at the close of the Middle Ages. Both even recognize the importance of this cultural pattern in stimulating economic growth, but they do not examine its role in a broader materialist culture. Nef sees a "cult of delight" as one of a number of cultural shifts occurring in the same period, though he does not attempt to excavate the common foundation for them all. And Sombart opposes the consumerism of the period to the asceticism described by Weber rather than identifying both as complementary forms of materialism, each encouraging greater use of wealth for social gain.[42]

In spite of these and other differences between previous studies and the present one, this book still owes a great debt to writers who have tried to understand the cultural transformation of the West from the Middle Ages, particularly those who established this transition as the classical problem in social theory. But by locating this transformation in religious or moral beliefs (as Weber, Durkheim, and Sombart do) or in the psychological relationship between Westerners and their material culture (as Simmel does), these authors have disregarded the material aspects of culture *production*. Even Simmel and Sombart, who study cultural artifacts as repositories of cultural values, tend to treat them as found objects rather than products of an economy, whose meanings are developed through the production process itself.[43]

The disregard for production as a source of social transformation was a conscious reaction by theorists against Marx's materialist analysis of Western history, one that makes Marx's work surprisingly vital for an analysis of cultural materialism. His emphasis on production combined with his insights into the meanings of commodities (in his work on commodity fetishism) suggests how cultural values could be designed into objects of production to give them economic value. Sahlins draws on this potential in Marxist analysis in his study of contemporary artifacts; he makes it relatively simple to see the interdependence of the social construction of meanings and the production process, tying the meanings of commodities (which Simmel recognized) to the organization of the economy.[44]

All this attention to the cultural transformation of the West may seem unnecessary to readers acquainted with literature that denies the distinctiveness of modern European culture by pointing to the economic rationality in precapitalist cultures, including Britain in the late Middle Ages.[45] But economic rationality was not so vital an element in distinguishing Western culture as many contemporary authors, or earlier ones like Weber and Simmel, believed. It was only a small part of the materialist culture that encouraged a distinctive pattern of economic growth in Europe and created the dramatic increase in wealth that permitted attachment to objects to become, for the first time, the *dominating* theme in the culture. This larger value shift allowed economic rationality to develop rapidly as one expression of concern with the material.

Although three forms of materialism will be discussed in this book, consumerism gets the greater part of the analytical attention. The reason is quite simple; technological and economic innovations are frequently cited in social theory as essential elements of social change, and even though their cultural character tends to be ignored, their essential contribution to modernization has never been underemphasized. However, the role of consumer tastes and commodity design in shaping demand, and through demand, patterns of economic development, has just begun to be revealed. The argument in this book is intended to show the interdependence of these three forms of materialism in producing industrial capitalism from early commercial capitalism, and it cannot be adequately made without more careful analysis of consumerism.

Before turning to the argument, it seems important to look at some of the basic terms used in it: printing, print, and prints. "Printing" is often treated as synonymous with "typography," describing the process of using type to mass produce a text. The term is being used here in its more general sense: the process of creating an impression by using some kind of stamp or mold, be it a woodblock or plate of type. The products of printing, by this definition, could equally well be a page of text or a picture. The noun "print" is being used to describe the product of typography, but the verb could mean either pictorial or typographic printing. The term "prints" describes graphics or pictorial prints, made on paper (for decoration or book illustration) or printed on cloth (e.g. calicoes). The great number of varied goods made by the printing process still show in their common names a debt to this technology and thus invite inspection as a set of cultural goods with a common technological heritage.

Of course, the point of this analysis is not merely to expand our conceptual understanding of what printing includes or what constitutes a print effect, and neither is it to document the role of consumerism in expanding the printing business in early modern Europe. It is to draw attention to a cultural shift that helped many businesses, including those that used printing, to increase in size and complexity. By this route, we may approach the importance of culture to the growth of capitalism.

CHAPTER TWO

Pictorial Prints and the Growth of Consumerism: Class and Cosmopolitanism in Early Modern Culture

A countless number of those small things and great things which combine to make up what we mean by comfort, we know to have first appeared in [fifteenth- or early sixteenth-century] Italy. . . . We read in the novelists of soft, elastic beds, of costly carpets and bedroom furniture. . . . We note with admiration the thousand of ways in which art ennobles luxury, not only adorning the massive sideboards or the light brackets with noble vases and clothing the wall with the moving splendour of tapestry, and covering the toilet-table with numberless graceful trifles. . . . All Western Europe, as soon as its wealth enabled it to do so, set to work in the same way at the close of the Middle Ages. —Jacob Burckhardt, *Civilization of the Renaissance in Italy*[1]

THE STARTLING beauty of Renaissance art has encouraged us to think of the material culture of the early modern period as comprised of aesthetically innovative objects designed to delight elites. This has drawn our attention away from the more mundane objects made in this era and from finding ways to analyze artifacts that are not particularly beautiful. But the common culture of the early modern period acted as an economic force of considerable power. The many exotic imported and novel domestic goods that appeared in markets of Western Europe were used to initiate new patterns of consumption that stimulated production and trade. To develop markets for goods, merchants began to define distinctive class cultures and a cosmopolitan pan-Europeanism, both of

An earlier version of the first part of this chapter appeared in *Theory and Society*, September 1979, under the title, "Mass Culture and the Modern World-System: The Rise of the Graphic Arts in the Fifteenth and Sixteenth Centuries."

which gave consumers new ways to use their purchases to make claims about their social position, furnishing them with reasons to use more manufactured goods.

Some results of this are clear. Many homes of the well-to-do in commercial centers, such as the Italian cities of Florence and Venice or northern towns such as Bruges and later Antwerp were turned into showplaces for elegant artifacts. They housed the jeweled goblets, fine tapestries, and paintings that displayed the highest standards of European (or often oriental) artistry and became the prized possessions of collectors for many generations. The homes of the less affluent became repositories for other novel consumer items—from prints to pots to cloth—which were often not aesthetically innovative but still were an economic force.[2]

International trade, primarily within Europe but also beyond its boundaries, was a necessary resource for and beneficiary of the cosmopolitanism in this new culture. Clocks and pins, prints and paintings, embroideries and ribbons, swords and knives, jugs and vases were common objects whose manufacture was driven by and helped to stimulate this trade. New consumer goods entering this system were increasingly designed to be attractive to buyers outside their region, nurturing a new geography of culture to complement the new system of trade.[3]

That a range of new consumer items was fashioned and bought in early modern Europe is taken for granted by scholars acquainted with this period, but most attribute little significance to it. The qualitative changes in the design of particular artifacts are not usually connected to quantitative changes in economic activity. But the standardization of demand resulting from the spread of common tastes within social classes and across geographical regions supported larger-scale production and economies of scale. Thus, the growth of consumerism affected economic development.[4]

Changes in consumption also helped to produce changes in the European social order. Opportunities for mobility were created by the profits from increased trade that threatened both the traditional hierarchy in European society and the egalitarianism within strata. By beginning to produce for the marketplace rather than their traditional local clients, some artisans found that they could make more goods and income than their traditional peers; at the same time, some merchants, taking goods to distant markets, gained enough wealth that their position within the traditional hierarchy became problematic. The freedom from tradition realized by both groups and the economic benefits that some of them derived from this freedom encouraged others to participate in manufacture for trade and in trade itself, augmenting the importance of trade to European social life and eventually providing the conditions for a revolution in material culture.

The consumers who bought these new artifacts might have been primarily interested in the beauty and novelty of their purchases, but they nonetheless showed a strong concern for spending their money wisely. Patrons who commissioned paintings in fourteenth- and fifteenth-century Florence often specified the kinds of pigment to be used to make sure an artist did not cut costs by using inferior materials. Later patrons started to demand that the artists they commissioned do some specified portion of the painting themselves rather than leave it to assistants. These elements in contracts for paintings indicate the interest of elite consumers in the monetary value of their purchases; they also show a shift in the primary basis for assessing value away from the materials used to more elusive ideas about the meaning of the design and authorship of work. Both kinds of contracts provide evidence that even the loveliest pieces of artwork were perceived at least in part as economic objects. The second kind of contractual arrangement also indicates that goods were increasingly inspected for what Marx called their exchange value: their equation with money spent, money earned, investments or savings.[5]

This economic perspective on goods was mirrored in a new attitude toward travel and trade, one that was taught explicitly in this period, as the following passage from Henry Peacham's *The Compleat Gentleman* suggests:

If therefore you intend to travel, you must first propound unto your self the end; which is either *ad voluptatem vel ad utilitatem*, pleasure or profit. For the first, every one naturally affecteth, and the fool himself is tickled with the sight of strange Towns, Towers, and Habits of people. Therefore, you must hold you to the other, which is profit.[6]

Not surprisingly, this new definition of value was resisted by many contemporaries of this period. They did not *have* to accept new ideas, and many continued advocating medieval ideas about economic practices, particularly those economic precepts that limited pursuit of profits or declared that economic matters must be tied to some socially integrative function. Many also publically scorned the growing distance between the prices that goods were getting in markets and what they took to be the true worth of those goods. They disliked, for instance, that the English were exporting used shoes to France, only to import and pay high prices for shoes that the French made from the old leather. But although these protests were plentiful, enough Europeans bought new goods at market prices to sustain a cultural shift, creating what Polanyi and Sahlins have described as modern Western culture: a culture dominated by economic values.[7]

The expansion of consumption in this period was stimulated in part by economic changes that put some surplus in the hands of, for instance, small farmers, giving them the wealth to become consumers. At the same time, increased consumption also depended on the shift in values that made it legitimate for manufacturers to seek to capture this surplus by providing the kinds of consumer goods that such consumers would want and could buy. It took an active and novel disregard for medieval notions of cultural propriety and economic activity to put this new pattern of behavior into motion and this new wealth into circulation.

Culture and Material Culture in Medieval Europe

In order to argue that European culture underwent a crucial transformation in the early modern period, it is necessary to describe, however briefly, the character of medieval culture and to contrast it with the patterns of culture that began to emerge in Europe during the fifteenth and sixteenth centuries. There are obvious pitfalls in attempting to do this, one being that the Middle Ages spanned over 700 years and that, in spite of the relative stability of its cultural forms, it did change, particularly during the renaissance of the twelfth century. It is also dangerous to write as if all the culture of the Middle Ages was cut from the same cloth, since there were huge differences between literate and popular (or oral) culture in the period. But because most scholars agree that there *was* a dramatic cultural shift around this time, one can set aside some of the subtleties that preoccupy specialists, and attend to the more blatant and persistent characteristics of medieval culture.

One was the fact that people from all social stations participated in the same popular culture, sharing songs, festivals, and pilgrimages. This integration stands in contrast to the strict social stratification of the period and may well have been encouraged by it. Without the status insecurities that make people self-conscious about who they are seen with, it may have been easier for people from all social stations to mix—not only to celebrate saints' days, but also to attend jousts and banquets, which were frequently open to all. The medieval fascination with death, a common theme in both songs and pictures, also expressed the deep communal sense felt in that period, the common vulnerability shared by everyone, and the inescapable limit of all human powers.[8]

Strict egalitarianism among peers was another aspect of medieval culture tied even more closely to the stratification system. In social organizations like guilds and monasteries, those of equal social rank were required to live in the same manner, taking no advantage over others. Guild masters, for example, had to follow closely a set of rules governing their manufactures and their conduct, which prevented any one guild master from producing more work than any other. This enforced egalitarianism among peers served to preserve the stratification by established social ranks.[9]

Medieval culture was also dramatically stable throughout its long ascendancy. Changes were almost imperceptible to those living during that period, creating an expectation that the future would be much like the present, turbulent and unpredictable but consistently so. The cyclical vision of life realized in popular images like the wheel of fortune and the wheel of life was a reflection of this world view. The wheel of fortune illustrated the uncertainties of the times, the ease with which fate could reverse life's course, and the wheel of life depicted the certainty of birth and death, the unchanging cycles. The Book of Hours was another cultural form that assumed a cyclical character, being, as it was, a religious calendar intended to be reused year after year.[10]

The stability of medieval culture seems to suggest that Europeans neither desired nor sought change, but the amount of technological innovation made in the Middle Ages contradicts this idea. Europeans seemed more than willing to find practical solutions to some problems in agriculture and war. They readily adopted technologies from other parts of the world, such as the stirrup and methods for making paper, while also experimenting with more local technological traditions, borrowing from antiquity ideas for water-wheels and clocks.[11]

The innovators who created the new technology in medieval Europe may not have fit standard sociological conceptions of traditional people because they thought practically, seeking ways to use their material culture for problem solving rather than living in fear of change. But unlike modern innovators, they did not evolve a systematic empirical science to support systematic technological innovation. Their theoretical science tended to be separate from the empirical, leaving their empirical science much like their technology in its pragmatic particularism. Alchemy, for example, was tied to the concrete aims of creating gold and eternal life, and attempted to reach these goals by exploring the particular character and uses of specific materials. Medieval culture as realized in science and technology was practically innovative but also oddly impotent, creating circumscribed changes that did not disturb the stability of medieval culture. The dual character of medieval technology was perhaps most clearly expressed in the medieval obsession with perpetual motion machines, an interest integrating the cyclical and the innovative strands in medieval culture.[12]

So far this discussion has treated medieval culture as a single system of objects and people, symbols and behavior. But it was essentially regional, particularly between 700 and 1100, when European trade was at an ebb. People throughout Europe might celebrate saints' days, but they did not observe the same ones. Areas had local saints whose festivals had special meaning and form, celebrated with local costumes and according to local custom. Even in the late Middle Ages, when the growth of cities and trade was reducing some of the isolation of regions of Europe, most of

European cultural life was still local, as was the economic life of the period.[13]

Another source of differentiation in medieval Europe was literacy. Everyone might have participated in the popular culture of the Middle Ages, listening to troubadors and attending mystery plays, but not everyone could read and participate in the intellectual life of the period. During the early Middle Ages the clergy was the keeper of the Great Tradition, attending to the remnants of Roman culture and its literary heritage. But by the twelfth and thirteenth centuries, with the growth of universities and the rediscovery of many classic texts, learning began to spread outside the clergy. Many members of the aristocracy, including women, learned to read and studied the books they could find, and a fair number of well-to-do urban artisans also acquired literacy and developed a taste for learning. While, by this time, the Great Tradition was spreading through the three estates of medieval social structure, it was still inaccessible to the majority of the population. Literacy was a kind of cultural dividing line, one that began by differentiating one social station, the clergy, from the others, but that increasingly divided those with enough wealth for schooling and books from those without it.[14] Along with the reestablishment of trade around the twelfth century, this movement in patterns of learning during the late Middle Ages was a harbinger of the modern economy and culture that would begin to grow in the fifteenth and sixteenth centuries. But the economic and cultural life known to most people during the late Middle Ages was still regional and stable.

Most important for this analysis, the level of material culture in the Middle Ages was low, even in the great medieval households where one might expect to find elaborate and extensive furnishings. In many such homes there were some books, beds, chests, chairs, and tapestries, but they were items reserved for the immediate family and distinguished visitors, not used by most inhabitants. Other members of the household used little more than stools to sit on and pallets for beds. At medieval banquets in the greatest houses there were frequently conspicuous displays of food, enormous pomp suffusing the ceremony, and even arrangements of silverware on sideboards. But at most banquets the level of material culture was low, with a few trestle tables and stools for furniture and shared bowls for food. Even at many elaborate occasions there were only a few objects on hand compared with the impressive displays of dishes, glasses, tables, chairs, linens, and decorations found at elegant dinners in the eighteenth century.[15]

The homes established by the wealthy in the trading towns of the late Middle Ages departed from this traditional medieval pattern. Many cultural historians have noted that these towns showed signs of a growing materialism, a greater concern for conspicuous consumption than had been traditional in Europe before that time.[16] This materialism was another harbinger of the culture that would expand with the trading networks at the close of the Middle Ages until it overshadowed other cultural values, becoming the materialist culture that would dominate Europe from the early modern period to the present.

Prints and the Growth of Consumerism

The best way to study the historical development of this pattern of consumerism is to analyze in some detail the appearance of some particular type of expressive material culture, i.e., an object whose symbolic content has little or no practical value.[17] Most types of printed goods would do for this purpose, but one does better than most: pictorial prints. Because pictures tend to be valued for nothing more than their decorative uses, they fit perfectly the definition of consumer goods as expressive artifacts. This is not to say that pictures do not and have not had practical uses; many pictorial prints of the early modern period were used to carry practical information, such as engineering plans or guides for making furniture. They indicate how utilitarian definitions of value as well as more purely expressive ones had a similar function: providing a cultural basis for establishing the economic value of consumer goods. The lack of a clear dividing line between capital and consumer goods does not destroy the value of looking at early prints as consumer goods.

Printing, of course, had a history before the early modern period. Like many of the other production processes refined and used extensively in the sixteenth and seventeenth centuries, printing had a medieval heritage. Europeans had been making some woodblock prints and block-books from the fourteenth century, but they made few of them and did not find or create a large market for them.[18] The development of the printing press, movable type, and plate engraving during the fifteenth and sixteenth centuries made printing a sophisticated technology for producing a wide variety of marketable goods.

Pictorial prints had a special place in the early history of printing: they were the first form of mass-produced images for popular markets. As such, they were an early form of mass culture that helped to cultivate consumerism in the lower echelons of society. Works of graphic art produced before the eighteenth century tend not to be considered by contemporary scholars as examples of mass culture; their antiquity and appearance in museum collections imbue them with all the trappings of fine art. But this view of prints reflects a social redefinition that began in the late seventeenth century, when middle-class collectors in Holland and France started treating prints as works of art which could be enjoyed, like paintings, both for their aesthetic merits and as investments.[19] Before this time, printmaking primarily involved images for a popular audience, works that were complements to rather than part of the new cosmopolitan artwork being developed for elite consumers.

While the histories of both printmaking and painting in early modern Europe are well known, that prints and paintings were pictorial forms with *distinctively different styles* in this period has been masked in the past. Most historians have not paid attention to the specific character of prints; they have either looked at prints as illustrations in books, and thus as an adjunct to the printed word rather than a distinct form of pictorial culture, or have subsumed the history of prints under the history of art, again minimizing their distinctiveness.[20]

There are some good reasons why scholars would subsume prints under these categories. The printed word and works of art have traditionally been treated as forms of high culture that were much more important than any kind of mass culture. Scholars may have been trying to elevate their subject matter by treating prints as either art or illustration. The confusion of prints with works of art may have an even more "sensible" basis, since art and mass culture in the fifteenth and sixteenth centuries had much in common. Many artists were also printmakers in the sixteenth century; in fact, some of them, like Albrecht Dürer, did much of their best work in prints. At the same time, printmakers and artists of the late fifteenth and early sixteenth centuries shared common political concerns that made their activities similar, each group establishing patterns of picture production outside the control of craft guilds. Artists and printmakers, in their own ways, were taking advantage of the economic changes of the period to shape new work practices and fashion new kinds of pictures for the growing ranks of consumers.

The history of the visual arts in early modern Europe (both prints and paintings) provides evidence of these complex and novel developments in Europe's material culture. It illustrates the growing cosmopolitanism in the pictures of the period, and the simultaneous development of fine art and mass culture as distinctively class-associated pictorial forms; it also shows how these innovations in the design of consumer goods originated from increased consumerism and helped to stimulate it. In this way, it suggests the link between this form of materialism and the growth of capitalism.

Elite and Mass Culture

In 1500. . . popular culture was everyone's culture; a second culture for the educated, and the only culture for everyone else. By 1800, however, in most parts of Europe, the clergy, the nobility, the [wealthy] merchants, the professional men—and their wives—had abandoned popular culture to the lower classes, from whom they were now separated, as never before, by profound differences in world view.[21]

While late medieval material culture was produced by artisans, working primarily within the guilds, manufacture in the early modern period took new forms as the growth of trade gave some artisans opportunities to leave the guilds and establish themselves as independent entrepreneurs. Some became artists, architects, and designers of other elite artifacts; others experimented with the production of new kinds of commodities for more common people, acting as the pinmakers, ironworkers, and pictorial printers of the period.

The development of a distinct group of elite culture producers in the early modern period is well known; the Renaissance is, of course, closely identified with the growth of the arts and the movement of artists from the guild to the workshop. Less well known is that many artisans began to produce new kinds of goods for mass consumption. They were one of the groups to create what Thirsk describes as the mass culture of the early modern period, the fruits of the "projects" developed in the fifteenth to sixteenth centuries:

A project was a practical scheme for exploiting material things through industry and ingenuity. . . . [These projects were] schemes to manufacture or produce on the farm, goods for consumption [primarily] at home. Since [these consumer goods] served the domestic market first and foremost, they were distributed through the kingdom without pomp or ceremony, and without leaving any statistical account. Such articles were hawked around the countryside on the backs of pedlars, or stowed by chapmEconsigned to carriers who maintained a regular service on the roads with carts and wagons, using the inns as bus-stops. We can never measure the scale of this trade for very few towns have preserved any toll or brokage books. Chapmen, trowmen, higglers and others distributed these wares more silently than the smugglers by moonlight.[22]

According to Thirsk, these projects (or, at least, the ones she studied in England) were direct responses to increased foreign trade: attempts to produce at home goods similar to those brought in from abroad. Because they were not traditional forms of manufacture, they developed outside the guilds and often in the hands of rural small entrepreneurs. And because they often were used to manufacture less expensive imitations of foreign goods, they usually created commodities meant for local markets and common people.[23]

Thirsk's analysis does not establish the existence of these projects throughout Europe, but it does at least locate them in England where one would not expect (reading the *Protestant Ethic*) a flowering of consumer goods or a consumerist culture. There is also evidence that similar schemes existed in other parts of Europe where they were supported, as English projects were, by small-scale investment and sometimes sponsorship, such as privileges or grants of monopolies. Printing businesses throughout Europe, for instance, share these features with the English projects that Thirsk describes.[24]

Thirsk's identification of these projects as commercial ventures embarked upon, in large part, by farmers and rural artisans with little capital and some small bit of spare labor seems to conflict with the view that farmers and other traditional people resisted the growth of the market economy and the elevation of market values in the early modern period. But, of course, many tenant farmers were thriving on the rising prices of agricultural products in this period, and many others were happy to find some new sources of extra income in the market economy. Their exploitation of these new commercial possibilities is easier to understand given Samuel Popkin's analysis of economic rationality in peasant life. He argues that the flaws and failures of the "moral economy" made peasants more amenable to politicoeconomic calculation than current conventional wisdom might lead us to expect.[25]

One might be reluctant to consider, as Thirsk does, hand-made copper pots and pins as forms of mass culture, since they were not mass-produced by machine. But her description of them in this way has some theoretical merit. They were, after all, generally made in quantity for sale at low prices; thus they became the culture of common people more often than of elites. The ribbons, stockings, and other kinds of textiles made in this period using technological innovations come very close to what we think of as mass culture; their production depended on machines and was made more efficient through technological innovation.

Pictorial printing should be considered one of these early projects, one that was used to manufacture goods that, even strictly speaking, should be called forms of mass culture. Printing may not have been developed and promoted by farmers (like many, although not all projects), but it was like many projects in using a new technology to produce inexpensive imitations of widely traded artifacts. Because of its effects on trade, printing was also like other projects in threatening and eventually replacing traditional forms of manufacture with new ones that thrived on and spread increased consumption in the lower levels of society.[26]

Guild Egalitarianism and Capitalism

It is well known that the guild system was being undermined in a variety of manufactures by the growing salience of trade in the early modern period, encouraging changes in the manufacture and design of material goods. The growth of the putting out system in sixteenth-century England is a case in point. As merchants gained greater control over the textile trade, they were able to direct artisans to manufacture the kinds of cloth that they wanted and discourage production of the goods that artisans traditionally made. This led to alterations in the kinds of cloth that English textile workers produced, making a staple of the so-called "new draperies." Similar changes in trade affected the production of luxury goods such as leather and silverware as the best artisans in these fields started to sell the work of others in addition to their own, becoming independent merchants as well as artisans. The story of pictorial printing in this period is only one of many that could be told to illustrate how the evolution of a new economic order in Europe was contributing to a revolution in material culture.[27]

But what in particular made artisans in the pictorial arts seek freedom from the guilds? The expanding trade of the fifteenth and sixteenth centuries may have made it possible for some picture producers to find markets for their work outside the guilds, but 'hat does not explain why artisans would have sought this free-uom. The craft guilds had been designed to protect local artisans from competition with outsiders, and the geographical expansion of trade would have increased the competition between foreign goods and local ones, presumably encouraging guild members to seek protection from their organizations. But the egalitarian policies of guilds often prevented well-known artisans from doing more work than other masters, restricting their ability to pursue economic self-interest. In addition, guild policies disallowing division of labor based on technical skills reduced artisans' abilities to explore production innovations. As Weber described it,

A guild is an organization of craft workers specialized in accordance with the type of occupation. It functions through undertaking two things, namely, internal regulation of work and monopolization against outsiders. It achieves its objective if everyone joins the guild who practices the craft in the location in question. . . . The spirit of the medieval western guild is most simply expressed in the proposition, guild policy is livelihood policy. . . . As to internal policy, the guild endeavored by every conceivable means to provide equality of opportunity for all guild members. . . . To realize this equality the development of capitalist powers must be opposed, especially by preventing the unequal growth of capital in the hands of individual masters and consequent differentiation among them; one master must not progress beyond another. . . . The guild maintained the position that the raw material must take the longest possible course in the individual shop, that the individual workman must keep the object worked upon in hand as long as possible. Hence it was required that the division of labor should be based on the final product and not on technical specialization of operations. . . . By all these measures the guilds opposed the development of large establishments within the guild-controlled industry.[28]

Artists and printmakers began to seek freedom from these regulations in order to exploit the economic possibilities of the period. Because of the limits imposed by guilds on the earnings of masters, one impulse toward freedom from the guilds came from the most esteemed craft workers. In northern Italy in the fifteenth century, rivalry among cities made local culture a matter of political concern; it brought the support of local aristocrats and merchants to the arts and created a demand for artworks that outstripped supply. For the best-known painters and sculptors, continuing to work under traditional regulation was not to their advantage. Once a new type of art consumer, the collector, appeared on the scene, artists were able to organize their work lives in new ways. Artists whose work was collected could set up their own workshops with a large group of apprentices and a high degree of division of labor to become more efficient suppliers. Their income, their productive activities, and their aspirations were increasingly determined by contracts rather than by guild standards.[29]

Print publishers too were able to set up their businesses outside the control of traditional artisan guilds in this same period, but they did it by taking advantage of the inability of craft guilds to control new manufactures (i.e., in the same way that most new projects established themselves outside guild regulation). Print publishers had an additional advantage in controlling their worklives which is rooted in the unique history of publishing: during the late Middle Ages in places where book production was under the control of universities, the publishing trade had been independent of the craft guilds. This is another reason why, when print publishers needed to employ skilled artisans from the guilds to do their woodcutting and engraving, they did not have to employ them under guild conditions.[30]

Of course, print publishers would not have been able to exploit this advantage unless they had been able to find workers willing to accept new work conditions. Luckily for them, the greatest masters were not the only ones discontented with the guilds in this period. Many apprentices and journeymen were unhappy with their subjugation to guild rules and guild masters; they were one source of the labor force needed in publishing. Their discontent was matched by the unhappiness of others who had not been able to join the guilds. As the guilds grew in political strength and attracted more potential entrants to their trades, their members developed policies (to keep the standard of living high) that extended the period of apprenticeship in which young workers were not paid for their services. This limited the number of people who could even become apprentices. By the sixteenth century, only those with independent incomes could survive the long apprenticeship; most others could not afford to do so.[31] This created a pool of disgruntled apprentices and would-be apprentices who were likely to have rejoiced at the chance to escape from guild regulation.

While the freedom of printers and unhappiness of many artisans may have brought printing to life in Europe outside the guild system, printing did not remain free of guild control forever. There were some unsuccessful fifteenth-century attempts to put pictorial printing under guild control, but it was not until toward the end of the sixteenth century that printers in England, France, and some parts of Italy established their own effective guilds. The printing business had expanded, and a glut of books appeared on the market that threatened even some of the most established printers. To reduce this threat, printers sought more power over their work and over those working in the print trade. The guilds they created were not like traditional craft guilds—they were more concerned with the regulation of trade than with the regulation of production—but they did begin to lay out formal patterns of control for masters over journeymen that set in motion a period of decline for workers in printing shops. In doing this, printers did not initiate total regulation of pictorial printmaking; some single-sheet pictures were made outside book publishing. But the movement did begin to alter the character of book publishing, and with it book illustration.[32]

The early freedom of publishing from guild control, however temporary, was crucial for establishing the printing business free from constraint by traditional codes governing manufacture. Guilds for regulating these new trades became important after the new businesses were established, when the risks inherent in the ventures seemed onerous.[33] Hence printing was much like many new forms of manufacture in the early modern period which began outside the guild structure but formed their own guilds after some initial success and some failures convinced entrepreneurs that they had something to protect.

The relative lack of early guild regulation, of course, did not guarantee that printing could develop freely. There were many attempts by the state and other political authorities to control publishing during its early history. Henri II in sixteenth-century France developed a campaign to stamp out heretical books that led to burnings of both printers and their books. Shortly afterwords Inquisitors in the Netherlands busied themselves with locating and preventing the publication of ideas sympathetic to the Reformation, searching the shops and confiscating the books and equipment of printers as distinguished as Christopher Plantin. Attempts at strict censorship such as these led to migrations of printers (like Plantin and Robert Estienne) to areas of Europe where they could work with less interference. English censorship also was quite severe at times, particularly under Charles I and the Star Chamber. Other political powers claimed the right to censor books but were more lax in doing so. For instance, Frankfurt had a board to review the content of all books published there, but perhaps because local authorities did not want to disrupt the printers working there, they were more tolerant in fact than they were in theory.[34]

Attempts at censorship tended to be directed toward control of the printed word more than printed pictures, but they sometimes also affected the flow of, for instance, religious cartoons. There were even some occasions when engravers were persecuted for their pictures.[35] But, by and large, owing to the ineffectiveness of political regulation as well as to the fact that censorship was less frequently directed toward pictorial prints than the printed word, in the late fifteenth and early sixteenth centuries designers of pictorial prints in fact found themselves freer than their counterparts in traditional craft guilds to experiment with the medium.

Print publishers, then, like their entrepreneurial counterparts in some other new manufactures realized not total but adequate freedom to allow them to be innovative producers of mass culture. They had access to skilled labor and the freedom to employ workers as they saw fit. And they saw fit to use capitalist organizational forms. Individual printers owned the woodcuts and engraving plates their employees made as well as their presses, giving themselves control over the means of production. In the fifteenth century printers tended to be their own publishers, initiating projects and seeing them through to completion, either hiring manuscript correctors or doing this work themselves, and overseeing the engraving, typesetting, and printing in their shops—acting, in other words, much like guild masters. But by the sixteenth century the division of labor increased as publishers hired other printers to put jobs on their presses. Pictorial printing was also increasingly divided into separate tasks: design, woodcutting or plate engraving, and printing. In this process, printers reduced the resemblance between craft manufacture of manuscript books and capitalist manufacture of printed ones.[36]

The artists and printmakers who established shops outside guild control in early modern Europe were taking advantage of the emerging systems of manufacture and international trade to create new kinds of pictures in Europe. With more efficient means of production, they helped create a proliferation of material culture;

by producing new types of goods (art and mass culture) for new types of consumers (the collector and nonaffluent), they helped spread the range of people recruited into the new consumerist culture.

Commercial Values and Commodity Design

European picture producers who explored the aesthetic freedom that this economic change unleashed were constrained by the problem of designing goods that would be commercially attractive; they had to consider how to use expressive meanings to create economic value. The expansion of the print trade and art production, as well as the differentiation of pictorial printers from artists, depended on finding consumers for the new kinds of pictures. Fine artists and commercial printmakers did this during the sixteenth century by designing goods to appeal to either elites or the masses, shaping distinctively class-based cultures that helped to attract more people to the system of conspicuous consumption.

We have already seen that nascent class cultures began to emerge in the late Middle Ages when the spread of learning started to disassociate literate culture from traditional social station and associate it more with having the wealth for an education, buying books, and finding the leisure to use them. In this way the Great Tradition of Western culture started to become the culture of the affluent, a distinct form of elite culture.

Fine art became part of this elite culture when it began to be associated with learning and thus tied to the Great Tradition. This shift in the social meaning of art occurred when the humanists began to absorb Greek ideas about the importance of aesthetic experience and combined them with their own mind/body dualism. They began to think of artists as intellectuals, conceptual geniuses, and peers. Since the humanists were the primary custodians of the Great Tradition in this period, their acceptance of artists as intellectuals raised the status of artists and their art.[37]

The attraction of humanist ideas to Europeans and the appeal of naturalism in the art of the times may well have reflected commercial values. Frederick Antal argues that close attention to the classics stemmed in part from an interest in Roman law for its support of trade, and that the growing naturalism in Renaissance painting mirrored the increasing rationality of the *haute bourgeoisie*. Michael Baxandall contends more specifically that Renaissance naturalism was a reflection of merchants' needs for careful measurement by eye, i.e., that it was a direct expression of the commercial enterprises that developed with trade. The naturalism associated with Renaissance art did, in fact, develop with the expansion of trade and creation of wealthy trading centers in Flanders and in the northern Italian cities.[38]

Fifteenth- and sixteenth-century Flemish paintings began to display the growing three-dimensionality and the more natural backgrounds that Baxandall associates with trade, while still retaining much traditional iconography. The naturalism that developed in northern Italy had a similar sense of depth and concern for volume, but it also explicitly expressed the growing alliance between humanists and artists. This work was more intellectual, displaying a closer relationship between human perception and the image quality of paintings; it helped to define artists as intellectual/conceptual geniuses as distinct from technically skilled artisans. Through their studies of perspective and anatomy, artists emphasized their role as intellectuals, pointing to the analytic skills they used in producing more naturalistic designs.[39]

The literature on prints by art historians documents a growth of naturalism also in pictorial prints in this period, but not the same pattern of increased naturalism evident in paintings. Certainly, there are echoes of Renaissance painting in prints by artists like Martin Schongauer in the North and Andrea Mantegna in the South; these men experimented with print techniques to produce more naturalistic imagery. Schongauer's *Saint Agnes*, for example, is elegant, technically refined, and more naturalistic in precisely the way that paintings were in this period. This piece and many others like it provide some basis for arguing that Renaissance prints were attempts to adapt graphic arts techniques to serve a new fine arts aesthetic. But most prints of the period were not made by great innovators like Schongauer; they were by less ambitious people who were creating simple images using basic printing techniques and less modern canons of taste. They were prints

Martin Schongauer, *St. Agnes*, c. 1475, engraving. BY PERMISSION OF THE NA-
TIONAL GALLERY OF ART, WASHINGTON, D.C., ROSENWALD COLLECTION (B-2621).

made by anonymous masters in Nuremberg and other cities that housed numerous small printing businesses.[40]

As fine art became the repository for the values of the Great Tradition, most prints carried values of the little tradition, bringing some medieval popular forms to nonelites in the early modern period. Most Renaissance prints were not collectors' items; they were thought to be of too little monetary value to require lasting aesthetic values. To be marketable, these pictures had to appeal to people who had had little access to pictures made by professionals and little education in the Great Tradition to influence their tastes. They probably sold best when they were made with the most traditional medieval imagery, which by then was easy to read.

These prints were pictures like the Master of Baalam's *Fool*, whose distorted frame, drawn in simple lines, floats in an undefined space. The pictures by the Master of the Power of Women also present only the simplest outlines of their subjects, line drawings that sketch nearly two-dimensional people in a similar space. These prints look, as David Kunzle suggests, like precursors to the modern comic book. They certainly resemble modern coloring books more than the best prints by Schongauer, Dürer or Mantegna. Many book illustrations, like the picture, *Christ before Pilot*, in Turrecremata's *Meditationes* were, in fact, meant to be used as guides by painters hired to hand-color (rather than illustrate) the text. In this sense, their simplicity was a direct reflection of publishers' efforts to make these pictures resemble medieval rather than contemporary arts.[41]

The description of these prints may make them sound like the most unsophisticated ones made in the period, but they were not. The illustration from the *Meditationes* shows a rudimentary concern for perspective, and the masters mentioned above were engravers, creating technically innovative works for the late fifteenth century. In different ways, these prints used techniques that could yield more naturalistic pictures, but they still resembled in form simple medieval images. They functioned to spread these traditional forms to new consumers. This was true even of some of the more sophisticated prints made by skilled engravers, such as Master ES. In his *Salvator Mundi* Christ is shown with a delicately

Christ Before Pilate, Turrecremata, *Meditationes,* Rome, 1473. Reproduced in Alfred Pollard, *Early Illustrated Books* (London: Kegan, Paul, Trench, Trubner, 1893). CENTRAL LIBRARY, UNIVERSITY OF CALIFORNIA, SAN DIEGO.

shaded face, but he is surrounded by a gothic latticework that holds his image in an elongated two-dimensional frame. This image is reminiscent of Simone Martini's Sienese courtly Gothic art, popular with the nobility and petty bourgeoisie in fourteenth-century Italy.[42] This print shows how printmakers of the fifteenth century used an outmoded art style to produce a form of printed mass culture. As Frederick Antal put it:

Conservative, uncultured sections [of the social order] were much more prone than the upper bourgeoisie to be governed both in their daily life and in their religious ideas by the old, symbolic, ungenetic process of thought which identified the externals of things with their reality, and on the basis of these outward marks discovered relations and created identities between the symbol and what was symbolised. Thus the symbolic and didactic art of the past, in which figures were represented not in their own right but as symbols of something else, could still persist, to a certain extent, among those sections at a time when this no longer suited

Master E.S., Salvator Mundi, c. 1440–1467, engraving. BY PERMISSION OF THE
NATIONAL GALLERY OF ART, WASHINGTON, D.C., ROSENWALD COLLECTION (B-22,
299).

the most progressive and rationalist part of the upper middle class. Whilst formerly the lower classes had probably been content with a vague understanding of these images, without grasping their every detail, the Church now made symbolic and allegorical art in every respect much more comprehensible to the masses, bringing it nearer to them in all its details.[43]

The conservatism of printed writing in the first century or so of printing has been noted in histories of print for years. Not only did early printers tend to reproduce traditional written forms, such as Bibles, Books of Hours, and the like, but they also tried to make them look like their handwritten counterparts by using traditional layouts and typefaces designed to resemble handwriting. In light of this, it should not be surprising to find some conservatism in early pictorial printing, a conservatism that led printers to concentrate on common medieval pictorial forms, such as playing cards and religious pictures. Some subjects for prints were not common to painting in this period (e.g., playing cards), but even when they employed themes that were used by Renaissance artists (such as religious ones), they were designed in traditional fashions, making them resemble medieval imagery.[44]

Emphasizing the stylistic continuities between fourteenth-century Gothic painting and late fifteenth-century prints may be deceptive since the important issue in designing the prints was making their content identifiable to a broad population. This led to a kind of standardization that was peculiar to this commercial style.[45]

The single sheet woodcuts seem to have been made for very simple people. The figures in them are no more than class symbols which stand for some particular saint or such an object of religious veneration as the Vernicle of the Sacred Heart. The identification of the personage represented is accomplished by the use of an attribute or sign that is specially connected with him. Well before the end of the century the cloven hoof of manufacture showed itself in these prints, for there are some that have changeable heads and attributes from little blocks dropped into slots left for the purpose in the bigger blocks. Thus different saints would have identical bodies, clothes, background and accessories, all printed from one identical block. The people for whom these prints were made obviously looked to them not for information but for the awakening of pious emotions.[46]

Players at Cards from Ingold, *Das gulden Spiel.* Augsburg: Günther Zaner, 1472. Reproduced in Alfred Pollard, *Early Illustrated Books* (London: Kegan Paul, Trench, Trubner, 1893). CENTRAL LIBRARY, UNIVERSITY OF CALIFORNIA, SAN DIEGO.

The illustrations in almanacs and other books produced in the period—illustrations meant to capture the attention of people who might not have been able to read easily—also display a simplicity paralleling that of the single sheet prints. Many of these illustrations conveyed little information and were not designed to clarify the texts with which they were printed. The illustration of the mandrake in the *Herbarium Apulei Platonici* (1481), a picture of a headless man with leafy hands, is one example of the decorative but less than accurate illustrations that accompanied some of these early texts. In other herbals, the same drawings would be used to illustrate different plants or different uses of plants, making the identification of plants through study of the illustrations impossible. Similar patterns appeared in other kinds of illustrated book. Sometimes the same woodcuts depicting a town or some

Illustration of a Mandrake from the *Herbarium Apulei Platonici*, 1481 (PML 25976 f.106 V). BY PERMISSION OF THE PIERPONT MORGAN LIBRARY, NEW YORK.

man would be used to illustrate both a piece of classical literature and a religious story. This is precisely what William Caxton did when he used illustrations from his *Cato* (1481) to illustrate his first edition of the *Mirror of the World* (1481). In these instances, prints were not used to convey information; they seem, rather, to have functioned simply as decoration. Another example from Caxton's work suggests this. Illustrations for the 1484 edition of *Can-

terbury Tales were not made to help the reader distinguish the major characters from one another, since the *same* woodcut was used, for instance, to represent the Merchant, the Franklin, and the Summoner. In this case, as well as others, printers inserted woodcuts to make the text a more attractive commodity (i.e., one that resembled more closely the elaborately hand-painted volumes being produced for wealthy patrons). There was little impetus to make these illustrations detailed or complex carriers of content; they were stylistic devices, attracting semiliterate readers to the

The Summoner from the General Prologue of Chaucer, *Canterbury Tales*. William Caxton, 1484 (PML 693). BY PERMISSION OF THE PIERPONT MORGAN LIBRARY, NEW YORK.

printed page and making inexpensive editions look more like elite books to nonelite consumers.[47]

Early book illustrations are interesting to compare to the paintings of the period because both types of artwork were of interest to publishers, particularly humanist publishers. On the one hand, paintings by artists were tied to the new learning of the period, gaining legitimacy for their high status from their association with ideas in the classic texts that were being reproduced at this time. On the other hand, publishers were using illustrations in a number of their books, including classic texts, to make them commercially attractive to the semiliterate. Both types of picture were gaining a new social significance in this period from book printing, but pictorial prints were appreciated for their commercial value while paintings of artists were appraised for their intellectual character.[48]

Accuracy and a Standard Syntax

To the extent that these simple prints began to be used as carriers of information and ideas, describing known places and objects, they had to present some recognizable figures and were pressed to become more naturalistic.[49] The simple decorative images common in the fifteenth century began to be replaced in the sixteenth with this new type of print. As they were given more intellectual functions, prints began to look more like Renaissance art, displaying a growing accuracy of representation. But they also remained traditional enough to separate them from fine art. They became a repository of divergent influences, which were integrated to establish a distinctive commercial style of pictorial representation.

The new naturalism in print design helped to differentiate the new mass culture from traditional medieval culture in both form and content. Pattern books, herbals, anatomies, engineering drawings, and maps were common in the sixteenth century, spreading enormous amounts of useful information. As they were increasingly tied to written texts and used to explicate texts (or vice versa), their informational capacity became increasingly important and of greater significance to printers.[50]

These new kinds of useful prints were not produced in quantities as great as traditional religious pictures, but they were more important in shaping the new character of mass culture. They were a new genre of picture that both called on and helped create a sharp contrast between medieval iconographic images and the practical diagrams of the early modern period. They drew on the emergent utilitarianism of the period and helped to provoke it by giving people a means for solving more of their practical problems. Their usefulness was predicated on a new social definition of pictures as carriers of accurate information. As a result, useful prints placed pressures on the informational capacity of the printing techniques, resulting in a kind of naturalism in print design, but not the kind of naturalism sought by fine artists. Accurate, detailed prints of practical subjects were simply more useful than ones with less information.[51]

The technical problems involved in trying to produce accurate information in prints made woodcuts progressively less useful than engravings in the sixteenth century. William Ivins describes these problems and their consequences:

In the course of the first half of the sixteenth century what I may call the informational pressure on the woodcut illustration, that is, the cramming of more and more lines and detailed information into the given areas, became notable. This resulted in immediate difficulty for printers. . . . Woodblocks, until the early years of the nineteenth century, were inked, as was type, not with rollers, as in our modern techniques, but by pounding them with large stuffed leather balls charged with ink. The least carelessness in the use of the balls produced spotty and clogged impressions. . . . This unevenness of impression could not be avoided by the printer of books with very fine cuts, because it came from the paper, which as made in those days was much smoother on one side than on the other. When the lines and the furrows in the paper were coarser than the lines on the block, the tops of the lines in the paper took more ink from the block than did the furrows between them. There are many fine textured woodcut book illustrations of the middle of the sixteenth century which were rendered almost illegible by the streakiness that came from this.

By the fifteen-fifties the woodcut had reached the limit of minuteness of work beyond which it could not go so long as there was no change in the techniques of paper-making and of inking the blocks. Although a few fifteenth-century books had been illustrated by engravings, it was not until about the middle of the sixteenth century that there began, slowly and sporadically at first and then with increasing commonness and regularity, the flood of books illustrated with engravings and etchings — processes which did not suffer from the limitations interposed by the paper and the method of inking.[52]

Engravings held their ink in grooves rather than on ridges and were made using much greater pressure than woodcuts, so they did not suffer from the same problems. But they were also more expensive, since they were cut from metal rather than wood and required greater skill to produce. Thus, that engravings became more common than woodblocks in the sixteenth century, rather than print designs becoming simpler when woodcuts could hold no more information, suggests that printers valued accuracy in their prints highly. If this were not enough evidence that accuracy was becoming a main value in print design, then the controversies that followed the wide-scale adoption of engravings would certainly make the point. Different engravers developed and used different systems for laying lines in their engravings to try to maximize the details of their subjects, some highlighting the textures of objects, others depicting the three-dimensional qualities of subjects, and still others emphasizing the outlines of engraved figures. The different systems all had their advantages and disadvantages, but all were designed to produce a higher level of information. The one system that gained predominance and became the standard system for laying engraving lines for the next two centuries was the "syntax" developed by Marcantonio Raimondi.[53]

Marcantonio produced a system using cross-hatchings, a kind of net, which, while poor in showing the surface details of objects, was easy to use for reproducing their topographical features. This probably assured its adoption, since an easy system allowed printers either to produce more engravings in their print shops or to hire people with a lower level of skill at lower wages to do their engraving.[54]

Marcantonio's syntax, then, was one solution to the problem of making accurate prints with maximum information. It was a technological innovation that evolved in response to the demand that prints be carriers of useful information, and that succeeded as an innovation because it was inexpensive to use and therefore helped keep engravings inexpensive enough to remain a form of mass culture. In addition, since engravers had an easy time laying lines with this system, they could make an old map design, or any work sloppy in its conception, look authoritative by giving it the technically polished appearance that came to characterize commercial culture for the next few hundred years.[55]

The emergence of fine art and mass culture as proto–class cultures, which had begun in the fifteenth century as a change in work routines, now by the end of the sixteenth was evident in the distinctive characteristics of the works themselves. A revolution in commerce had given rise to new and distinctive cultural forms designed to take advantage of and thus necessarily to reflect the emergent system of social stratification in European countries.

Dürer and the New Consumer Culture

The articulation of novel elite and mass cultural forms was not a product of some disembodied welling-up of social forces but a pattern created by the action of individuals who were using the economic opportunities of the times to make new goods and to design them for the consumers of the period. The social processes described in general terms above are evidenced in the lives of particular sixteenth-century graphic and fine artists. Of course, not all artists and printmakers freed themselves from guild restrictions, were able to do innovative work, and found monetary reward for it; but those who were more adept at exploiting the opportunities of their times (or better located for doing so) illustrate in their lives how economic changes encouraged new patterns of picture-making. Dürer is one such person.

It may seem odd to discuss Dürer in an argument that has so far stressed the differentiation of printmaking from fine art, since Dürer is well known for working in both media. Yet his life suggests how these two separate traditions were interdependent innovations of the period.

Dürer was born in Nuremberg in 1471, the son of a goldsmith and godson to Anton Koberger, the greatest printer of that period. He learned goldsmithing from his father and woodcutting from his godfather but expressed enough interest in painting to be apprenticed to a painter (Michael Wolgemut) who had worked for Koberger. He studied with Wolgemut to make painting his trade, and in doing so he learned something quite unusual for a German art student of that period: he learned to associate painting with printmaking.[56]

Before this period, woodcutting in general and book illustration in particular were still quite simple. Illustrations for the best books were still hand made. Koberger was unusual in hiring painters like Wolgemut to make book illustrations, and in trying to make illustration a more central and interesting part of the book. Because of his early association with Koberger and Wolgemut, Dürer had an unusual training that affected his work from the beginning, from the time he became a journeyman and began to travel through the principalities of what would become Germany.[57]

Art historians do not agree on many of the details of his early travels and work, but it seems likely that his travels kept him in Germany and that he worked for printers producing woodcuts. In 1492 he seems to have arrived in Colmar, where he met the brother of the famous engraver, Martin Schongauer. Dürer could not have studied with Schongauer, who had recently died, but his brother may have taught Dürer engraving.[58] In any case, Dürer seems to have developed his skills in printmaking (both woodcutting and engraving) during these early years while he was still not able to work for himself.

On his return to Nuremberg Dürer may have expected to become a master craftsman in a painter's guild, but in the years he was away from Nuremberg painting had become redefined as a free or liberal art and no longer a trade. This definition of art that seems to have migrated from northern Italy, changing the conditions of picture-making from the medieval ones Dürer had known as a boy.[59]

Soon Dürer, perhaps interested in the transformation of art in Italy or simply escaping the plague in Nuremberg, left for Italy to study the work of Italian Renaissance painters. There are records placing him in Venice in 1494, making copies of Italian art. The next year he returned to Nuremberg, and found Elector Frederick the Wise of Saxony interested in becoming his patron. Thus he embarked upon a prolific period of printmaking during which he produced many of his most famous woodcuts, including the large *Apocalypse* and *Adam and Eve*. He also made his first engraving, the first engraving known to have been made in Nuremberg.[60]

Dürer's fascination with Italy and Italian art continued, and he returned to Italy in 1505, staying there for over a year, enjoying the life of a celebrity and continuing his studies. By this time he was investigating body proportions and looking at their expression in Italian art. He returned to Nuremberg in 1507, set up his own workshop, and received from Anton Koberger full access to a printing press.[61] He began another fruitful period of producing prints, but his work changed as he began to reserve his woodcuts for books and to do more original works of engraving. H. T. Musper notes:

Without any apparent reasonable explanation suddenly shortly before the middle of the second decade of the sixteenth century, after having virtually given up individual woodcuts, Dürer produced the three great master engravings on which so much of his fame rests [*Knight, Death, and the Devil* in 1513, and in 1514 both *Saint Jerome in his Study* and *Melancholia.*][62]

Dürer's shift of interest from woodcuts to engravings does not seem difficult to explain. He was probably a wise enough businessman to have noticed that print publishers were finding greater use for engravings than woodcuts. This inference seems plausible because Dürer clearly realized prints were salable commodities when he used them to pay expenses during a trip to the Netherlands in 1520. He recorded the transactions in his journal in the following businesslike style:

Sebald Fischer bought of me at Antwerp sixteen "Small Passions" for 4 florins, thirty-two of the large books for 8 florins, also twenty half-sheets of all kinds taken together at 1 florin to the value of 3 florins, and again 51–4 florins' worth of quarter sheets, forty-five of all kinds at 1 florin, and eight miscellaneous leaves at 1 florin; it is paid.[63]

Albrecht Dürer, *Riders on the Four Horses from the Apocalypse*, c. 1495. THE
METROPOLITAN MUSEUM OF ART, NEW YORK.

Dürer was a man who took advantage of all the new opportunities available to designers of pictorial images. He produced both prints and paintings, had his own workshop, traveled extensively, had an international reputation (which seems to have made his trips to Italy enormously pleasurable), enjoyed the patronage of an aristocrat, could sell his prints on the street in many areas of Europe, went to Italy to copy the work he admired, and generally seems to have recognized and exploited all the new opportunities for artists. He seems very much the creature of his times, when the evolving international economy was creating changing possibilities for artists' lives and life-styles.

Dürer was also the ultimate printmaker of his period, using that medium with a level of skill and sophistication that made him an unusual figure in the art world of the time and that made his prints influential in establishing the distinctive character of the graphic arts. His prints displayed, for example, a mixture of medieval and modern elements that has encouraged art historians to label him a transitional figure, bridging two styles at the moment of change. But his pictures were also articulating the commercial style of printmaking described above: the use of familiar medieval imagery with a Renaissance naturalism. Given Dürer's explicit awareness of and interest in prints as commercial commodities, it should not be surprising to find elements of the commercially profitable style of printmaking in his print designs (and, for that matter, to see effects of this style in his paintings).[64]

Because of his influence Dürer may have helped to establish the distinctive commercial aesthetic for pictorial printing. There is an apparent irony in this, i.e., in having an artist help to define a commercial aesthetic. But it makes perfect sense for the period, since artists, as the intellectuals of pictorial culture, were expected to translate aesthetic experiments into theories of art. Dürer's interest in *codifying* an aesthetic for prints, then, reflected a general concern among artists of this period for delineating the proper methods of representation—an interest commonly expressed in treatises on anatomy or perspective. Intellectual exercises of this sort were encouraged by the humanist definition of artists, but they had more practical importance as a way to conventionalize art-making. In this period, after all, the division of labor in workshops was increasing the productivity of artists. Conventions that described procedures for drawing the human body or suggesting depth, then, were enormously useful for coordinating the activities of the many apprentices who were likely to be involved in the production of a given piece.[65] Under these circumstances, it is no wonder that artists like Dürer and Marcantonio were encouraged by their role as artists to articulate formulas for picture-making. The delineation of a mass cultural aesthetic, i.e., the use of advanced techniques for producing conventional imagery, was little more than an extension of this movement in painting; it was similarly designed for and useful in increasing the production of pictures.

A scholar quoting Dürer on these issues suggests that his ideas were odd, but they seem, rather, to express current sixteenth-century ideas about the arts, both fine and commercial.

A few ideas do, admittedly, strike us as rather odd. For one, his certainty that only the artist can tell us what is good, and that, at best, most people can only grasp that something is beautiful. This, surprisingly, goes along with his insistence that wholly unlearned common folk should be allowed to pass judgment because "they are able to recognize if a thing has been done very clumsily, even though they have no way of knowing if it is good."[66]

What Dürer describes is a rationale for emphasizing technique in production of mass culture, i.e., for developing precisely the kind of technical finish on works that Marcantonio's system provided for prints. In this way, he delineates the basis for a commercial aesthetic, helping to bring a mass culture to life and increasing the range of pictures available not only to the wealthy patrons of the fine arts, but also to more common consumers.

Cosmopolitan Patterns of Culture

Prints helped in the geographic spread of consumerism by carrying designs for artifacts over broad areas, shaping international patterns of taste. Of course, trade was the underlying cause of this internationalism; it permitted the movements of artisans, artifacts, patrons, and raw materials that integrated consumers from different regions into a pan-European culture. But prints had a special role in this cultural integration, in part because they were easy to transport and in part because they had become easy to read. Trade in books about architectural planning, for instance, could cultivate cosmopolitan tastes in buildings in a way that trade in either artisans or raw materials alone could not. By the end of the sixteenth century, the commercial style of printmaking had already been established as an international style. The technically polished and highly conventionalized images in prints were so familiar that the cross-hatching was no longer a problem for most viewers, who were accustomed to it and found it less visible than the content of the pictures. Prints might have been less interesting than they were the century before, but they could communicate very clearly, making them an effective means of fashioning a European cultural heritage and international patterns of culture.[67]

By the end of the sixteenth century uses of prints also were beginning to change as book illustration became a more sophisticated method of communication, one central to the production of the best books. The new illustrations, found particularly in books on nature, architecture, drawing, and engineering, were unlike their simple predecessors. Rather than attracting semiliterate audiences by relieving the tedium of the verbal text, they were meant instead to supply pertinent information and to aid the expert in understanding the ideas in the writings. Hence these illustrations became a part of elite culture.[68]

More precisely, illustrations of this sort were part of an elite international culture. Like the "new draperies" and other successful projects developed originally to serve local markets, they had expanded into international trade and had become available to Europeans in all regions. They were not so prestigious as paintings, but they were in demand because they were useful to elites as information carriers.

As careful preparation became more common, book illustrations became more attractive in their own right, and the sale of illustrations as separate single-sheet prints increased. Their dual value as intellectual tools and as consumer goods gave them and the information they contained a broader market, increasing their potency to shape European vision.[69]

International trade in elite books and book illustrations was large enough to encourage publishers throughout Europe to continue improving the quality of the illustrations in their best books, and sustained a lively trade in woodblocks and engraved plates as well. When publishing businesses failed or discontinued their use of plates or woodblocks, they sold them, not only to local firms but also to publishing houses in other countries. This trade in plates and blocks added to the internationalism of printing, as did the practice of pirating illustrations along with texts for books. Publishers might not always duplicate the original illustrations for a pirated edition of some foreign book, but they frequently made smaller versions of the illustrations for less expensive editions.[70] Between the trade in plates and blocks and the copies made of illustrations, there was wide dissemination of the content of book illustrations, creating standardized images that were shared throughout Western Europe.

The Great Tradition

These movements in prints affected the development of both the Great Tradition and regional little traditions of European culture: as they made the revived classical heritage more accessible, they also made regional cultural variations visible as sources of ideas for a cosmopolitan European culture. The first part of this pattern is obvious in the history of the Baroque:

Although Rome was its birthplace, the Baroque style soon became international. Among the artists who helped bring this about, the great Flemish painter, Peter Paul Rubens (1577–1640) holds a place of unique importance. It might be said that he finished what Dürer had started a hundred years earlier—the breakdown of the artistic barriers between North and South.[71]

The barriers broken down by both international trade and the Baroque created "world" systems of economics and culture, ones that had roots in the changes of the fifteenth century but that only blossomed in the seventeenth. The cultural effects of expanded trade and capitalist development, as Fernand Braudel suggests, were most apparent in the elite culture of this period, i.e., in the culture of those persons who were most directly involved in the expanding international capitalist economy. The aristocrats and high-level merchants in this period were the ones most interested in establishing links between the culture they consumed and classical culture; they took themselves to be the new caretakers of the Great Tradition of Western culture and used their displays of wealth to make this claim.[72]

William Ivins argued that prints of classical and Renaissance art, being mass produced and spread throughout Europe in this period, were used to define the classical heritage for Europeans. They carried the images of past artworks to new patrons throughout the continent, many of whom could not see the originals themselves. Baroque artists took advantage of the resulting market for printed reproductions and the lack of clear line dividing Renaissance and Baroque art by adding prints of their own works to the flow of pictures and using them to attract art collectors. Rubens was one of the artists taking fullest advantage of this opportunity. He made numerous title pages for publishers and some single-sheet prints; more important he also had reproductions of his own paintings made by his own engravers and sold under his supervision. Thus Rubens was able to direct the dissemination of his work, bringing it to the attention of patrons who might be induced to sponsor paintings. Rubens successfully used this method to increase his wealth and fame, exploiting the new legitimacy of, and elite interest in, printed reproductions of artworks.[73]

The Little Tradition

With the spread of the Baroque and classical art through books and reproductions, regional cultural traditions became less effective as systems of local control over elite culture than they had been in the past, but they did not disappear. They became instead both a source of ideas for the growing cosmopolitan culture and a basis for rebelling against the hegemony of the Great Tradition in shaping culture. Their significance for European culture did not diminish but did change.

While increased trade encouraged international styles of fine art in the late sixteenth and seventeenth centuries, it did not decrease the variety of local goods that elites could or did consume. In fact, the opposite was the case. Trade in books about local designs and artifacts increased the variety of goods available on the market. And it made what had previously been regional types of goods, both elite and popular, models for the design of entirely novel goods.

Some of these new designs came from the distinctive customs of traditional regional elites. These included peculiar ways of organizing rooms within a manor house or ways of dressing to display social rank. Regional forms were obvious resources for anyone wanting to make innovations in the international elite culture; they were already associated with high social rank, and they were novelties for consumers outside of their regions. Designs for some articles, such as upholstered chairs and courtly apparel, could not be dictated by classical culture because their roots were more recent, and these used regional elite forms.

The regional forms and the international ones developing at the same time helped to define each in terms of the other. This is why, for instance, regional costume was codified for the first time in the sixteenth century. Because the articulation of specifically regional designs was only valuable to consumers when more cosmopolitan dress was attainable, many of these regional forms were self-consciously made in this period. The cultivation of regional forms was often inspired as a reaction against the homogenizing effects of the international culture, but their wide spread resulted in expansion of the latter.

Some forms of *mass* culture from regional little traditions became the foundation of successful projects. The popularity of these goods, usually based on practical advantages, could make them major commodities on the world market. They might not have had the importance of elite forms in defining the reigning aesthetics for a pan-European culture, but they did provide the means for further commercial expansion and growing cosmopolitanism.

Books, as we have seen, were successful projects that found practical use within the international cultural arena. They acted as a conduit between regional and cosmopolitan cultural worlds. For instance, costume books, which catalogued the variations in dress that Europeans encountered on their own continent and abroad, became quite popular items in the sixteenth century. Cesare Vecellio's *Habiti antichi et moderni di tutto il Mondo* was among the finest examples of this genre, illustrating how new information about design variations was giving Europeans a new cosmopolitan view of cultural differences and a novel self-consciousness about local traditions.[74]

Just as international trade (and trade in books and prints) helped artisans to draw on regional cultural forms, disruptions of trade encouraged further differentiation of regional cultures. The political struggles that accompanied, for instance, state-formation, the Reformation, and overseas expansion periodically threw artisans back on their local traditions. Trade crises created both temporary and permanent losses of resources: a lack, for instance, of foreign raw materials, a loss of skills due to the expulsion of foreign artisans (or artisans with the wrong religious affiliation), or a lack of new ideas resulting from reduced trade in the artifacts themselves. The frequency of these disruptions made this regional differentiation a common source of innovation and important to the cultural fabric of the times. The pursuit of diverse design traditions created a variety in European material culture that eventually fed the cosmopolitan culture of elites, producing a complexity that a spread of classical ideas alone could not have fashioned.

The Reformation is known to have disrupted traffic between Italy and Protestant countries, helping to encourage regional differentiation. The resulting isolation of Protestant areas was temporary, but it did last long enough to help cultivate, for instance, disdain among some Protestants for the flamboyant religious and mythological (or "pagan") subjects that were central to the Catholic Baroque and a complementary interest in local little traditions as sources for humbler and more authentic design.[75]

Much of Dutch art of the seventeenth century, many of the landscapes, portraits, and "genre" paintings of everyday life, showed little or no debt to the Catholic Baroque; they were direct outgrowths of a regional cultural tradition from the Middle Ages that sanctioned the depiction of morality tales about everyday activities. These pictures displayed the Protestant dislike of the monumental themes and subjects that dominated most of the art in

Catholic Europe and documented the interest in commerce that was then dominating Dutch life. Major forms of property, from land to homes to jewelry and decorative objects, were central images in these Dutch paintings.[76]

There is a story (probably apocryphal but apt enough to deserve telling) about the popularity of still-life paintings of floral arrangements in this period. A seventeenth-century Dutchman commissioned a painting of some tulips at the height of the Dutch mania for these flowers. He wanted the painting, he claimed, because buying a picture of tulips was cheaper than acquiring the bulbs themselves. Given the price of the bulbs during this fad and also given the surplus of artists in seventeenth-century Holland, there may be some truth to this story.[77] But it also shows how a taste for consumer commodities could have contributed to an interest in paintings that depicted them. Moreover, in locating some of the appeal of genre paintings in their displays of commodities, this story suggests why these types of paintings, in spite of their distinctively northern qualities, could have had international appeal, making this regional type of artifact a prime candidate for incorporation into an international European culture.

In fact, genre paintings were not, as one is frequently led to suspect, a monopoly of the Dutch in the seventeenth century. Some elements of this northern tradition had been found in the art of southern Europe as early as the fifteenth century, when Flemish painting became influential in southern Europe. The Habsburg empire helped to spread this influence even further, encouraging, for instance, the development of Spanish "vanitas" paintings, a southern equivalent of this northern "genre" form. The Dutch cultivation of this style in the seventeenth century simply brought it to the attention of more northern Europeans, particularly the English and French. Thus, although these Dutch paintings seemed the essence of regional culture in the seventeenth century, they were, in fact, one type of regional culture that had already begun and would continue to be spread throughout Europe.[78]

Dutch art became particularly easy to imitate after Dutch independence from the Habsburg empire, when Amsterdam, and to a lesser extent Leyden, became publishing centers, and the Dutch

Jan Davidsz de Heem, *Vase of Flowers*, 1649. BY PERMISSION OF THE NATIONAL GALLERY OF ART, ANDREW MELLON FUND.

put out large numbers of emblem books (the iconological bases for many genre pictures). These emblem books contained pictures and poems illustrating morality lessons. The following passage from one of the emblem books that Christopher Plantin put out in English gives some of the flavor of these ditties:

And he that lik'd to spende his time at dice,
This law in Rome, Servrs did prouide:
That euerie man, shoulde deeme him as a vice,
And of his Landes, an other shoulde be guide:
Like Lawes beside, did diuers more deuise,
And wisdom still, againste such unthriftes cries.[79]

The Dutch also put out pattern books containing decorations for furniture and the interiors of houses, decorations that influenced these and other forms of nonclassical elite culture. The widespread popularity of these books (and copies of them made in other countries) assured that artists throughout Europe could produce similar kinds of artifacts.[80]

The story of these Dutch publications is one of many that can illustrate how printed works helped to connect Catholic and Protestant Europe, making the cultural differentiation of these areas less complete than one might at first suspect. Books that had already brought humanist ideas about art to Holland and England before the Reformation provided a continuing influence on Protestant art after the Reformation, sustaining, for example, an interest in mythological subjects that, although diminished, was not entirely dissipated by Reformation ideas or loss of trade with Italy. It was revived, among other places, in many of Rembrandt's paintings and prints. Books even continued to carry ideas and images across religious boundaries when more direct traffic between Catholic and Protestant areas was reduced. This trade in books had perhaps its clearest effect on the history of English architecture in the seventeenth century, when books by Serlio, Palladio, and others were used as the basis for a new English classicism (and influenced, particularly, the work of Inigo Jones).[81]

Trade in single-sheet prints also affected art in this period. Rembrandt, for instance, was able to combine northern and southern elements in his paintings, in spite of the fact that he did little travelling, because he collected prints and used print collecting to learn about the cultural currents that he could not experience directly.[82] In his case, single-sheet prints were central to his production of artworks in a cosmopolitan style.

Besides the direct effect of art reproductions on the artwork of this period, there were indirect effects from a variety of types of il-

Elevation from *The Designs of Inigo Jones.* London: B. White, 1770. SPECIAL
COLLECTIONS, UNIVERSITY OF CALIFORNIA, SAN DIEGO.

lustration. Pictures in herbals, for instance, were used as designs
for embroideries as well as plans for laying out garden beds. Similarly, John Evelyn's *Sylva,* a book on trees that was published in
England in the second half of the seventeenth century, was used
by furniture makers to choose the proper kinds of woods for furniture or inlay, and used by the designers of great Baroque gar-

dens for choosing and locating both fruit and decorative trees. In addition, books on Alexandrian water mechanics, intended to be used as classic scientific works, were guides for engineering the grottoes that were popular in gardens in the sixteenth and seventeenth centuries. In the same time period, prints of world maps became the models for murals and tapestries. Added to all the ways in which culture was directly shaped by books, these more indirect patterns show the subtle but strong role of prints in producing a shared cosmopolitan culture of elites in the early modern period.[83]

Material and Ideational Culture

This discussion, which has emphasized the growing integration in designs for material culture, stands in contrast to the usual descriptions of culture in this period, which describe it as fragmented. While this analysis has so far dissected only material culture, these patterns hold equally well for ideas. The ideological aspects of political and religious movements like state-formation and the Reformation divided Europeans in some ways, but they integrated them in others. To the extent that they dissolved medieval patterns of thought, they undermined not only some of the unifying elements in traditional "Christian" culture but also some of the medieval regional differences. The Counterreformation had a similar dual effect on European beliefs. Although it developed because of and to highlight the differences between Catholicism and Protestantism, it ended up creating greater homogeneity among Catholics when it led to a standardization of religious practices after the Council of Trent. Similarly, efforts to create states in early modern Europe led to new patterns of cultural integration after the dominant groups in the new states began to suppress regional autonomy and cultural differences in order to establish their national hegemony.[84]

These movements did not produce complete homogeneity in European culture any more than trade created a unified material culture; in fact, in tending to make regional variations more apparent, they sometimes helped to sustain them. But the new political and religious thought did help to promote greater internationalism in ideational culture, in the same way that trade created greater cosmopolitanism in material culture; the competition between alternatives stimulated imitation of competing patterns, which reduced differences. Trade, in both cases, helped to make what were originally quite different cultures into variations within a common cultural system.

Trade, then, made it difficult for any political, lingual, religious, or other boundary to be totally effective in promoting fragmentation. And, as was true for material culture, printed works had a special role in ideational integration. While books were used in propagating some of the ideas that created struggles in this period (like the Reformation), they also spread humanism and ideas for the new science, i.e., ideas that were creating new forms of internationalism in European thought.

Political and religious censorship, privileges or monopolistic rights over publishing particular books, restrictions on the importation of books, and limits on trade engendered by language differences all seemed to circumscribe the influence of printed works. But books still had increasing power over European thought in the early modern period in spite of all the restrictions placed on their production and distribution. The growing use of the vernacular in print (which limited the language groups books could reach) and censorship laws, both of which erected regional barriers to the movement of ideas, did not prevent books from producing a broader ideational culture. Books originally published in one vernacular, for instance, were often pirated by publishers in other countries, translated (which could be done relatively easily), and put on the market in a new edition. Particularly during the first few centuries of printing, when printers depended on local grants of monopolies to protect and regulate their businesses, publishers without such monopolies often needed to pirate books simply to sustain their businesses; they probably also felt justified in copying books that were protected only within some distant town or circumscribed region. Pirating spread the content of books well beyond the boundaries of local markets, making the ideas contained in these books part of European culture.[85]

State censorship laws similarly stimulated as well as limited the movement of ideas in print, since censorship encouraged the development of unauthorized publication and distribution. John Wolfe, for instance, began his business as a non-privileged printer in England by reprinting and exporting to Italy those Italian books that had been prohibited by the Church. By locating this foreign market for his books, he was able to circumvent the restrictions on publishing in England that gave privileges to a small number of printers to publish for the English market. He also learned, as other publishers did, that one could frequently make more money pirating books than producing new ones, since for pirated editions publishers did not have to pay for the original preparation of the manuscript or for the right to publish the work. His experience demonstrates how precisely those censorship laws, restrictions on trade, and language differences that would seem most fragmenting to European culture in this period could have had the opposite effect, increasing the cultural uniformity in Europe.[86]

Consumer Culture

New kinds of production and trade in material culture then, acted as a counterweight to the sources of cultural fragmentation, increasing the cosmopolitanism of European culture. The movement of *goods* could be such a powerful cultural force because the increased production and use of consumer commodities was helping to join both rich and poor into similar market relations and gathering together buyers throughout Europe into common patterns of taste. The new patterns of consumption of these novel goods brought to life a cultural system that, because it tapped and bred new levels and types of demand, was particularly suited to and encouraging of capitalist development.

The consumers who became enmeshed in this new culture ranged in type from the high-level aristocrats, trying to sustain medieval notions of aristocratic largesse in a world of increasingly elaborate and expensive material culture, to the Dutch merchants using English cloth to save some money (so they could invest the rest), to the English farmer buying Dutch pins because they were harder than local equivalents. The desires of new consumers and the patterns of their purchases stimulated new economic activity in Europe in specific ways: by discouraging hoarding, thus making new surplus a more potent economic force; by creating the broad patterns of taste that would support larger-scale production and trade; and by increasing the general level of demand for goods by making a greater proportion of the population consumers than had been typical in the past.

The impetus to design new consumer goods to take advantage of economic changes in this period provided opportunities for cultural innovation. The cultural creativity that this situation unleashed was striking, particularly during the Renaissance, but it was also clearly limited, circumscribed by the drive to use meaning to create profit, i.e., to tie cultural activity to economic purposes. The new kinds of goods that flourished in this atmosphere were commercial successes, items that provided buyers with the kinds of meanings they wanted to purchase: ideas in books, the presence of people in portraits, access to tulips in paintings, or definitions of status in the collection of some variety of these objects. The growth of such consumerism, then, was instrumental in creating a fundamental shift in the locus of meaning in European social process, placing it in the world of goods and the economic activities that gave birth to them and shaped the patterns of their distribution.

CHAPTER THREE

A New World-Picture: Maps as Capital Goods for the Modern World System

And he who doubteth but a simple Fisher-man of Barking knoweth Barking Creeke, better then the best Nauigator or Master in this lande; so who doubteth but these simple men doth know their owne places at home. But if they should come out of the *Ocean* sea to seek our chanel to come vnto ye riuer of *Thames*, I am of that opinion, that a number of them, doth but grope as a blinde man doth, & if that they doe hit wel, that it is but by chaunce, and not by cunning that is in him. —William Bourne, *Regiment of the Sea*[1]

ONE REASON why Weber's thesis about the Protestant ethic and capitalism seems so plausible is that an ideology with a title as awesome as the "Protestant ethic"—one evoking fire and brimstone—seems potent enough to usher in as powerful and demanding an economic order as capitalism. In contrast, the thesis argued in this book is counterintuitive in locating the culture of capitalism in some of the humblest and most innocuous items that our culture has produced: pins and laces, pictures and cooking pots.

The importance of material culture to the growth of capitalism is perhaps more plausible when we stop looking at consumer goods and turn our attention to capital goods, particularly the technological innovations that were used to enhance trade. Some of these were as modest as, if not pins, then at least cooking pots. Sextants were rather compact items with a powerful effect on trade; cannons might have been a bit larger, but they were rather simple innovations in material culture that gave European traders advantages over, for instance, their Arab competitors in the trade with the East.

Technologies, like heaven and hell, have large reputations in Western culture. In fact, technological innovations have sustained almost to the present day the aura of miraculous power that even religions seem to have lost. Saying that technological innovation has contributed to the growth of capitalism makes such obvious sense to those steeped in this tradition that it hardly seems to need demonstration. Conveniently, this view of technology also fits the general thesis of this book: that innovations in material culture in the early modern period were central to the growth of capitalism. But the term "technology" as it is usually used is really not appropriate for describing the innovations that affected patterns of economic development in early modern Europe.

The word simply has too many meanings. On the one hand, it conjures up images of clattering machines in large factories; on the other, it can refer to writing systems and other *techniques* that are neither directly connected to manufacturing nor embedded in a particular piece of material culture. The line between technique and technology is too blurred to distinguish forms of material culture designed for pursuing economic advantages from either other cultural objects or nonmaterial cultural forms.

Similar problems arise in using the term "capital goods" to describe objects with specific economic purposes, not only because the term assumes the existence of a particular economic system (capitalism) but also because the term is frequently used to distinguish practical objects from consumer goods, even though, as was suggested in chapter one, the line between them is not at all clear. The first problem is raised by Fernand Braudel when he argues that the expanding trade of the early modern period was not a form of capitalist development in itself, but only provided the levels of economic activity that could *support* capitalist enterprise.[2] How, then, can we describe the cannon, new ships, and other innovations in material culture designed to improve trade? Are they "capital goods"? The answer seems to be yes—not because Braudel is wrong in distinguishing the commercial revolution from capitalist development, but because once Europeans used these objects to gain competitive advantages in trade, they also increased the amount of capital necessary to make ocean commerce a successful venture. In this way as well as others, the innovations in "capital goods" increased capitalist development.

The other problem with the term "capital goods" is equally sticky but simple to solve. While the capital goods that were increasingly invented and used in the early modern period may not have constituted a set of items distinguishable from all consumer goods, they were still identifiable as items designed specifically to have economic uses. They might have been put to other uses, but their economic potential was written into their physical structure. For these reasons and because it makes specific reference to "goods," the term capital goods is more appropriate for an analysis of material culture than "technology." Hence that term is used here to describe the innovations in material culture that were *specifically designed to act as economic tools.*

The geographical documents published and distributed in the late sixteenth century were a type of "capital good" whose proliferation in print and wide distribution affected the international balance of power by changing patterns of control over world trade. Most scholars (and perhaps most readers) would tend to think of these publications as carriers of ideas, without considering how their physical form affected either their character or the effects of the information they contained. But their forms shaped their possible functions. Maps and geographical writings, as information fixed in a permanent form, replaced both memory and advice in accumulating and transmitting this information, and they also helped to pass it from one individual to the next without loss of accuracy. Records of this sort could even be reviewed, compared, and revised with an ease and accuracy unparalleled by oral accounts. In these ways and probably others, the information put in these documents was more useful than the same information carried by word of mouth.

Maps and geographical writings became particularly salient in the fifteenth and sixteenth centuries, when overseas exploration was revealing vast new areas of the world to Europeans, and when improved surveying techniques were revealing increasing details about European geography. It would have been difficult for Iberians to expand their trade if they had had to rely exclusively on memory to guide their ships, and it would have been silly to survey either estates or regions of Europe for politicoeconomic purposes (such as assessing taxes or rents) without recording the results. Making accurate maps and pilots, then, facilitated the reorganization of patterns of trade and political control.

Maps and geographical writings had circulated in small quantities in manuscript form before they began to be published, but they were difficult to reproduce and their use was not highly developed. Most medieval travelers did not use maps. Navigators on fishing or merchant vessels relied primarily on memory and experience to plot their courses, and European land travelers tended to embark on their journeys with little more than advice from others or their own experience to guide them. There was even some active resistance to the use of maps, particularly on the part of fishermen and merchants who wanted to monopolize geographic information to protect their interests.[3]

By the beginning of the sixteenth century, a growing number of manuscript maps and printed maps or geographical writings were appearing, although few travelers actually used them; the Iberians, who had started to collect geographical documents during the early stages of exploration, secreted their maps and writings to try to secure their proprietary rights over trade routes. When the Italians and Germans began to use print more frequently to reproduce larger numbers of these documents in the sixteenth century, such traditional monopolies started to be disturbed. And in the late sixteenth and early seventeenth centuries, the Dutch published numerous atlases and books on navigation, initiating what we would call today the free flow of geographical information.[4]

Printed geographical information was not the only innovation in material culture with important consequences for European expansion. Innovations in and increased production of ships, guns, and navigational equipment helped give Europeans the material resources they needed to reach overseas trading centers and secure the rights to trade there. Printed works were simply one part of a multifaceted shift in material culture that contributed to the growth of an international capitalist economy initiated and controlled by Europeans.

Ships, weapons, sails, and maps had existed in Europe before the early modern period, but their designs changed as they were tailored to the pursuit of profits through trade. The ships built in this period were now armed with cannon, giving Europeans the military power to make this trade a commercial success. They were also rigged in new ways with sails that made them more versatile for ocean voyaging. These design innovations could be (and usually have been) seen as responses to the technical problems of engaging in this new type of trade, but they also can and should be recognized as modifications made to give their users (and usually the countries that used them) an edge in world trade. Innovations in ship design were politicoeconomic as well as technical expressions, responses to a specific kind of world economy as well as to the natural world.[5]

The new geographical writings that appeared in this period also displayed both politicoeconomic and technical concerns. Many sets of sailing directions, ostensibly meant to inform navigators about the shape of land masses and the character of oceans, also explicitly advocated trade as a means for national economic development. Moreover, many of the land maps of Europe emphasized the estates, waterways, and political boundaries that constituted the politicoeconomic dimensions of European geography. These geographical documents were among the many innovations in capital goods that were specifically designed to gain economic advantages in a political competition over the emerging economic order.

The importance of geographical information in the political and economic reorganization of early modern Europe can be seen in the following passage from John Evelyn's 1674 book on commerce:

It was Commerce, and Navigation (the Daughter of Peace, and good Intelligence) that gave Reputation to the most noble of our Native-Staples, WOOL, exceedingly Improv'd by Forreigners. . . . They are not therefore Small Matters, you see, which Men so much contend about, when they striue to Improve Commerce, and, by degrees, promote the Art of Navigation, and set the empire in the Deep, from whence they have found to flow such notable Advantages.[6]

Contemporaries of Evelyn, like Richard Hakluyt, Jan Huygen van Linschoten, and others also felt that the tools of navigation, including maps and travel chronicles, were vital resources for the pursuit of national wealth through international trade.[7]

The publication of geographical writings, charts, and maps played a role in two processes that Immanuel Wallerstein takes as central to the growth of a new economy: (1) the failure of the Habsburg empire, and (2) the establishment of European states. Wallerstein identifies these changes as essential to the system of competing European states that fostered the rise of capitalism.[8]

Although Wallerstein's thesis has generated considerable controversy, his model is particularly useful for analysis of geographical documents because he has derived from Braudel a concern for the geography of economic organization that has informed his view of the world economy. While the study here is dependent on this kind of analysis (since it suggests a close connection between geography and economy), it does not require that all aspects of Wallerstein's approach to the topic be correct. Wallerstein's basic argument, that the modern world system was an economic order based on a geographical division of labor supported by political and religious divisions, has not in itself been widely contested. Only the details of how this system is constructed are questioned, and they are not at issue here. What is important here is that a geographical division of labor was produced with the aid of geographical documents.

Wallerstein argues that the resulting balance of economic power between states distinguished the social organization of the new world economy from that of earlier empires. This new economic order allowed capitalist growth to increase in Europe as it never had in land-based empires because the fate of the world economy was not dependent on the stability of one political order.

Wallerstein explains the development of this new world system in sixteenth-century Europe entirely in economic terms. I shall demonstrate here that innovations in capital goods, specifically changes in the design and distribution of geographical documents, were a prerequisite to the geographical division of labor that Wallerstein describes. In other words, changes in the material culture of Europe had an important role in the formation of the new world economic system.

Manuscripts and Ocean Empires

A casual reading of fifteenth- and sixteenth-century geographical history might suggest that printed maps, charts, and other geographical information had little, if anything, to do with the formation of the modern world system, since much of the early Portuguese and Spanish exploration, which first opened the possi-

bility of a world system, predated widespread publication of geographical information. In fact, the period when geographical
information was first being printed in any quantity (c. 1550) was
also the period in which both Portugal and Spain were beginning
to lose their monopoly over overseas empires. But that is precisely
the point: publication of geographical information undermined
Portuguese and Spanish control of the world's oceans, making it
easier for other countries to participate in world trade. This was
one reason for Spain's failure to establish a Christian empire that
included all of Europe and the New World.

The formation of a modern world system centered around the
Atlantic was to some extent dependent on early explorers' opening that ocean, but it was even more dependent on the fact that
an empire uniting all of the regions engaged in this trade did not
develop. Formation of such an empire in sixteenth-century Europe
was not unlikely. As Braudel suggests, when cities were no longer
large enough politicoeconomic units to regulate the broader patterns of trade, sovereign states or empires had to develop. Either a
French or Habsburg empire seemed the most likely possibility.
The failure of both of these attempts at empire made the formation of the modern world system possible.[9]

Charles V forged the last great early modern empire on continental Europe, uniting within it Spain, the Netherlands, and parts
of Italy and Germany. He did this by exploiting two advantages
he had over other European leaders: (1) his control of the strong
financial centers in northern Europe, which provided for the bank-
ing needs of the empire; and (2) the Spanish hold on the New
World, which provided bullion. The Habsburg empire that
Charles created collapsed when Phillip II could hold on to neither
of these prizes. The resources of the empire had been expended
first in the struggle with France and, most critically, during the
revolt of the Netherlands, when the Dutch freed themselves from
Spain and became a formidable sea power in their own right, ri-
valing their Iberian predecessors.[10]

The Portuguese initiated European overseas expansion, first by
exploring and colonizing Madeira and the Azores, and later by
creating trade routes down the African coast. We do not know
with any accuracy the reasons for these Portuguese activities, but

we do know that Prince Henry the Navigator took a personal interest in exploring Africa and supported such explorations.[11]

Henry did more than simply encourage a few Portuguese to venture far from home; he helped to accumulate the material resources for doing so. With his help the Portuguese not only directed money toward expansion but also created innovations in material culture to facilitate his projects.[12]

Ralph Davis has pointed out that the Portuguese began expansion into the Atlantic using square-rigged ships that could not tack against the wind. As a result, they were limited in their ability to go south along the African coast where the northwest trade winds began. If square-rigged ships went that far south, they had to sail way out into the Atlantic with the trades to make their way back to Portugal. Only after the earliest African voyages were successfully made under these difficult circumstances did the Portuguese develop from Arab models in the Mediterranean the lateen-rigged caravel that facilitated the later voyages of exploration.[13]

A number of scholars have mentioned that Henry set precedents for future exploration by supporting a fusion of Mediterranean and Atlantic cultural traditions in the design of ships and their use. They argue that caravels were a hybrid mix of the small Mediterranean fighting ship and the large Atlantic merchant vessel, representing a cultural convergence in Europe. This same convergence of cultural influences shaped another Portuguese innovation: the increased development of geographical documents for Portuguese voyages. Portuguese charts combined the Mediterranean portolan tradition (of making accurate, manuscript coastal charts) with practical experience in the Atlantic. As in the case of caravels, the Portuguese drew on the cultural resources of both the Atlantic and Mediterranean to make new kinds of capital goods that could facilitate a shift in patterns of European trade.[14]

Innovations in capital goods, such as the development of new ship designs and the widespread use of guns on the new ships, have frequently been pointed to as central factors in the success of European expansion. Carlo Cipolla, for instance, argues that innovations in guns and ships made Europeans invulnerable to enemies in other parts of the world. In contrast, Portuguese use of maps and geographical writings seems much less influential. After all, medieval portolan-type charts had already existed, and some had even contained information about the Atlantic coast of Europe. It also seems possible at first glance that the Portuguese could have made their voyages without making maps of what they had found so far. But a look at what happened to other Europeans when they tried to sail down or around Africa without using these Portuguese records and the number of times that other Europeans tried to capture Portuguese pilots and copy their records puts this kind of assumption in question. It seems likely that monopoly in this area temporarily made the Portuguese and, later, the Spanish expeditions free from other European competition. Without European competition, Iberians could and did create vast ocean empires; they might not have been able to conquer all the land masses they encountered or even keep the seas free of pirates, but they could and did make oceans their property both on paper and to a large extent in practice.[15]

This is not to say that the design and use of geographical documents was the only or even the primary cause of expansion. On the contrary, a broad pattern of innovation in capital goods facilitated early changes in patterns of Portuguese trade. The virtue of focusing on geographical documents is that their symbolic meanings tend to be easily read, making it relatively simple to see in their designs the growing definition of them as economic resources, as material solutions to the politicoeconomic problems of expanding and controlling commerce.

Portuguese Exploration and Cartography. When Henry the Navigator began his sponsorship of expeditions down the African coast, he hired the son of a famous cartographer to train Portuguese pilots: Master Jacome, whose father, Abraham Cresques, had been the author of the Catalan Atlas of 1375.[16] The atlas was not, as one might expect, a collection of maps but rather one large sheet which integrated much of the medieval knowledge of the world; it was compiled from the information in Marco Polo's writings, as well as from the experiences of Venetian and Genoese merchants who traded in the Levant. This atlas was made in the style of the portolan charts fashioned in the Middle Ages primari-

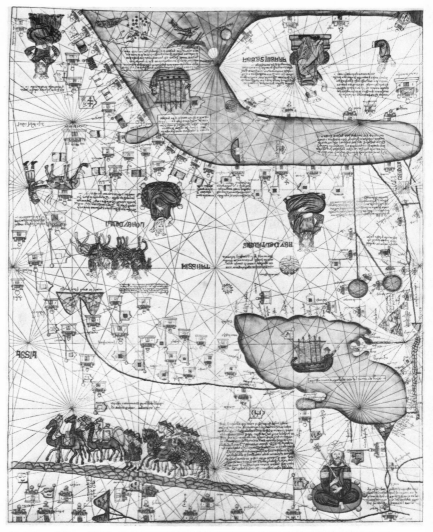

Catalan Atlas, 1375. REPRODUCED BY PERMISSION OF THE BRITISH LIBRARY.

ly for merchants and navigators who traded in the Mediterranean, which depicted major ports, rivers, and coastlines in the Mediterranean and sometimes the Atlantic coast of Europe. The Catalan Atlas added to this well-known stock of information new material about the East, but it was still a traditional chart made for merchant shipping, not for the general public.[17]

Master Jacome's position in Henry's entourage and his association with the Catalan Atlas suggests that the portolan cartographic tradition was the major source of Portuguese information about the world as well as the style of cartography the Portuguese would use to record their observations of new parts of the world. Appropriately, these records were designed to provide the kind of information useful to merchants in trade; thus, they were easy to adapt for new voyages embarked upon for the same purposes.

To appreciate fully the distinctiveness of this commercial orientation within the portolan tradition, we should contrast the geographical information in these maps with that from the other major medieval traditions: patristic geography and mythological travel writings. Patristic geography produced the Christian maps of the world that were most familiar to the public in the Middle Ages. They depicted the earth as a flat circle divided by a cross with its center in Jerusalem. These so-called "T and O" maps were given that name because they looked like circles divided by a T (often lying on its side) which segmented the circle into three parts, representing Europe (in the northwest), Africa (in the southwest) and Asia (in the east). The sacred world view that these maps represented was such a strong force in European culture that they continued to be used even after the introduction of portolan charts and the rediscovery of Ptolemy's more empirical maps. The more accurate maps did not have the same ideological value, and early geographical discoveries could be absorbed into the traditional form. By adding some complexity to the shape of the T, treating the Mediterranean as the trunk of the T and interpreting the Red Sea and Black Sea as its arms, patristic geographers could revise their maps in the face of new information about the geography of Europe and Asia without compromising the ideological value of these images. Only the discovery of America and recognition that it was a fourth continent finally brought an end to patristic geography.[18]

Medieval travel writings tended to be less empirical than portolan charts, presumably because they were as much a form of entertainment as a source of information. Yet they opened up the world to Europeans in a way that patristic geography did not; they described parts of the world as unknown, where T and O maps had seen the world as known a priori. Travel writings provided reasons, then, for exploring the rest of the world more thoroughly. Marco Polo and other careful chroniclers brought relatively accurate information about the East to Europe, and more fanciful writers enchanted the world beyond European reach, making it an attractive place to contemplate or try to see. The Mandeville papers and other travel lore brought to Europe a body of mythology about exotic islands in the Atlantic and idyllic lands to be found in the East. The Mandeville papers, for example, included descriptions of the land of Prester John, a mythological Christian kingdom somewhere in Ethiopia or India which Henry the Navigator seemed to want to reach.[19] The possibility of finding this Christian king, establishing trade with him, and joining military forces with him to fight the Turks provided a Christian ideology for exploration that a Portuguese chronicler, Azurara, attributed to Henry:

It is meet that in this present chapter we should know his [Henry's] purpose in doing [great things]. . . . Because he also had a wish to know the land that lay beyond the isles of Canary and that Cape called Bojador, for that up to his time, neither by writings, nor by the memory of man, was known with any certainty the nature of the land beyond that Cape. . . . And seeing also that no other prince took any pains in this matter, he sent out his own ships against those parts, to have manifest certainty of them all. . . . And this was the first reason of his action. The second reason was that if there chanced to be in those lands some population of Christians, or some havens, into which it would be possible to sail without peril, many kinds of merchandise might be brought to this realm, which would find a ready market, and reasonably so, because no other people of these parts traded with them, not yet any other that were known; and also the products of this realm might be taken there, which traffic would bring great profit to our countrymen. The third reason was that, as it was said that the power of the Moors in that land of Africa was very much greater than was commonly supposed, and that there were no Christians among them, nor any other race of men; and because every wise man is obliged by natural prudence to wish for a knowledge ᴊɪ the power of his enemy; therefore the said Lord Infant exerted himself to cause this to be fully discovered and to make it known determinately how far the power of those infidels extended. The fourth reason was because during the one and thirty years he had warred against the Moors, he had never found a Christian king, nor a lord outside this land, who for the love of our Lord Jesus Christ would aid him in the said war. Therefore he sought to know if there were in those parts any Christian princes. . . . [20]

Although Azurara does not mention the name of Prester John, the model of the Christian prince who could help trade and fight the Moors seemed based on the Prester John myth. One can see in this document how the rhetoric of medieval mythology and the medieval pattern of holy wars were used to explain the expansion that occurred under Henry's direction.

Henry, then, while using *existing* medieval myth and symbolism to motivate exploration, developed *novel* kinds of geographical documents to aid navigation down the coast of Africa. In fact, he brought some Italian cartographers to Portugal to copy charts and maps for pilots, and to incorporate new information from successful voyages into existing maps. Thus, he set up a system for producing new kinds of maps, importing traditional Mediterranean portolan-making skills and applying them to plan and document voyages into the unfamiliar waters of the Atlantic.[21]

Henry's use of cartographers illustrates what seems to have been a policy of accumulating geographical documents. But he also apparently banned their dissemination. With this he helped to establish a precedent for other Iberians, making it seem good practice to try to monopolize information—to use geographic documents as an economic resource, much as craft mysteries were secreted and used. Thus, Henry's policies toward cartographic records sustained both innovation in material culture and traditionalism in its use.

The pilots from Portuguese ships and the Italian cartographers in Portugal may well have produced a series of charts that recorded the information from the Henrician period of exploration, but no such records have been preserved. What does remain is a group of charts produced in other parts of Europe that appear to have been copied from Portuguese ones. The 1448 Andrea Bianco chart contains some of the information about the African coast that was picked up in Henrician voyages; but the writing on it is English, and it seems to have been made in London. There are also some chronicles describing Portuguese voyages that came out in manuscript form around the same time, including the 1450 Azurara manuscript on Guinea quoted above. The relatively rare pieces of manuscript writing and charts that remain from this period to this day give the contemporary scholar some basis for understanding the period of Henry's dominance over European expansion, but they also indicate how little data reached the public on the momentous naval adventures of this period. The veil of secrecy that Henry had wanted was relatively well maintained.[22]

By the beginning of the sixteenth century, when Henry's period of exploration was over, manuscript maps and writings containing the fruits of Portuguese expansion began to proliferate. The audience for these works must have been relatively small, since the number of manuscript copies was limited, but at least the era of greatest secrecy was over. It should be no surprise that more information about the early discoveries would be available then to non-Portuguese, since by the end of the fifteenth century a greater number of Europeans from diverse parts of Europe were participating in the trade and new explorations that the Henrician period had opened up. Columbus had inaugurated Spanish exploration of the New World, independent merchants from Italy were on Portuguese ships trading on the Guinea coast, and explorers and traders were bringing back goods from new lands in growing quantities. Under these circumstances total secrecy about overseas trips would have been impossible to maintain.[23]

The early sixteenth-century maps and writings about Portuguese expansion may have been seen by few people, but they opened up a new flow of geographical documents. For instance, the 1502 Cantino map, which provided the first accurate depiction of the whole African coastline, was produced for the Duke of Ferrera by a Portuguese cartographer who was obviously ignoring his king's ban on divulging information about the discoveries. This leaking of documents was significant because it led to eventual publication. The 1502–4 Caneiro map, which seems to have been copied from the Cantino map, was used as a model for Waldseemüller's early printed maps based on the discoveries, first the 1507 single sheet *Weltkarte* and later the new maps in his 1513 *Ptolemy* (the latter being one of the first printed sets of maps to bring new geographical findings into the commercial market).

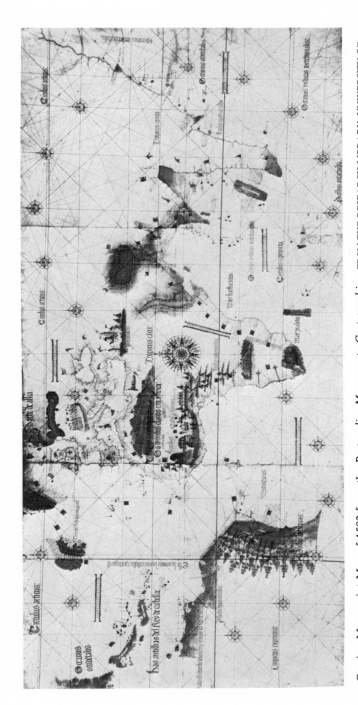

Cantino Manuscript Map of 1502 from the *Portugaliae Monumenta Cartographica*. FROM THE RESEARCH LIBRARY, UNIVERSITY OF CALIFORNIA, LOS ANGELES.

Together the Cantino and Caneiro maps represented a hinge joining (1) the manuscript map-making tradition, based on information from the discoveries that was meant to be secret, to (2) early
map printing for commercial dissemination.[24]

The 1507 *Paesi* collection of geographical writings was another
important document from the period of transition to print, since it
made public descriptions of explorations which had previously
been unknown.[25] It was published in Italy to become widely distributed and translated into many languages. But since it contained information about Spanish activities in the Americas as
well as about Portuguese voyages to Africa, India, and the Spice
Islands, discussing it now puts us out of chronological order. We
must first take a look at Columbus' voyages and the beginning of
Spanish exploration of the New World.

Spanish Cartography and the Erosion of Secrecy. Columbus was an
important figure in both the history of early exploration and the
history of early geographical writings. He wrote a diary of his first
voyage, parts of which were included in the short "Columbus letter" which was printed in many editions in a variety of languages
from his first return to Spain until the end of the century. This
letter was one of the first truly popular pieces of modern geographical writing. It demonstrated the potential market of this
whole genre of sixteenth-century literature, but it did not stimulate widespread publication of writings or charts showing accurate
details of Spanish or Portuguese exploration, in part because the
Spanish were still trying to keep this type of information secret.
Columbus' journal, which was a more extensive and accurate account of his trip, seems to have fallen victim to these policies; it
was kept secret and subsequently lost. Because Columbus' writings were both secreted and published, they are another example
of the mixed treatment of geographical information in the transitional period.[26]

The Columbian cycle of voyages (from 1492 to about 1515)
yielded massive amounts of new information about the size of the
world and the shape of the Americas. Though the Spanish tried to
keep details of these voyages secret, they also encouraged the creation of records, not simply the secret maps but also histories that

could demonstrate the vision of the Spanish monarchs in sponsoring the voyages. Because of this ambivalent attitude, there remain today a number of documents that describe Spanish activities in the Americas, some of which reached the public eye in the sixteenth century and some of which did not. One important document that was not published is the Juan de la Cosa map of the Americas. Juan de la Cosa was a cartographer/cosmographer who seems to have been on Columbus' second and perhaps third voyages, recording his observations and using them to produce a manuscript map (sometime between 1500 and 1508) that was among the first to show with any accuracy the shape of northern and central America and the islands of the Caribbean. About the same time, some other information about early voyages was going into print, including the *Paesi* collection of chronicles about Spanish and Portuguese expeditions. Thus, the Spanish policy of keeping detailed geographical information from the public was partially successful, giving some protection to the Spanish hold over world trade, but not succeeding, as Portuguese policies had, in keeping descriptive accounts of exploration out of print.[27]

In the same period (the first decade of the sixteenth century) the Castilian court set up the Casa de Contracion, a department of commerce that was to oversee exploration and house in secrecy accurate documents of discovery. An account of this institution and the training of pilots there was taken from a Spanish pilot and translated by Richard Grinville in 1585. It then appeared in Hakluyt's *Voyages*:

First they make suit unto the Pilot Major (who at this present is called Alonzo de Chiavez) that he would admit them to examination. . . . Hereupon the Pilot major commandeth the party to be examined, to give information that he is a mariner, and well practiced in those parts, about which hee desireth to be examined. . . . They do come to a certaine house which the kings reader hath appointed unto him for the same purpose, at eight of the clocke in the morning: and there they stay two houres, and two houres likewise in the afternoone: in one of which houres Zamorano [the reader in navigation] readeth unto them, and in the other they aske one another many particulars concerning the art of navigation in the presence of the said kings reader. . . . And having heard the kings reader those two moneths, they resort them unto the

hall of examination which is in the Contraction house, where there are
assembled the Pilot major and divers other pilots, to the number 25 at
least. . . . Then the Pilot major commandeth the examinate to spread a
sea-chart upon the table, and in the presence of the other pilots to de-
part or shewe the course from the barre of Sant Lucar to the Canarie-Is-
lands, and from thence to the Indies, till he come to that place whereof
he is to bee examined, and then also returne backe to the barre of Sant
Lucar in Spaine, from whence he departed. Also the Pilot major asketh
him, if when he saileth upon the sea, he be taken with a contrary wind,
what remedie he is to use, that his ship be not too much turmoiled upon
the sea? And the examinate answereth him as well as he can.[28]

A master world map, the Padron Real, was also located in the
Casa de Contracion and kept up to date by Portuguese cosmographers, such as Diogo Ribeiro, who were brought in for this purpose and to prepare sea charts for Spanish-sponsored expeditions.[29]
While the Padron Real was meant to be kept secret, much of the
information recorded on it was reproduced for the use of navigators, so it was not so secret as the Spanish might have hoped.
This became obvious later in the century when cartographers from
other parts of Europe made efforts to get copies of some of these
early charts and appear to have had some success in doing so.

It was not until between about 1520 and 1550, however, that
the Spanish actually began to lose control of the new information.
The reason for this change and the period in which it occurred
lies primarily in two factors: the spread of printing in Europe and
the Habsburg empire. Between 1510 and 1550 there was enormous growth in European printing businesses, which made publication of new materials more likely than it had been in the past.
But it was Spain's involvement in the Habsburg empire after 1519
that made the geographical information more available for publishers to use. Spanish expeditions became the business of Europeans in Italy, Germany, and the Netherlands, giving merchants in
these areas important interests in Spanish conquests and the right
to know something about them. Around 1540 printers in the map-
making areas of Italy began to put large amounts of current geographical information in printed form. As these efforts proved
profitable, similar ones followed.[30] By 1550 the information that
the Spanish had tried to keep to themselves to sustain their su-

premacy in the Western oceans had become available to potential explorers in most areas of Europe. Charles V's attempts to create an empire on the continent of Europe began to undermine the future of Spain's overseas empire. Because of the successes of the conquistadores in this period, there seems to be no sign of a decline in the Spanish empire, but Spain's ability to keep other Europeans out of the Americas and her areas of the East were diminished when others knew as much about the geography of these areas as the Spanish did.

Print and Geographical Information

Both the Spanish and the Portuguese stimulated the production of geographical documents, thus injecting greater materialism into the process of ocean exploration, but they also tried to inhibit trade in the documents they produced, seeing more profits in monopolizing rather than selling these goods. But with the growth of printing it was not long before the monopoly was disrupted. Publishers found a good market for maps, charts, and travel chronicles and saw profits in developing their trade. By mass-producing maps and chronicles, they increased the scale of the materialism associated with overseas trade, and by trading extensively in these goods, they brought many of the new documents from early voyages to the eyes of interested audiences, breaking the Iberian monopoly over the information they contained.

Most scholars who have studied sixteenth-century cartography have missed this point; some even suggest that because many of the printed geographical pieces from the sixteenth century did not contain information brought back from ocean voyages, printing did not have great consequences for the spread of geographical information. For example, Lucien Febvre and Henri-Jean Martin argue that the European reading public's image of the world was by and large unaffected by the new geographical discoveries yielded by European expansion. They contend that the public must not have been interested in this material because many surviving manuscripts (both charts and writings) were not put into print.[31] In making such an argument, these authors are assuming that whether works did or did not appear in print in the sixteenth century depended on popular interest (a dubious assumption even in the present day) and that only massive dissemination of information could create an effect.

Febvre and Martin reach such a conclusion because they assume that printed geographical works could only have *cultural* or *intellectual* effects on European life. If they had considered the economic uses of these documents, they would have realized that, precisely because these items could be used as capital goods, they did not need to reach a large audience to stimulate social change. They only needed to catch the attention of those merchants or aristocrats interested in sponsoring new forays into the world's oceans.

J. H. Elliott also argues that Europeans tended to write and read little about the new areas of the world brought to light by discovery, but he suggests that this was because finding exotic new lands, including a new continent filled with novel plants, animals, and peoples, was too startling to absorb immediately. Instead of suggesting that Europeans were not interested in these novelties, he claims that they were so shocked by their revolutionary significance that they could only gradually integrate them into their intellectual traditions. In saying this, Elliott is suggesting that even a small amount of information about something as surprising as a new continent could have enormous intellectual consequences.[32]

Elizabeth Eisenstein has developed a persuasive argument to explain the enormous effects of small-scale printing on European intellectual life; she attributes them to the preservative powers of print. New knowledge (either newly formulated or dug out from the past) was less likely to be lost once it was mass-produced; then it could be used by contemporaries and also become a permanent heritage for future generations to use.[33]

The fate of many manuscript charts and chronicles from the era of early expansion tends to support her argument. Columbus' original journal, for instance, has been lost forever, along with many charts from the period of Henry the Navigator. These pieces were lost in spite of (or perhaps more accurately, because of) the value placed on them. Efforts to monopolize their information inhibited their reproduction. Printing helped to change this pattern by providing the means to make early maps, charts, and written works into permanent documents available to groups which had had no part in their original design.

Not surprisingly, Italian and Flemish publishers, rather than their Spanish and Portuguese counterparts, were most interested in and effective at reproducing geographical works in the fifteenth and early sixteenth centuries. The Spanish and Portuguese did publish some works on their own presses, even while their governments were trying to keep much of this information secret, but they were not the ones who put out the popular *Paesi* collection, the Columbus letter, or the early Ptolemaic works. Non-Iberians were the ones who took the information hoarded by the Spanish and Portuguese and made it a resource shared by many Europeans.[34]

This was true in part because geographical publishing was simply one small part of the publishing business, a business that was dominated by non-Iberians. Most geographical writings put into print came out where book publishing was strongest, and were put into print for many of the same reasons that other works were. Cosmography interested publishers at first because it was part of the classical heritage that was being rediscovered and recorded at that time. Early book publishers liked to produce classics of this sort or religious works—in large part because the Church and state would sponsor them, but also because these genres had vital constituencies. Religious works had a wide public appeal that made them the most profitable genre, and classical works had the devoted following of humanist scholars to promote (if not always manage) their publication. It should not be surprising, then, that the first piece of cartography or geography introduced in print was Ptolemy's *Geographica*, a classic text brought out in the late fifteenth century along with hundreds of other works of interest to the humanists.[35]

Ptolemy's work was the first and most published geographical classic; more important, it set a standard for contemporary geography, since it embodied the scientific approach to geography. Ptolemy provided a model for depicting a round world on a flat surface; he divided it into 360 degrees around the North Pole and

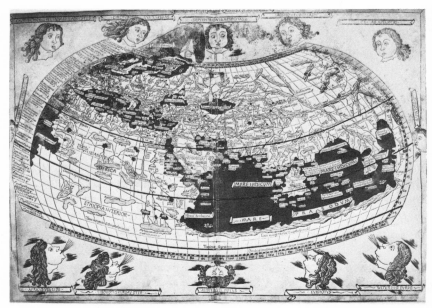

World Map from Claudius Ptolomaeus, *Cosmographia*, Ulm, 1482. BY PERMIS-SION OF THE RARE BOOK DIVISION, NEW YORK PUBLIC LIBRARY, ASTOR, LENOX, AND TILDEN FOUNDATIONS.

located parallel meridians around the equator and to the north and south of this line.

These qualities in Ptolemaic maps gave them lasting influence by stimulating greater concern among early modern mapmakers with the problems of projection and the size and shape of the world. But they also introduced an image of the world that had been or was soon to be proven inaccurate by Iberian travels. Ptolemy had not conceived of a cape around the bottom of Africa, but rather had envisioned the base of Africa as part of a great southern continent. He had also underestimated the size of the globe and not anticipated the discovery of the New World.

Thus, the publishing of the *Geographica* did not alter the distribution of *accurate* information on the subject. Published Ptolemaic maps from the fifteenth century were kept true to Ptolemy's original conception of the world and were unaffected by the Iberian discoveries. It was not until the sixteenth century that Europeans began to publish geographical documents for their economic value, when the organization of both the publishing business and European political geography began to change.[36]

Between 1500 and around 1515 European publishing began to expand. During the first half-century of publishing in Europe (c. 1450–1500), there was a massive growth in the number and location of printers and print shops, but there was little organization to the book trade. Hence there were frequent gluts of unwanted books on the market, and many books did not reach the audiences that might have been interested in them. Around the turn of the century there was a crisis in the book trade in Venice, a major publishing center. It shut down many businesses, but it also led to better organization of book distribution as agents from the major publishing houses began to contact booksellers in distant cities around Europe to increase their sales. With this period of market consolidation, the publishing business began to expand and new kinds of work appeared, among them new types of books on geography, containing more contemporary material. Peter Martyr's *Libretto* describing Columbus' voyages appeared in 1505 and was reprinted in numerous editions after that time; the *Paesi* collection already mentioned was published in this period; and Vespucci's *Mundus Novus* also appeared around this same time (the last was written as a letter to Lorenzo de' Medici and typical of much of the literature of this period, since it described the new discoveries in a letter form). The apex of this period of geographical printing was the 1513 publication of the Ptolemy with illustrations by Waldseemüller based on the Caneiro map. The maps in this volume were a combination of classical and contemporary geography; new maps supplemented traditional Ptolemaic ones.[37]

While the 1500–15 period of expansion for the publishing business brought some contemporary cartographic and geographic information into print, it did not revolutionize public images of the world; it only brought small amounts of new information to a relatively small public. It was not until the second period of expansion in publishing, around 1540–50, that massive amounts of new information reached the reading public.[38] Like the earlier one, this second expansion in printing had economic origins. In the first half of the sixteenth century, the book trade began to be centered at the annual fair in Frankfurt. While this center of exchange helped to organize the book trade, it also made it clear that most booksellers could not keep track of all the new works produced in the print shops of Europe. The larger publishing houses, as a result, began to produce catalogs to circulate at the fair (c. 1540). During this same period, inflation created rapid price rises and some rapid capital accumulation. The book trade seems to have ridden a swell in the 1540–50 decade, beginning a second period of rapid growth in the book business which brought with it a great increase in geographical publishing. Febvre and Martin provide a basis for understanding the scale of this increase with some figures on the geography books printed in France before 1610:[39]

Dates	Number of works
to 1550	83
1551–1570	70
1571–1580	82
1581–1590	76
1591–1600	54
1601–1609	112

The authors attribute the reduction after 1590 to wars.

The patterns of geographical publishing followed the general pattern of book publishing, expanding with general growth in the number of books put out and emanating from different cities as the center for publishing shifted. Again Febvre and Martin present evidence about the location of printing establishments that provides the baseline for this assertion. They claim that in 1480 there were 50 print shops in Italy, 30 in Germany, 5 in Switzerland, 2 in Bohemia, 9 in France, 8 in Holland, 5 in Belgium, 8 in Spain, 1 in Poland, and 4 in England. By 1480 Venice was the center for printing both in Italy and throughout Europe. Between 1495 and 1497, of the 1,821 editions of books known to be published in that year, 441 were from Venice, with 181 from Paris and 95 from Lyons (the two other areas with a large number of publications that year). The absolute number of books published is not possible to estimate, since the size of book editions in the

1490s varied widely, from less than 100 books to 3,000 or more; one can only assume that the cities that put out the largest number of editions also put out the greatest number of books.[40]

In the fifteenth and early sixteenth centuries, Italy was not only the major publishing region but also a cartographic center. Since the Middle Ages, it had been the primary site for production of the portolan-type charts used by seamen trading in the Mediterranean. Thus the Italians had an established tradition of making maps as capital goods, which they modified only slightly to include them in the printing business. It follows, then, that Italy was the first large producer of printed geographical information based on the discoveries. The Columbus letter, Peter Martyr's *Libretto*, the *Paesi* collection, Roselli maps, and many other of the more famous early sixteenth-century publications were first printed by Italians. The 1513 Ptolemy was from Germany, and other bits of geographical publishing were from France, but by and large the most widely known and used of printed geography came out of Italy. Work produced by the publishing houses in Portugal and Spain, which might seem destined for wide circulation, was manufactured in a peripheral area of the printing business and proved of lesser importance.[41]

In the sixteenth century Venice's position in publishing began to be eroded by the expansion of print businesses in the commercial centers of northern Europe, particularly the Netherlands. Antwerp was becoming the commercial center of all Europe at the same time that Plantin set up there the largest and most famous of all the early publishing houses.[42]

Antwerp's commercial vitality was increased by its position as the center for Charles V's empire, the place where most of the economic activity surrounding Spanish expansion was conducted. Antwerp supported the Baltic trade in wood and arms that made Spanish overseas expansion easier, and provided both much of the capital for Spain's empire and most of the marketing mechanisms needed for European trade in the goods yielded by expansion. As the center of the empire Antwerp was also a center for information, the place where news of activities from all parts of the empire would go, including the information about overseas expansion that made Antwerp a rich source for cartography.[43]

The greatest cartographer from the Low Countries, Gerhard Mercator, was a citizen of Antwerp during Charles V's reign and a member of the intellectual circle that surrounded the emperor. He was also a friend of another of the leading figures in cartography from the Netherlands, Abraham Ortelius. These two men seem to have been appropriately located for making cartographic history. They both put out atlases around the end of the sixteenth century that became standard European sources of information about geography previously found only in Iberian charts; in doing so, they started the era of preeminence in cartography for the Low Countries, the so-called age of atlases.[44]

The age of atlases reached its height in the Netherlands but it had roots in Italy. Around 1568 or 1569 an unknown Italian developed the idea of an atlas of maps, covering all the areas of the world, that would be made in (or folded to) the same size and bound into one volume. Those who produced volumes according to this Italian formula compiled sets of diverse maps, culled from a variety of sources and designed by different cartographers, until they had large collections (of 233 maps in one instance); these they arranged in the traditional Ptolemaic order and issued in one book.[45]

Shortly after the first Italian atlases were published, Abraham Ortelius published his own *Theatrum orbis terrarum* (1570) in Antwerp. Ortelius was a cartographer and bookseller who decided to use his skills in mapmaking to produce an atlas. He was acquainted with many of the leading cartographers of his day and traveled extensively to collect from them the most accurate available documents. Like the Italian atlas-makers before him, he assembled a set of maps to cover all parts of the world, but he surpassed them in two ways: he collected only modern maps and engraved them all in one style, citing their sources at the bottom. The result was formally like Italian atlases but quite different in substance. All the maps looked alike and (more important) contained no Ptolemaic influence. In this sense, the *Theatrum* was the first wholly modern atlas. It was immediately popular and reprinted by Christopher Plantin.[46]

The popularity of the atlas is logical given the fact that it was produced in a commercial center and *the* center for world trade,

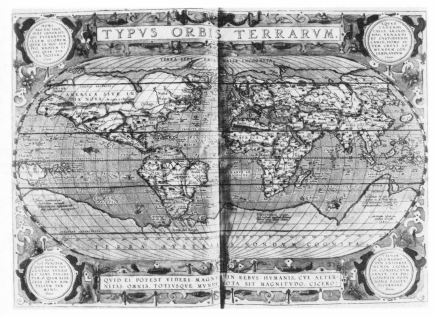

Typus Orbis Terrarum from Ortelius, *Theatrum Mundi*, 1606. REPRODUCED BY PERMISSION OF THE HUNTINGTON LIBRARY, SAN MARINO, CALIFORNIA.

where navigators, merchants, and intellectuals all would find the material compelling. To the extent that it contained the most recent (or at least not the most ancient) geographical information, it was a particularly attractive commodity that reflected and even glorified the activities of explorers and their sponsors.

Mercator was primarily responsible for producing the second great modern atlas. He made only three sections of it before his death in 1594, but in them he established a form for the maps that made this atlas unique. He used a new projection system that compensated for the curvature of the earth so that navigators could draw straight lines to chart their courses. He did this by expanding the land masses at the poles in relation to those at the equator. The resulting charts looked unusual, but they were much better suited to the needs of ocean travelers. They were also suited for use in practical navigation, since they contained information in current Spanish and Portuguese charts. Yet, for all its virtues, this atlas did not receive the immediate popularity that greeted Ortelius' atlas. Its incompleteness probably accounts for this—the *Atlas* only covered Europe and the North Atlantic in its original three volumes—although the odd look of the maps may have been a contributing factor. In any case, once it was expanded by Jodocus Hondius, it too was in great demand. Hondius acquired Mercator's plates in 1602, added new plates, and brought out the first of many Mercator-Hondius atlases in Amsterdam in 1606.[47]

The age of atlases in the Netherlands roughly coincided with the Netherlands' revolt against Spain. The Spanish sack of Antwerp ended its reign as the center for geographical publishing, as it pushed all the best publishers from that city. Hondius left for England and Mercator went to Duisburg to live under the protection of the Duke of Cleve. When the northern provinces became independent, some cartographers like Ortelius returned to Antwerp to resume work, but many others (and many map publishers) moved to Amsterdam, including Jodocus Hondius.[48]

Europe from the Mercator-Hondius *Historia Mundi*, 1635. REPRODUCED BY PERMISSION OF THE HUNTINGTON LIBRARY, SAN MARINO, CALIFORNIA.

Hondius and his successors/competitors (such as Petrus Plancius and the Blaeus—William Janszoon, Johann, and Cornelius)
helped to establish Amsterdam as the cartographic center of Europe. They also made it the publishing center that introduced to
the European reading public much previously little-known information about Spanish and Portuguese expansion. The independent
citizens of the north, now that they were free of the Habsburg empire, were free to profit from the publication of Iberian geographical findings by exploring their commercial value in international
markets.[49]

Dutch publications from the age of atlases were obviously impressive intellectual documents with enormous economic significance. Yet they were also interesting as commodities. Most were
clearly consumer goods, made for sale to the general reading public. The majority of maps in the atlases (or on single sheets) were
lavishly designed so they would attract readers from among the
merchants, bankers, and other elites that were interested in trade
but not involved in the technical side of navigation.[50] This does
not mean that these works were not also used as capital goods.
What is remarkable about many of these publications is that they
contained both technical and general information in the same volume and were clearly meant to appeal to a dual readership.

There is evidence that both general readers and practical
seamen did, in fact, read these books. Henry Peacham, for example, wrote in 1661 that, because travel was an essential part of a
gentleman's education, a young man should study cosmography.
He specifically mentions Ortelius, Hondius, Copernicus, Mercator,
and Dee, among others, as authors of important works on the
subject that could provide the gentleman with the appropriate education. Since his prescriptions are so clearly directed to young
men with more interest in commerce and pleasure-seeking than serious study, his admonitions suggest one use for this information
by general readers.[51]

Some of the seventeenth-century books of sailing directions and
other navigational writings also seemed to be designed for casual
readers because they contained information that had no practical
uses. The first volume of Samuel Purchas' *Hakluytus Posthumus*,
for instance, contains a number of historical maps and descrip-

tions of voyages made by the ancients.[52] In the seventeenth century, when the book was published, this information could have had no useful purpose for navigators or seamen; it was the kind that would appeal to the serious scholar of cosmography and to the lay educated reader. The inclusion of such descriptions, then, helps to identify the work as intended, at least in part, for the general reading public.

However, Purchas' work was also intended for the cosmographer or navigator, since many of the chronicles and illustrations were simply too technical and detailed to interest others. For instance, in the first chapter of book 5, part I, Purchas says, "the Ilands are falsely laid in most charts, laying too much to the West,"[53] a comment that not only shows the author's knowledge about and interest in nuances of cartography but displays a concern for details of interest to the expert. The same pattern is apparent in his inclusion of chronicles that contain detailed information on compass variation, water depths, and descriptions of shorelines.

The coexistence of such comments and historical descriptions within the same manuscript suggests that the work was not meant as either a consumer item or an economic resource. Rather, this book and its counterparts were intended to serve both purposes, to provide the kinds of geographical information that would make them both general geographical texts and guides to practical navigation.

The more extreme kind of geographical writing that only a navigator or scholar could bear to read is illustrated in Thomas Herbert's *Some Yeares Travels*. This book contains pictures of islands and harbors from the most useful perspective, as one would see them from the ocean, and continually compares the findings from his voyages with those described previously. The book is filled with data taken from soundings and measurements of currents, precisely the information most helpful to a navigator and precisely the kind of thing an educated gentleman did not need to know.

By this, under 13 degrees we are parrellel with *Sierra Leon* a Cape land upon the Lybian Shore, by old Geographers improperly cal'd Deorum currus, Fronns Africae, Tagazza and Zanquebai in *Thevet* and *Marolius*.[54]

In another section he says:

Six leagues North-East from the last land, we discried another Ile, full of
Palmeto trees; the current here set us 20 leagues forward in 24 houres,
the latitude of the Ile 16 degrees and a halfe, longitude 21 degrees and
28 minutes thus shaped.[55]

This is the language increasingly found in European travel
books of the seventeenth century and later, when the general
shape of the world and its seas and continents was known, and
when the interests of specialists and general readers began to di-
verge. The technical language of the specialist then developed as a
distinctive voice in the cartography literature.

The resulting writing style so offended Daniel Defoe that he
parodied it in his *A New Voyage Round the World by a Course
that never failed before*.[56] His ridicule was an appropriate response, since many travel books in his time and slightly earlier
were still intended for general as well as specialist readers.
Throughout the sixteenth century and much of the seventeenth,
most travel books were clearly designed for both audiences; their
maps had elegant cartouches, and their stories, even when they
contained useful information, were not so technical that they lost
the flow of the narrative. It was the disappearance of this style
that Defoe seems to lament.

Many early travel publications were made so decorative and en-
tertaining that they may not strike contemporary readers as tools
for navigation and trade. The sixteenth-century atlases, world
maps, and chronicles also contained so little technical information
compared to the counterparts a century later that in hindsight
they appear too vague to have had practical value; but this was
not the case. Robert Thorne's book about the Portuguese in the
spice islands, written in 1527 for the ambassador to Henry VIII
and published by Hakluyt in his *Voyages*, describes the *political*
value of rough world maps in this period:

I have caused that your Lordship shall receive herewith a little Mappe or
Carde of the world: the which I feare me, shall put your Lordship to
more labour to understand, then me to make it. . . . And the sayd coasts
of the Sea are all set [here] justly after the maner and forme as they lie,
as the navigation approveth them throughout all the Card, save onely

the coastes and Isles of the Spicerie of the Emperour which is from over against the 160. to the 215. degrees of longitude, For these coastes and situations of the Islands, every of the Cosmographers and pilots of Portingal and Spayne do set after their purpose. The Spaniards more toward the Orient, because they should appeare to Appertain to the Emperour: & the Portingals more toward the Occident, for that they should fal within their jurisdiction. So that the pilots and navigants thither, which in such cases should declare the truth, by their industrie do set them falsly every one to favor his prince.[57]

This author clearly acknowledges the politicoeconomic significance of roughly locating land masses during the period of early expansion when the Pope was dividing up the world into Portuguese and Spanish territorries.

There is also evidence that contemporaries considered these rough documents useful for economically inspired adventures, such as finding new trade routes. There is, for example, a bill for the charts and navigational instruments that Martin Frobisher bought for his first attempt to locate the Northwest Passage (in 1576). For this difficult project he accumulated surprising amounts of general information, not only general maps, such as the Mercator world map of 1569 (and some other, unspecified printed maps), but also some more general printed works, such as a French book on cosmography by André Thevet and William Cunningham's *Cosmographicall Glasse* (1559); these comprised the library that Frobisher took to sea with him when he was attempting the technically complex task of locating a new major trading route to the East.[58] Even the basic cosmological information contained in atlases and world maps could be important to world trade.

There were, in fact, a variety of early practical uses for general world maps. For one thing, they were attractive gifts for those considering sponsoring a voyage. They could be used to indicate the possible time and costs involved in voyages, the distances from one area of the world to the next, the best routes for reaching a particular destination. They may not have been adequate in themselves for finding a harbor or water on a particular coast, but they could help gather the funds needed to reach that coast. This is obvious in the fact that Sebastian Cabot offered to make a world map in order to encourage sponsorship for a voyage to find the Northwest Passage.[59]

Hence there was a ready market throughout Europe for the atlases published in the Netherlands, which, however general their information, still had a value for European expansion. The Dutch also took the lead in publishing many other kinds of geographical documents in the late sixteenth and early seventeenth century. The popular success of the atlases helped to support cartographic and cosmological publishing in general, so that there was an economic base for the dissemination of much more detailed information about the world's coastlines and oceans.

Some evidence of the economic significance of seventeenth-century Dutch publication of practical navigational information comes from studies of English hand-drawn charts that were used in navigation during the sixteenth and early seventeenth centuries. These charts were hand copied for English navigators from printed Dutch charts. The tradition of hand-drawing charts for ocean voyages had not yet died in England, but the sources for much information in these charts were works being published and distributed by the Dutch. These hand-drawn charts were also beginning to be supplemented by the printed rutters or pilots published by both the English and the Dutch in the sixteenth and seventeenth centuries. Pierre Garcie's rutter was translated into English in 1528. In 1657 Joseph Moxon's *The Waggoner*, based on a book of sea charts printed earlier in that century by the Dutchman, Pieter Goos, was published and became a standard item on English ships.[60]

The importance of geographical documents to expansion is also apparent in a new genre of geographical writing that appeared in the late sixteenth and early seventeenth centuries, advocating national development through international trade. Richard Hakluyt in England and Jan Huygen van Linschoten in Amsterdam were the major authors in this genre.[61] They collected existing maps, charts, and geographical/navigational writings and published them with the express intention of stimulating expeditions by their compatriots. Linschoten, for example, traveled to Portugal to gather the most accurate Iberian maps, charts, and chronicles, and supplemented them with his own careful geographical and navigational notes, gathered during a trip to India on a Portuguese ship. The result was a publication with enormous practical value for Dutch expeditions. As J. H. Parry notes:

Linschoten's sailing directions supplied exactly what the Dutch needed. Dutch sailors were already sailing to the East in Portuguese ships; but the yarns of deck-hands—even of officers—do not amount to a reliable guide for navigators. Such a guide was now available. The first Dutch fleet using Linschoten's sailing directions sailed in 1595.[62]

Linschoten's *Itinerario* was translated into English and published as his *Discourses* in 1598 by John Wolfe. This edition contained all the useful information that had been placed in the Dutch version, including a wide variety of plates. The plates were illustrations for the chronicles, including portraits of natives found in different parts of the world as well as the crucial maps and pictures of landfalls that were such a valuable part of Linschoten's

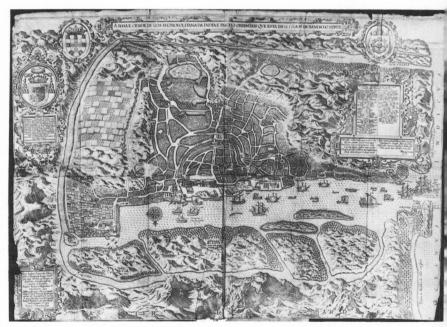

Map of Goa from Linschoten, *Discourses*, 1598. BY PERMISSION OF THE HOUGHTON LIBRARY, HARVARD UNIVERSITY.

book. For example, a large map of Goa was a detailed guide to the harbor and a street map of the town. The plates of landfalls included some pictures of harbor entrances as they might be seen from the sea; they were presented with text describing their virtues as havens for European trying to survive the long and dangerous voyages to strange parts of the world. The material on Saint Helena is a case in point. A picture of the island (drawn as one might see it from the sea) was captioned with the following note:

The Island of Ste Helena full of Sweet and pleasaunt ayre fructfull ground and fresh water but not inhabited: a good refreshing for those yt come ovt of east India it lyeth under 16 degrees on the South Syde of the equinotiall lyne.[63]

The introduction to book 2 of Linschoten's volume, the section that describes the Americas, displays Linschoten's practical interests in the problems that Europeans had in long-distance travel.

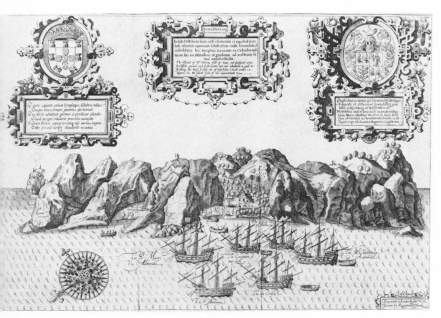

Ste. Helena from Linschoten, *Discourses*, 1598. BY PERMISSION OF THE HOUGHTON LIBRARY, HARVARD UNIVERSITY.

When the authoure of this booke, as also the Printer, had bestowed and used with great labor and charges herein, to set forth some perfect cards of *America* because that often times the Indian Shippes in their failing out or returning home, do fall upon those Coasts, specially Brasilia, which herein is most discovered, they thought it most expedient therewith to place a brief description of the same countries, thereby to show the readers' the principall places therein, whereunto at this day most ships do traffike, hoping they will take it in good part.[64]

It may be that Dutch interest in the Americas was less benign than this, but the possibilities of being blown off course and ending up by Brazil when rounding the Cape of Good Hope were great enough at least to make sense of Linschoten's suggestion.

Linschoten's work as originally published contained four sections: (1) on his own voyages, (2) on the voyages to India made by the Portuguese pilot, Diego Alfonso, (3) on the Americas, and (4) on sources of income to the Spanish Crown. This fourth "booke" on Spanish income may seem out of place, but it was there to suggest, if obliquely, the wealth that could be acquired through ocean voyaging; it made Linschoten's work into a piece of politicoeconomic advocacy, detailing the commercial value of using his guide. The English translation helped to spread reliable geographical information and his attitude toward expansion to the English as they were developing a taste for expansion.[65]

After the English translation appeared, some still felt the English were disadvantaged in being unable to talk to Linschoten himself and ask questions about his travels. This, in large part, is what inspired John Davis to follow in Linschoten's footsteps by making a voyage to the East Indies as a pilot on a foreign ship. Linschoten had traveled on a Portuguese vessel; Davis went on a Dutch one. He too brought back a description of his voyage, one published in 1601. Ironically, Davis took this trip because he did not trust printed information to be as complete as oral accounts of experiences; but he decided to make the voyage after reading Dutch books on geography, and produced from his travels another geographical/navigational text.[66]

As I mentioned earlier, by late in the seventeenth century even more useful information was beginning to appear in print. Thematic maps like Halley's map of trade winds and magnetic varia-

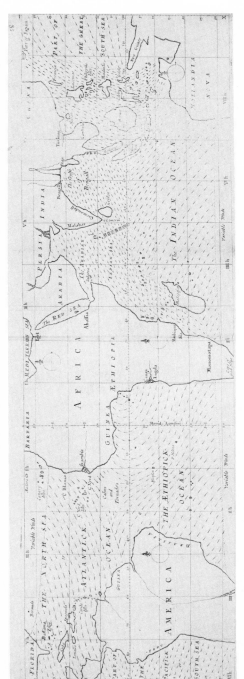

Map of the Trade Winds by Halley, 1686. REPRODUCED BY PERMISSION OF THE BRITISH LIBRARY.

tions as well as Kircher's map of ocean currents helped navigators make long-distance voyages with greater accuracy and safety. John Seller's sea charts and pilots, also published in the late seventeenth century, helped to bring both Portuguese and Dutch geographical information into England. The importance of this expanding literature to sea captains even early in the seventeenth century is indicated by John Smith in his *Sea Grammar* of 1627, where he mentions a collection of books to read for ocean sailing. He includes in this list Edward Wright's *Certaine Errors of Navigation*, John Davis' *The Seaman's Secrets*, and Willem Blaeu's *The Sea Mirrour*, all of which were available to English pilots by this time.[67]

By the end of the seventeenth century, then, the Dutch and the British both had gathered and spread in print the kind of geographical information that was directly useful for international trade, and they had used it for this purpose. That these countries became major powers in the European political arena through their success in world trade at precisely this time suggests the importance of new geographical documents to the political economy of the period.

Perhaps new printed geographical writings did not affect the thinking of *most* Europeans in the sixteenth and seventeenth centuries, but Italian and Dutch publications from the period seem to have been particularly potent in changing the political life in Europe by altering the spread of maps and travel writings. They made it easier for readers outside of the Habsburg empire to use geographical documents as capital goods to pursue their states' economic and political purposes within the growing international economy.

State Geography and the Modern World System

Maps and geographical documents may have been used most dramatically to carve out patterns of control over world commerce, creating through competition what the Pope had tried to establish by fiat when he divided the world between Spain and Portugal, but they were also used strategically in struggles for political control of the European continent. They could mark territories, delineate their boundaries, and depict their contents; thus they were useful to governments for centralizing political authority and controlling the economy through regulation of land use and commerce.

A number of scholars have already noted that publication in general had an important role in state formation in the early modern period. To the extent that state-authorized books were written in a particular vernacular, they could promote a national language. To the extent that the central government could control what was published, it could assure, in spite of the limits of effective censorship, that the flow of information in the country would tend to support the state and its policies. Works on law, political theory, and national history, all of which seem to have been popular in sixteenth- and seventeenth-century Europe, tended to help centralize administrative control in European states. Printed works on law, for instance, might have at first tended to formalize and standardize local laws, but were later used to unify national legal systems under a common code. Books on political theory were used even more consistently in the service of states, furnishing ideologies and policies for organizing the political process. National histories were another source of ideology for emerging states, outlining what their authors identified as the deep cultural, spiritual, or geographical unity of particular countries. In these ways and others, publications aided the general process of state formation.[68]

What was the particular role of geographical literature in this process? It sometimes contributed to the cultural integration of emerging states by forming an image of a state or region that inhabitants could begin to identify as theirs. On other occasions, maps and geographical writings were practical tools for the centralization of authority, providing information for tax assessment and military planning in emerging states. They were also used for developing economic policies, suggesting possible drainage projects or ways to improve transportation that would affect economic development in the state. Frequently, they did all three.[69]

Europe in 1500 had around 500 more or less independent political units;[70] so the process of state formation was more often one of incorporation than differentiation, a centralization rather than decentralization of authority. Integration of some set of regions within a state required that new political authorities master enormous amounts of information about the territories coming under their control. They needed to know, for instance, what local political customs were, where traditional legal centers or seats were located, and how to defend a new state's borders from military threat. To solve these problems they needed, besides political skills, simple information—some of which could be supplied by accurate surveys.

State formation was also part of an economic reorganization of Europe, one that gave new meanings to material resources, including land itself. New land-use policies, from drainage projects to enclosures, encouraged surveys of land. Together, the political and economic value of geographical information bred a new desire for surveys that was conveniently met by the professional surveyors who were, just at that time, refining their skills for these tasks.

The politics of state formation required banding together different ethnic groups, principalities, and social classes into political wholes. Under these conditions, surveys were frequently used to shape patterns of political domination (i.e., to create what Michael Hechter has labeled internal colonialism).[71] Once political, economic, and cultural life was organized in the interest of certain groups, their ability to maintain control was strengthened; hence they had a deep desire to use tools like surveys to subordinate and control less advantaged groups. The industry and agriculture that the state promoted, the state policies toward internal and external trade (among other factors) were important in allocating advantages to groups and were all affected by surveys.

Surveys were particularly valuable allocation tools because they could easily be used to serve the interests of both central administrators and landlords. Estate surveys, for example, could present information about the value of estates to governments for tax assessments and to landlords for use in determining rents. Such coincidences of interest were of no small importance to state formation. As Charles Tilly suggests,[72] the consolidation of political units in Europe would not have been possible without the cooperation of the landlords, whose power was great enough to make them essential in forming central governments. Because kings needed to win their support, governments manipulated the land-use policies which directly affected landlords to make them, at least in part, political as well as economic policies.

Maps describing the land masses of Europe, like the geographical images made of other parts of the world, were thus politicoeconomic visions and resources. They were designed to address the politicoeconomic problems of the time and helped to make European states vital units of economic activity within an international system.

Linking new interest in map-making with state formation in the early modern period is not at all difficult, since most of the major surveys from this period were authorized, if not sponsored, by central governments with the clear purpose of establishing the character of their state's (or empire's) territory. Some were produced as part of national histories, advocating the development of a particular state. The works of Jean Bodin, John Speed, and Bishop Leslie fall into this category. Bishop Leslie's maps of Scotland (1578) were part of a chronicle history of the lands that expressed strong support of Mary Queen of Scots. This book illustrates how such maps were used for political purposes during the struggle over European political boundaries.[73]

While some politically motivated geographical documents were created to produce nationalist sentiments, most were used in more practical ways to centralize authority in large political units, including both the Habsburg empire and emerging European states. Perhaps the best known of these works are the county maps of England and Wales produced by Christopher Saxton and John Norden. Saxton's county atlas, produced between 1574 and 1579, and Norden's maps, made during the 1590s, were particularly early examples of printed maps based on original surveys.[74] For this reason, they provide valuable data about how maps of this sort came originally to be sponsored and to what ends they were used.

Saxton's county maps were produced by royal authority and with the financial support of Thomas Seckford, Master of the Court of Requests and Surveys of the Court of Wards and Liveries under Queen Elizabeth. They apparently gained their practical, political significance through their use in taxation and military planning. George Owen has argued that the inequitable distribution of the tax burden by counties in this period can be attributed to a misreading of Saxton's maps. He suggests that administrators did not understand that Saxton's maps were drawn in different scales; their resulting assumption that the counties were of roughly equal size led to these tax inequities.[75]

Saxton's maps also seemed to have been used for military purposes. At least, some scholars argue that a general map of England and Wales that Saxton made as the frontpiece to his county atlas was the basis for the Quartermaster map that Wenceslaus Hollar put out in 1644 and that was used by Parliamentary forces during the Civil War. In addition, the interest of Lord Treasurer William Burghley in surveys (and particularly Saxton's work), although probably influenced by his exposure to estate surveys, was motivated more directly by his fears of foreign invasion and his hope of using surveys for military planning.[76]

Another reason why Saxton's project received such lofty and secure support was that he was producing an English atlas in the age of atlases. For commercial as well as nationalistic reasons, this project was a desired innovation to the English. The commercial success of the atlas and maps from it was great enough, in fact, that it helped to make this atlas the prototype for most subsequent maps of the British Isles, establishing the county (the unit that Saxton's surveyed for each map) as the normal cartographic unit for depicting the region.[77]

John Norden had a quite different experience in surveying the English counties. Unlike Saxton, he initially found it difficult to secure sponsorship for his work and (in part as a consequence) he was very slow in his efforts to complete and publish the surveys. He did, in the end, receive a warrant for his work from the crown, and he did manage to find commercial outlets for his county maps, but he was not able to produce the kind of glorious atlas that Saxton did. Norden did not produce all the maps he intended (surveying some counties without ever making the maps), nor was he able to put out his maps in large formats. In the end, the small size of his books may have made them even more commercially attractive than Saxton's large books, but they were initially less influential because they did not have the same political potency.[78]

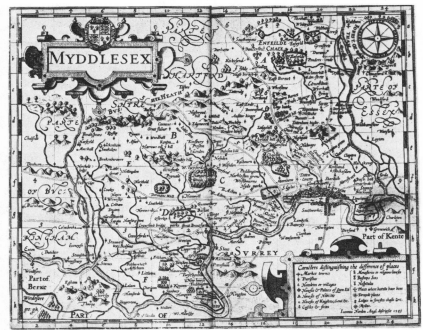

Map of Middlesex from John Norden, *Speculi Britanniae*, 1593. REPRODUCED BY PERMISSION OF THE HUNTINGTON LIBRARY, SAN MARINO, CALIFORNIA.

While Norden found it difficult to receive political legitimation for his work, he did make some innovations in map-making that were worthy of note. He paid even greater attention than Saxton to the economic significance of land areas, and therefore provided kinds of practical information that were not available elsewhere. One of his more famous innovations was depicting roads on his maps, a useful feature that eventually became a standard aspect of regional mapping. But it was only a small part of Norden's efforts to describe and analyze the economic resources of England's counties. His more general concerns can be gleaned from the following passage taken from his *Description of Essex*:

This shire is moste fatt, frutefull, and full of profitable thinges, exceeding (as farr as I can finde) anie other shire, for the generall comodeties, and the plentie. . . . The hundreds of Rocheforde, Denge, Dansye, or

Dansing, which lye on the sowth-este parte of the shire, yelde milke, but-
ter, and cheese in admirable aboundance: and in those partes are the
great and huge cheeses made, wondered at for their massiuenes and
thicknes. The second quarter of the shire may be saide to contayne the
hundreds of Lexden, Hinckforde, Dunmow and Froswell, which lye in
the northe parte of the Shire. And theis abounde greatelie with hopps, a
comodetie of greate and continuall use, but draweth with in an
inconuenience: the distruction of younge springes. In theis hundreds also
are manie and good feedinges, and corne in resonable measure.[79]

Norden continues in this vein until he has described the major
crops or land-use patterns within the shire. This information gave
his survey a particular slant, a view of the land of England as the
economic resource that many entrepreneurs in agriculture were
finding it to be.

Any discussion of Norden's and Saxton's work should make it
clear that these two surveyors were primarily private entrepreneurs who were hired by landowners to survey their estates. The
skills that they developed were hewn in this service rather than
public service, and private practice was probably what encouraged
Norden to see land in the commercial terms apparent in his county surveys. In addition, it was private work that supported the
men, particularly Norden, who was less able to find government
financing. But the survey work that they did in the service of the
government or with government warrant produced the major
published surveys of this period and made images of the British
Isles part of the public record and imagination.[80]

Surveys of this sort were being made in a variety of places at
the command of various central governments in the sixteenth century. Charles V, for example, sponsored surveys/maps of the territories under his control. The superiority of Flemish cartography in
the period plus the importance given to cartography by Iberians
helped to stimulate mapping of the Habsburg empire. This interest yielded, among other pieces, the famous Caerte van Oostlant
by Cornelius Anthonisz, which was frequently copied after its
original publication. Phillip II also showed an interest in surveying and mapping when he ordered a survey of Spain and Portugal
which was completed around 1585. These maps, like the regional
maps made by Saxton and Norden, were based on original survey

material, but, unlike the English atlases, they seem to have been made separately and by different surveyors. The map of Portugal from the 1585 survey, for instance, is much more accurate than the one of Spain, but the method by which it was produced is not known, probably because the Portuguese were still treating all geographical information as secret.[81]

The Aretin map of Bohemia used during the Thirty Years' War, although the details of its production are also unknown, illustrates how surveys (other than the Quartermaster map) were used for military purposes. Paul Aretin was a Moravian land surveyor who apparently made this map without using original survey material. What is interesting about the map is its hydrographics, showing the major waterways in Bohemia (the transportation system of particular use in the seventeenth century) and its depiction of the administrative divisions of the country into fifteen regions (the kind of political information relevant for the military). The map in itself is not extraordinary, but rather represents a compiled survey of a country that was inaccurate by modern standards but detailed enough to aid the military in planning their actions.[82]

Political uses of geographical information were not new to the sixteenth and seventeenth centuries. In fifteenth-century Venice the Council of Ten ordered surveys of the various principalities under its control,[83] presumably to help in assessing and collecting taxes and defending the territory from attack. What was new was the proliferation of documents that printing made possible, and the growing interest in these documents that resulted from the problems of territory created by state formation.

The use of maps for delineating transportation systems was also an ongoing project that had expanded rapidly in the period. While charts of waterways became common with the portolans, and depictions of at least major rivers on maps were not new, there were few maps of roads *inside* Europe before Norden's time. Some pilgrims' maps were made in the late Middle Ages, but they were rare. During the sixteenth century, however, a large number of single-sheet maps and road atlases—collections of maps with written descriptions—began to be produced. Before Norden's county maps there were some of trade routes through Germany (the spine of Europe). They were somewhat crude in their depictions/descriptions of the routes, sometimes only suggesting the relationship between topography and roads, but they show a growing awareness of the importance of internal transportation systems to the expansion of European commerce. In the seventeenth century, the French depicted their road systems in national surveys, trying, for the first time, to record systematically the transportation resources of the state.[84] Here we begin to see concern for rationalizing and simplifying internal transportation as a way of diminishing regional control over commerce and increasing the state's role in regulating national trade. Eli Heckscher has pointed out the problems involved in the process of nationalizing transportation—that state administrations were less successful in regularizing internal transport than they may have hoped—but while he has reservations about the progress made in this direction, Heckscher does not deny that progress was made. Maps of the period showing road systems within states were both a reflection of the problem and a tool for achieving more rational state transportation systems.[85]

Political maps, maps of transportation systems, and military maps (as well as the geographical writings that paralleled all these pictorial forms) were all traditional ways of using geographical documents for the benefit of a political administration. Estate surveys were a less developed form that became more common and more precise as the growth of European states helped to initiate changes in patterns of land use in Western Europe. So long as estates were traditional parcels of land used in traditional ways, no one needed to know their exact dimensions; their shape, size, and uses were roughly and traditionally known. But when new parcels of land, such as the Church lands in England, came into the hands of government, when traditional estates were divided into smaller parcels and rented out to tenants, and when forests were cut, fens drained, or fields cultivated in new ways, the measurement of land and descriptions of topography and soil fertility had to be more precise. This is evident in a seventeenth-century English document legitimating enclosures:

Commons, which lie open undivided, every man may furnish with what sort of cattle he liketh *sans* number, which is an occasion that the richer sort of people by surcharging the commons do eat up both their own part and their poor neighbors', which commons, if they were divided and made into severals, then every man might know his own, and dispose thereof as he should think good for his best profit which otherwise they cannot do. . . . For the manner how to proceed in this great affair, with our duty and under reformation be it spoken, it would then be thus: a commission would be awarded from his Majesty to certain honest, discreet and serviceable gentlemen . . . and an exquisite surveyor. . . . The place where to begin his Majesty may do well, as we think to set this practicable business on foot within his Highness's county of York for there the commons, moors, forest grounds, and chases be spacious and large. . . . And for the encroachments which are daily made upon the King's wastes without his Highness privity, permission or benefit (without innumerable), it is thought fit *salvo semper meliori judicio* that his Majesty should award another commission to the forenamed commissioners, thereby giving them power to enquire by jury who have transgressed in this kind, to survey the same by the foresaid surveyors, and to give unto them full power to impose a moderate rent.[86]

Similarly, a survey of crown lands made in 1607 was involved in James I's plan to drain the fens on his Hatfield Chase and other nearby properties. This project was entertained and developed over a sixty-year period, gaining impetus in 1630 when Cornelius Vermuyden was hired as the engineer for the project and was brought into a company of Adventurers that was formed for the job. Disputes over the land and the Civil War disrupted the project, but by the 1660s, some of the lands were drained and being cultivated.[87] Here again, changes in land-use plans were both stimulated and facilitated by surveying.

Surveys were also used in this period by landlords to fit the rent of tenant farmers to the fertility of the soil; as Lawrence Stone notes in his analysis of the finances of the earls of Salisbury:

The first of the two great pasture ranches was Brigstock Parks in Northamptonshire. It has already been explained how the first Earl acquired the property from the Crown and ruthlessly enclosed it in the face of bitter local opposition. In 1612 all the 2,200 acres were let for twenty-four years to come to a single tenant at a rent of 1,209 pounds a year. When this lease expired in 1636 a new policy was adopted. As early as 1632–3 a complete new survey was made and a map drawn, and when the lease expired 380 pounds was spent on fresh enclosures dividing up the old closes. Thanks to the survey it was possible to vary the rent according to the quality of the ground, and a mass of new twenty-one year leases were made for the individual closes, at rents that ranged from 12 shillings to twenty-two shillings an acre.[88]

When inflation of land prices made land more valuable, the reasons for making surveys increased, as differences in the sizes of properties that might previously have been considered small suddenly became economically significant. With both larger and smaller land parcels needing measurement, two different kinds of surveying technique had to be developed. Surveyors had to be more accurate in small measurements, and they had to develop ways to make accurate measurements over long distances. In the sixteenth century they developed methods of triangulation that could meet both needs. They also began to standardize measurements, so that interpretation of the survey could be as accurate as the survey itself.[89]

The dual political and technical significance of such surveys is conveyed in John Norden's seventeenth-century book, *Surveiors Dialogue*. A. W. Richeson describes the book in the following manner:

The first section in the surveyor's discussion with the farmer points out the need for surveys and clears up the dissatisfaction with the surveyor on the part of the farmer and the tenant. The farmer feels that surveying is a recent innovation by the lord of the manor to obtain greater rents from his tenants, a feeling expressed in his statement, "But I Maruaille how such great persons did before Surveying came up: for this is an upstart art found out of late, both measuring and plotting." On the other hand, the surveyor explains to the tenant that the value of grain had increased in equal or greater proportion with respect to rents, and therefore the land is more valuable, requiring more accurate surveys. The author then reminds the lord of his obligations to his tenants. . . . Norden's surveyor goes around the entire manor and then around each field using the plane table, although he points out that other instruments may be used. . . . After giving the necessary geometry relating to various types of figures the author explains how land area may be found.[90]

This passage makes it clear that the development of more accurate surveying techniques was not simply a technical issue. The techniques used to make surveys were developed to meet needs arising from political and economic changes. Surveys, like other devices used to create national unity and more uniform ways of controlling economic activity within the state, were clearly used to benefit primarily those who already had advantages rather than the disadvantaged.

The political significance of careful land measurement was also clear in William Petty's survey of Ireland in 1655–56. This survey was commissioned by the government after Cromwell's conquest of Ireland to plan the distribution of forfeited Irish land to the English soldiers who had fought there. The land settlement was desired not only as a means of paying the soldiers but also as a way to keep a military presence there. Petty, who was known primarily for his work as a mathematician (and particularly a mathematical economist), had been trained in mathematics by studying navigation at sea. This apparently qualified him to make a technically advanced survey of Irish lands, and he displayed his qualifications by criticizing a previous survey made for the same purpose:

That although the way of surrounding each parcell of forfeited lands, with deduction both of the unprofitable and unforfeited land, and of paying fourty-five shillings per thousand acres for the neat forfeited and profitable land only, doeth much excell the preceeding way of surrounding whole barronyes at forty shillings per thousand, both in respect of rate and usefullness of such admeasurement, yet there hath been exhibited unto us against the said present way of survey, severall defects and inconveniences: the heads whereof are briefly as followeth:

1st. The admeasurement by surround of great parcells is more uncertaine and nice than that of small, and the proof or examination of the one is much more difficult and chargeable then the other.

2dly. The not paying for the measuring of included unprofitable land will be such a byas to the surveyor's judgement, as may tempt him to returne the same for profitable [etc.].[91]

Instead Petty offered:

To admeasure all the forfeited lands within the three provinces, according to the naturall, artificiall, and civill bounds thereoff, and whereby the said land is distinguished into wood, bog, mountaine, arable, meadow, and pasture; moreover to add and sett out such auxiliary lines and lymits as may facillitate and ascertaine the intended finall subdivision without any readmeasurement.[92]

Here again the desire for an accurate survey was closely tied to political policies, to a pattern of internal colonialism, but what is particularly interesting is that the political meaning of the survey was overshadowed by technical concerns about how to make it accurate. Petty's history of his survey is filled with comments about the problems of measurement and completely overlooks the political problems that had provided the original impetus for the work.

Petty's apparent obfuscation of the political meaning of his activities was motivated by the conventions of seventeenth-century science, which were beginning to affect the theory and practice of geography. As we will see in the next chapter, techniques for analysis were consciously separated from the meaning of the conclusions reached by them. But the power of geographical documents over the changing political economy of Europe was quite apparent in that surveys of Europe were consistently used for rationalizing land-use, commerce, taxation, or military control.

A New Image of the World

The development of more accurate surveying techniques in the late seventeenth century began an era of extensive national surveys, initiated by the French.[93] These projects were clearly the culmination of efforts to make land measurement exact and were tied to other advances in science. But they were also expressions of a politicoeconomic order that made the state seem the natural unit of geographical analysis. A new image of the European continent based on the current political economy replaced the older classical and religious imagery.

Pictures of Europe's new political geography became a familiar sight not just to those who administered governments and dominated economic life, but also to those subject to them. The many successful mapsellers trading in these articles could not have been

Johannes Vermeer, *Lady with a Lute*. THE METROPOLITAN MUSEUM OF ART, BE-
QUEST OF COLLIS P. HUNTINGTON, 1925. ALL RIGHTS RESERVED.

supported by the purchases of scholars and administrators alone.
World atlases, mass-produced and sold as consumer goods,
reached part of the reading public; single-sheet maps of the European continent, nations, and their counties carried the politicoeconomic imagery to a larger audience. Maps started to be used
for wall decorations. Many seventeenth-century Dutch households
painted by Vermeer contain wall maps of Holland or Europe.

And recent evidence that Vermeer used a *camera obscura* to help him record precisely what he saw in these homes suggests that his paintings indeed reflect the popularity of maps as decorations.[94]

Thus single-sheet maps seem to have become common consumer goods as they were also becoming important political tools and capital goods. With public spread of this material, a process that had begun with the accumulation of new accurate geographical information during Portuguese expansion and continued with increased publication of geographical documents in the late sixteenth and early seventeenth centuries reached its logical conclusion. The development of sophisticated surveying techniques was rapid; the fact that geographical documents could be used for politicoeconomic purposes was clear; and the transformation of the European political economy facilitated by the dissemination of geographical documents (more efficient agricultural production, increased trade within Europe, and competition for international trade among European states) was well in progress. The politicoeconomic transformation of Europe in the early modern period was not caused by the proliferation of geographical materials alone, but neither were maps merely passive reflections of this change. Europe's new economic order was made possible by broad changes in material culture of which the production of geographical records was a part.

Scientific Materialism: The Book of Nature and the Growth of Rational Calculation

Philosophy is written in this grand book, the universe, which stands continually open to our gaze. But the book cannot be understood unless one first learns to comprehend the language and read the letters in which it is composed. It is written in the language of mathematics, and its characters are triangles, circles and other geometric figures without which it is humanly impossible to understand a single word of it; without these, one wanders about in a dark labyrinth. —Galileo, *The Assayer*, 1623[1]

WHY DID seventeenth-century scientists—not simply Galileo, but also Boyle, Sprat, and Descartes—describe nature in metaphors such as the "book of the world" or the "text of creation"? With one or two exceptions,[2] historians of science have not furnished answers; perhaps they thought it a shallow metaphor, suggesting only that scientists found nature a proper object of study. But it has greater significance. It hints at the link between materialist thought in early modern science and the obsession with artifacts described in the last two chapters as this era's cultural materialism. The metaphor suggests that perceptions of nature and of natural processes (which in this period were said to include economic activity) were linked to the development and use of printed books in scholarly research.[3] When scholars not only used books in their work but also began to see their world *as* a book, they made this artifact a symbolic as well as practical factor in European intellectual life. Why they would do this is best explained as part of the growing obsession with objects.

Materialist thought has frequently been identified as a source of capitalist development. Max Weber, the leading exponent of the theory, argued that the particular form of materialist thinking developed by Protestants in the early modern period (usually called entrepreneurialism) led to the shift in values necessary for making capitalist enterprise the center of economic life in the West. Weber claimed that this materialism resulted when Protestants imputed spiritual value to economic success and sanctified the pursuit of profit.[4]

While this level of legitimacy for profit-taking was new, the materialism was not; it had its roots in the materialism of the Renaissance, which was used to legitimate dramatically high levels of consumption and trade. Renaissance materialism predated the Reformation and helped to bring it about. The growth of the publishing business, which was supported by the interest of collectors in books, eventually made it easy and logical for Protestants to advocate universal literacy and direct study of the Bible. The availability of printed Bibles allowed Protestants to develop a theology that required private religious study and to create a new pattern of biblical exegesis. The new empiricism and precision they brought to the reading of biblical text affected their views of all analytic activities, including scientific research and economic analysis. Protestant materialism, from this perspective, was not a novel invention (as Weber suggested), but rather acted as a bridge between a Renaissance heritage of cultural materialism and the scientific materialism used to analyze nature and economic processes in the seventeenth century.

In providing a new vision of both the natural world and economic processes, materialist thought helped to encourage and shape European efforts to dominate nature and to use natural resources for the accumulation of wealth. In this way, the materialist thought that Weber labeled rational calculation, whether applied to economic problems or to problems in the natural sciences, aided and shaped capitalist development.

By the Weberian tradition materialist thought is equated with economic rationality;[5] here, materialist thought or rationality is used in a broader sense, to refer to the careful measurement and evaluation of many aspects of the material world. By this definition, it includes the natural sciences usually identified as the locus of scientific materialism in the seventeenth century and the scientific economics used in economic planning during this period. Rationality of this sort thus encompasses the the natural and the social sciences, both pure and applied forms of rational calculation.[6]

Scientific materialism as a mode of thinking arose from a differentiation of the material realm, a world of objects, from the ideal or spiritual realm, the former becoming the knowable universe and the domain of science. The material realm was seen as open to direct inspection, as the passage from Galileo quoted above suggests; it was also assumed to be orderly and ordered in a way that could be recognized through study.[7] This perspective dissociated nature from the ineffable, placing the former directly within human grasp. The natural world, seen from that perspective, was not a labyrinth; it was a single system of finite materials and forces that was ready for human comprehension and manipulation; it was no longer God, but only God's handiwork.

The cultural materialism of the early modern period, in contrast, was a *value* system that legitimated accumulation of consumer and capital goods. It shared with scientific materialism a shift of attention away from the spiritual to the material or practical; it also shared impulses for the domination of the material world.

In spite of these seemingly obvious parallels, there would be little point in examining the "book of nature" metaphor in great detail if Raymond Williams and other scholars had not written specifically that these two materialisms have historically shared nothing but an unfortunate use of the same word and a similar balance of attention to objects. Although it may be hard to believe that sheer coincidence accounts for the development of scientific materialism when cultural materialism was flowering in Europe,[8] this assumption apparently has gone unchallenged. The use of metaphors like the "text of creation" by seventeenth-century scientists (reducing the universe to a bit of material culture) makes the notion of historical accident seem even more unlikely, and provides a basis for challenging it.

Protestant thought linked cultural with scientific materialism when it articulated a model of study that took material evidence as the true basis for knowledge and that derogated speculation not based on such evidence. This model of study was derived from Renaissance humanism, with its parallel interests in direct study of original texts and the use of mathematics to document observations.[9] The difference was that the Protestants added the authority of religious legitimation to their ideas about scholarship;

when they referred to "the Book," they meant God's rather than merely Aristotle's or Ptolemy's. Ironically, this theory placed God's spirit (or absolute truth) in matter (the Book or book of nature) and denied that the human spirit had any intuitive or subjective access to God's will.

The book of nature shares many similarities with the other great metaphor for nature current in this period, the great clockwork. Many scholars have pointed to the clockwork as *the* symbol of a mechanistic view of nature, identifying it with the essence of scientific materialism.[10] They have not emphasized that the clockwork, like the book, was a form of material culture with a special connection to Protestant values. But Lynn White, Jr. has demonstrated that the clock represented the Protestant virtues of temperance and rationality even before the Reformation.[11] Seen in this light, the great clockwork image, as much as the book of nature metaphor, connects cultural and scientific materialism through what came to be known as Protestant values.[12]

These images are interesting in their own right, but they are more interesting for their insights into the perceptions of nature that early modern scientists shared. For instance, Galileo in the passage quoted above uses the book of nature metaphor to tell the reader *how to see the world*, as measured and measurable, a knowable entity, something that can be understood through careful textual analysis using the language of mathematics. Galileo uses this metaphor, then, not to argue that a materialist science is the only route to knowledge, but to propose the methods for such a science: reducing nature to its material aspects—those that can be measured, since they take up space or consist of motion—and producing a mathematical model of it.[13]

To understand how the book of nature metaphor influenced the thought of seventeenth-century scientists like Galileo requires using the kind of thematic analysis of scientific thought advocated by Gerald Holton.[14] Holton argues that, while the objective content of scientific discoveries may or may not have obvious connection to the social environment, the subjective aspects of scientific thought—scientists' goals, standards, attitudes toward nature, and conceptions of their own work—are deeply embedded in the social fabric. Thus, the image of nature as a book would, in

Holton's view, constitute a subjective theme shaping scientific thought and linking this thought to patterns of culture.

Holton's approach is particularly useful to sociologists of knowledge who are interested in understanding connections between ideas and their social contexts. It goes beyond attempts to link the social characteristics of knowers directly to their ideas, and suggests that images may be embodied in traditions of knowledge, intervening between social contexts and social actions, affecting all those working with those traditions, whatever their other social characteristics. It suggests that, whether they were Protestants or Catholics, scientists who thought of nature as a book were influenced in their perceptions of nature by Protestant values.[15] Galileo, of course, was not a Protestant scientist, but like many Catholics he was steeped in a tradition of humanist scholarship that was similarly devoted to direct observation and study of original texts.[16] The continuity between Catholic humanism and Protestant scholarship may have been obscured for ideological reasons during and slightly after the Reformation, but the compatibility of the work done by Protestant and Catholic scientists was, in part, due to this earlier similarity of purpose. Common ideas about scholarship and its proper conduct, based on the use of printed texts, spanned religious barriers, enabling Catholic scholars to adopt a vision of nature and mode of study that was primarily cultivated by Protestants.

The line of development in European thought traced here— from humanism to Protestantism to modern science—is the subject of Elizabeth Eisenstein's book on printing and social change.[17] She too finds the book of nature metaphor an important symbol, which links developments in science to other intellectual currents through the common relationship to print. She argues that print gave scholars the means to retain, study, and build upon a shared body of knowledge; the availability of texts brought to light contradictions and omissions in past work that encouraged intellectuals to develop new ideas. But that does not explain why they created the particular line of theoretical thinking that they did. It does not show how scholars used print as a guide to the perception of nature through the book of nature metaphor. Hence, it does not indicate the connection between the cultural materialism that was supporting the proliferation of printed texts and the materialism in the scientific theories of the early modern period.

Expressive Characteristics of Print(s)

In contrast, a number of scholars who have studied cognitive effects of printing have drawn connections between the structure of printed texts and patterns in early modern scientific thought.[18] In doing this they have suggested (apparently unwittingly) that there was interaction between cultural and scientific materialism. They have found in print a material basis for (1) an emphasis on empirical study, (2) a conception of the universe as a closed system, and (3) the decontextualization of the material from the spiritual, the separation of natural laws from supernatural forces or human desires.

Because these authors have not directly confronted the issue of how these two kinds of materialism could be connected, they have not posited a theoretical justification for the connection. But they still have managed to identify important ways in which printing helped to shape the character of early modern science.

The notion that print was an essential precursor of the empiricism in modern science is the thesis of William Ivins' book on visual prints.[19] He claims that the development of science and technology was inhibited before the sixteenth century because before that time there was no way for people to share observations. Without the repeatable print, he argues, there could be no widespread dissemination of observations that would allow people living in different areas to assess one another's generalizations from observation. Words are wonderful symbols for categories of objects, but they cannot capture the unique qualities of one member of a category—at least, verbal descriptions are often clumsy conveyors of such information. While for many intellectual purposes scholars are only interested in generalizations, scientists frequently need documents of particular observations. They must be able to show the particular facts that lead to generalizations, and they must be able to convey the facts to others, so that colleagues can replicate their studies. The repeatable prints that became common and easy to produce after the fifteenth century provided a means of conveying work to others. This, Ivins argues, was crucial to the development of the sciences, particularly the biological sciences.

As evidence for this thesis he notes that the Greeks, for all their scholarly achievements, were unable to develop the biological sciences. They depended on copyists to reproduce pictures by hand —usually from previous drawings—and they could not be sure that copies of copies of pictures drawn from life would show the relevant features of a given plant. To illustrate this point he describes what Pliny the Elder had to say about Greek botany in his *Natural History*.

The Greek botanists realized the necessity of visual statements to give their verbal statements intelligibility. They tried to use pictures for the purpose, but their only ways of making pictures were utterly unable to repeat their visual statements wholly and exactly. The result was such a distortion at the hands of the successive copyists that the copies become not a help but an obstacle to the clarification and the making precise of their verbal descriptions. And so the Greek botanists gave up trying to use illustrations in their treatises and tried to get along as best they could with words. But, with words alone, they were unable to describe their plants in such a way that they could be recognized—for the same things bore different names in different places and the same names meant different things in different places. So, finally, the Greek botanists gave up even trying to describe their plants in words, and contented themselves by giving all the names they knew for each plant and then told what human ailments it was good for. In other words, there was a complete breakdown of scientific description and analysis once it was confined to words without demonstrative pictures.[20]

Ivins points to sixteenth-century herbals to illustrate his thesis, arguing that printed illustrations for herbals became more accurate during the sixteenth century because people realized their value in the identification of medicinal plants. Thus pictorial printing made possible greater empiricism in the biological sciences in the early modern period by providing the means for exactly reproducing evidence from observations.

In contrast, Walter Ong and Alvin Gouldner pay greater attention to the form of printed books as discrete pieces of material culture with their own internal order or form.[21] They see in these

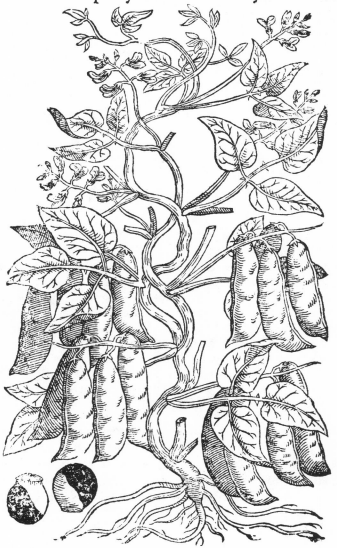

7 *Phaseolus Ægyptiacus.*
The party coloured Kidney Beane of Egypt.

Kidney Bean in John Gerarde, *The Herball*, 1597. SPECIAL COLLECTIONS, UNIVERSITY OF CALIFORNIA, SAN DIEGO.

characteristics of printed texts the basis for closed-system models in science and the separation of scientific thought from lived life.

Ong sees much of this effect in the growing emphasis on the visual character of written communication:

> the Renaissance fixed its attention on material visually stored and retrievable. Its lexical and linguistic base was not an orally possessed language as such, but a body of texts—a controlled and closed field, at least in principle more or less explicitly bounded. The Renaissance preoccupation with texts, inherited from the Middle Ages, but intensified by print, tended to shift the focus for verbalization from the world of sound to the surface of the page, from the aural to the visual.[22]

The disjuncture between the sound of talk and the look of the printed page, Ong argues, helped make writing and talking seem distinctly different forms of communication.

Ong suggests that written language, and particularly the printed word, alienated verbal communication from everyday life, giving the text a unity and clear boundaries which made it appear to be a closed system. Printing made it possible for texts to be arranged in paragraphs and indexed by page, ordering print in ways that speech or hand-copied books could not be ordered. This internal orderliness furthered the impression that texts were complete systems.[23] The sense of closure, Ong argues, was important to sixteenth- and seventeenth-century scientific thought.

> The tendency to closure had to do with a state of mind encouraged by print and its way of suggesting that knowledge, and thus indirectly actuality itself, could somehow be packaged. Though of course there were other factors at work besides print, it would appear that many if not most of the other factors can be related dynamically to print. In *System and Structure* Anthony Wilden has discussed some of the ways in which widely dominant Cartesian and Newtonian frames of reference relied on "closed-system energy models of reality." . . . The closed system paradigm was encouraged by the new science of the sixteenth and seventeenth centuries in its reliance on seemingly closed-system mathematics: the physical universe was assimilated to a closed system, or, rather, a system of systems, each operating on purely mathematical laws.[24]

Gouldner's work on print complements Ong's, looking at the changes in the forms of rational discourse that arose with the decontextualization of words and their closure in print.[25] He suggests that the decontextualization of the printed word required authors to make more elaborate and extensive arguments, since they could not see how their readers were responding to their ideas or what assumptions about the subject readers might hold and use against them. Moreover, readers could examine texts more carefully for flaws than they could rapid speech.

With the spread of printing, then, the structure of what is regarded as a convincing argument begins to assume a specific character. This involves the idea of a full explication of all the assumptions necessary to support the conclusions. This, too, becomes an important rule in the emerging grammar of modern rational discourse. The fullest exemplification of this idea, with its structure of axioms and theorems, is the geometric proof which becomes the concrete paradigm of that ideal of rational discourse.[26]

Authors increasingly replace the dialogue with arguments designed to stand on their own. Writers make arguments that seem absolute in order to protect themselves from criticism from the reader. Readers, unable to approach writers directly, and faced with well-armored positions in texts, are left to evaluate written ideas on their face value. In this way, the text is given an autonomous life, carrying a message as a disembodied truth. This, to Gouldner, is the form of modern rational discourse, the language of positivism.

In sum, according to Ivins, Ong, and Gouldner, the emphasis on observation, the use of mechanical, mathematical, or other closed-system models, and the belief in the possibility of an objective or positivist science represent ways of thinking which could only develop fully after the introduction of printing. What these authors (with the exception of Gouldner) do not elaborate is that these modes of thinking also represent uses of printing developed not by technological but by cultural innovators: those who were designing and articulating the new patterns of materialist culture.

The development of printing, as earlier chapters of this book have suggested, created problems of meaning of the sort created by other innovations in production and trade. Printers and readers were faced with deciding what print meant and what it was good for. Print technology did not in itself dictate its meanings or uses; printers rather than presses chose to reproduce classic texts and made these books representative of the category "book"; patrons rather than typefaces supported the reproduction of new manuscripts and defined some new directions in European intellectual development; religious leaders rather than new inks encouraged the mass production of Bibles for private study and changed the relationship of some Christians to their religious beliefs.

Cultural factors, then, helped to define the meanings and uses of print in early modern Europe. That is why patterns of printing developed quite differently there than they did in China. Fundamental characteristics of the writing system and educational tradition in China had profound importance in shaping the uses of this technology.

For instance, the sheer number of characters needed to write in Chinese limited the value of the printing press as a mass production technology. Although the Chinese invented moveable type, they could never exploit its commercial possibilities as was done in the West. By the seventeenth century, Chinese printers had become efficient manufacturers of blockbooks, and could put out relatively inexpensive editions of books, but were limited in the audience they could reach. Just as the writing system created a technical barrier for printers, the intricate nuances of the classical tongue constituted a learning problem for the population.[27]

The elitism and conservatism in Chinese scholarship also shaped patterns of literacy and the use of the press. There was an ancient tradition in China of putting authoritative versions of texts on stone and making rubbings from them to produce exact copies of the works. This print tradition seems to have taught Chinese scholars to consider printed works a means for creating and maintaining scholarly standards, a view of print that suited the elitist tendencies of the mandarin class and encouraged official control over the publication of scholarly works.[28]

These practices did not prevent the development of popular forms of literature in China. By the Sung period independent publishers were putting out popular works. But even by the seventeenth century, when novels were a common form, they were still reaching only a small portion of the population and were not meant to be used to achieve mass literacy.[29]

In contrast, European publishers and intellectuals early on began to consider the commercial and social possibilities of mass literacy. Printers like William Caxton in fifteenth-century England designed books for semiliterate audiences by reproducing familiar stories in the vernacular and printing them with many illustrations. In Italy in the same period intellectuals argued the virtues and vices of mass literacy and education using printed texts, seeing in the mass production of books using moveable type a potential for disrupting or improving upon existing social relations. And Reformation theologians made literacy a burning political and religious issue, formulating ambitious designs for mass printing and education.[30] All these groups helped to give the printed book in Europe a special range of meanings that it could not acquire in this period in China.

Protestants were the most notable social innovators to make early use of print as a mass medium and to define its character in Europe; hence any attempt to understand the consequences of the book of nature metaphor for early modern science should begin by studying Protestant uses of print. Gouldner, unlike the other authors described above, is aware of the importance of Protestantism in shaping the effects of print. He is particularly sensitive to the role of Protestants in encouraging vernacular publication. He cites Michael Walzer in suggesting that vernacular publishing democratized communications and made possible the use of printing for mass dissemination of ideas.[31] Thus, he intuitively realizes, though he does not argue it, that Protestantism somehow played a vital role in linking the material culture of print to the print effects that shaped scientific materialism.[32]

Protestantism, Print(s), and Science

It is well known that Protestants played an important role in developing the meanings and uses of print; they were early in taking advantage of the medium and thus in shaping ideas about its proper use. Their successes in using print to spread their ideas also helped to suggest what printing was good for. In other words, their way of using print to participate in the cultural materialism of the early modern period set precedents for scholarship that affected the behavior of many people, Protestant and Catholic. As the following poem from an emblem book suggests, they began to equate ignorance with evil and book learning with salvation.

Though Sathan striue, with all his maine, and mighte,
To hide the truthe, and dimme the lawe diuine:
Yet to his worde, the Lorde doth giue such lighte,
That to East, and West, the same doth shine:
And those, that are so happie for to looke,
Saluation finde, within that blessed booke.[33]

Most historians of the Reformation imply that Reformation leaders turned to print because of their belief that everyone should have direct access to the Bible, and should be able to make their own judgments about theological debates. But there is ample evidence that, in advocating detachment from traditional institutions and institutionally sanctioned beliefs, along with self-discipline and self-education through independent study, Protestants were forging a theology that could only have been possible at a point in history when books could be produced in relatively large numbers. Protestant attitudes toward study encouraged fuller use of print; Protestants put the Bible in the vernacular so people without extensive education could read it, and they used the press to spread of their own religious ideas.[34]

The rebelliousness of Protestantism was deeply embedded in its use of language. Luther's use of vernacular was offensive to the Church, and Calvin's publication of his ideas brought about strict religious censorship of books in many countries, particularly France under Henri II. Luther's and Calvin's activities were not threatening simply because of the substance of their new ideas about religion but also because they had new ideas about *how* to spread religious thinking.[35]

Elizabeth Eisenstein writes about the importance of the press to Protestantism, arguing that wide dissemination of religious documents raised questions about current religious ideas.[36] Scholars suddenly found that different translations of the Bible presented conflicting messages. These differences had been somewhat masked in the past by inaccuracies in the reproduction of manuscripts; the fact that print could exactly reproduce a particular version of the Bible meant that comparison among versions was simplified. The result was greater theological confusion when the obvious differences called into question the true meaning of the text. This confusion fueled the Protestant skepticism about religious authorities and supported their contention that people should read the Bible directly and make their own interpretations of it. In this way, Protestant thought was directly tied to the problems in theology resulting from the reproduction of religious texts.

Protestant interest in spreading education (literacy) was an obvious extension of interest in private study of the Bible.[37] While there is a substantial literature that discusses Protestant interest in education, much of it suggests that Protestant values alone were responsible. Kenneth Lockridge, for example, published a carefully designed study of literacy in the United States in which he finds that literacy in the Massachusetts Bay Colony was much higher than in Virginia in the early eighteenth century. While the former had a literacy rate of close to 80 percent by the middle of that century, the latter had high rates of literacy only among the upper classes. This pattern, he argues, results from the greater emphasis on education among Puritans.[38] He is carefully circumspect about the weaknesses of his data and the problem of generalizing from them, but he never examines the patterns of publication in the two colonies. If he had, he would have noticed that the Massachusetts Bay Colony had between two and six active printers in the seventeenth and eighteenth centuries when Virginia had none, making books both more expensive and scarce in Virginia than Massachusetts. In both colonies printers were viewed as troublesome types, but in the Bay Colony, they were seen as a necessary evil. Printing skills gave members of this colony the material resources they needed to support their belief in the value of literacy. While it can be argued that publishing was more common in Massachusetts than Virginia because of Puritan interest in print, this is not the argument that Lockridge makes. He does not put the Protestant interest in education within the context of a larger pattern of Protestant use of print.[39]

Protestant uses of print affected both religious and secular applications of the medium. During the seventeenth century, Protestant publishers in Northern Europe began to take over the larger share of the publishing business where Catholic censorship was displaced. This pattern is manifested, among other places, in the fate of the German book trade. As we saw earlier, Germany had been an international center for the book trade since Gutenberg's time. By the late sixteenth and early seventeenth centuries, the book fairs in Germany had become major gathering places for both publishers and scholars.[40]

The declining appearance of foreign books at the German book fairs, which began with the Thirty Years' War, continued when other methods for distributing books were developed in the later seventeenth century. This change is attributed by James Thompson to the growing importance of Protestant publishing.[41] Since the majority of Protestant books were written in the vernacular, they tended to be traded locally, while Catholic books were in Latin and could have international distribution. As a result, he argues, the decline of German book fairs as centers for international trade was in part due to Protestant domination of German publishing. Between 1675 and 1700 the number of books in the vernacular began to exceed the number printed in Latin as Protestant publishing began to gain ascendancy over Catholic publishing.

By 1675 there is a marked distinction visible between Leipzig and Frankfort. The former is the center of the national trade, the latter of the international. With the decline of international trade and the increase of the North German (vernacular) Protestant production over the South German (Latin) Catholic production, we get the change of the book trade from Frankfort to Leipzig. The fair organization ceases to be important. . . . [42]

Protestants' contributions to publishing, added to their ideas about scholarship, made this group particularly powerful in shaping European ideas about what books were and how they should be used.

146 SCIENTIFIC MATERIALISM

The Word of God

To Luther, Zwingli, Calvin and less renowned Reformation leaders, the Bible was the sole religious authority. They criticized Catholicism for its lack of fidelity to this text and they taught their followers to study and respect it as the direct manifestation of God's Will. They specifically defined the Bible as a closed system in Ong's sense by claiming it as the *only* manifestation of God's Word. Luther first became angry with the Church when its leaders tried to elaborate rules of conduct beyond those which could be supported by scripture, arguing that Christians should disengage themselves from the Church and refuse to support this heresy.[43] Calvin described the scriptures as eternal, containing God's messages to mankind, a set of ideas too pure to be revised by mere mortals. He suggested that some biblical stories might be allegorical, as they were composed for a popular audience, but their messages or truths were clear and could neither be discarded nor changed.[44]

Protestant ideas also treated the Bible as objective truth, claiming it to be divine revelation and not infused with human errors of judgment or fact. They took the variety of translations as indication of the possible corruption of the text under human hands, but Calvin, at least, believed that the true message of the book was apparent through this haze of differences and ambiguities. Thus, he argued that the message of the Bible had no worldly context; it was a decontextualized and thoroughly elaborated statement of objective truth.[45]

When Calvin and Luther wrote about the freedom that faithful Christians could find as a consequence of their faith, they meant, besides freedom from the rules of Catholicism, freedom to read God's Word directly without relying on interpreters. Humans might not be able to know God's full mysteries, but they could look directly at his words (scriptures) and deeds (Creation) to recognize his wonders and learn about his Will. Believers could then free themselves from incorrect information about God that they might hear from others.

The emphasis on direct study of God's words and deeds is not unlike the emphasis on direct observation that Ivins says was made possible by prints. While Reformation leaders tended to discount direct study of Creation, e.g., observation of the natural world to understand God, (a fact to be discussed later in the chapter), they treated the text of the scriptures as *evidence* of God that deserved exact communication. Just as Ivins claims pictures became meaningless as they were distorted by sloppy copyists, so Luther and Calvin claimed that biblical teachings became obscured by inaccurate Catholic interpreters.[46]

Protestant leaders also advocated translation and mass distribution of the Bible along with mass literacy campaigns to make the Bible available to all the faithful. They wanted this evidence of God's Will to be shared by believers so that each one could evaluate the quality of religious ideas against the absolute authority. Again, this message is reminiscent of Ivins' argument in advocating the use of specific evidence to compare with theory, placing highest regard on direct encounters with evidence. In sum, then, the characteristics that Protestants attributed to the ideas in the Bible were precisely those that Ivins, Ong, and Gouldner identify as effects of print on scientific thought. It is evidence that the Protestant model of biblical exegesis set a precedent for later forms of study, including seventeenth-century science.[47]

There is another reason to link biblical study to scientific research in the early modern period. In Calvin's theology, the Word and Creation were the two direct manifestations of God. Each was a revelation and contained God's truth; both could be studied directly for knowledge of God; each was a closed system of revelation which could not be changed by mortals; and both were objective manifestations of God's Will and Glory. The difference between the two (to Calvin) was that God's words were easier to understand than his deeds. He writes:

Though the light which presents itself to all eyes, both in heaven and in earth, is more than sufficient to deprive the ingratitude of men of every excuse—since God, in order to involve all mankind in the same guilt, sets before them all, without exception, an exhibition of his majesty delineated in the creatures—yet we need another and better assistance properly to direct us to the Creator of the world. Therefore he has not unnecessarily added the light of his word to make himself known unto salvation, and has honored with this privilege those whom he intended to unite in a more close and familiar connection with himself. . . . For, as persons who are old or whose eyes are by any means becoming dim, if you show them the most beautiful book, though they perceive something written but can scarcely read two words together, yet, by the assistance of spectacles, will begin to read distinctly—so the Scripture, collecting in our minds the otherwise confused notions of deity, dispels the darkness and gives us clear view of the true God.[48]

The parallel Calvin draws between the revelations of Creation and the Word, in spite of his conviction that the Word is easier to understand, suggests how scientific study could have been continuous with the textual analysis of the Bible that characterized Reformation scholarship. Yet it also suggests how science broke with this tradition in making the revelation of creation, the book of nature, the object of study.

Protestantism and Science

Although many scholars have discussed the role of Protestantism in the scientific revolution of the seventeenth century, they have not agreed about its importance.[49] Scholars who have argued that this revolution was made possible by Protestantism have been criticized by others who have argued the opposite—that the individual gifts of scientists in conjunction with their exposure to the intellectual heritages of the Middle Ages and the Ancients produced this revolution. Among the scholars who find the large proportions of Protestants among early scientists too important a pattern to ignore, there have been debates about the differences among Protestants which make a simple relationship between Protestantism and science difficult to imagine.[50]

Elizabeth Eisenstein has drawn a very clear connection between early modern science and Protestantism through the publishing industry, pointing out that Protestants put out the vast majority of scientific works.[51] Scientific publishing tended to become centralized in the Netherlands in the seventeenth century, after the Dutch had won their independence from Spain and while Catholic censorship was still limiting scientific publishing in other parts of Europe. In this way, Protestant publishers contributed to and profited from the so-called scientific revolution.

The intensity of the debates among those who have questioned the role of Protestantism in early modern science and the importance of printing to science have tended to obscure the important questions that should be answered by this type of research: (1) why so many people turned to scientific inquiry in the seventeenth century, and (2) how seventeenth-century scientists developed a new kind of scientific thought.[52]

The first question, which seems the simpler of the two to answer, has stimulated its own debate. Scholars have found causes of the scientific revolution in such disparate factors as economic demands, developments in the arts and mathematics, political movements in the period and religious changes. All these arguments are attractive but some more than others.[53]

Developments in the arts and mathematics that profited from the classical revival during the fifteenth and sixteenth centuries were surely important to the scientific revolution, but they do not explain why seventeenth-century scientists rejected the work of the ancients or why people became increasingly attracted by scientific inquiry in that century. Similarly, studies of political development in this period may show parallels between scientific and political thought but not why scholars became more interested in science than other intellectual pursuits during the seventeenth century. This process of elimination leaves the role of economics and Protestantism in encouraging new interest in science as the most serious explanations, but it does not reveal a way to *understand* the role of these two factors.[54]

The last section of this chapter argued that it would have required little cognitive change on the part of Protestants to turn from studying the scriptures to examining Creation in their search for God's Will, but it does not explain why they would make this shift. And the literature which posits that economic needs for technological development fostered scientific research does not explain how so many Protestant scientists found their way into early modern science. Another form of economic and religious argument is needed to explain this shift, one provided in part by William Innis, Barbara Shapiro, and Wallerstein.[55]

Innis describes the scientific revolution as a change in the focus of scholarship from theology to science as a result of the stalemate between Catholic and Protestant theology. Science afforded people a way out of this useless debate. Shapiro refines this argument by demonstrating that most seventeenth-century English scientists were moderate Protestants who were exhausted by theological battles and did not have vested interests (as radical Protestants did) in continuing the revolutionary fervor of the Protestant movement.[56]

This argument and the period in which this transition occurred make more sense in the context of Wallerstein's analysis of the Reformation. He contends that the conflict between Protestantism and Catholicism created an ideological schism between the more developed and less developed parts of Europe. He suggests that the barrier between the Protestant commercial north and Catholic agrarian south helped sustain the economic inequality between these two areas, an inequality necessary for the modern world economy.[57]

By this model it makes sense that the Catholic-Protestant theological conflict would diminish once their division of Europe approximated the economic divisions there. The theological arguments were useless at this point because they were settled by the creation of economic boundaries. Science, by this argument, became the new alternative scholarship, the new revolutionary discipline, taking a role previously held by Protestant theology and calling (as Protestant theology had before) for the creation of new ideas through independent study—but now ideas that could be directly applied to economic competition.

Both Protestantism and scientific thought supported a curious combination of discipline and rebelliousness in their adherents. Merton has stressed the discipline required in Protestants which was maintained by some seventeenth-century scientists. As a counterargument to Merton's thesis, Lewis Feuer uses data that suggests scientists were often more hedonistic than disciplined.[58] This hedonism was a flagrant rebellion against social mores. These two images need not be contradictory if one takes seriously Michael Walzer's ideas about Protestantism as a revolutionary movement. What Merton and Feuer describe as opposite types of personal characteristics could be integrated and depicted as a kind of revolutionary discipline, a subversive attitude toward the status quo, an experimental attitude which required some discipline to achieve and maintain. Both Protestantism and scientific method called for detachment from established belief and self-discipline as a way to focus attention on the Word or the world rather than traditional wisdom. Descartes expressed the character of this revolutionary discipline for a scientist in the early seventeenth century:

"And this is why, as soon as my age permitted me to quit my preceptors," he says, "I entirely gave up the study of letters; and resolving to seek no other science than that which I could find in myself or else in the great book of the world, I employed the remainder of my youth in travel, in seeing courts and camps, in frequenting people of diverse humors and conditions, . . . above all in endeavoring to draw profitable reflection from what I saw. For it seemed to me that I should meet with more truth in the reasonings which each man makes in his own affairs, and which if wrong would be speedily punished by failure, than in those reasonings which the philosopher makes his study."[59]

The contrast between the scientist's independent observation and religious independence is even more clearly illustrated by Francis Bacon's idea that one should turn away from the Word and theological debate to observation and the understanding of nature.[60]

This notion suggests one of the important differences between Protestantism and scientific experimentation; while the former was revolutionary in its use of words, the latter was revolutionary in its use of pictures and perception.[61] But both were ways of creating new ideas which contributed to the destruction of an old order, in part by making independent study and thought an accepted social form. Each won this freedom by turning to a text, the Bible or the book of nature, as an authority greater than any human one. By disciplining themselves to be true to their text, scientists and Protestants liberated their thought from established patterns, producing their innovations in both theology and science.

Protestant theologians were like the humanist scholars who preceded them in placing authority in ancient texts (the works of either the Greeks or the Patriarchs),[62] but Protestant scientists who carried the resulting empirical attitude into the study of nature saw themselves as creating a decisive break with the classical tradition; hence William Gilbert could write in the preface to *De Magnete*:

To you alone, true philosophers, ingenuous minds, who not only in books but in things themselves look for knowledge, have I dedicated these foundations of magnetic science—a new style of philosophizing. This natural philosophy (*physiologia*) is almost a new thing, unheard-of before; a very few writers have simply published some meagre accounts of certain magnetic forces. Therefore we do not at all quote the ancients and the Greeks as our supporters, for neither can paltry Greek argumentation demonstrate the truth more subtly nor Greek terms more effectively, nor can both elucidate it better. Our doctrine of the loadstone is contradictory of most of the principles and axioms of the Greeks.[63]

A sense of mission in conducting their research and their feeling that they were being pious by accepting the discipline of a new empiricism are also apparent in the writings of other Protestant scientists, such as Robert Boyle.[64] This feeling of legitimacy for innovative research was one of the central contributions of Protestantism to scientific materialism, tying cultural and philosophical materialism together as keys to intellectual change.

The Book of Nature

Scientific thinking could replace theological scholarship without offending the devout when it could be viewed as a continuation of the same reform movement. Thomas Sprat, one of the founders of the Royal Society, suggests this when he says:

The Church of England will not only be safe amidst the consequences of a Rational Age, but amidst all the improvements of Knowledge, and the subversion of old Opinions about Nature, and introduction of new ways of Reasoning thereon. This will be evident, when we behold the agreement that is between the present Design of the Royal Society, and that of our Church at its beginning. They both may lay equal claim to the word Reformation; the one having compass'd it in Religion, the other purposing it in Philosophy. They both have taken a like course to bring this about; each of them passing by the corrupt Copies, and referring themselves to the perfect Originals for their instruction; the one to the Scriptures, the other to the large volume of the Creatures. They are both

unjustly accus'd by their enemies of the same crimes of having forsaken
the Ancient Traditions, and ventur'd on Novelties. They both suppose
alike, that their Ancestors might err; and yet retain a sufficient reverence
for them. They both follow the great Praecept of the Apostle, of Trying
all things. Such is the Harmony between their Interests and Tempers.[65]

But what precisely could it mean to scientists to think of themselves as studying the "text of creation" or the "volume of the
creatures?" On one level, they thought they were studying a revelation, a manifestation of God's Will with ultimate authority
much like the Bible. To some like Boyle and Newton, the only
higher authority was the Bible,[66] and to others, like Galileo, even
the Bible was less authoritative about creation than the book of
nature that revealed creation itself.

I think that in discussion of physical problems we ought to begin not
from the authority of scriptural passages, but from sense-experiences and
necessary demonstration. . . . Nor is God any less excellently revealed in
Nature's actions than in the sacred statements of the Bible.[67]

Whether scientists considered the text of creation nearly or
completely equal to the Bible, they still took it as more authoritative than any human opinion or idea. In this sense, the book of
nature was a revelation in its own right, whose study was a religious as well as intellectual act. For some, this study was necessary for proper interpretation of the Bible. Boyle suggested this
when he said:

The Scripture being so full of allusions to and comparisons borrowed
from the properties of the creatures, that there are many texts not clearly
intelligible without some knowledge of them [the creatures].[68]

While not all the scientists of the period were looking for inge-
nious ways to make scientific study of value for biblical exegesis,
many felt that the Word and Works were comparable revelations.
Holton says of Kepler:

For next to the Lutheran God, revealed to him directly in the words of
the Bible, there stands the Pythagorean God, embodied in the immedia-
cy of observable nature and in the mathematical harmonies of the solar
system whose design Kepler himself had traced—a God "whom in the
contemplation of the universe I can grasp, as it were, with my very
hands."[69]

To Newton, studying the book of nature could have the same effect as reading the Bible; it could *provoke* religious belief by exposing people to God as the primary force in nature. To these particular seventeenth-century scientists, at least, defining their work as study of the text of creation meant they were doing religious as well as intellectual work, learning about their God by finding His patterns in nature.[70] They saw spiritual value in the study of the material universe.

The English Puritans, who were active in the development of English science during the seventeenth century, clearly articulated their sense of mission in pursuing scientific analysis. Charles Webster argues that, because millenarian Puritans felt that the end of the world was near and that the faithful would soon be restored to their dominion over nature, they began exploring new areas of research to prepare for the final day.[71] John Beale, the Baconian writer on orchards, suggested this when he wrote in a letter to Samuel Hartlib around 1658:

And as Man is thus by Light [the Bible] restord to the dominion over his own house, soe, by Magnalia [the miraculous patterns of nature] that are brought to light, Hee is restord to a dominion over all the beasts of the field, over the birds of the ayre and over the fishes of the Sea. Here you must adde the discovery of, dominion over all the Workes of God; the conversion of Stones into Metalls and back againe; of poisons into powerful Medicines, of bushes, thornes and thickets into Wine and Oyle, and of all the Elements to take such guise as Man by divine Wisdome commands. . . . And let all these Naturale, Artificiall and Spiritual Wonders bee allwayes recorded to the prayse of the Most High.[72]

Puritan intellectuals in the Baconian tradition, preparing to restore the earth to a garden of Eden, felt compelled to explore nature because of the impending millennium. They felt that God, besides giving them new intellectual tools for doing their work, was exposing them to so many mysteries of nature that they could clearly see that the end was near. As Bacon said in *Cogitata et Visa*:

It would disgrace us, now that the wide spaces of the material globe, the lands and seas, have been broached and explored, if the limits of the intellectual globe should be set by the narrow discoveries of the Ancients.

Nor are these two enterprises, the opening up of the earth and the opening up of the sciences linked and yoked together in a trivial way. . . . Not only reason but prophecy connects the two.[73]

English Puritans deserve some special note because they also developed scientific economics at this time,[74] perhaps because of their belief that the well-being of the population in the coming perfect state depended on this kind of social knowledge. Robert Boyle, for instance, attributed spiritual importance to maintaining material comfort when he said:

Outward Goods make not to the Essence of Felicity but are necessary to it's Eminence: that is, they are not absolutely requisite for the Beeing of a happy-man: but they conduce extreamely to his Wel-being. For the Being of Felicity consists in the Habitude of Virtue: expressing it self by frequent Axioms: but certainly the Operations of that Habitude cannot be so wel exercised without those accessory helps.[75]

While concern for material well-being may have stimulated seventeenth-century economic theorists to conduct their studies, it did not define their work as science. For this, they drew on Bacon's idea that nature appeared in two guises: "Nature free" and "Nature vexed and disturbed" by human production.[76] This idea paved the way for more explicit analysis of economic patterns as natural phenomena, as extensions of those natural processes that the physical sciences explored.

Many natural scientists started to become interested in and write on economic questions in this period. Some of them were drawn to such questions by their special technical expertise on metallurgy and minting coins; many others simply felt free to write on topics that interested them. They might have had no particular scholarly training to approach economic questions, but they were able to bring all their experiences in scientific research to their economic work. Copernicus was perhaps the earliest of them, and Newton perhaps the most famous, writing about economics because of his experiences working at the Mint. But neither was a great innovator in economics. That is why it is perhaps more important for this analysis that many of the writers who gained large reputations for economic writings had received scientific training; Nicholas Barbon, William Petty, and John Locke were among the men in this category, ones who were trained in medicine but established themselves as major writers on economics. Each of them, in his own way, seemed to use his scientific training to formulate a more systematic economics.[77]

Thinking of nature as an authoritative and revelatory text, as I noted earlier, required scientists to be true to that text, to assign a higher place to what they could see by direct observation of nature than to what they might hear from other people. This emphasis on direct observation resurfaced in the seventeenth century as a cornerstone of the new science.[78] Kepler's and Harvey's work particularly embody the new empiricism, demonstrating an effort to base scientific knowledge on careful observation and a concomitant lack of trust in scholarly theorizing not based on careful observation.[79] While some historians have argued that this empiricism came from Greek thought and was not particularly new to the sixteenth and seventeenth centuries, Holton describes how it differed from classical forms:

Where in classical thought the quantitative results of experience were used largely to fill out a specific pattern set by a priori necessity, the new attitude permits the results of experience to reveal in themselves whatever pattern nature has in fact chosen from the infinite set of possibilities.[80]

To seventeenth-century scientists who saw nature as a revelation, being true to the text of nature would be close to a moral necessity, something the Greeks would not have felt. Their materialism was not just one way to approach nature but rather the spiritually sanctified way. Thus, shaping an empirically grounded science was a virtue.

Another consequence of thinking of nature as a text was that scientists conceived of the natural world as a whole, a single and encompassing statement of creation, a closed system. Kepler described the heavens as a great clockwork; Galileo suggested that all the natural world was regulated by the same natural laws, ones written in the language of mathematics. Harvey even described the movement of the blood in mechanical terms, suggesting that human beings were part of the single system of nature.[81] That is why he could think of the action of the heart on blood in the following terms:

Frontispiece of *Ptolemy*, 1496. Reproduced in Alfred Pollard, *Early Illustrated Books* (London: Kegan Paul, Trench, Trubner, 1893). CENTRAL LIBRARY, UNIVERSITY OF CALIFORNIA, SAN DIEGO.

Just as water, by force and impulsion of a *sipho* [fire-pump] is driven aloft through pipes of lead, we may observe and distinguish all the forcings of the Engine, even though it be a good way off, in the flux of the water when it passes out, the order, increase, end and vehemency of every stroke.[82]

Harvey did not develop this mechanical image of the heart and the movement of the blood in ignorance of the mechanistic models of the universe that were being developed in the same general period. In fact, he saw his efforts as compatible with the astronomer's work; "so the heart is the beginning of life, the Sun of the Microcosm, as for the sake of comparison the Sun deserves to be call'd the heart of the world."[83]

Descartes was also articulating a theory of the circulation of the blood just as Harvey was writing up his theory. Descartes described the circulatory system as a "still" or distillation apparatus. The heart in this system would heat the blood so it would evaporate and move to the other parts of the body where it would cool and return to the heart again. This image was more closely allied with Greek thought than Harvey's, but it was also grounded in the machines of the period.[84] In contrast, Greek imagery about the movement of the blood was grounded in natural processes.

It was likened to the movement of the tides which perpetually ebbed and flowed. For the Greek in particular, it seemed analogous to the movement of the sea by Scylla and Charybdis. The tissues of the body were thought to use up the natural and vital spirits inherent in the venous and arterial blood as the fields used up supplies of rain. So in Aristotle we find an adumbration of a circular movement of the blood which has nothing whatever to do with the physiological circulation described by Harvey: that the rain falling upon the earth returns to the heavens by evaporation.[85]

The distinct contrast between the naturalistic analogies drawn by Greek scientists and both Harvey's and Descartes' mechanistic imagery helps to highlight the novelty of seventeenth-century scientific thought.

Isaac Newton is frequently identified, along with Descartes, as a perpetrator of a mechanistic view of nature. It is generally well known, for instance, that Newton considered God as the creator, a designer of a single natural world, one based on mathematical principles. Because Newton's mechanistic image of the universe was so complete, he was accused of being Godless and felt compelled to make his ideas about God a clearer part of his scientific thought. But because his perceptions of the natural world were so carefully tied to a mathematical, mechanistic model, the God he wrote about with such admiration appeared as a mechanic.[86]

With the development of these mathematical/mechanical systems, reality was described as a system not devoid of change (because it was primarily a system of motion) but, in Edwin Burtt's terms, one almost devoid of people. "Man appears for the first time in the history of thought as an irrelevant spectator and insignificant effect of the great mathematical system which is the substance of reality."[87] In the seventeenth-century scientist's view, the universe was defined in material terms—in terms of its measurable features—and the human spirit was not found in it.

The natural world described by these scientists, the one devoid of human beings as vital and central actors, was meant to be objective by its lack of special attention to people and its isolation from the world of human activity and frailty. Galileo describes this in his *Dialogues*:

If what we are discussing were a point of law or of the humanities, in which neither true nor false exists, one might trust in subtlety of mind or readiness of tongue and in the greater experience of the writers, and expect him who excelled in those things to make his reasoning more plausible, and one might judge it to be the best. But in the natural sciences, whose conclusions are true and necessary and have nothing to do with human will, one must take care not to place oneself in the defense of error; for here a thousand Demosthenes and a thousand Aristotles would be left in the lurch by every mediocre wit who happened to hit upon the truth for himself.[88]

These ideas about scientific knowledge might seem self-contradictory, given Galileo's rhetorical gifts, but they would also seem sensible to anyone who was predisposed to seeing nature as a sacred text.[89] The content of any text by definition is decontextualized, but the message of a sacred text, a revelation, is necessarily of a different order from common human knowledge. To natural scientists of this period, from Galileo to Kepler to Harvey, Boyle, and Newton, the truth of nature appears in mathematical laws, a special language of nature that distinguishes the true revelation of creation from common human experience of nature. Because the true message of nature is eternal, necessarily lying outside of human, mortal life, it is fitting that it be written in its own language rather than the language of ordinary discourse.[90]

Kepler expresses this view when he claims that nature contains mathematical harmonies which scientists can learn to recognize and isolate from the noise of experience. These harmonies exist in nature and are to be found through direct observation of the text of creation, but their beautiful simplicity is revealed in their separateness from ordinary experience.[91]

Newton similarly takes scientific research to be the search for eternal truths to be found as simple mathematical rules of nature in the empirical world. Hence he encourages scientists to study only those aspects of the natural world that are quantifiable and can yield simple laws in the mathematical language. This does not mean that Newton (or any other seventeenth-century scientist) did not recognize the importance of nonobjective factors in scientific inquiry; he only suggested that what distinguished scientific knowledge was that it took the form of simple mathematical statements which appeared objectively true. Real science was to Newton that body of knowledge that could be decontextualized without loss of accuracy because it was not dependent for its meaning on imperfect speculations of the human mind.[92] Thus, Newton was the ultimate spokesman of the new scientific materialism.

While this mechanistic image of the world was most evident in physical and biological sciences, it was also apparent in social scientific thought. One can find leaders in this area of research, including Samuel Hartlib, making comments such as this:

He that can look upon the frame of the whole State, and see the constitution of all the parts thereof, and doth know what strength and weaknesse thereof is, and whence it doth proceed; and can, as in a perfect modell of a Coelestiall Globe, observe all the motions of the spheres thereof; or as in a Watch, see how all the wheels turn and worke one upon another for such and such ends, he only can fundamentally know what may and ought to be designed; or can be effected in that State for the increase of the Glory, and the settlement of Felicity thereof with Power according to Righteousness.[93]

In this case, natural and politicoeconomic processes were equated through mechanistic metaphors. Anatomistic metaphors were used even more frequently by economic writers to suggest the parallels between these two areas of inquiry. Nicholas Barbon, for one, wrote that the movement of goods was the "circulation" within the "body" of trade that gave it "life." In a similar way, when Sir William Petty wrote about the movement of money, he equated it with the circulation of the blood. His metaphor was so distinctly modeled on the natural sciences that Gweneth Whitteridege has felt confident in arguing that his model of circulation was drawn from Galen. But even if a classical model was not the source for this image (and it seems just as possible that Descartes's theory was the source), the metaphor still indicates how Petty was trying to equate natural and economic processes.[94]

Other means were used to show parallels between the social and natural sciences. Locke, for instance, argued that human behavior, since it was natural, had to be orderly in just the way that other natural processes were:

Aquinas says that all that happens in things created is the subject-matter of the eternal law, and, following Hippocrates, "each thing both in small and in great fulfilleth the task which destiny hath set down", that is to say nothing, no matter how great, ever deviates from the law prescribed to it. This being so, it does not seem that man alone is independent of laws while everything else is bound.[95]

By treating the book of nature as authoritative, seventeenth-century scientists made it seem possible for human beings to gain authoritative knowledge of nature by learning to read the text. Moreover, they wrote as though they had achieved this level of understanding, using the form of modern rational discourse, mathematical proof, and extensive arguments to show the necessity of their theories. In doing this they were much like Calvin. He wanted Christians to read the Bible as the authoritative text on God's Will so that they could gain authoritative knowledge of God which would lead them to reject papal authority and become

Protestants. They would do this when they recognized the truth of what he was saying about religion. Seventeenth-century scientists sought authoritative knowledge of God in the text of nature and found what they took to be just that. They thought they found true knowledge of the universe and would bring scholars to respect their new science more than the science of the Greeks or medieval scholars. That modern historians write about a scientific revolution in this period as the beginning of modern science suggests that they came close to realizing their aims.

Material Culture, Metaphor, and Thought

Gerald Holton associates modern science in the seventeenth century with the ability and desire to distinguish those aspects of the natural world that could be quantified (or understood in mathematical terms and with mathematical precision) from those that could not. He argues that what made this new science distinctively modern was that scientists excluded from their domain those natural phenomena that could not be known accurately and empirically. This helped science to shed many superstitious and mystical elements that had limited its progress.[96]

While Holton developed these ideas to describe changes in the physical sciences, a parallel model holds for economics. Economic writers, much like physical scientists, were removing remnants of traditional morality and attachments to personal interests from their rhetoric (and sometimes their theories) by using measures of the material world to document their ideas. At least, William Letwin argues that economics became scientific in the seventeenth century because writers wanted to impress on their readers that they were not simply promoting their own interests in advocating a particular economic theory or policy. Even though many of these authors claimed, perhaps in earnest, that they were presenting their ideas for humanitarian rather than personal reasons, their ideas were frequently impugned by readers who recognized their names and their roles as important businessmen and/or politicians. At first, Letwin argues, they responded to this problem by writing their tracts anonymously, forcing the reader to take the ideas at face value by removing evidence about the author. But this practice did not suffice, since readers could (and did) remain skeptical about an author's intent even without knowing anything specific about that particular author. The only recourse left for serious students of the economy was to make their writings seem scientific or objective. This, by Letwin's account, provided the motivation for writers to separate their economic ideas from practical interests. This is why, he suggests, Petty tried to stress mathematical measurement of economic processes in his "political arithmetic"; and this is why Locke and others tried to focus their policies for recoinage on the issue of how currencies gain their value. The resulting literature had all the characteristics of scientific thinking that Ivins, Ong, and Gouldner describe. It was based on empirical evidence and framed into closed–system models that were decontextualized from the rest of social process. In this sense, economics literature developed a scientific rhetoric just as natural science writings did in that period.[97]

Changes in the rhetoric of science reflected the desire to purify scientific knowledge and make it unlike more speculative forms of human thought. This attitude toward scientific study shared many similarities with the purifying program laid out by Protestant theologians. They wanted to limit their Christianity to practices that were specifically supported by the Bible. They too rejected traditional authority, which they thought speculative and tainted by the limitations of human nature, and looked for direct evidence of God's Will in his words. Thus, both Protestant theologians and early modern scientists were using a kind of philosophical materialism to build their theoretical systems. The difference is that the Protestants were building their theory on practices (particularly study of the Bible) which were deeply rooted in the cultural materialism of the early modern period.

Because of this materialism in Protestantism and because of the link between Protestantism and science one can trace a connection between early modern science and the cultural materialism of that period. It was not only tied to this materialism through the increasing use of scientific equipment for conducting research; it was not even tied to it primarily through scientists' increased access to and use of printed texts in their work;[98] it was born from this materialism through the images that scientists used in perceiving nature, in the way that they likened nature to books and clocks, not just as literary devices but as guides for understanding the natural world.

The text of nature to seventeenth-century scientists was, in sociological terms, a reality, but it was not simply a reality symbolically defined; it was a reality grounded in the material world and cultural materialism of the period, in the increased production of many artifacts, including books. Printed texts were numerous and their uses were as concrete as they were patterned. Scientists' conception of the natural world as a book, then, was built from the material resources available at that time as well as from philosophical meanings.

While the material culture of the early modern period was potent in shaping scientists' views of nature, the new science was powerful in transforming the European economy and its material life. Some work in the natural sciences, such as William Gilbert's discoveries about magnetism, was directly useful for economic expansion; sailors troubled by magnetic variations could use Gilbert's findings to interpret their compass readings. Similarly, astronomical data was used by navigators trying to locate their positions at sea by the position of the stars. And while the natural sciences seemed to have had little effect on the manufacturing changes of the seventeenth and eighteenth centuries (because the machines used to create these changes were not derived from scientific theories but from practical experiments), as we will see in the next two chapters, scientific economic thinking played an important part in these changes.

The new form of economic analysis stimulated capitalist development, but not in the way discussed by Weber. The scientific economic theories described by Letwin were not the source of an entrepreneurial spirit; rather, they were policies for the state. Weber does not pay special attention to states as economic actors. He seems to have assumed that states were like any other entrepreneurial group, a sensible enough assumption on the surface, since states did act very much like late medieval cities in developing mercantilist doctrines and trying to control their economies through trade. But they developed and acted on mercantilist policies in a distinctive way. States were large political arenas in which numerous diverse and newly assembled interest groups clashed, producing loud discussions of political differences. Their size and diversity made the politics of policy-making particularly complex and consequential for large numbers of people.

As a result, policy-makers acting in states were often forced to argue their ideas publically and suffer public discussion of their strengths and weaknesses. Letwin's theory suggests that this change had a profound effect on economic thinking when questions were raised about the motives of economic writers. It led them to seek new kinds of arguments for their positions, ones that seemed based on scientific principles. Hence this type of economic reasoning emerged directly from the particular problems of developing *state* economic policies.

This kind of economic analysis was unique; it attempted to make the momentous economic changes of the period a kind of social resource for the state in much the way that the natural world was beginning to be made a natural resource for business. Scientific materialism, then, helped to give rise to shared understandings of the new economic order and the use of nature to shape it that would encourage innovations in material culture. It was the kind of materialism that was used to interpret and create increased consumption and new uses of innovative capital goods in manufacture and trade.

CHAPTER FIVE

Culture and Industrialization, Part I: The Fashion for Calicoes

In Ages of Old
We traded for Gold,
Our Merchants were Thriving
And Wealthy
We had Silks for our Store,
Warm Wool for our Poor,
And Drugs for the Sick and
Unhealthy
And Drugs for the Sick and
Unhealthy.

But now . . .

They're so Callico wise,
Their own Growth they despise,
And without an enquiry, "Who
Made'em?"

Cloath the Rich and the Poor,
The Chaste and the Whore,
And the Beggar's a Callico
Madam.

O! this Draggle-tail Callico
Madam.

Every Jilt of the Town
Gets a Callico Gown;
Our Own Manufack's out of
Fashion;
No Country of Wool
Was ever so Dull,
'Tis a test of the Brains of the
Nation:
O! the test of the Brains of the
Nation . . .

—Verses from "The Weaver's Complaint against the Callico Madams," 1719[1]

THE GROWING number of consumer goods brought to Europe from distant parts of the world in the early modern period were generally incorporated quite painlessly into what the historian John Nef called the Renaissance "cult of delight," a hedonist culture embracing surprises and sumptuousness. Exotic novelties fit well into this culture, particularly when they seemed economically harmless, or beneficial fancies interesting only small groups of consumers or local artisans who wanted to copy them for new manufacturing projects. Nef argues that this legitimation for consumption, in combination with developments in science and technology, provided the cultural environment that allowed European industrialization.[2]

Nef's argument makes good sense to modern readers looking at the past; it also would have found some followers among economic thinkers of the period. Nicholas Barbon, the projector and economic theorist, argued that the desire for goods was beneficial for economic growth and that it could expand enormously as more people were able to develop a taste for consumer luxuries.[3]

While Barbon and Nef assumed a more-or-less smooth relationship between consumers and producers, this relationship was anything but smooth during the economically troubled seventeenth and eighteenth centuries. Moreover, the power of consumerism was probably greatest when it threatened the economic status quo by undermining traditional forms of manufacture. Then it acted as both an incentive to innovators and a source of punishment for those who did not innovate.

The popularity of imported goods like the printed cotton calico fabrics brought from India created just such a spur to change. When calicoes became fashionable among consumers, who prized them over locally produced fabrics, they created a crisis for artisans in the textile trades, who found them very difficult to imitate. Calicoes became a target for various politicoeconomic protests, from riots to the "complaint" in the quotation above, but the protests were not adequate to prevent the desires of consumers from initiating a wave of technological experiments that finally were used to restructure textile manufacture.

This movement would not have developed without the growth of materialism in Europe, manifested among elite consumers in a growing concern about dress. As trade brought to market (from different regions of the world) both exotic fabrics and clothes tailored in a variety of styles, the affluent were offered new choices in clothing which they used to express their wealth. They dressed, on the whole, more elaborately than before and changed their styles of dress with a rapidity that Thorstein Veblen would call a form of conspicuous waste. With this they established the modern form of fashion or fashionable change.[4]

Wanting to dress well and to change styles of dress may have increased demand, but it also gave rise to systems of taste in clothing which limited the kinds of fabrics that fashionable people were interested in wearing. When fashionable Britons developed a taste for fabrics, like calicoes, that local artisans could not easily make, they seemed to threaten the wool trade, Britain's central in-

Painted Hanging, Seventeenth-century Indian (28.78.4). THE METROPOLITAN MU-
SEUM OF ART, GIFT OF HARRY WEARNE, 1928. ALL RIGHTS RESERVED.

dustry. By mercantilist doctrine, this meant that they were imperiling the entire development of their country. Tastes in fabrics, then, created an apparent contradiction between capitalist development in England and the development of consumerism,[5] precipitating a political and economic crisis in England that was partially resolved by restriction of calico imports but not fully resolved until machines were invented to produce inexpensive printed cotton cloth.

Many scholars have argued that the astronomical growth of cotton production in eighteenth-century England was the beginning of England's industrial revolution. Even critics of this view acknowledge the special role of cotton in the economic changes of this period.[6] Demonstrating the strong impact of the fashion for calicoes on British cotton manufacturing, therefore, provides one method for seeing the role of materialism in the industrial revolution.

Because this analysis emphasizes fashion and public taste as elements shaping consumerist demand, the evidence for it must include finishing as well as production processes. For consumers, the finishing of a product may be a crucial factor in its selection, for it may be the designs on a fabric or the details on a cast-iron stove that attract potential buyers. Similarly, it was the colorful printing on calicoes as well as their light weight that gave these fabrics their fashionable appeal.[7] Most writings on the eighteenth-century cotton industry neglect finishing processes, and instead point to innovations in spinning and weaving as the prime movers in its economic development. Even the writings which take cultural factors more seriously also tend to ignore finishing, pointing to entrepreneurialism, not consumerism, as the cultural shift supporting industrialization. But a full cultural understanding of industrialization requires attention to the finishing of cotton cloth. After all, part of what made some eighteenth-century entrepreneurs successful was their ability to tap fashions and provide the finished goods that fashion (or other systems of taste) favored.[8]

This argument, then, concentrates on two problems: how development of a general system of fashionable change in Europe led to the particular fashion for calicoes in the late seventeenth and early eighteenth centuries, and how demand for calicoes shaped the growth of Britain's cotton industry. Each issue is so complicated that it will be examined separately, the first in this chapter and the second in the next.

Fashion and Materialism

"Fashion" is used here to refer not to general interest in dressing well but rather to a concern for dressing according to a style that is temporarily favored. The word "temporarily" implies that styles of dress change, and change rapidly enough that staying up to date in dress is a problem. As a result, people who want to be fashionable must continually monitor what others are wearing to determine how they will dress.

In the late Middle Ages clothes were certainly meaningful parts of material culture, expressing the major lines of medieval social stratification, but styles of dress did not change rapidly. Various occupations had their own particular costumes, and social stations displayed marked differences in the sumptuousness of their clothing. Other variations in dress resulted from the fact that most cloth and clothing tended to be locally manufactured. But medieval costume was primarily stable, regional, and stratified.[9]

Within this relatively stable structure of dress there were some changes in medieval clothing occasioned by technical innovations, such as the invention of the button. With buttons, some clothes became more form-fitting than the draped modes of the early Middle Ages. Along with less dramatic changes in the length and shape of sleeves as well as changes of headdress from one age to the next, these technical changes provide the clues for dating medieval clothing within different periods. Over all, however, styles of clothing remained remarkably stable throughout the Middle Ages.[10]

The first major break in the pattern began in the fourteenth century, after Philip the Bold of Burgundy married Margaret, daughter of the Count of Flanders, and began a process of integrating Flanders and adjoining principalities into a Burgundian commonwealth that extended from the Flemish center of commerce, Bruges, to Burgundy itself, along south-central France.

This area lay directly along the spine of Europe when the Mediterranean trade was at its height and was spreading both goods and commercial interests through this corridor to the North Sea and to England. Burgundy, at the center of the trade, was enriched by it and made culturally more materialistic by the flow of commodities into its markets. Members of that rich court took increased interest in their clothes, adorning themselves with much more elaborate costumes to display their growing wealth. By the middle of the fifteenth century, they were making extensive use of furs and the black cloth manufactured in Flanders (particularly in men's clothing) to articulate a distinctive fashion. Some aristocrats in other parts of Europe copied the Burgundian initiative, and spread this style of dress through the spine of Europe, establishing fashionable change as a distinct pattern of elite culture.[11]

The sense of authority in dress felt by those who followed fashion is expressed in a story that Michael Baxandall recounts about King Alfonso of Naples, which was told originally by the Florentine bookseller Vespasiano da Bisticci:

There was a Sienese ambassador at Naples who was, as the Sienese tend to be, very grand. Now King Alfonso usually dressed [according to proper Burgundian fashion] in black, with just a buckle in his cap and a gold chain round his neck; he did not use brocades or silk clothes much. This ambassador however dressed in gold brocade, very rich, and when he came to see the King he always wore this gold brocade. Among his own people the King often made fun of these brocade clothes. One day he said, laughing to one of his gentlemen, "I think we should change the colour of that brocade." So he arranged to give audience one day in a mean little room. . . . And on that day [the Sienese ambassador's brocade] was so handled and rubbed, not just by the other ambassadors, but by the King himself, that when they came out of the room no-one could help laughing when they saw the brocade, because it was crimson now, with the pile all crushed and the gold fallen off it, just yellow silk left: it looked the ugliest rag in the world. When he saw him go out of the room with his brocade all ruined and messed, the King could not stop laughing. . . . [12]

Late in the fifteenth century and early in the sixteenth, after the Burgundian territory was absorbed by the Habsburg empire but while the Mediterranean trade was still strong, Italian modes

Petrus Christus, *St. Eligius*, Fifteenth century. THE METROPOLITAN MUSEUM OF
ART, ROBERT LEHMAN COLLECTION, 1975. ALL RIGHTS RESERVED.

came into fashion and were copied widely by elites throughout
Europe. Most elite clothing started to be made with the silks and
brocades imported from this area, carrying with them both in
style and in substance indications of a new cosmopolitan pattern
of stylish dress. By the end of that century, however, Spanish
styles started to reign over European dress. Clothes became stiffer,
once again dominated by black fabrics, and more elaborately dec-

Damisella Travulsia in *De Claris Mulieribus*, Ferrara, 1477. Reproduced in Alfred Pollard, *Early Illustrated Books*, (London: Kegan Paul, Trench, Trubner, 1893). CENTRAL LIBRARY, UNIVERSITY OF CALIFORNIA, SAN DIEGO.

orated with leatherwork and embroideries in the Spanish style. With this switch, the center of fashion moved to the Atlantic along with world trade, indicating the interdependence of fashion and changes in commerce.[13]

These dynamics in styles of dress were documented in the pictures of the period. The portrait of Damisella Trivulzia from *De Claris Mulieribus* shows the lines and sumptuousness of Italian fashion at the end of the fifteenth century, the simple drapery combined with a love of jewelry, embroidery, or other decoration. Bronzino's *Portrait of a Young Man* also shows the effects of this style, but indicates the growing Spanish influence on fashion in the sixteenth century, particularly in the posture of the young

Bronzino, *Portrait of a Young Man*, c. 1540. THE METROPOLITAN MUSEUM OF ART, BEQUEST OF MRS. H. O. HAVEMEYER, 1929, THE H. O. HAVEMEYER COLLECTION.

Titian, *Portrait of a Man in a Red Cap.* COPYRIGHT, THE FRICK COLLECTION, NEW
YORK.

man and the predominance of black in his dress. Titian's *Portrait
of a Man with Red Cap* also shows Italian influence on dress, particularly in the cap, linen shirt, and drapery. But the portrait also
shows some of the Germanic influence that came between the Italian and Spanish periods of domination. That trend, which seemed
to appear with the power of the Fuggers over European economic
activity, produced the broad shoulders and extensive use of furs
associated with the dress of Henry VIII in England.

Perhaps the most important point to be made about fashion in the fifteenth and sixteenth centuries is that the fashion-conscious of the period (particularly those in England, France, and Italy whose love of decoration made them particularly expressive of swings in style) were beginning to be ashamed of wearing outdated clothes. This was the first indication that people would conform so precisely to the dictates of fashion that they would abandon their clothing simply for reasons of style.[14] Henry Peacham said of the fashion-conscious in the seventeenth century:

Moreover, as among the Spanish and Dutch, one fashion of Apparel still observed amongst them, argueth a constancy of mind and humour: so their [the French] chang and variety, their vainness and levity; for every two year their fashion altereth. And the English (as their apes) think it great pride, to be like unto them, and to follow them in all their vanities.[15]

Temporal correlations between concern about fashion and commercial activity in the fourteenth to sixteenth centuries suggest that the new interest in fashion during the late Middle Ages and early modern period was a pattern of materialism stemming from trade. It is not hard to imagine *how* the expansion of trade, first in the fourteenth century and increasingly in the sixteenth, could have contributed to a change in habits of dress. Trade gave people greater exposure to foreign styles of clothing than they had known before; in addition, it gave elites access to the fabrics and furs they needed if they wanted to copy these styles.[16] One can see in the development of fashionable change evidence of how increased movement of goods in Europe created a pattern of cultural diffusion and innovation.

The relationship between expanded trade and clothing is not unlike the relationship between trade and the kinds of pictorial representation discussed in earlier chapters of this book. There had always been some European trade in both pictures and fabrics. What changed in the sixteenth century was the size and shape of the trade. With the expansion of trade, picture producers, for instance, were freed to experiment with new cultural forms designed for consumption by social groups that had had little previous access to pictorial goods. Something similar was true for clothing. Increased trade made previously rare imported fabrics available to a larger portion of the population and thus allowed tailors to make new kinds of goods for a broader market. The converse was true as well. At the same time that trade was facilitating innovations in picture-making and dress, changes in fashion and picture production were facilitating increases in trade. Each innovation allowed merchants to identify some goods as up-to-date designs, stimulating sales of those items. With innovations in both design and merchandising feeding one another, there were increases both in the pace of cultural change and in the size of the groups affected by it.[17]

Quentin Bell suggests that the change in elite treatment of clothing in the early modern period resulted from the development of modern capitalism. He claims that conflicts arose between the middle class and aristocracy when capitalism began to change the stratification system. Rapid changes in fashionable modes of dress were one expression of this conflict. Because the middle class was a relatively new class without a traditional culture of its own (and no traditional dress within the medieval scheme), it suffered status anxieties that led some members of the class to imitate aristocratic modes of dress. This allowed them to express their sense of high social standing (vis-à-vis the majority of the population), but it also confounded the use of dress to denote traditional social standing. The resulting confusion of aristocrats with wealthy merchants spurred the aristocracy to seek out new fashions to distinguish themselves from their imitators. This conflict gave rise to the short-lived patterns of dress that we now call fashion.[18]

There are a number of problems with Bell's formulation, among them his insistence that the middle class was imitating the aristocracy rather than vice versa. Particularly during the period of Puritan dominance in England, pronounced middle class values were imposed on the dress of the aristocracy.[19] But saying this does not destroy his model of class conflict and fashion; it only suggests that changes in fashion did not always go from the top down but also could go from the middle class to the aristocracy when the former had the political and economic power to define fashion.

Another problem with Bell's argument is that he specifically denies that increased trade had anything at all to do with fashionable change. This seems absurd because of the importance of trade to the availability of styles of dress and fabrics, and because it ignores the role of trade in defining the relationship between the middle class and aristocracy. After all, merchants were the ones providing aristocrats with choices for their clothing, and aristocratic desire to be fashionable provided a large proportion of the demand for the goods traded by merchants.

Another problem with Bell's theory is that it ignores the geographical patterns of innovation and imitation in fashionable change. Geographical centers of fashion developed in the early modern period where new modes of dress were introduced and then diffused to other regions of Europe. In other words, fashion developed cores and peripheries in much the same way that Wallerstein suggests commerce did.[20] The growing international division of labor was creating a hierarchy of regions within Europe as well as the hierarchies within the regions themselves, giving the reigning groups of core states higher prestige than both their counterparts in the peripheries and social inferiors in the core. This hierarchy found expression in fashion. The fashions that developed in a core could come from different social ranks, but whatever ranks were not dominating fashion then became peripheral to that fashion along with people of all social rank outside the core. Once fashions moved towards the peripheries, those in the center would seek new fashions to distinguish them from their imitators.

The pattern of cultural innovation based on this structure helped to enrich cosmopolitan elite culture with designs from regional little traditions as different regions became cultural cores. They could temporarily affect, for instance, the costume of elites living in many regions of Europe, but they would eventually lose their power as both economic and cultural competition reorganized relations among the regions. In this way, each of these fashions reigned over European dress but was subsequently replaced with new designs.

During the early modern period, the center of fashion moved through a variety of different locations. In the sixteenth century fashion first emanated from Italy, and then Spain. In the seventeenth century Holland was the first fashion center, but it soon lost power and was eclipsed by France. Centers of fashion followed the centers of commerce in Europe, moving with the shifts in the economic balance of power, creating innovations in patterns of material culture where goods were flowing most freely.

The close association between commercial centers and cultural dominance in fashion is easier to appreciate once one recognizes that fashion was not part of the Great Tradition. Italy was the constant geographical center for classical culture in this period because it had been the center of the Roman empire, and it was also the center for the Renaissance and Baroque styles of art that had been identified as heirs to that tradition. But new forms of culture, like fashion, which had little classical precedent, did not have such a stable center. They were, instead, oriented toward whatever area of Europe was providing the greatest cultural innovation through dominance in manufacture and trade. Hence commercial centers also became cultural centers, particularly for the new cosmopolitan culture of elites being drawn from local little traditions.

International trade was producing, then, a new kind of cosmopolitan culture in the early modern period. This is part of what made being fashionable attractive to both aspiring merchants and local aristocrats. It offered a kind of cosmopolitan prestige that local culture could not provide, helping to drive a cultural wedge between regional, medieval social forms and modern social patterns.

Because of its novelty, fashion may have been appealing to its proponents, but it was also threatening to many other Europeans. Like the free trade ideology for economics that was opposed by many economic thinkers because it so clearly discarded traditional paternalism in trade,[21] fashion was threatening to traditionalists because it represented a new cultural and economic order. In fact, the set of values conveyed by fashionable dress was seen as disruptive enough to stimulate the passage of sumptuary laws.

Sumptuary Laws and Patterns of Dress

The European sumptuary laws, passed in the fourteenth to seventeenth centuries primarily to restrict innovations in dress, provide evidence about the growth of fashion. Sumptuary laws, as a legal genre, were intended to restrict conspicuous consumption, i.e., public displays of wealth through impressive amounts or kinds of consumption. Some of these laws limited the amounts of eating or drinking one could do in public, but most were designed primarily to regulate patterns of dress.

The earliest sumptuary laws appear in Italy and England in the fourteenth century, at precisely the time when Burgundian fashion was influencing costume in these areas. These sumptuary laws outlined the types of cloth and style of dress appropriate for each social station; they also proscribed overdressing, and restricted the use of imported fabrics and decorations to the highest levels of the aristocracy. In these ways, early sumptuary laws attempted to reimpose by legislation the medieval codes of dress that were being threatened by the first signs of modern fashion.[22]

The 1337 English law forbidding the wearing of clothes made with foreign cloth was one of the earliest signs of the upcoming sumptuary legislation, revealing its connection to the growth of trade in Europe. But this act was not the kind of sumptuary law that would soon carefully delineate appropriate dress. In 1363 the first true piece of English sumptuary legislation was enacted in response to a petition of 1362 which read:

Since many necessaries within the kingdom have been greatly increased in price because divers people of divers conditions use divers apparel not pertaining to their estate; that is to say, yeomen use the apparel of craftsmen, and craftsmen the apparel of valets, and valets the apparel of squires, and squires the apparel of knights; . . . therefore the below-mentioned merchandise sells at greater prices than it was accustomed to, and the wealth of the kingdom is destroyed, to the great damage of the Lords and Commons. For which they pray a remedy. . . . [23]

The act that resulted from this petition put a top price on the cloth to be used by grooms, yeomen, and craftsmen, stating that they could not wear "precious stones, cloth of silver, silk, girdles, knives, buttons, rings, brooches, chains, etc. of gold or silver and embroidered silken clothing."[24] While gentlemen below the rank of knight and merchants with low income were also prohibited from wearing the fancy goods listed above (but could wear more expensive cloth), gentlemen with higher incomes and well-to-do

Man's cape, red cut brocaded velvet silk, Italy (Florence?), c. 1480 (M.66.11).
LOS ANGELES COUNTY MUSEUM OF ART, COSTUME COUNCIL FUND.

merchants were allowed some furs and silks within prescribed limits. The lower ranks of knight could dress better than both the wealthy merchants and gentlemen of high rank, while the wealthiest knights could wear anything except gold cloth and certain types of furs and embroideries. Because this law was repealed the following year, it may seem to have little historical consequence, but acts modeled after it were passed again in the fifteenth and sixteenth centuries. The height of sumptuary laws in England was reached in the sixteenth century, when wearing velvets, fine silks, furs, embroideries, and particularly red and purple velvets was proscribed for all but the highest ranks.[25]

Such laws clearly attempted to enforce the use of clothes to express social station in much the way the medieval clothing norms had organized dress. They were specifically designed to eliminate the spread of concern for fashionable attire through the social ranks, particularly the demand for fancy imported goods such as silks, velvets, and furs.

During the sixteenth century the lower ranks were limited in their clothing to local, heavy fabrics made with natural color (or, in some cases, clothes dyed all blue). The bright and elaborately decorated clothes fashionable in this period and covered by most sumptuary laws were inaccessible to many peasants and artisans, who needed workclothes and could afford little more. The fancy imported goods that were making possible new fashions and sumptuous decoration on clothes were primarily the province of the middle class and aristocracy.[26]

This is important to note since much of the rhetoric used to support the passage of sumptuary laws (including that in the quotation above) suggested that all the ranks in society were being blurred by changes in styles of dress. What is perhaps more accurate is that the lower ranks were remaining, on the whole, true to the medieval structure of costume, but that the medieval structure itself was being threatened by the new uses of clothing by the upper ranks. Aristocrats and merchants were now frequently using clothes not to show their traditional social position but to display their new wealth and to show their cosmopolitan aspirations by participating in a Europe-wide system of fashionable change.

The enormous proliferation of sumptuary legislation in sixteenth-century Europe can be explained as a reaction against this new system of fashion. Not surprisingly, the laws regulating consumption were not effective in stopping changes in dress because they were not and could not be easily enforced. By the seventeenth century the proliferation of sumptuary laws was still continuing on the Continent (particularly in Eastern Europe), but all sumptuary legislation in England was repealed.[27]

Fashion and Trade

Sumptuary laws in England were repealed and fashion was given full sway there just as Indian printed calicoes were first being imported into England. Calicoes did not become immediately popular; they did not play a large role in English fashion or economic life in the first half of the seventeenth century. But during that period, the power of fashion as a cultural system was growing as sumptuousness was losing its bad reputation. Numerous writers, including Nicholas Barbon, were defining consumption as a stimulant to trade:

Fashion or the alteration of Dress, is a great Promoter of *Trade*, because it occasions the Expence of Cloaths, before the Old ones are worn out: It is the Spirit and Life of *Trade*; It makes Circulation, and gives a Value by Turns, to all sorts of Commodities; keeps the great Body of *Trade* in Motion; it is an Invention to Dress a Man, as if he Lived in a perpetual Spring; he never sees the Autumn of his Cloaths: The following of the Fashion, Is a Respect paid to the Prince and his Court, by approving of his Choice in the shape of the Dress. It lyes under an ill Name amongst many Grave and Sober People, but without any Just Cause; for those that Exclaim against the Vanity of the New Fashion, and at the same time, commend the Decency of the Old one, forget the every Old Fashion was once New, and then the same Argument might have been used against it.[28]

Robert Boyle even went so far as to argue that there was some spiritual as well as material virtue to consumption:

God has furnish't Man with . . . a Multiplicity of Desires; & whereas other Creatures are content with those few obvious & easily attainable Necessarys that Nature has almost every where provided for them; In Man alone every sense has numerous greedy Appetites, for the most part for Superfluitys and Daintys; that for the satisfaction of all these various Desires, he might be oblig'd with an inquisitive Industry and range, anatomize & ransacke Nature & by that concern'd survey come to a more exquisite Knowledge of the Workes of it, & consequently Profounder Admiration of the Omniscient Author.[29]

These passages indicate that many analysts in this period saw a compatibility between the demand shaped by fashion and expansion of manufacture and trade. Trade and fashion had come to be identified as mutually supportive—which is not surprising, since the history of English economic development in the early modern period is closely tied to the wool trade. Wool was England's major industry, and England's primary item of exchange with the Continent. Significantly, trade in woolens was also the area of British economic activity most affected by fashion.

In the fourteenth century England was connected to the Continent primarily through the wool trade with Flanders. This trade brought England into contact with the system of fashion evolving from Burgundy in that period and embedded England's economic development in trade with the rest of Europe. At this stage England was primarily providing wool for European manufacturers in exchange for goods such as timber from the Baltic, furs from the Levant, and Flemish textiles. The wool trade was important for English economic expansion, but it was not really essential to the English economy until the sixteenth century. At that point England had more need to import goods to further internal economic development (such as bringing in lumber to make ships). In addition, the British had more completely specialized their economic life, so that international trade in wool and woolens was an enterprise on which the whole English economy depended.[30]

The growth of fashion also made the cloth trade more important in the sixteenth century. Fashionable Britons had greater demand for imported fabrics, and fashionable people on the Continent wanted the fine English woolens. The good reputation of English wools was part of what made this trade successful[31] through the seventeenth and even into the early eighteenth century:

The Antiquity of Wooll in this Kingdom hath been beyond the memory of Man, that accustomed use hath always been observed to make it the Seat of our wise and learned Judges, in the sight of our Noble Peers, within the place where all whosom Laws are established for the good Government of this Kingdom; so that no Kingdom whatsoever can speak so happily of this benefit as this Realm; who findeth it the rich mans increase, and the poor mans Comfort. . . . [Now] it is this time the glory of our Traffick, and maintenance of our poor, many hundred Thousadds [sic] depend wholly on the same, whose bread is gained by these employments; it affords Rayment, nay, rich Robes for the greatest Princes, and also warm clothing for the meanest personages, and no part unprofitable or deceitful in it, but often abused by the wicked practices of deceitful people.[32]

While Britons were primarily wool exporters and importers of fancy fabrics, they did make some fine linens and silks in the sixteenth century. There is a contested story that, when Huguenot artisans came to England in the sixteenth and seventeenth centuries, they introduced French techniques for producing these fine fabrics and stimulated the manufacture of these goods. It is quite clear that Huguenots played an important role in the London silk industry, developing designs for fancy figured silks and introducing finishing techniques that permitted Britons to produce kinds of silks that they had not been able to manufacture before. It is less clear that Huguenots made any changes in techniques for linen manufacture, although it seems that they brought skilled labor to the industry that did stimulate production. But none of this activity created a large enough silk or linen industry in England (or some might say a sophisticated enough industry) to make English silk or linen that could meet demand at home or be exported.[33]

In the sixteenth century the British were also making some fustians, cotton-linen materials entirely different from the fine linens worked on by Huguenots. Fustians were generally very rough fabrics used by lower classes (or ranks) in the areas near their manufacture. The cheap fabric was an alternative to the inexpensive woolens which had been the traditional fabric for the English peasant and low-level artisan.[34]

Cultivation of woad, which was used to make a blue dye, also increased in the sixteenth century. From this era, inexpensive cloth made in England could be found in blue as well as natural colors. The dramatic success of woad-growing projects enhanced the development of dyeing in Britain in this period, but it did not make England a major fabric-finishing country. The British still sent most of their fine wool fabrics to the Continent to be finished before finding export markets there.[35]

Into this picture of textile production and trade and into the world of fashion, members of the British East India Company brought calicoes. They added another element to the already complicated arrangements of international and internal production and trade that were moving fashions, fabrics, and patterns of political and economic influence through England, Europe, and beyond.

The Calico Trade

Britain's East India Company was one of many European trading companies pursuing the economic fruits of overseas exploration and contributing to the formation of a new economic order in this period. This company and its counterparts helped to create the patterns of imports and exports that brought about a new international division of labor. Within this system, European companies that traded with Asia and the Americas were supposed to bring raw materials into Europe and take finished goods out. Certainly England's East India Company made efforts to do exactly that but often found it impossible to follow this pattern. It frequently had to use England's gold to buy Indian goods, since there was little market for European manufactures in India, particularly for English woolens. The East India Company also broke the standard pattern of trade by importing calicoes; they were finished goods, not raw materials. But the breach of common practice that the calico trade manifested did not seem to have any notable consequences in the early seventeenth century, because when calicoes first arrived in England through the East India Company, hardly anyone used them.[36]

The earliest records that mention imports of calicoes into England suggest that they had little immediate economic or cultural significance. Records of the East India Company show that some company employees took calicoes home for their own use and to give to their friends, but they reveal the small size of the market for these goods. Some calicoes also found their way into France in the early seventeenth century. The oldest remaining calicoes in Europe are in France, but these early pieces are rare because their importation was immediately banned when they gained some popularity there. The demand for calicoes was limited until the English fashion for this fabric blossomed toward the end of the seventeenth century. In the early and middle third of the century there was no such fashion.[37]

If simply supplying calicoes to England did not immediately produce an interest in calicoes for fashionable attire, how did the fashion finally develop? To answer this question we must turn again to the history of fashion to see what changes in taste were occurring in the seventeenth century that might have affected the change. This complex story will be simplified here by focusing on the ways that the cosmopolitan system of fashion affected British patterns of dress, and narrowing the analysis of fashionable change to its manifestation in England.

The changing centers of fashion in early modern Europe produced waves of styles of dress in Britain. In the early seventeenth

Frans Hals, *The Merrymakers at Shrovetide*, 1580–1666. THE METROPOLITAN MU-
SEUM OF ART, BEQUEST OF BENJAMIN ALTMAN, 1914. ALL RIGHTS RESERVED.

century, as Italian and then Spanish influence on fashion throughout Europe began to decline, Dutch fashions began to have more
influence, encouraging more simple and comfortable clothing, a
theme in dress that was picked up by the Puritans in England.
This tendency in dress did not (as stereotypes might suggest)

eliminate sumptuousness. On the contrary, many Britons, including wealthy Puritans, wore very expensive, bright, and elaborate clothes. What is most characteristic of English dress in this period is its diversity. As European fashion was becoming less clearly organized around a single center, British fashion was becoming decentralized. The frequently noted simplicity of English fashion associated with the rural life of the gentry is apparent in this period, along with both severely simple clothes usually associated with Puritan dress and the elaborate clothing associated with courtly dress.[38]

But the decentralized quality of English fashion in the early and mid-seventeenth century was being countered by the growing centralization of English cultural, political, and economic life in London. Late in that century, the court life of the Restoration provided a focus for English fashion just as Louis XIV's court was becoming the center for fashion in Europe.[39]

Charles II was a great admirer of the French court and helped to introduce French fashions into England. He and his court were flamboyant, fashionable, and true to the trends in fashion under Louis XIV. During Charles's reign, the styles of the European Baroque were brought into England.[40] Samuel Fortrey suggested this in 1663:

But most of these evils [from using too many imported goods] would be easily prevented, if only his Majesty would be pleased to commend to his people, by his own example, the esteem and value he hath of his own commodities, in which the greatest Courtier may be as honourably clad, as in the best dress Paris, or a French tailor can put him in; besides it seems to be more honourable for a King of England rather to become a pattern to his own people, than to conform to the humours and fancies of other nations; especially when it is so much to his prejudice.[41]

Those who were following French fashion and could afford it used imported French fabrics for their clothes. They showed a particular preference for the figured silks (for which the French were renowned), but they also used a variety of satins, velvets, and brocades. Since Britons produced very small quantities of these fabrics, following the fashion meant depending primarily on imported goods. Fashionable dressers probably preferred to wear imported textiles for their cosmopolitan air and for the fact that

Lord and Lady Clapham, painted wooden dolls in the fashions of the day, late seventeenth-century (T846-T847–1974). COURTESY OF THE VICTORIA AND ALBERT MUSEUM, LONDON.

imported fabrics had been considered more prestigious since the Middle Ages.

Because of the special meanings of imported silks, when restrictions were put on French imports in 1678, halting the trade in French fabrics, a vacuum was created. There was an unmet demand for elegant imported cloth. It was at this moment that calicoes began to gain both new prestige and new use. At first they were used to make linings for clothing made with a more traditional elegant cloth (like silks). But increasingly, calicoes appeared as the primary fabric in dresses, particularly in dresses meant to be worn exclusively at home. Even this limitation on their use started to diminish, however, and calicoes became a standard, if not always the preferred, textile in fashionable clothing.[42]

What was there to calicoes that made them an acceptable alternative to fine French fabrics? The answer to the question is complicated and depends on a multilayered interpretation of fashionable change.

The popularity of calicoes for fashionable attire has to be partially explained by the limited alternatives available to Britons at that time. While they could still find some silks and brocades from areas of Europe other than France (and still preferred to wear them in the seventeenth century), their choices were limited enough that their ability to use novelties for fashionable change was restricted. Local British fabrics were also available, including some fine wools and silks, but most local fabrics were simply not fine enough for high fashion.

In contrast, calicoes embodied characteristics of the traditional elite fabrics. They were very light, sheer, and soft, like fine silks. Silk, of course, had a long history of identification with the highest nobility. It was, one might say, a noble cloth. To the extent that calicoes resembled silks, they took on an association with the nobility.[43] Calicoes were also figured with floral designs in a variety of colors. In the history of English fashion it is clear that flowered designs in embroideries, silks, and brocades had a long association with the nobility. Thus, the patterns on calicoes too made them look more like elite fabrics than the plain clothing worn by the lower ranks.[44]

In the seventeenth century, lightness of fabric and floral patterns were also particularly fashionable. When calicoes first were being used for fashionable dress in Britain, women were wearing clothing that had many pleats and multiple layers, a style of dress the French had designed for silks. To create the proper shapes for the clothes, women had to wear lighter fabrics like silks or calicoes. The dresses made in this period were also frequently cut from fabric covered with baroque floral designs, designs produced in brighter colors than had been normal for floral patterns earlier in the century and during the Elizabethan period. Calicoes shared this use of bright floral patterns, although the floral designs on French brocades and embroideries were much more formal and stylized and did not have the "natural" flavor of calico prints. The differences between the designs of calico prints and baroque

Silk dress by A. M. Garthwaite, English, Spitalfields, 1744 (T.264-1966) COURTE-
SY OF THE VICTORIA AND ALBERT MUSEUM, LONDON.

fabric designs might have made calicoes appealing as a novelty that sufficiently resembled silk to be used in the same styles of dress. This argument gains some credence because of the recognizable influence of oriental designs on rococo patterns.[45]

The British were also told that fine cottons were treated by Indian elites as equal to or better than fine silks. Lewis Roberts made this point in describing trade on the Chormandel coast:

the principle *Commodities* that this city [Musulipatan] is noted to be famous for, are those excellent *fine Cotton Linens*, made herein in great abundance, and of all colours, and interwoven with divers sorts of Loom-works and flowers, very fine and cunningly wrought, and therefore much worn in *India*, and better esteemed here than *Silk*, as indeed being both found finer and richer, and used by the greatest women in those parts for their clothing. . . . [46]

Another difference between Indian calicoes and European fabrics may have also contributed to the fashion for calicoes. Calicoes were much more practical than fancy linens and silks. They were cheaper and easy to wash. These characteristics may not have been of much interest to the aristocracy (since cleanliness was not particularly an aristocratic virtue in this period), but they certainly contributed to the attractiveness of calicoes to the middle class. This meant that calicoes had even stronger appeal to the middle class than any fabric imported from Europe; they embodied the look of elite fabrics appropriate to the fashions of the time, yet were inexpensive and easy to wear and clean.[47]

Almost immediately after the 1688 revolution, calicoes became fashionable fabrics for Britons of all social classes. Before the fashion for calicoes, some members of the urban lower class had taken to wearing them, primarily because of their low cost and easy wear. When the fashion spread their use to the middle class and aristocracy, calicoes could be seen in some of the clothing worn by people of all social classes. They might not have been used in the best dresses worn by the most fashionable Britons, but they were in a wide array of wardrobes. This gave calicoes (and their more expensive cousins, the hand-painted chintzes) an unusual kind of popularity, a breadth of appeal and use that was unprecedented. Defoe commented on this pattern by bemoaning the

Detail of Hanging, border scene, painted and printed, seventeenth century, Indo-Persian (20.79). THE METROPOLITAN MUSEUM OF ART, GIFT OF MRS. ALBERT BLUM, 1920. ALL RIGHTS RESERVED.

fact that one could no longer tell ladies from their servants by their dress.[48] Pope also wrote sarcastically on this fashion in his not-too-flattering *Of Characters of Women*:

> She, while her lover pants upon her breast,
> Can mark the figures on an Indian chest;
> And when she sees her friend in deep despair,
> Observes how much chintz exceeds mohair.[49]

Many people also began to use calicoes to decorate their houses. The development of modern fireplaces in the sixteenth century and their widespread adoption during the building boom of the early seventeenth century had begun to change fashions in home decoration, allowing people to use fabrics on their walls, floors, and furniture as well as on their beds without fear of ruining them with fireplace smoke. Calicoes became widely used for home decoration, particularly when word spread that Queen Mary had used calicoes to decorate a bedchamber.[50]

There is some question whether the sudden popularity of calicoes in this period was due entirely to restrictions on French imports or whether it was also the result of East India Company policies. In the mid-seventeenth century, merchants from that company began to take patterns from European textiles to India, giving them to Indian artisans to copy on printed cotton. Some evidence suggests that this practice helped Indian chintzes to catch the eye of European aristocrats. Other evidence suggests that this policy was a disaster because Indian artisans paid no attention to the patterns they were told to imitate. Eighteenth-century Indian fabrics and European fancy embroidery from this and earlier periods resemble one another enough to suggest that there was some design exchange. But even so, it is difficult to assess the importance of this design syncretism to the fashion for calicoes in England. Certainly, the use of European motifs must have been some help in associating the look and feel of this fabric with the silks and linens previously worn by aristocrats.[51]

Calicoes were probably popular also because there was nothing quite like them in Europe. There was little production of cotton fabric in this period and little fabric printing that yielded wash-

Palampour Bedspread (RIHS 1962.7.2). BY PERMISSION OF THE RHODE ISLAND
HISTORICAL SOCIETY (PHOTO BY GEORGE HENDERSON).

able colors. Some artisans in Germany and England as early as
the fifteenth century had used wallpaper printing techniques to
print on fabrics for clothes, but until nearly the end of the seventeenth they had not yet learned how to combine printing techniques with mordants and dyes to make permanent designs.

Instead they printed with oil base inks that would dissolve when the fabrics were washed.[52] Nor could they make the fabrics to print on inexpensively. British artisans did not have a tradition of cotton spinning that would yield the strong cotton warp yarns needed to make pure cotton cloth. Even if they learned to do this kind of spinning, the resulting cloth would be more expensive because Indian artisans had a much lower standard of living. For this reason it was more profitable for merchants to import Indian cottons than to encourage British manufacture of them using existing technology.[53] This gave Indian calicoes a special place in the English textile trade. They were the one fabric that had no competitors and that enjoyed popularity with all classes.

Calicoes gained in popularity during the late seventeenth century, when local silk and woolen manufacturers were experiencing a sharp slump in trade. The precise reasons for the slump are not clear, although fluctuations in the seventeenth-century British economy were common.[54] But textile workers thought they knew the cause; they blamed the fashion for calicoes. By identifying calicoes as a threat to traditional textile manufacture in Britain, they labeled it as dangerous to the British economy itself and stimulated a search for solutions to the problem. This is probably part of what inspired the best-known English mercantilist, Thomas Mun, in *England's Treasure by Forraign Trade* to blame consumers for England's economic problems. He did not completely condemn conspicuous consumption of imported goods, but he did call for restraint in the use of expensive imports:

Lastly, all kind of Bounty and Pomp is not to be avoided, for if we should become so frugal that we would use few or no Forraign wares, how shall we then vent our own Commodities? What will become of our Ships, Mariners, Munitions, our poor Artificers, and many others? doe we hope that other Countreys wil afford us money for All our Wares, without buying or bartering for Some of their? this would provide a vain expectation. . . . Again the more pomp of Building, Apparel, and the like, in the Nobility, Gentry, and other able persons, cannot impoverish the Kingdome; if it be done with curious and costly works upon our Materials, and by our own People, it will maintain the poor with the purse of the rich, which is the best distribution of the Common-Wealth.[55]

Mercantilist Restriction on the Calico Trade

Because of their fashionable connotations, calicoes not only gained economic value but also took on politicoeconomic significance. There was nothing particular in the designs that made them political symbols to textile manufacturers in Britain (although their designs had everything to do with their fashion). What gave them political significance was that Indians produced them and Britons consumed them rather than locally produced fabrics.[56]

The political meaning of calicoes constituted a second-order symbolism based on their use, just as the meaning of "the book" as a closed system of thought was a kind of second-order symbolism based on Protestant use of printed texts. In both cases the objects were given these second-order meanings without specific reference to the varying character of their contents, so that a calico with a tree-of-life design was no less offensive than a simple flowered one and a book on religion was no more or less of a closed system than a book on law. It was the *structural* meaning of the textiles and texts, their use in defining the relationship between believers and their God or Indian and British artisans, that gave them this second level of social significance.

Efforts were made to limit or stop imports of calicoes in late seventeenth- and early eighteenth-century Britain when textile producers, particularly those in the silk and woolen trades, saw calicoes as a threat to their businesses and thought that the government could protect them. The British government had already passed a number of bills that limited trade with both other European countries and British colonies, ending a period when free-trade ideas were starting to find advocates.[57] British regulation of the calico trade, then, was part of a resurgence of mercantilist protectionism.

Mercantilism has been described by some scholars as the economic manifestation of nationalism, but many others have objected to this characterization. Although there is no accepted definition of mercantilism, it seems best described as a strategy used by governments to make patterns of trade favorable to their national economies. Viewed in this way, mercantilism can be described as an economic expression of the politics of materialism, an attempt to regulate political relations to serve material interests. But those who advocated such policies also treated mercantilism as an economic theory. They tried to create with it something close to a national economic philosophy favoring national solidarity, economic autonomy, and expansion.[58]

In sixteenth- and seventeenth-century Europe the fate of national economies was closely tied to international trade, so something like a national economic policy became salient. Political leaders faced pressure to achieve good returns on trade. In England there was particular interest in formulating national economic policies on the part of Puritan political leaders who hoped to realize their utopian dreams through the state. They saw the enrichment of their country at the expense of Catholic countries as an indication of their special favor in God's eyes, and they considered the economic improvement of the English population as central to establishing the perfect state.[59]

One way in which politicians hoped to enrich their countries was by making the terms of their trade with other states as favorable as possible. Mercantilist policies were one approach to reaching this goal. They reflected a particular view of the world economy, a sense that states were increasingly important as economic units but limited in their ability to control their own economies because their fates rested on their positions vis-à-vis other countries within a world economy.[60] Their vulnerability to market forces was an underlying theme of the economic literature of the times.

Wallerstein's model of the modern world system provides a language for understanding the vulnerability that policymakers of the sixteenth and seventeenth centuries seem to have felt. Wallerstein suggests that sixteenth-century increases in trade were producing economically unequal areas in the world and shaping an international division of labor. Strong core states were emerging in areas of Europe with the greatest economic advantages, but they were developing in competition with other core states. As they became increasingly specialized in industrial manufacture, drawing on the raw materials and food supplies from peripheries (in Europe and outside), they gained economic advantages that could help sustain their autonomy but at the same time they became more dependent on other regions for the resources they needed. In this situation, all the regions of Europe, even the richest, were subject to competition and felt vulnerable because of their dependence on outsiders.[61]

Strong core states, England among them, tried to develop economic policies to sustain their dominance. Their problem, if they wanted to maintain dominance, was to avoid becoming dependent on trade in manufactured goods, particularly trade with other core states. Theorists who advocated free trade saw the route to autonomy in the pursuit of the highest levels of trade, i.e., in following the Dutch model for achieving political and economic independence through the freest practice of commerce and successful competition to control trade. Mercantilist ideas, on the other hand, were based more on French precedent. Mercantilists presumed that core states could sometimes lose in open competition. They felt that it was the government's duty to reduce the negative effects of unfavorable trade balances by prohibiting any trade that seemed detrimental to the state's economic development. Some of this mercantilist defensiveness and interest in the French experience appear in the description by the rather crude mercantilist, Gerard de Malynes, of the effects of trade on the movements of bullion:

But we may well observe, that the greatest part of the silver which commeth from the West *Indies*, is transported into the East *Indies*; where diuerse nations now trafficking for spices, cause the price thereof to rise in those countries: who buying deare, must sell according, or else prove to be small gainers, as the sequell of that trade will manifest. Gold is chiefly exhausted in all countries by the trade of silkes, which caused the Frenchmen to prohibite the bringing in of any into *France*, where diuers stuffes of silke, as velvets, satin, grogaines, and such like are made by the inhabitants.[62]

Although French mercantilist policies might have inspired English mercantilists, Dutch economic and political successes were too impressive for sophisticated mercantilists to ignore. This is why Thomas Mun said:

For since [the Dutch] have cast off the yoke of Spanish slavery, how wonderfully are they improved in all humane policy? What great means have they obtained to defend their liberty against the power of so great an Enemy? and is not all this performed by their continual industry in the trade of Merchandise? [63]

But unlike the free traders of the seventeenth century, Mun praises Dutch strength not to admire it but to argue that the English were making it possible. He claimed that the Dutch were taking advantage of their friendly relations with England by exploiting English fisheries and carrying goods to English ports. In this way, he presented the Dutch not as models but rather as enemies of England in world competition for economic power, whose rise should be curbed by mercantilist restriction.

Mercantilist policies such as these were plausible in the period because core states like England could produce their own manufactured goods and freely prohibit the importation of many foreign wares, without endangering their economy. Hence they were in a position to restrict trade in many items when they felt it was detrimental to the local economy. What remained a problem for mercantilists was deciding when trade was detrimental to the kingdom and how to limit it. Thus mercantilist doctrines came in a variety of forms. The two primary forms in seventeenth-century Britain were bullionism and balance-of-trade theory.[64] Early in the century the major issue of debate was bullionism, i.e., the direction of flow of bullion either into or out of the state. Later greater emphasis was put on the balance of trade in commodities but both sets of ideas stressed the use of restrictions on the movements of goods.[65] Bullionists like Malynes presented their ideas with the following kind of logic:

A prouident and wise Prince therefore will rather conclude this: Are things growne deare, through the abundance of gold and silver of late years? then is it most requisite for me to procure to participate of that abundance, as much as lieth in my power, and to accumulate treasure for me and my subjects by importation of gold and silver, and preuention of the transportation of any.[66]

In contrast, Thomas Mun wrote:

It is not therefore the keeping of our money in the Kingdom, but the necessity and use of our wares in forraign Countries, and our want of their

Commodities that causeth the vent and consumption on all sides which makes a quick and ample Trade. . . . The conclusion of this business is briefly thus, That as the Treasure which is brought into the Realm by the ballance of our forraign trade is that money which doth abide with us, and by which we are enriched, so by plenty of money thus gotten (and no otherwise) do our Lands improve. For when the Merchants hath a good dispatch beyond the Seas for his Cloth and other wares, he doth presently return to buy up the greater quantity, which raiseth the price of our Woolls and other commodities, and consequently doth improve the Landlords Rents as the Leases expire daily: And also by this means money being gained, and brought more abundantly into the Kingdom, it doth enable many men to buy Lands, which will make them the dearer.[67]

Mun, then, did not identify the welfare of the state with the amount of bullion acquired but with the amount of profit merchants could accumulate and bring home to increase land values in England. Both this model of economic development and the bullionist one attempted, in their own ways, to define and locate patterns of trade as the basis for a state's wealth.

Describing these ideas in abstract terms may seem to imply that British mercantilist thought was a detached perspective on economic policy, but nothing could be farther from the facts. Mercantilist policies were *political* policies, bills enacted because of pressures from the varied interest groups within Britain that were seeking economic advantages through legislation. The mercantilist laws were frequently compromise solutions to problems debated among conflicting interests groups—merchants in monopolistic trading companies versus local manufacturers, free merchants versus landowners, etc. The main line of conflict in this period was between merchant and landowner interests, since merchants and landowners were the two most politically powerful groups in England. But the definition of their interests, the degree of unity within each group, and the degree of conflict between the two camps could vary widely depending on the issue under debate. Thomas Mun, for instance, wrote his pamphlet on the East Indian trade (the source of the quotation above) not out of some abstract desire to understand it but rather out of his desire to maintain it. He was a director of the East India Company and was arguing for the trading practices of that company. It is likely that his equation of national wealth with high land values was a political as

well as an analytic choice; a coalition of merchants and landowners could keep this trade alive, and any friction between them
could help bring on its demise.[68]

But however self-serving these ideas might have been, they were
found more attractive in this period than free-trade ideas, probably because, whatever their origins or shapes, they tended to argue that the welfare of the state depended on its well-being as a
single economic unit within a world economy. Their emphasis on
solidarity and autonomy was a great source of appeal. It stood in
contrast to the free-trade emphasis on the economic interests of
particular merchants. This contrast was pointed out by a promi-
nent mercantilist writing under the pseudonym "Philopatris":

> Trading merchants while they are in the busie and eager prosecution of
> their particular Trades, although they be very wise and good Men, are
> not always the best Judges of Trade, as it relates to the Profit or Power
> of a Kingdom. The reason may be, because their Eyes are so continually
> fixt, and their minds intent upon what makes for their peculiar Gain or
> Loss, that they have not leisure to expatiate or turn their thoughts to
> what is most Advantageous to the Kingdom in general.[69]

In the seventeenth century British economic policies were developed to regulate trade with other European countries, and with
the colonies and trading stations that Europeans had established
in other parts of the world. These two types of trading policy
were quite different, but both worked to sustain Britain's position
as a core state.

The earliest English mercantilist policies were directed toward
the Dutch, trying to diminish Dutch control over British trade.
The British prohibited the export of unfinished woolens to be finished in Holland in order to encourage the growth of wool
finishing trades in England. This policy, known as the Cockayne
project, was soon retracted because it disastrously encouraged the
Dutch to promote their own textile production and reduced the
continental demand for British cloth. The British fared a bit better
as mercantilists when they passed the successful series of Navigation Acts requiring, among other things, that goods imported to
Britain or the colonies be carried by British ships. These efforts
were successful in reducing Dutch control of trade because the

British were equipped to do their own shipping and *could* supplant the Dutch in this area.[70]

Mercantilist restrictions were also placed on the importation of French goods. Trade with the French was prohibited during much of the seventeenth century. The countries were enemies, and French goods tended to be luxury items not available in Britain, just the kinds of goods whose popularity threatened the balance of trade with France.[71]

In these policies toward trade with the Dutch and French, Britain expressed concern about maintaining its economic autonomy and avoiding the dependencies that could have threatened its position as a core state. Political leaders of the period may not have realized their policies in just these terms, but they did express ongoing concern about the terms of trade and saw in these terms advantages and disadvantages for their country's national development. When considering trade with other European states with similar levels of economic development, they were particularly and specifically concerned about the threat of finished imports to local industries.

Phyllis Deane and W. A. Cole argue that such mercantilist thinking flourished in the late seventeenth and early eighteenth century because of the growth of colonial trade.[72] If Britain was to be economically independent from European nations, it needed markets and sources of raw materials outside the European arena. The establishment of colonies furnished just this and as a result may have helped to bring about the resurgence of mercantilist doctrine in the late seventeenth century. As Henry Robinson, the merchant and economic writer, suggested:

wee [should] enlarge our Forraigne Plantations, and get farther footing in Barbarie, East and West Indies, with other Countries wheresoever it may be compassed. Not onley that wee may the better provide our selves of Canvas for Sailes, Masts, Timber, with all other things necessary for shipping within our own Dominions; but also in that a little spot of ground, as England is, with its Dominions, if it does not inlarge them, in future generations, it feare me, will be found inconsiderable in respect of Spain, Portugall, the United Providences, or any other European Nation, which shall have arrived to, and be armed with five or ten times a greater strength, power, and riches, either from their Asian, African, or American Dominions.[73]

Colonies were useful alternative trading partners as long as they could be prevented from competing with the British in trade among the colonies. The mercantilist policies Britain developed to regulate colonial trade, then, tended to encourage increasing dependence of the colonies on British trade. This kind of policy was articulated by Benjamin Worsley as part of his effort to analyze the consequences of colonial expansion. The historian of science, Charles Webster, has said of him:

Worsley became the ideologue of [the Council of Trade] during the years preceding the Navigation Act [of 1650]. It is apparent from his writings on Virginia that he came to believe that the encouragement of English shipping, even more than free ports, was fundamental to the expansion of England's trade. He recognized that the control of colonial trade would not only be to the advantage of English shipping, it would also impose a political settlement on the recalcitrant American and West Indian colonies. This policy secured the support of both imperialistically inclined politicians and the interloping colonial merchants. . . . The initial response to the expansionist position was the Act of 1650, which aimed to reduce Virginia and three other American colonies to conformity by completely prohibiting their trading with foreign ships. In addition a licensing system was introduced to control personnel carried to all English plantations. Finally, the Council of State asserted its authority to control the appointment of governors and other officers in the colonies.[74]

The Navigation Acts, then, besides restricting Dutch trade with Britain and the colonies, limited trade among the colonies themselves; this, of course, did not please the colonists in North America, since it clearly conflicted with their economic interests. Similarly, when Irish grain and beef were competing with British production, their export was prohibited, and when the British needed timber for ship building, the Irish became suppliers of wood, increasing their dependency on trade with Britain. In these cases and others, British economic policies encouraged trade with the colonies on terms that increased British autonomy and their dependency.[75]

The Indian calico trade developed in this atmosphere of mercantilist protectionism. Trade with India was always a problem to seventeenth-century mercantilists. There was, as I stated earlier, little market in India for British goods; so trade with India always involved the loss of British bullion. Even though Indian goods bought with this bullion could be sold for more in Europe and the other colonies, on bullionist principles the Indian trade appeared unwise. And no matter how this trade was arranged, it still seemed to produce autonomy rather than dependency for India.[76]

East India Company merchants were able to argue effectively to Parliament that the trade was profitable, even though it did not yield its profits through a form of trade that the British recognized as beneficial. "Philopatris" argued, for instance, that imports of Indian silks were good for England because they reduced imports of European silks. Reexport, he suggested, was even more beneficial because Indian silks competed for markets with the silks produced in Italy, France, Holland, and Flanders. In other words, he tried to suggest that this trade increased English autonomy from other core states and even helped to reduce the control of other states over European manufacture and trade in silk. These arguments held sway for a while, but they did not dispel the doubt and suspicion that surrounded trade with India.[77]

The East India Company actually increased public distrust of trade with India because of its status as a monopoly (which many Britons did not like) and because of political problems within the company itself. All this weakened the legitimacy of the company in its attempts to keep trade with India as open as possible. That is one of the reasons that East India trade and export of bullion through it were repeatedly mentioned in documents discussing crises in the textile trade in the seventeenth century. Thus, when the woolen and silk interests in Britain felt threatened by the popularity of calicoes and felt these goods were undercutting local textile production, their views resonated with popular distrust of the company and gained political force.[78]

The debates about calicoes lined up merchants against a coalition of landowners and artisans who had interests in the woolen trade. As a way of balancing these interests, duties were imposed on calico imports first in 1664, then with a 10 percent increase in

1685. But a general recession in the 1690s which created widespread unemployment among textile workers (whose jobs may have been partially affected by the loss of some home and export markets to calicoes) brought this controversy to a head.[79]

The 1696–1700 calico controversy began with petitions from the "silk weavers of Norwich, the say-makers and the worsted yarn makers of Norfolk and Cambridge" requesting restrictions on calicoes. Their petition was debated in Parliament and the press but was not acted upon and was finally dropped.[80] In 1699 another bill was introduced which was finally passed and became effective on September 29, 1701. It read, "All manufactured silks, Bengalls and stuffs mixed with silk or herba of the manufacture of Persea, China or East Indies and all Calicoes painted, dyed, printed or stained there which are or shall be imported into the kingdom of England, dominion of Walles and town of Berwick-On-Tweed, can not be worn or otherwise used within this kingdom."[81]

The 1700 bill started a new period of printed calico production in which plain cotton fabric was imported from India and was printed in England. This pattern made calicoes even cheaper than before because the duties on plain cotton goods were dropped. The law did not, then, disrupt East India Company trade; there was a great demand for plain cottons and cotton yarn. The local linen finishers were happy with the arrangement, since they were the ones who developed the skills and equipment to finish the calicoes. But the woolen and silk interests were not appeased because calicoes were still widely available, and they were not even satisfied when a new excise tax was placed on goods printed in England.[82] They had good reason to be dissatisfied; cotton cloth enjoyed a popularity that woolens and silks did not. To workers in the woolen and silk trades, calicoes became a symbol of their decline and *the* cause of their economic hardship.

In the summer of 1719 they started to riot. The economic historian Parakunnel Thomas, quoting a less than sympathetic contemporary, wrote:

The peaceable citizens of London were roused from the slumbers by the rude shouts of mutinous weavers who had come from Spital-fields. There were as many as 2,000 of them—"a mixed rabble of weavers, pickpockets, housebreakers, scoundrel Papists and Jacobites." They assembled in several companies and went about the streets tearing calicoes off the women's backs and throwing *aqua fortis* on their clothes.[83]

This "calico chasing" continued intermittently from June to September of that year. The weavers' protests were fortified by the publication of pamphlets describing their frustrations with the calico trade and the company's interest in sustaining it. They claimed that the East India Company did not need to trade in calicoes to survive, but local artisans needed the good health of Britain's wool and silk manufacture to sustain themselves.[84]

In 1720 Parliament passed a bill to appease the weavers and stop calico chasing. The act prohibited the consumption of all printed cotton fabric "except muslin, neckcloths, fustians or calicoes dyed all blue."[85] The bill prohibited the multicolored printed cottons which had drawn the eyes and the money of the English of various social classes and which Britons could not make as easily or cheaply for themselves. It still allowed the import of calicoes for reexport (which provided some opportunities for smuggling them into Britain), but it struck a blow directly at calicoes' competition with locally produced fabrics by outlawing new consumption of calicoes. By restricting the use of calicoes, it also served to discourage the development of British calico production, but since Britons could not then produce calicoes inexpensively, the restriction was not a deterrent to local manufacture.

The woolen and silk weavers had won what they wanted—effective restriction on competition—but they had not gotten what they needed to end the threat of calicoes to their livelihoods. To do this they would have had to end the fashion for calicoes or develop a totally local industry which could provide British artisans with jobs while also competing effectively with Indian calicoes. Calicoes remained fashionable even after their restriction, perhaps more so once they became scarce. Soon after the 1720 bill went into effect, people began to appear again in calico clothing. They may have worn old clothes, clothes made from old wall coverings (or palampoors) or new dresses cut from smuggled fabric; in any case, calicoes had retained their special meaning to people, so calico clothing returned when people felt safe in wearing it.[86]

Some aspiring entrepreneurs saw this situation as a great opportunity to provide fabrics which resembled calicoes. At least, some linen manufacturers seemed to recognize the basis for the fashion, namely the similarities between fine cottons and the traditional linens and silks of the aristocracy. The fustian branch of the linen industry began to develop new designs—stripes and checks—which were colorful, light, and inexpensive enough to attract some of those who had favored calicoes, particularly in the colonial markets. Since geometrical designs on cloth had been alternating in popularity with floral patterns, stripes and checks could serve many of the same functions as flowered calicoes. Fustian makers also began to experiment with producing a range of all–cotton fabrics made with double-twist cotton warp. With this warp they made velverets and other cotton velvets, popular imitations of fashionable velvets (another of the fabrics that had been restricted in use under sumptuary laws because it represented an elite type of cloth).[87]

Stripes, checks, and cotton velvets enjoyed wide popularity as reasonable substitutes for elite cloth, but they did not completely replace calicoes as fashionably desirable. Floral fabrics were still the vogue for clothing and were more popular for home decoration. Some fustian makers, then, were not content to experiment with these new fabrics; they wanted to find methods for producing calicoes. While they were sometimes successful in making attractive cloth, they had a number of problems doing so. They had difficulty printing on local fustians, which were made with two kinds of fiber, because the dye would not always be absorbed at the same rate by the two fibers. They even had troubles when they tried to make a pure cotton cloth (calling it "fustian" so that they would not be fined for making cotton fabric) because they could not make anything as inexpensive as Indian calicoes. Attempts to develop large calico-producing enterprises failed entirely in this period because most of those who developed schemes to found a local calico industry were ignorant of the problems involved.[88] But the number and intensity of the efforts to imitate or replace calicoes were a tribute to both the power of public taste in manufacture and the power of mercantilist policies to encourage national economic autonomy through self-sufficient manufacturing. In other words, they illustrate the strength of both the cultural and political manifestations of materialism in this period. Defoe described the growth of calico imitations in the following terms:

The late Acts of prohibiting the Use and wearing of painted Callicoes, either in Cloths, Equipages or House Furniture, was without Question aim'd at improving of our Woollen Manufacture, and in Part it had an Effect that way. But the Humour of the People running another way, and being used to, and pleased with the light, easy and gay Dress of the Callicoes, the Callicoe Printers fell to Work to imitate those Callicoes, by making the same Stamps and Impressions, and with the same Beauty of Colours upon the Linen, and that this fell upon two particular Branches of Linen, call'd *Scots* Cloth and *Irish* Linen: I need not take any Pains to prove this. The Consequence is also evident, (viz) That the Linen Manufacture both in *Scotland* and in *Ireland* are considerably encreas'd upon that Occasion, and many hundred thousand Ells of Linen are yearly imported from *Scotland* and *Ireland*, and printed in *England*, more than ever were before; so that this is an Article wholly new in Trade, and indeed the Printing it self is wholly new; for it is but a few Years since no such thing as painting or printing of Linen or Callicoe was known in *England*; all being supply'd [from India] so cheap, and perform'd so very fine, that nothing but a Prohibition of the foreign printed Callicoes could raise it to a Manufacture at Home.[89]

Defoe catalogs the positive effects of the calico ban on the linen industries in Scotland and Ireland, but does not mention that these fine results did not yield a cloth that could compete with calicoes. Linens were just too expensive. The failure to produce a British fabric which could compete on an open market with Indian calicoes was due to the limits of British craft skills in bleaching and dyeing and the lack of any technique for producing fine, strong, inexpensive cotton warp. The will for local production of printed cottons was there, but there was no way to produce them within traditional forms of craft manufacture. Britons needed to change their mode of production to create a competitive cotton industry, and this they were soon to do.

CHAPTER SIX

Culture and Industrialization, Part II: The British Cotton Industry

The great revolution of capital importance was that of printed calico. The combined effort of science and art was needed to force a difficult and unpromising material, cotton, to bear every day so many brilliant transformations and then, when it was thus transformed, to distribute it everywhere and to put it within the range of the poor. —Carlo Cipolla[1]

THE CALICO crisis was rooted in two major forms of the emerging materialism of the early modern period: specifically, the growth of fashion and the development of economic policies based on scientific economics. This crisis was only eradicated by the cultivation of a third form of materialism in manufacture: the creation of capital goods to increase efficiency in producing the consumer goods in demand on the world market.

The contradiction created by the fashion for Indian calicoes in England and by the British inability to create a comparable cloth was a problem that was not finally overcome until the British found the means to make similar cotton cloth at a lower cost. Only then were they able to profit from the fashion. They eventually accomplished this goal by responding to mercantilist doctrine in a new way, by turning away from attempts to control trade politically and turning toward the development of new capital goods to achieve that mercantilist's dream: a favorable balance of trade.

As I showed in chapter 3, long before the eighteenth century Europeans had turned to innovations in capital goods to solve their trading problems. They had even developed some production machinery by that time: equipment to replace human labor power, such as, water-driven beaters for making pulp for paper, and machines for replacing human skills, like the printing press. But most of these innovations had little economic significance, since they were peripheral to state economies. When printing machinery was used to replace copyists' skills, for example, it did not substantially change patterns of trade; the demand for printed pictures and writings was simply not that great. When the British created new equipment and chemicals for producing cotton calicoes, however, they were not only solving immediate production problems but changing Britain's major industry. In doing so, they were also developing a new approach to the trade problem: designing production machinery to adjust the balance of trade. In their success at making innovations to produce the most desired textiles, they created a new model for world economic competition.

Europeans began with one advantage over Indians in making printed fabric; they were skilled at printing with a press. This skill was specifically appropriate for the problem of making printed fabrics. Moreover, it represented a general advantage that European culture provided to its artisans: a tradition of designing new capital goods for resolving production difficulties. When they developed mechanical and chemical solutions to their major problems in calico production (spinning, weaving, and dyeing), Britons were using their cultural resources to gain world supremacy over cotton production and trade. They were calling on their belief in human dominion over nature as well as their medieval tradition of innovation to manage their position in the world economy.

In elaborating this part of their cultural tradition, these innovators also enhanced the materialism of European social life. In Polanyi's terms, they were again placing social solidarity second to the manipulation of material resources for material gain. With the industrialization of textile manufacture, the machine rather than the worker became the favored source of profits. It became the solution to the economic problems of nations, the means for creating those goods which were in demand and which would give their manufacturers power in the international market.

The techniques developed for competing with Indian craft manufacture were ones that necessarily devalued human skills by replacing them. Since they affected all artisans who possessed those skills, regardless of nationality, they destroyed the craft structure of British cloth manufacture. As a result, what had originated as an attempt to make British textile production strong in relation to the Indian craft structure resulted in the development of a new form of manufacture in England that helped to undermine traditional British textile production.

Making a cloth comparable to Indian calicoes in Britain required two types of innovation. First, Britons had to find some way to make cloth competitively priced and equal in quality to Indian cottons. As we have seen, cotton cloth was desirable in itself because of its light weight and easy care; in addition, it was to textile printing what paper had been to the development of print(s). Britons could not develop fabric printing without having some fabric to print on, and wool, their traditional major textile, was too rough a fabric to take printed designs well; it was also difficult to dye. Linens shared many of the same problems. The finest grades of linen could be used as a print-carrying cloth, but fine linen, like silk, was too expensive to compete with Indian calicoes. Cotton could be cheap enough for this purpose if the labor involved in producing the cotton cloth could be minimized. Thus, when Britons searched for ways to produce a printable fabric to make calico cloth, they had to find ways to improve cotton manufacture and diminish its costs.[2]

Second, Britons could not make printed cottons without improving their printing and dyeing. Britons were particularly backward in fabric finishing, having relied so heavily on the Flemish for this part of textile manufacture. One indication of their backwardness is the fact that the earliest attempts at calico printing in Britain were made by Huguenot refugees, who were the only ones knowledgeable enough about mordants and dyes to begin to copy Indian goods. But even French artisans had difficulty developing sophisticated techniques for printing calicoes. The Indians' long history of textile dyeing had given them a distinct advantage over all Europeans. They worked with a wide variety of dyes and mordants and were very sophisticated about the techniques of multiple dyeing that could yield multicolor patterns. Since Indians protected this information as caste secrets, Britons had to search out comparable techniques on their own.[3]

The British faced two dramatically different types of problem when they tried to surpass the Indians in textile manufacture. Innovations in dyeing were conceptually complex, dependent on developments in applied chemistry, but they were relatively simple to implement because their use did not threaten a traditional group of fabric finishers in Britain. In contrast, spinning or weaving machinery was relatively easy to design, since it only required applying known mechanical principles to a new set of problems, but introducing this machinery into textile manufacture was socially disruptive. It replaced skilled artisans and thus threatened the autonomy and economic well-being of skilled craft workers.[4]

Given the character of the problems raised by new textile production equipment, it may seem ironic that many of the innovators who transformed spinning and weaving in Britain were rural artisans, people whose peers in the textile trade were likely to be adversely affected by the new machinery. Their actions would seem inexplicable were it not for the fact that the social position of artisans was already threatened by the growing power of merchants in manufacture. Before the introduction of new spinning and weaving equipment, the putting-out system was instituted in textile production by merchants able to pour capital into this area of manufacture. In other trades, craft manufacture within the guild system was also going into decline as merchants took the control away from artisans. To follow the flow of capital into textile manufacture with an infusion of capital goods was a logical step.[5] Rural artisans, living in the areas most affected by the putting-out system, may have recognized most clearly the transforming effects of this infusion of capital, and noticed that they could protect themselves from the worst of its effects by developing technical innovations that they could use to control their livelihoods. They may have become pioneers in this change to avoid being its victims.

Innovations in Spinning and Weaving

From the Middle Ages, artisans had been the carriers of instrument- and machine-making skills. They had been major participants in the proliferation of machines of the fourteenth and fifteenth centuries; they had been the clockmakers and makers of navigation instruments in the fourteenth to sixteenth centuries; they had worked with scientists in instrument-building during the scientific revolution of the seventeenth century; and some had even worked on the innovations in pumps and smelting that changed mining and metallurgy in the seventeenth century. In the textile industry itself, artisans had worked with and on the simple machines already used for spinning and weaving, gaining technical knowledge about that craft in the process of practicing it.[6]

This technological tradition carried by craftworkers was both augmented and altered by the scientific materialism of the seventeenth century. It was bolstered by the idea that the material world could be understood and manipulated by human beings, and it was also legitimated by the Puritan contention that changes in material circumstances could help to usher in a better world. As Cressy Dymock wrote in 1651:

the Reformation of States in civil affairs for the most part, is not compassed without violence and disturbances: But Inventions make all men happy without either injury or dammage to any one single person. Furthermore, new Inventions are as it were new Creations, and imitations of God's own works.[7]

The success of existing inventions in changing the character of European life was important in giving invention this sacred significance:

Again, it were good to take notice of the vertue, efficacy, and consequences of Invention, which are scarce more conspicuous in any, then in these three, unknown to the Auncients, and whose beginning (although but of late) are obscure and unrenowned, to wit, the Art of Printing, Gunpowder, and the Marriner's Needle. For these three have changed the face of things throughout the whole world. The first in the matter of Learning, the second in that of War, and the last in Navigation: From whence has followed an innumerable change of things, so that no Empire, no Sect, no Constellation seemeth to have had a greater influence on humane affairs, then these Mechanical Inventions have had.[8]

This new definition of machines as a modern source of social improvement was not only apparent among the educated elites of the period (the scientists, theologians, and politicians quoted here and described in the last two chapters), but also among the artisans who would bring it to the project of innovation itself. Because rural artisans traditionally enjoyed high status and increasingly reached a high level self-education after Puritan rural literacy drives, they were in a position to profit from new intellectual currents as well as the latest scientific and mechanical experiments.[9]

Every weaving district had its weaver-poets, biologists, mathematicians, musicians, geologists, botanists: the old weaver in *Mary Barton* is certainly drawn from the life. There are northern museums and natural history societies which still possess records or collections of lepidoptera built up by weavers; while there are accounts of weavers in isolated villages who taught themselves geometry by chalking on their flagstones and who were eager to discuss differential calculus.[10]

Rural tradesmen could scour printed literature on science and engineering to improve their machine-making abilities and skills, and they could also join scientific societies. The Baconians who founded the Royal Society and other scientific societies in England specifically encouraged artisans to join because of their skills in designing equipment for experiments and because of their trade skills and knowledge, which the Baconians defined as useful for solving both practical and theoretical problems.[11]

While, in these ways, intellectual currents were acting as a source of encouragement for innovation, successful innovations themselves were another source. Innovations in agriculture were particularly effective in bringing to rural areas evidence that careful observation of nature and technological innovation could increase profits. Surveyors like John Norden helped to carry these ideas into the country.

To preseue or augment Reuenues, there must be meanes: the means are wrought by Knowledge; Knowledge had by Experience; Experience by view, and due observation of the particulars, by which Reuenues does or may arise. Wherein are to be considered the Quantities, and Qualities of Land, with the present Rents, and estimate values by a reasonable improouement. . . . [For an example of an improvement,] though this plot of ground be very leuell by apparence, yet if it were tried by a true leuell, it would be found to be declining towards yonder forlorne brooke, which you see is stopt vp with weedes, that it permitteth not the water conuenient passe. Therefore the first worke is, to rid the sewer or chief water-course, and then shall you see, that the grounds neere the cleansed brooke, will become more drie, by the moisture soaking into the sewer.[12]

The spread of new ideas in agricultural production and the publication of scientific information may have helped to bring to rural artisans the ideas and attitudes they needed to become technological innovators, but it was the economic changes of the period, threatening their livelihoods, that seems to have finally encouraged some artisans to apply their machine-making skills to problems of craft manufacture. Innovation was one obvious way for artisans to use their assets to solve their own problems.

The textile trade, being one of the crafts most dramatically affected by the growing export market, was an obvious place to begin. Traditional historical descriptions of the putting-out system in British textile manufacture during this period consistently note how artisans lost autonomy, status, and control of this manufacture because guild control, particularly in rural areas, became so weak that merchants found it easy to employ common laborers to replace craft workers. Artisans continuing to practice their trade in this situation were put on a par with common laborers, and lost control of their craft mysteries to merchants who spread them to workers over whom the artisans had no control.[13]

Their loss of control over the skills of their trade left artisans without control over the work process or the value of their work. In periods of prosperity they might enjoy high wages, but in periods of recession they could no longer reduce their output and still be assured of working. Merchants could simply decide not to employ them.[14]

In contrast, those artisans who knew how to make machines had skills that had not suffered the degradation of traditional textile manufacturing techniques. Rural artisans living in the period of the putting-out system who were aware of the loss of status by their colleagues in the textile trade but who also had machine-building skills could prevent the decline in their own status and autonomy by using these resources.[15]

The tradition of using machines in textile production existed long before the industrial revolution. Spinners and weavers had used the hand loom and spinning wheel since the Middle Ages. The exact history of the hand loom is not known, but there are indications of its use in the fourteenth century, and it probably had its origins well before that. The spinning wheel seems to date from the fifteenth century, although it too had ancestors from an earlier part of the medieval period. The silk winding machine for making silk thread had a slightly different history; although it was not known in Britain until the seventeenth century, it seems to have been developed in Italy in the fourteenth. Thus, well before the industrial revolution European artisans in the textile trades were using machines developed in the Middle Ages for some parts of the production process.[16]

By the sixteenth century, new economic ideas were beginning to encourage increased innovation in capital goods. New mining equipment, types of ships, and navigational aids were improving patterns of manufacture and trade, and new machines were being used in the textile industry. The Dutch smallwares loom and the frame knitting machine were two of these innovations, designed to reduce the labor for rapid production of particular types of textiles and to increase productivity in existing areas of manufacture. But they were not intended either to produce new kinds of cloth or to correct imbalances in the textile trade. The smallwares loom produced up to six different ribbons in the same loom at the same time. The knitting machine was similar in that it could make an entire row of stitches with the same series of movements a hand knitter would use to make one stitch. These machines did not improve on or replace the medieval textile production machines but simply added to the number of tasks that artisans could now accomplish using a machine.[17] The problem facing potential innovators in the eighteenth century was to design machines that could make the basic processes of spinning and weaving even more efficient and to make this equipment appropriate for producing the most desirable types of cloth.

In sum, the artisans who made eighteenth-century textile production machines had both the resources and the reasons for participating in machine-making. They had (1) a tradition of toolmaking; (2) exposure to a new vision of nature resulting from the scientific revolution; and (3) indications that British textiles were beginning to fail on the world market. They also found that inventions could make an inventor less vulnerable to the whims of merchants; if their machines proved useful, artisans could protect their knowledge of the invention through secrecy in its use, maintaining their control over the value of their work.[18] Artisans might not have been able, at that time, to monopolize craft mysteries, but some could use the same logic in keeping secret the design of machines, reproducing for themselves some of the ideal characteristics of the independent artisan's life which they saw their peers losing completely.

If this desire for some level of autonomy by artisans made innovations in capital goods meaningful and desirable, then it may be that an attempt to produce good work conditions for the few may have completed the change to the factory system for the many.[19] But it does not explain why innovators fashioned the particular machines that they did. To explain how some projects could have been more meaningful to artisans than others requires examination of the specific eighteenth-century inventions and their early applications in textile manufacture.

Production Machines and Textile Manufacture

The innovations that gave birth to the British cotton industry and brought an end to craft forms of textile manufacture in Britain were fashioned not by grand visionaries but by individual innovators seeking to provide themselves with secure and lucrative positions within a changing economy. Although, by convention, we refer to these men as innovators, most of them were not trying to generate change. In fact, many of them were attempting to bolster traditional forms of textile production in England by making machines to augment wool and silk production. But their innovations were applied to the production of cotton cloth, or were replaced by other innovations that helped to establish a British cotton industry.[20] That these individual and diverse efforts gave rise to a new mode of production that made cotton cloth England's major textile indicates the magnitude of the structural problem that textile manufacturing machines resolved.

Most discussions of the development of machines for textile production in Britain posit an economic need for machines and assume that innovators responded directly to this need. But there were two stages to the innovation in textile machinery; the first machines were designed to improve wool or silk production and the second to produce cotton cloth. The tension between Britain's wool and silk trades and the fashion for calicoes was expressed in production machinery, reflected in the designs for textile manufacturing equipment. This conclusion should not be surprising, since the machines were artifacts that necessarily carried cultural meanings in their forms. Historians of technology routinely suggest this when they write like art historians, describing the social conditions conducive to innovation and the social characteristics of innovators that affect their work. While they do not usually inspect the social iconography of the machines themselves, their art-historical style suggests that iconographic analysis should be possible.[21]

Since we are used to thinking of consumer goods as expressive artifacts, it is commonplace, if not simple, to study their symbolic meanings. It is easier to think of production machines as expressive artifacts if we remember that the line between capital and consumer goods is not at all clear. Once we acknowledge this, we can compare, for instance, pictorial prints to spinning machines as similar forms of European material culture. Both kinds of objects had medieval heritages but were increasingly used after the expansion of European trade, when artisans used them to established new occupations through the development of new commodities. The major difference was that production machinery devised in this period had greater impact on the production of other commodities than most new consumer goods did.

Eighteenth-century rural artisans began the mechanical transformation of the textile trade when they started to redesign machines for performing the basic processes of weaving, spinning, and knitting. They began this project fully realizing that their efforts could alter the fundamental character of textile manufacture, but they designed the machines to maintain the traditional economic order by supporting the woolen branch of the textile industry. This is clear in the pattern of early innovations.

In 1733 John Kay, a reedmaker from near Bury, patented his flying shuttle, an apparatus designed to change standard practices for manufacturing broad fabrics. Until Kay's machine was introduced, weavers either had to limit the breadth of their fabric to the reach of their arms or, when making broad cloths, employ a second weaver to help push the shuttle through the warp by hand. Kay's flying shuttle was a mechanism that would throw the shuttle through the warp (using a little hammer to start it) when the weaver pulled a string located in the center of the loom. The mechanism made broad fabrics easier and cheaper to produce, successfully increasing the manufacture of a desirable cloth. More important, it turned out to increase the speed of the weaving process itself.[22]

Paul (occupation unclear) and Wyatt (a carpenter, from Lichfield) patented an early spinning machine that could both roll out wool and give it a good twist, making wool thread good enough for weaving. The machine was sold and put to use by a variety of people, but it was mechanically unreliable. While it set a precedent for machine spinning (one that seems to have been copied later), it did not immediately replace wheel spinning.[23] But it did show that innovators were seeking mechanical means to improve the wool trade in this early period of invention.

In 1759 Strutt (a wheelwright and farmer) patented a mechanism for modifying the knitting frame, his so-called rib-knitting machine. It was less a machine than an attachment that could be put on a knitting frame; it could twist alternate stitches, producing a stretchable ribbed knit, the kind of knit most useful for mass-producing stockings.[24]

These early eighteenth-century mechanisms were innovative in attempting to change the basic processes for manufacturing textiles, but they were also conservative in that they were designed to serve the traditional woolen, linen, and silk trades. The conservatism of these early machines is often lost in histories of innovation because by the end of the century, all three were being used to produce cotton goods. But their intended uses reveal something about their meanings to their designers. In contrast, the machines designed in the later portion of the eighteenth century were explicitly meant for use in cotton manufacture.

The traditional argument used to explain the development of spinning machines in the late eighteenth century is that the rib-knitter and the flying shuttle increased the demand for yarn beyond what local spinners could provide, creating an imbalance that could only be eliminated with new (and effective) spinning machines. This argument probably has some truth to it, since there is plenty of evidence that yarn was scarce and hard to get at this time, but it ignores the facts that Strutt's machine was used primarily to make silk stockings and that Kay's flying shuttle was adopted primarily for weaving bays, a woolen fabric.[25] How did they create a demand for spinning machines used primarily to make cotton yarn?

The obvious missing piece in the picture is a shortage of cotton yarn, independent of the demand created by new technology. There was still an active fashion for colorful cotton fabrics in the early eighteenth century that was being satisfied to some extent by the stripes and checks produced by the fustian industry. Hence there was a demand for this yarn that had been filled by imports from India, until the collapse of the Mughal Empire at the beginning of the eighteenth century and the unrest in India during the first half of that century. This threatened both the fustian industry and the cotton branch of the hosiery trade. L. C. A. Knowles identifies this problem as the primary impetus for inventing cotton spinning machinery and one that was, at least, another source of the yarn shortages.[26]

The yarn shortages caused by the disruption of trade with India could have had symbolic as well as practical meaning, underscoring Britain's continuing dependence on trade with India, while increasing demand for British cotton thread. Hence they may have played an inordinately powerful role in changing the character of innovation in this period. A desire to reduce British dependence on imports could be another factor explaining why innovators turned away from improvements in wool production (which had not reduced demand for cottons) toward the production of inexpensive British cotton thread.

Two of the machines that revolutionized spinning and ended these shortages, the spinning jenny and the waterframe, were developed almost simultaneously in the 1760s for the specific purpose of making cotton thread. The former was developed by James Hargreaves, a weaver from Stanhill, and the latter by Richard Arkwright, the wig-maker and dyer. Both were mechanically and economically successful machines, immediately adopted and used, but each had its own characteristic advantages and disadvantages.[27]

The spinning jenny was a good machine for producing soft cotton weft for fustians; while it did not pull the fibers or twist them enough to make good cotton warp, it did make weft in large quantities. The jenny had the advantages of being very simple to use and relatively inexpensive to buy. For these reasons and because it required no outside power source, it was appropriate for spinners to use in their homes without significantly altering their life styles.[28]

Arkwright's waterframe could draw the cotton out firmly and give it a good twist, making a fine, strong cotton warp. This thread was as good for weaving and knitting as the ordinary grades of Indian cotton yarn being used for these purposes, but it could not be made without an outside source of power. Thus, production of thread in the waterframe led to centralization of work in the factory. Because Arkwright's machines could produce greater quantities of spun cotton than the jenny and could make precisely the kind of cotton warp that Britons had been unable to produce inexpensively by hand, it became the preferred piece of spinning equipment.[29]

The design of Arkwright's machine was not technically novel. It resembled the one used by Paul and Wyatt for their spinning machine, and both some contemporaries and later historians suggest that Arkwright copied their machine. But its consequences were revolutionary because it finally gave the British the ability to make fabrics competitive with Indian cottons, and did it in a way that centralized production, helping to foster the factory system for textile manufacture.[30]

Soon after he completed the development of the waterframe, and designed the carding and slubbing machines necessary for preparing cotton for spinning, Arkwright started a firm for manufacturing calicoes. Arkwright had originally spun cotton yarn for the hosiery trade in Nottingham, but he found himself both producing more yarn than local manufacturers could consume and unable to sell his yarn to fustian dealers, who accused him of patenting an invention based on the Paul-Wyatt design. So Arkwright decided to manufacture calicoes, petitioning Parliament to exempt him from the 1720 prohibition on calicoes and gaining that permission in 1774.[31]

Given the vehemence of the opposition to calicoes in 1720, Arkwright's relative ease in getting permission to sell calicoes seems to require some explanation. Probably the major reason was the collapse of the Mughal Empire, which had finally made India economically and politically dependent on Britain and no longer in a position to maintain its importance in the world market for cloth. In addition, the fustian industry had been growing tremendously since the prohibition of calicoes, making cotton cloth, or at least mixed cotton-linen cloth, more familiar as a local industry of some value to the nation. Whatever the mix of reasons, Arkwright's idea for making British calicoes did not sound so outrageous in 1774 as it would have in 1720, and it eventually became the basis for the first successful scheme to mass-produce the fabric that Britons had been wanting to produce for over fifty years.[32]

Samuel Crompton's mule was the last of the new eighteenth-century spinning machines. It produced the finest yarn of all the inventions, yarn that was as fine, if not finer, than that in the best grades of Indian muslins. The mule, like the waterframe, was a machine that could only be used in factories, since it was bulky and expensive, required power, and needed a number of people to attend it. But the mule was also the ultimate piece of spinning machinery; it could do inexpensively and easily what only the best Indian artisans could do by hand.[33]

With the introduction of this machine and the end of the prohibition on the use of pure cotton fabrics in Britain, the era of restriction on cotton fabrics was over. Ended also was the identification of British economic interests with woolen and silk production. This change had been signaled by the development of more efficient looms and spinning machines, but it took a few more innovations in finishing processes to prepare the British for making bright, colorful, and inexpensive cotton cloth that could compete successfully in the world market.

Innovations In Fabric Finishing

Since the fashion for calicoes was based partly on the appeal of their bright colors and designs, the processes used to decorate fabrics were important to the growth of calico production. But learning how to finish cottons to make them appeal to consumers was a practical as well as aesthetic problem that British textile manufacturers had some difficulties solving.

They had little problem printing on cloth; Europeans had been printing on fabric before they began printing on paper, and they had a wealth of experience and skill in pictorial printing to guide them in producing either the blocks or plates for textile printing. In fact, before trying to imitate calicoes Europeans had experimented with a number of methods of printing fabrics for clothing; as I noted earlier, Germans were early in using oil-based inks (made for paper printing) to apply designs to fabrics, making

Tan linen printed in green, German, Rhenish, fifteenth century (09.50.1092). THE METROPOLITAN MUSEUM OF ART, ROGERS FUND, 1909.

cloth in the fifteenth century that was sometimes attractive but could not be washed without ruining the design. The British and particularly the Flemish had experimented with pressure-printing designs on fabrics, using a woodblock to crush velvets and using the pressure of a woodblock on silks to stretch the threads and create a pattern.

These early experiments were attempts to make inexpensive reproductions of more elegant cloth. The fabrics made with oil-based inks replicated some embroidery designs at low cost, though without either the beauty of embroideries or the practical virtues of washable textiles. Crushed woolen velvets, made with fabric less expensive than silk, had impressed on them the types of design typically found on silk cut velvets. They evolved into quite handsome fabrics, but they never gained the popularity of calicoes or other cottons. The silks decorated with pressure patterns were also less than wholly successful commercially; they were made with an expensive fabric and were poor copies of figured silks.[34]

Nonetheless, Europeans still had enormous printing skills to use in applying dyes, and with these they eventually surpassed the Indians. Indian artisans used paper screens to outline designs on chintzes, and used woodblocks on cheaper calicoes, but many of their dyes were applied by hand. This meant that when Britons learned effective means to apply dyes with the printing press, they were much better equipped to finish fabrics with great speed and in great quantities. This was particularly true after they invented roller equipment for continuous printing on cloth.[35] But that was a late development; when the calico ban was lifted in 1774 and mass production of cottons began, Britons did not have the skills for bleaching large quantities of cloth or dyeing it in a wide array of colors with rapid speed and at low cost.[36]

The importance of these skills for promoting English textiles is not difficult to establish. Europeans had long associated elaborate decorations on clothing with higher social station, and they had already begun to develop an interest in decorated oriental fabrics when small pieces of silk and other fine goods were brought to Europe through the Levant, well before the East India Company trade. The admiration that the British felt for printed calicoes, then, had some antecedent in a long-standing respect for Asian

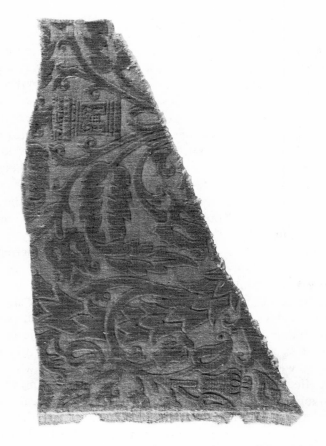

Flemish pressure-printed woolen velvet, sixteenth century (M.66.11). BY PERMISSION OF THE LOS ANGELES COUNTY MUSEUM OF ART.

fabric-finishing. There is evidence for this argument in a poem about English dyes and dyers printed in Geffrey Whitney's sixteenth-century emblem book:

> The dier, loe, in smoke, and heate doth toile,
>   Mennes fickle minds to please, with sundrie hues:
> And though hee learne newe collours still to boile,
> Yet Varying men, woulde faine some newer choose:
>   And seeke for that, which arte can not deuise,

When that the ould, mighte verie well suffise. . . .
Now straungers, who their countries still commende,
And make vs muse, with colours they recite:
Maye thinke our lande, small choise of hues doth lende.
Bycause so fewe, of manie I doe write.
    Yet let them knowe, my Aucthor these presentes,
    Inoughe for those, whome reason still contentes.
But say wee lacke, their herbes, their wormes, their flies,
And want the meanes: their gallant hues to frame.
Yet Englande, hath her store of orient dies,
And eeke therein, a DYER most of fame,
    Who alwaies hathe so fine, and fresh, a hewe,
    That in their lands, the like is not to vewe.[37]

The British had long identified their dyeing skills as deficient, but the level of skill did not improve in the face of criticism. One reason is that innovations in this area were particularly difficult. Cotton production problems had mechanical solutions, but finishing problems were problems in applied chemistry whose solutions required experimentation. Scientists and nonscientists both became involved in finding improved bleaching and dyeing methods in the eighteenth century, and their collaboration was crucial to the growth of the cotton industry.

Much has been written about the importance of science to the innovations used in the industrial revolution. Many authors have claimed that the discovery of eighteenth-century machines and materials for industrial development were quite unconnected to the changes in science that occurred in the seventeenth and eighteenth centuries; they argue that scientists and practical innovators were engaged in quite different projects which kept them from learning much from one another. According to this model, scientists were interested in studying the natural world in order to understand it, while inventors were interested in changing material culture even if they did not understand how they were doing it.[38]

There is some validity to this argument. Scientists and inventors tended to come from different social classes and to have different conceptions of the value and proper use of their findings. Science was practiced primarily among elites who conceived of their work as intellectual investigation leading to discoveries that should be published and spread to everyone. In contrast, mechanical innovations tended to be made by nonelites, artisans or merchants, who thought technological experimentation was practical or craft work that should be kept secret so the inventor could profit from the innovation.[39]

Because those who designed the new eighteenth-century textile machinery were almost exclusively artisans who worked without consulting or collaborating with scientists, the distinction between them may seem crucial for analyzing all the important innovation in this period. Yet, as A. E. Musson and Eric Robinson point out, there were also areas where interaction between scientists and inventors helped to locate the raw materials and tecnhniques necessary for new manufacture. The advances in bleaching and dyeing that facilitated fabric finishing belong in this category.[40]

Those who developed new processes for bleaching and dyeing fabrics were either aware of or participants in new developments in chemistry. For example, an apothecary, Thomas Henry, who worked on the development of new bleaching techniques and a theory of dyes also translated Lavoisier's *Essays, Physical and Chemical* into English. He and other nonscientists spoke frequently of the value of scientific discoveries for facilitating innovations in applied chemistry, advocating a pattern of collaboration that was to become commonplace in the nineteenth century.[41] Applied chemistry was one area where scientists and practical innovators gained a great deal from their interaction. The connections established between them in the Royal Society and its local versions, such as the Lunar Society of Birmingham and the Literary and Philosophical Society of Manchester, turned out to be particularly useful for those exploring chemical problems, helping to shape a pattern of mutual aid that would increasingly tie basic research to practical problems.[42]

Scientists and inventors could be joined in the search for the chemistry of bleaching and dyeing because this project appealed to both social groups. Understanding the chemical properties of substances and their reactions with other substances was a salient intellectual problem; trying to improve methods for bleaching and dyeing was important to those who wanted to profit from British calico production. Making calicoes was a technically complex task, requiring multiple stages of dyeing and bleaching; thus it was also a complex process to understand, providing a variety of intellectual puzzles and chemical reactions to analyze. Preparing the fabric to carry dyes presented one set of problems, and applying mordants and dyes in the elaborate sequences required for calico-printing by the Indian model presented entirely different ones. The stages in fabric preparation are described by R. Patterson:

Traditional European Method for Preparing Cloth for Printing or Dyeing

1. Bucking—soaking cloth in an alkali solution.
2. Washing.
3. Souring—soaking in a vat of sour milk or buttermilk.
4. Washing.
5. Crofting—putting the fabric in the sun to bleach for about two weeks.
6. Repeating the bucking, souring and crofting about six times.[43]

All these chemical processes were used just to bleach the cloth before printing. John Irwin and Katherine Brett describe the even more elaborate stages of calico-printing first used by Indians and imitated by Europeans:

The Indian Process for Dyeing Calicoes

1. Drawing or printing outline of design on fabric, using acetate of iron as a mordant for black and alum solution tinted with sappan wood as a mordant for red.
2. Dipping cloth into a vat filled with red dye (chay, a madder type dye) to bring out the reds and blacks.
3. Bleaching the cloth to whiten the background.
4. Using wax to cover the parts of the fabric not wanted blue.
5. Dipping cloth into a vat of indigo.
6. Removing wax with boiling water.
7. Using mordants of alum, strong for red, weak for pink and alum with iron added for violet.
8. Putting cloth in a vat of red dye for the second time.
9. Bleaching.
10. Adding yellow dye by hand, on white parts for yellow and on blue to make green.[44]

The eighteenth-century Britons who were trying to make calicoes did not know how to make many of the dyes they needed, or the mordants they had to use with the press to bring out colorful designs with the dyes. They were also hampered in mass-producing fabrics by their primitive bleaching process. The latter problem was particularly serious after the seventeenth century when inflation made the price of land rise dramatically, since bleaching by traditional methods required that fabrics be stretched outside on the ground for long periods of time.

Experiments to improve bleaching methods continued well into the nineteenth century as the growth of the cotton industry made improvements more profitable. But by the end of the eighteenth century much progress had been made, mainly because of experimentation with three agents: oil of vitriol (sulphuric acid), alkali (soda or sodium carbonate), and chlorine.

Oil of vitriol was a substance known to all chemists, but its usefulness in textile bleaching was not recognized until the late eighteenth century. The first vitriol works in England was set up by Joshua Ward in 1733 probably to meet the needs of metalworkers nearby. Around 1750 people first realized that they could use vitriol in bleaching to replace sour milk or buttermilk. John Roebuck, a doctor with extensive scientific training and partner in a vitriol plant, seems to have been the first to discover the use of vitriol for souring, but Francis Home was the first man who publicized this process in the 1756 book, *The Art of Bleaching*. Home's writings emphasized the speed of vitriol in the souring process: "the milk takes five days to perform its task, but the vitriol sours do it in as many hours, nay, perhaps in as many minutes."[45] Vitriol found many uses in calico manufacture, souring being only one of them.

Bleachers found it admirable as a substitute for the sour milk formerly used, and after the discovery of chlorine it became an essential in the preparation of chemical bleaches. Calico-printers also used it as a sour and in the production of citrus acid. It was used by dyers to render indigo soluable, in the preparation of mordants and in many other ways.[46]

"Alkali" or "soda" was another important substance for finishing cottons, one made in the seventeenth century by a process known as "kelping" or burning kelp to yield a mild and relatively inexpensive soda for bleaching. In the late eighteenth century a number of scientists and technicians began to apply scientific ideas to the manufacture of alkali, trying to synthesize it, and in the 1780s, a Frenchman named Guyston de Morveau developed a way to make synthetic soda from sodium sulphate. But it was a process invented by another Frenchman, Nicolas Leblanc, in 1787 that became the backbone of the heavy chemical industry. Leblanc used sulphuric acid to decompose common table salt, mixing the resulting chemical with chalk and charcoal and heating the mixture to make "black ash." When water was added to this ash, the soda could be leached out and recovered by evaporation. This process made inexpensive soda widely available with the help of the "oil of vitriol" that was already being manufactured. The Leblanc process was brought to Britain in the early nineteenth century, and soda works were established to meet the needs of soapmakers, textile finishers, and others.[47]

Chlorine bleach was one of the true discoveries of the eighteenth century that revolutionized textile finishing. Chemists in this period were particularly interested in studying gases (owing to their rejection of the alchemical view that air was the only gas). A Swedish chemist named Carl Scheele was the first to discover chlorine gas (in 1774), but it took the French chemist, Claude-Louis Berthollet, to realize that chlorine was a powerful bleach and to stimulate a variety of experiments in France and England to develop ways to use chlorine for textile bleaching. The problem in using chlorine for industrial bleaching was that the gas would escape from a bleaching vat and was dangerous to workers. Charles Tennant, a bleacher working with the Scotish inventor George Macintosh, finally combined lime with chlorine to make the first bleaching powder that was both easy to transport and safe to use in factories.[48] Chlorine bleach was eventually produced as a byproduct of Leblanc's soda-making process; then textile bleaching became fast and inexpensive,[49] so that rapid finishing of mass-produced cottons was possible. More dramatically than other chemical innovations in fabric finishing in this period, the development of chlorine bleach demonstrates how scientists and practical innovators interacted to produce synthetic chemicals for industry.

Few new dyes or mordants were made synthetically in the eighteenth century, but many old ones that had not previously been produced in England began to be manufactured there, and started to be produced in larger quantities and with greater efficiency. Hence it is legitimate to claim that this part of fabric finishing underwent important changes in eighteenth-century England that facilitated inexpensive calico-printing. In fact, because more was known about dyes and mordants on the Continent that in Britain and Scotland, improved dyeing in the British Isles depended primarily on importing either foreign dyeing techniques or information from scientific experiments made on the Continent, but the result was the formation of a cotton-finishing capacity in Britain that was crucial to the expansion of cotton production there.

One way to study these improvements in dyeing techniques is to look at the work done by the father-and-son industrialists George and Charles Macintosh. Although many others made contributions to this art, the Macintoshes and their collaborators made so many changes in all the areas of chemical fabric finishing and did so much to bring the most needed dyes and mordants into Britain that their contributions were central to improvements in British fabric-finishing in the eighteenth and early nineteenth centuries.[50]

George Macintosh began dye-making when he was asked to manage a cudbear or blue dye works; he was involved in a variety of chemical experiments to improve fabric finishing, including the invention of water-repellent Macintosh coats, but he left to his son Charles many of the improvements that proved useful to calico-making. This process began in 1786, when Charles, who had just begun to work for his father, took a trip to the Continent, and noticed that the Dutch were making the mordant lead acetate, using British raw materials. When he returned he began to manufacture this mordant in Scotland to supply it at reduced cost to British dyers. In the late eighteenth century, the Macintoshes also became interested in manufacturing a dye called Turkey red. The madder red used both in India and in France was far superior to other red dyes. They brought a dyer, Papillon, from France and began a madder works, the first in Britain.[51]

While Charles was active in the family firm, the Macintoshes also developed new dyeing methods that reduced the costs of fabric finishing, particularly calico-printing. For instance, in the 1780s, Charles found that acetate of lime could be used to replace the more costly "sugar of lead" or lead acetate in the "red color liquor" (of acetate and alum) and began to produce this cheaper acetate, reducing the cost of red dyeing. Charles also found a way to produce alum from the aluminous shale in coal mining waste, thereby reducing dramatically the cost of what had been one of the most expensive and desired of the mordants. In addition, in the early nineteenth century he developed a process for calico-printing with Prussian blue using an iron sulphate mordant and a potassium ferrocyanide vat to make blue designs. This reduced the need to use wax and indigo in calico-printing. Charles thus combined his knowledge of chemistry and the chemical feats of scientists on the Continent to make new chemicals to reduce the cost or difficulty of dyeing cottons in Britain.[52]

The improvements in finishing that resulted from these and other experiments facilitated the growth of Britain's calico manufacture, reducing the cost and increasing the speed of finishing cottons enough to make mass production possible. The new flexibility in designing fabrics created by this new ease of finishing allowed finishers to vary the look of their fabrics whenever they noticed subtle changes in demand. It gave them the skills to produce the goods that were particularly attractive in the marketplace, to follow fashion and profit from it. The new chemicals and machines for cotton manufacture were then ready to be used to follow fashion and make clever entrepreneurs into captains of industry.

Designing for Mass Markets

The many small entrepreneurs in the textile industry in the eighteenth century faced numerous boom and bust periods. Their businesses generally expanded rapidly, but the market was so uncertain from month to month that many companies with too many debts and little capital were going out of business during the short recessions that spotted those decades.[53] In this unstable economic climate, entrepreneurs had to be sensitive to even subtle changes in demand to build up their businesses.

The early cotton entrepreneurs were using changing methods of production to meet this fluctuating demand. On the one hand, they were introducing more machines into textile manufacture and centralizing more of their production, encountering numerous political and economic problems in the process. On the other hand, they were making goods for a broader market of consumers linked in that volatile system of imitation and innovation known as fashion. Under these conditions, entrepreneurs had to try to use the new equipment to manufacture the kinds of cloth that consumers wanted to buy. A Scottish muslin weaver put it this way:

As the muslin trade depends principally on fancy goods, it is absolutely necessary that the manufacturers go to London to see Fashions and get new patterns. It is necessary that they be on the spot themselves to see which way the whims of the moment points, and be enabled to form new things that will hit the varying taste of the times.[54]

The entrepreneurs in the textile trade during this period tended to handle all aspects of their businesses. They found their own sources of raw materials, organized the work processes in the factories, found sources of credit or capital to run their organizations, ordered or designed the machines their workers used, and arranged for their goods to be marketed. Charles Wilson has suggested that the most successful of these entrepreneurs were the ones who were sensitive enough to public taste to make the particular kinds of goods that consumers wanted to buy.[55] Without this sensitivity their organizational skills, use of capital goods, or access to either money or inexpensive raw materials did them little good.

Because London was the center for fashion in Britain and the city where imports from foreign countries arrived, it was the major center for trade in textiles in the late eighteenth century. Cotton manufacturers in and around Lancashire sent their goods to London to be sold and received back information and advice about the kinds of cloth selling there.[56] The following message from Bury's London agent illustrates the character of this type of exchange:

If you have not good cloths for the furniture do not print a single piece more until there are some good pieces bought and if you have nothing for the printers to do in the meantime, let them go away, this is my positive orders to you, on no account put a furniture print to work but on the very best cloths—the work that you have doing lately in garments is the worst in the trade, all the orders are returned on our hands.[57]

The largest cotton producers tended to rent or buy warehouses in London where they could store goods and show them to potential buyers. Some others went into a partnership or agreement with London merchants to sell their cloth, and the least well-to-do would give their fabrics to London merchants to sell on commission. Whatever the particulars of the arrangements, merchants in London were the ones to market textiles for most British and foreign trade, and to give producers feedback on the quality and design of their goods and how the goods did in the marketplace.[58]

The extent to which cotton manufacturers depended on London agents to trace subtle changes in demand suggests how unstable the market for cottons was from about 1780 through the first decade of the nineteenth century, and to what extent manufacturers found themselves economically vulnerable when they did not adequately anticipate the desires of their customers. But the reason that many entrepreneurs amassed great fortunes in this unstable climate was that the demand for British cottons was generally expanding as both home and foreign markets increased in size.

Some of the increased demand for cottons in the last decades of the eighteenth century resulted from a spreading fashion for British cottons within the home market. During the 1780s and 1790s the principal demand for British cotton goods came from the middle and working classes. In 1786 Robert Peel, speaking for some other printers, said that "3 parts of 4 of printed goods are consumed by the lower classes of people." The upper class maintained a taste for imported cloth and used Indian muslins and imported silks until the 1790s. At that point they began to show an interest in British calicoes and muslins, just as improved spinning on the mule made British muslins as fine and much less expensive than imported muslins, and improved designs for printed fabrics made local fabrics more appealing to elites.[59]

Changes in fashion in the eighties and nineties also contributed to the popularity of muslins and calicoes. After the French revolution, the English began to act as models for European fashion.

The greater design simplicity of English dress may have made it seem more appropriate for the times, and the fear French aristocrats had of wearing fashionable dress may have made them glad to leave innovations in fashion to others. Women's dresses became simpler as bustles began to replace hooped skirts; later even these were abandoned for the fine pleats or gathers that led to the empire gown. Men's clothes also were simplified; they became more tailored and less elaborate than earlier French fashions. The new designs favored decorative and light cotton cloth and were frequently made with English calicoes. During the eighties, calico shirts were the vogue for men and calico aprons, caps, and petticoats enjoyed wide popularity among women. Even when calicoes became less popular for clothing as finer muslins were developed, English cottons remained the most fashionable fabrics, and calicoes simply were used more often for home furnishings.[60]

With the development of English muslins, British fabrics became competitive on the world market with Indian goods, and British exports began to rise dramatically. Joseph Smith and Robert Peel provided the following analysis of the success of cotton exports to Europe:

The principal advantage of the English cotton trade arises from our machines for both spinning and printing[;] by means of these we can print not only cheaper and better but we save more than half of the colors which before we wasted. It is impossible to say how soon foreign countries may obtain these machines, but even then, the experience we have in the use of them would give us such an advantage that I should not fear the competition. With respect to colours and taste, I think we are on a par with any other country.[61]

The increasing demand for British cottons helped to make the sale of cottons much more complex. By the late 1780s manufacture and selling had become more clearly differentiated as the agents and merchants who specialized in selling cloth sought out new ways to organize their work. These changes were most apparent outside the London area.

When the cotton industry was first growing in Britain, some cotton manufacturers set up warehouses in the towns where they

Copper plate impression for textile printing by Talwin and Foster, English, late eighteenth century (N1943-2). COURTESY OF THE VICTORIA AND ALBERT MUSEUM, LONDON.

had their factories. Salesmen from these warehouses would not only show cloth to prospective buyers who came to the warehouses, but they also took samples of their wares to fairs and marketdays in the countryside, some salesmen even going abroad to find outlets for their goods.[62]

When some of these traveling salesmen found that they could sell more goods in Manchester than they could in the towns scattered over the Midlands and the North, they set up warehouses in Manchester, wholesale outlets that were still close enough to the site of cotton production to make shipping costs low but that centralized Midlands and Northern sales. Centralization affected other aspects of the cotton trade when finishers moved from London to Manchester in order to place themselves closer to the site of manufacture. With this move, Manchester became a center for textile trade that so successfully rivaled London that by the end of the eighteenth century many London cloth merchants were sending their agents to Manchester.[63]

In the early nineteenth century Manchester began to take a larger role than London in cloth exporting. The entrance of Manchester merchants into this trade was in part the result of their position close to manufacturing centers and their position near the West coast, which facilitated trade to Africa and the Americas. The growing reliance of British manufacturers on cotton wool from the Americas was also somewhat responsible for this shift, but it was initially due more to the growing difference between the kinds of cottons sold in the two markets. London had remained the center of fashion and trade in fine goods, while Manchester became the center for the more popular and less fine goods that comprised the bulk of the cotton trade at home and abroad. As sales in Africa and the Americas expanded vis-à-vis exports to Europe, Manchester interest in this trade grew because Manchester merchants supplied the desired types of goods at lower costs.[64]

Calicoes played an important role in the rise of this dual market just as they had in the development of textile production and finishing innovations. Printed cottons remained the most popular goods in this period; muslins and calicoes together were the most produced cotton fabrics (see the table on p. 240).

Of the printed cottons consumed in England (or at least the ones that were taxed there) printed calicoes made in Britain were the ones to show the greatest growth in the last two decades of the eighteenth century (see the graph). It should not be surprising that British calicoes were the type of fabric which enjoyed the major growth with the adoption of machines for cotton manufacture. After all, they were the kind of cloth for which many of these innovations had been made, and they were also the kind of cloth most favored by the mass market because of their broad (cross-class as well as cross-cultural) appeal. This is why calicoes were favored by early entrepreneurs seeking to make themselves into captains of industry in the late eighteenth and early nineteenth centuries.[65]

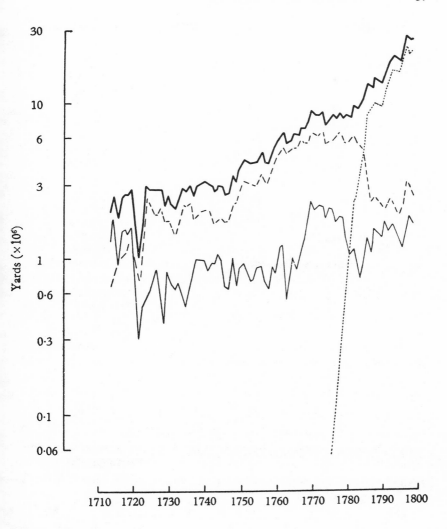

Printed Goods Charged with Duty, 1713–1798
———— total printed goods;
———— printed linens, cotton-linens and stuffs;
– – – foreign calicoes;
. . . . . British calicoes

Source: Customs Library, Excise Revenue Accounts; reprinted from Phyllis Deane and W. A. Cole, *British Economic Growth 1688–1959* (Cambridge: Cambridge University Press, 1967), p. 54.

P. Colquhoun's Estimates of Production 1787 & 1789 (revised by N.J. Smelser)

1787 Estimate Branch	lb. consumed
Calicoes and Muslins	10,440,000
Fustians	5,400,000
Mixture—Silk and linen	1,800,000
Hosiery	1,350,000
Candlewicks	1,350,000
Cotton waste	2,260,000
	22,600,000

1789 Estimate	
Calicoes and Muslins	13,000,000
Fustians	6,500,000
Silk mixed goods, checks, etc.	1,500,000
Hosiery	1,800,000
Candlewicks	1,700,000
Cotton waste and dirt removed	3,000,000
	27,500,00

Materialism and the Cotton Industry

The growth of the British cotton industry resulted from a contradiction between the demands of fashion and the perceived welfare of the British economy. The resulting system of production was one that both assumed and depended on high levels of demand, demand that was originally defined by a European system of fashionable change but that was augmented by the spread of fashions to colonial markets.

This new system of production was organized around the use of machines for a large part of the manufacturing process, creating a kind of economic dependence on objects, capital goods, for generating economic growth. This use of capital goods was distinctive in both its character and its economic consequences; it was designed to create the consumer goods in demand on international markets and to adjust the balance of trade. The innovations were materialistic not only because they were material solutions to practical problems, but also because they were used (in different ways) to serve the material interests of individual entrepreneurs, consumers, and the state.

In these ways, the growth of the British cotton industry was linked to the growing materialism of the early modern period. It was stimulated by demand for cottons created by that pattern of conspicuous consumption known as fashion; it was accomplished by the creation of new forms of material culture, new machines and chemicals that could speed up and cut costs of textile production. In addition, it was instituted to solve a problem in the British economy, a problem defined in material terms. The growth of the British cotton industry was, then, perhaps as much the logical consequence of the growth of materialist tendencies in European society as an outcome of economic forces put into play by the development of the international capitalist economy.

The effects of this revolution on material culture appeared in the everyday objects and routine events found in the lives of Britons; they were markedly different from what they had been at the beginning of the eighteenth century. Some changes in the material environment were created by the growth of factories, expansion of urban areas, creation of new forms of transportation, and growth of new ports, i.e., in the obvious consequences of the industrial revolution. But there were also more subtle and small-scale changes. As people's clothing and household goods changed, so did the character of their daily lives. Changes in the fabrics used in clothing encouraged new patterns of washing and greater personal cleanliness. Changes in home life participated in a redefinition of families and sex roles along with the more commonly recognized pattern of differentiating the home from the workplace.

Changes in the design of goods—not simply changes in design to follow fashion but the development of designs for mass production—transformed the *look* of the material environment. As more people's homes and bodies were filled or covered with mass-produced goods copied from the designs for elite goods, the appearance of class differences became less pronounced.[66] Social stratification did not disappear from view, but it began to become less distinct and more subtle in appearance. The same happened to some extent with regional and even national differences in material culture as trade in mass-produced goods increased. The look, feel, and routines of everyday life veered imperceptibly with each new yard of cloth to arrive at the London or Manchester market.

These changes are some of the evidence that scholars use when they define materialism or mass culture as a child of the industrial revolution. It is easy to associate material culture, as many sociologists have, with the mass societies engendered by industrialization.[67] But the changes in the production and distribution of goods that we call the industrial revolution would not have occurred if a prior materialist culture had not already made sense of increased production to both entrepreneurs and consumers. It was the culture of the early modern period that helped to explain and encourage increased economic activity, including the development of mass production machinery and the necessary materials for manufacturing consumer goods.

CHAPTER SEVEN

Materialism and Social Change

FROM THE perspective of a twentieth-century analyst, the materialism in the early modern period may seem quite unlike the materialist tendencies in contemporary Western societies. Sixteenth-century farm families using a few cast iron pots, buying ribbons to decorate their clothing or hair, and using newly surveyed and reclaimed land to raise their crops may seem only distant relatives of today's *hautes bourgeois* living in luxurious homes and working in large corporations with huge inventories of plant and equipment. The two types may have lived in eras dominated by the same materialistic culture, but each has lived according to cultural forms specific to its social rank and its own historical period. The differences in their lives help to highlight the quantitative and qualitative differences in the material culture of these two eras, but they also tend to mask continuities that have resulted from a common cultural tradition. By looking at forms of materialism that appeared in early modern Europe and have persisted to the present day, one can trace the origins and evolution of this tradition and clarify its relationship to contemporary materialism.

Finding the origins of this culture in the early modern period suggests that materialism and capitalism developed interdependently. The first three studies in the book clarify this mutual reinforcement. They show how consumerism, innovations in capital goods, and materialist thought developed originally in conjunction with early capitalist socioeconomic forms. The first, for instance, shows how the design of new consumer goods was linked to the emergence of the peculiar forms of social stratification resulting from capitalism. Manufacturers did not intentionally produce a pattern of stratification in objects to enhance the development of the new social order, but when they attempted to tailor objects to different income groups to increase their profits, they effectively mirrored and ratified the social system. They cultivated cosmopolitan tastes among elites and produced a taste for less expensive commodities among nonelites, helping to create aesthetic and life-style differences between the two groups. At the same time, they increased the demand for goods coming from both these parts of the population, favoring more efficient forms of capitalist production. Pierre Bourdieu and Jean Baudrillard, among others,[1] have found similar class stratification inscribed in contemporary artifacts and have attributed them to similar concerns about marketing; in the same vein, literature on contemporary cultural imperialism points to ongoing tensions between regionalism and internationalism in patterns of culture and domination. All this work is testimony to the continuing importance of the stratification of consumer goods to contemporary life and suggests the value of tracing its historical origins.

The second study shows how the development of innovative capital goods was also important for capitalist expansion. Specifically, it shows how access to the new goods designed in the early modern period for use as economic resources affected the relationship among nations in the emerging world economy. By tying economic expansion to the use of objects, Europeans increased the amount of capital necessary for economic competition and made differences in the development and use of artifacts central to both the economic welfare of states and the ability of individual entrepreneurs to enrich themselves. This pattern again can be found in the contemporary situation. In steel manufacture and other industries where technological innovation has continued to change manufacturing practices, patterns of international trade and the relationship of nations within the world economy have been closely tied to patterns of innovation.

The third study shows that new patterns of thought were part of this materialist culture and affected capitalist development. It demonstrates how the obsession with objects that is commonly associated with cultural materialism evolved in early modern Europe into a new scientific attitude: an emphasis on empirical evidence and closed-system or "objective" models of explanation. To the extent that the new science helped to redefine nature as a resource for manufacture and was used to analyze and plan the economic activities of nations within the world economy, the scientific attitude also contributed to capitalism. That nations still fund research in the natural sciences and hire expert economic planners to guide their decisions is testimony to the continuing importance attributed to scientific thinking for state economic development.

The last two chapters demonstrate most dramatically the value of studying the early evidence of materialist culture to understand contemporary society, but in a different way. They suggest how the three aspects of materialism could have provided the cultural prerequisites for the eighteenth-century industrial revolution. Given the close identification of contemporary materialism with industrial manufacture, this attempt to show the interdependence of the two is particularly valuable. We tend to think of materialism as a consequence rather than a cause of industrialization, and so we underestimate the potency of material culture in shaping the contemporary economic environment. This study shows how the tensions arising between the desires of consumers and the defined needs of the state for economic development spurred the search for innovations in manufacture that were used to develop industrial forms of production.

My argument has been presented with evidence from the history of printing, a history which, while providing an unusually broad perspective on materialism in the period, does not necessarily contain conclusive evidence about the role of materialism in the industrial revolution. It does provide a novel look at the growth of Britain's cotton industry, but its value for unveiling the cultural underpinnings of industrial development in general cannot depend on this evidence alone.

The researchers who have dominated the search for causes of the industrial revolution, economists and economic historians, are not in agreement about when (much less how) industrialization began. There are, of course, many scholars, including Rostow, Smelser, and Mantoux, who have treated the astronomical growth of cotton manufacture in late eighteenth- and early nineteenth-century Britain as the prime mover in the industrial revolution, arguing that this spurt of industrial growth started a chain of events which transformed Britain's economy and made Britain into the first industrialized country. Their arguments have been challenged most dramatically by Phyllis Deane and W. A. Cole, who argue that cotton manufacture accounted for only a small amount of Britain's national income in the period, and therefore could not have triggered such an enormous economic revolution. They suggest instead that expansion of British agriculture increased demand at home for both domestically produced goods and imports; when the imports expanded the economies of other countries, they helped to create greater demand for exported British goods which then supported expansion in Britain.[2]

Rostow, among others, has defended the traditional association of the cotton industry with the eighteenth-century industrial revolution.[3] He has apparently accepted Deane and Cole's statistics on the role of the cotton industry in Britain's national income in the eighteenth and nineteenth centuries. But he has criticized the authors for using an explanation of the industrial revolution based on "demand," arguing against all theories of demand (either demand created by agricultural expansion of the sort that Deane and Cole describe, or demand produced by population increases, i.e., the type of demand that many other authors see as essential to the industrial revolution). Rostow argues instead that "take-off" in eighteenth-century Britain was an artifact of technological change.[4]

The analysis made so far in this book suggests that these two theses, for all their differences, share a common characteristic: considering only levels of demand and innovation, and neglecting their qualitative aspects. Rostow does not consider the importance of public taste in goods or growing interest in the use of machines for solving practical problems as motives for the technological innovations of the eighteenth and nineteenth centuries. And Deane and Cole cannot suggest *why* the domestic population in Britain would have used the extra money it gained from the rise in agricultural production to buy consumer goods made newly available on the market, such as printed cotton fabrics.[5]

This lack of attention to cultural factors affecting industrial development is a little disturbing just as a matter of principle, since it treats the people involved in this transformation as though they had no interest in making sense of their experiences. It also inhibits the process of historical analysis by encouraging scholars to think, for instance, that technological innovation and demand for goods were separate phenomena. If in fact the studies presented here are not misleading, then demand, technological innovation, and entrepreneurialism were different faces of the same cultural system. Hence central issues in contemporary debates about industrialization may be based on false dichotomies.

Marxist historians, who have provided alternative explanations of the industrialization of Britain during the eighteenth century, also tend to ignore cultural factors. While Marxist scholars may have a more systematic model of how economic changes led to the industrial revolution, they have difficulty in identifying exactly why, for instance, the cotton industry was transformed when it was, since they have been reluctant to assign causality to the culture of capitalism. By treating culture as entirely epiphenomenal, they have not seen how early cultural changes embedded in the transition from feudalism to capitalism (such as the growth of fashion) put pressures on particular forms of manufacture (such as textiles) to supply new goods for a European cosmopolitan culture. In other words, these scholars have not recognized how the new cultural forms evolving in the early stages of capitalism created public demands that furthered economic changes. There is certainly some basis for developing such an analysis using a Marxist frame (based on Marx's discussion of commodity fetishism), but this possibility has not been exploited by Marxist scholars of the industrial revolution. It is unfortunate that it has not, since an understanding of the relationship between capitalism and its material culture can explain more exactly the rise of British cotton manufacture in the eighteenth century as an early stage of the industrial revolution.[6]

This is not to say that all historians have ignored the qualitative aspect of demand as a factor in Britain's industrial revolution. Elizabeth Gilboy and Harold Perkin, for instance, have both claimed that the development of fashion, as a system of social emulation, created a demand for goods that provided markets elastic enough for industrial expansion. Gilboy emphasizes the elasticity of the markets created this way, and Perkin uses this argument to suggest that the relative egalitarianism of British culture was particularly conducive to industrial development because it made social emulation a strong cultural force.[7]

The problem with these arguments is that, while they acknowledge the importance of cultural factors to increased demand, they do not convey the complex interplay of forces linking social emulation with the demand for goods. They tend to look only at (and for) those situations in which increased demand contributed to economic expansion, and not the opposite. As a result, they tend to overlook situations in which demand favored imported rather than locally produced goods and hence acted as a barrier rather than a resource for the industrialization of a particular country. Since demand for internationally marketed goods could sometimes stimulate and sometimes inhibit a nation's development, patterns of taste that shaped international demand tended to promote expansion in areas producing fashionable items at the expense of those regions where fashion demanded the extensive use of imports. For this reason, the cosmopolitan cultural systems that grew up with international trade were dangerously powerful economic forces.

This theoretical attention to cultural factors affecting the growth of the British cotton industry may not seem terribly useful to those scholars who dismiss cultural explanations entirely or who believe that the cotton industry was not the point of takeoff for the industrial revolution. But the play of cultural factors extracted here from the case of the cotton industry deserves some careful attention for two reasons. First, the aspects of materialism isolated and examined here are precisely the factors most frequently associated with the industrial revolution. Demand, innovation, and entrepreneurialism (as they are usually identified) are at the center of all debates on this subject. What this analysis provides is some vision of their roots in a common culture that permeated Western culture and made industrialization seem a reasonable thing to pursue. Second, the patterns of interaction among these three forms of materialism that I have only been able to sketch clearly in the history of the cotton industry seem to have had analogs in other areas of industrial expansion. The systems of taste shaping demand, the patterns of economic analysis used in planning, and the capital innovations used to start new industries, so visibly potent in cotton manufacture, were also apparent in pottery and iron manufacture.[8] In all three cases it seems that the innovations used to establish industries were designed to meet demand for imports that was thought to be limiting consumption of locally produced goods. The possible ubiquity of this pattern is provocative, suggesting in a more general way how this culture could have stimulated change.

In the case of the pottery industry, increased demand for ceramics in Britain began in the seventeenth century when tea became a fashionable beverage, and when changes in table manners increased the number of dishes included in a proper dinner service. These fashions created a demand for ceramics, but not for British pottery; the eighteenth-century English wanted oriental porcelains or the fine ceramics made on the Continent. As a result, the fashion prescribing the use of more tableware did not create the kind of demand that favored expansion of British manufacture, but rather, the kind that could make the British more dependent either on goods from major European producers of ceramics, such as Holland and France (Britain's rivals), or on goods brought in from the colonial trade, which helped to make colonial artisans competitive with their British counterparts. This demand could be harnessed to serve British pottery-making only when Britons developed the salt-firing process for improving the strength of their pottery and the printing techniques for applying patterns of glaze to china. These innovations helped to give British pottery the durability and beauty to make it competitive with foreign goods, reducing imports and increasing the export of British goods.[9]

Perkin, in describing the growth of this industry, points frequently to N. McKendrick's evidence that fashion played a large role in bringing about changes in pottery-making. He suggests that Wedgwood's pottery became widely popular after it found favor among aristocrats whose tastes were imitated by others. What Perkin does not mention, but McKendrick does, is that Wedgwood continually used innovative techniques to keep his products in step with subtle changes in fashion. He used these techniques not only to tap demand in England but to tap the international demand that was making fine china desirable throughout the European core states.[10]

Even this brief sketch indicates the striking parallels between the cultural factors affecting the growth of cotton and of ceramics manufacture in the eighteenth and nineteenth centuries. While the structural similarities in the development of the two industries are too obvious to dismiss altogether, they cannot be used to establish some general relationship between culture and industrialization because, no matter how lucrative the pottery trade was for some entrepreneurs, it was not a major element in British economic expansion.

Iron refining, however, is an area of agreed-upon importance to the industrial revolution. Britons had to develop new methods to refine and use iron when the old craft method of refining, heating with charcoal, became difficult and expensive as Britain began to run out of wood. This problem was exacerbated by a new demand for iron products for household goods, building materials, engine manufacture, and military equipment. Like the demand for calicoes, it seemed to be an economic problem rather than a boon as long as it forced the British to import more iron. The British could profit from it only when they could meet the new demand with their own iron, i.e., after they transformed the process so that they could purify iron ore with coal rather than charcoal fires.[11]

Patterns of changing tastes again played a crucial role in the push toward innovation. Part of the demand for iron, for instance, derived from the building boom and changes in taste for household design in the seventeenth and eighteenth centuries. The building boom itself created demand for items like nails and hinges that were basic to the construction process; the demand for fireplaces with iron firebacks (which improved their heating efficiency) and for iron grates in which to burn coal were evidence of the new ideas about home design that were creating new uses for iron. Iron stoves and iron pots were used more often during this period, the former making it possible to cook with coal and the latter providing a less expensive form of cookware. None of these items were fashionable in the sense that calicoes or fine china were; they did not represent luxuries of the upper classes. The increasing use of these goods reflected either changes in taste or the evolution of a kind of consumerism that fit the pocketbooks of the less affluent.[12]

Additional demand for iron developed out of increased use of new capital goods in manufacturing. Machines, and particularly engines, were commonly used capital goods that were made in part or entirely from iron. They were of growing importance to the iron-founders of this period, becoming important staples in the diet of British manufacturers.[13]

Military battles, like economic ones, depended increasingly in the seventeenth and eighteenth centuries on the superior equipment of one side, so that the production of hardware for the military became an important part of the iron trade. In fact, the single largest type of demand for iron products was for military equipment, such as the cannons and cannonballs that were primary means of waging war.[14]

None of these major sources of increased demand for iron really parallels the kind of fashion that created the strong demand for textiles and ceramics. But all three sources of new demand for iron goods represent demand based on a growing *materialism*, whether the desire for more and better household goods or an increased dependency on machines for commerce and war. The latter two sources of demand represent changing fashions of a different sort, novel ideas about the proper means of achieving military victories and economic goals. They may not be matters of "taste" in the common sense of that term, but they do represent new ideas about using an expanding material culture for politicoeconomic advantage.

The new tastes for iron led to innovations in refining when the lack of any traditional method for producing iron without charcoal became a more aggravating problem. Increased demand pushed Britons to import so much iron that it seemed to jeopardize their economic autonomy. Britain found itself becoming dependent on Sweden, Russia, and America for pig iron and importing growing amounts of Dutch cast iron. Neither of these patterns of trade was appealing to British mercantilists, who did not savor increased imports from their trading rival, Holland, and particularly disliked dependence on products from British colonies.[15]

The problem of importing Dutch cast iron was solved with the earliest successful experiments in refining with coke. Abraham Darby, who made these experiments, used the iron he produced with his coke-refining process to cast iron pots, firebacks, and coal grates. These goods met the consumer demand in Britain that had been met by Dutch goods in the past, and also satisfied demand for these items in the colonies and parts of the Continent.[16] The first set of experiments was successful enough to reduce imports of Dutch ironwork and improve the British balance of trade. But it alone could not eliminate the British need to import iron; the "pigs" produced using the first Darby coke-firing process were not good for making wrought-iron products.

British fear of becoming dependent on imported pig iron, particularly on imports from the colonies, was great enough to stimulate the passage of mercantilist restrictions on trade in iron from the American colonies. Although there is no evidence that without restrictions the American colonists would have surpassed Britons in iron production, fear of this possibility (based on the superior supply of iron ore and trees in the colonies) led to the passage of mercantilist restrictions on the trade.[17] While these restrictions may have reduced anxiety, fear of colonial advantage in the iron trade was only removed when additional experiments made by the Darby family and others increased the quality of pig iron that could be made with coal fires. This innovation destroyed the advantages of imported pig iron and reduced British dependence on iron imports for all sorts of ironwork, from cutlery to cannons.

The change in manufacturing even began to make English iron products more desirable than competitive goods on the world market. Defoe suggested this when he wrote:

It is not many Years since the best Scissors, the best Knives, and the best Razors were made in *France*, and the like of the fine Watches, Tweezers, and other small Ware; nothing is more evident in Trade and the Time, than that the best Knife Blades, Scissors, Surgeons Instruments, Watches, Clocks, Jacks and Locks that are in the World, and especially Toys and gay Things are made in *England*, and in *London* in particular; and our Custom-house Books, will make it appear, that we send daily great Quantitites of wrought Iron and Brass into *Holland*, *France, Italy, Venice,* and to all Parts of *Germany, Poland,* and *Muscovy.*[18]

The political and technical history of iron refining in England bears strong resemblance to the calico controversy. It shows again how increased home demand seemed to favor first continental and later colonial trade rather than domestic economic expansion. Mercantilist legislation was then enacted to stall this unfavorable trade, and innovations in capital goods were made to reverse its effects. In the case of iron refining one cannot find as clear evidence of changing patterns of trade as one finds in the case of cotton manufacture. Iron refining in the Americas was never as advanced as cotton production in India, and British imports of iron from the colonies were never on the scale of calico imports. But the similarity of the fears in both cases and the legislative response to them do help to sketch how patterns of demand could and did create problems of symbolic politics for Britons which spurred them both to enact laws restricting trade and to innovate to change manufacture.

What is shared in these cases is a structure of meanings. When patterns of taste shifted, creating new demand for goods like calicoes, teapots, cast-iron grates, and cannons, and when the new types of demand seemed to favor the economic growth of either other core states or the colonies to the detriment of British industries, Britons faced what they took to be a crisis in trade. Mercantilist restrictions might temporarily reduce their anxiety, but only changes in demand or methods of production would solve the problem. In iron production and textile manufacture Britons seemed to be trying to resolve the crisis by developing new machines and chemical processes to transform their methods of producing the desired goods.

From this perspective, the industrial revolution was culturally a "mercantilist" strategy for solving Britain's economic worries, used to induce further colonial dependency and British autonomy by making Britain the producer of the goods most desired on the world market. After the growth of British cotton manufacture, India became a cotton fabric importer rather than exporter. And after coal replaced charcoal refining in Britain, Americans increasingly imported British iron.[19] Changes in production could have these strategic effects by providing the goods favored by fashion at low prices and equal or higher quality than other areas could produce. British goods started to be desired products in the United States, Germany, India, and to some extent in Britain's European adversary, France.

Thoughts and desires, dreams and fears, designs and plans were not peripheral to this economic revolution; they were part of its core. In simplest terms, they were manifested in the interaction of three distinct types of materialism: (1) a materialist view of the meaning of trade; (2) innovations in capital goods, a materialist means for increasing productivity; and (3) materialist systems of consumption. Understanding how these forms developed in the early modern period is one means for excavating the cultural underpinnings of industrial capitalism.

While the studies presented in this book give only general evidence about materialism before the industrial revolution, evidence based on an analysis of only one kind of good, printed objects, they do indicate quite clearly that these three types of materialism had some role in increasing the economic expansion of Europe. In the Middle Ages most Europeans believed that the most beneficial form of trade was hoarding, bringing in goods from other places to store and be used by families or communities when needed, but in the early modern period Europeans began to think of trade as an opportunity to make exchanges for profit. This redefinition of objects stimulated economic activity.[20]

The history of cartography presented earlier in this book illustrates this change in the use of commodities. During the fourteenth and fifteenth centuries Europeans tried to hoard maps and geographical writings, attempting to increase their strength by monopolizing these goods and the information they contained. But with the advent of printing and the growth of new forms of economic thought, the idea of *profiting* from the exchange of maps and writings became both feasible and more legitimate, opening a new era in the history of cartography and overseas expansion. Here one can clearly recognize a shift in orientation toward movements in material culture, as designing goods to gain economic value from their exchange replaced the pattern of hoarding goods or sharing them only among those with whom one wanted to create or sustain social bonds.

The development of novel consumer goods was part of the same process. One can see in the history of the pictures made during the early modern period evidence of how Europeans began increasing the exchange value of objects by designing them to fit broad patterns of taste. This impulse and the dual system of commodity design that it engendered also increased trade; it broadened the range of people engaged in patterns of consumption and added to the demand for new goods.

Continuities between the changing meanings of consumer commodities and capital goods (specifically, popular prints and maps) are worth noting because they illustrate another point made in chapter 1: that these two categories of objects are not and have not been mutually exclusive. When European materialism transformed the meaning of manufacture, it affected not only the manufacture of consumer commodities but also the development of mechanical and chemical innovations. Europeans had already become accustomed to creating mechanical solutions to practical problems in the Middle Ages; but in the early modern period, they used this proclivity to serve the developing materialist culture. They devised the style of using innovations to define, promote, and sustain economic growth; in other words, they self-consciously developed capital goods to manipulate the economy.

The Portuguese use of capital goods during early expansion provides evidence of this changing meaning of capital goods. At first, the Portuguese used innovations to aid in overseas expansion, but they did it in a way that was distinctly medieval. For instance, when they developed new kinds of maps, ships and sails, they used these material innovations to engage in a Holy War with the Islamic Empire. They also used these innovations in medieval ways when they secreted maps and travel writings as they would craft "mysteries." Thus, they made the new equipment compatible with medieval culture, even while they used it for capitalist expansion. But once the innovations were used to find economic benefits and were exchanged in the trading system as profitable commodities, they were stripped of the medieval meanings. They became part of the materialist culture of the early modern period.

This new culture was earmarked by its internationalism. New consumer commodities and capital goods (decorative prints and maps) created an international form of European culture, a common material and symbolic heritage with which all Europeans could identify and work. The dissemination in print of techniques for sailing the world's oceans and the spread of fashions and tastes were both elements of this culture, and they directly affected economic development by shaping competition among core states in Europe. They gave different states more equal access to the equipment they needed for expanding their trade and confronted them with common problems of manufacture arising from international patterns of demand. Machines as well as textiles (capital and consumer goods) were now spread rather than hoarded, traded for profit. The competition among European states, then, was in part made keen by the similarities in their capabilities and problems.

The growth of the "free trade" movement and further industrial development in Europe started a new era for European social life, as innovations in manufacture and trade started to become the primary basis for competition among the core states. States began to focus more on developing technical differences that would give them the edge in this trade. In the seventeenth century they did this primarily by improving transportation, but with the eighteenth-century industrial revolution, Europeans learned that they could gain an edge in trade by more efficient production of goods in demand on the world market.[21]

These economic changes, then, were closely tied to the fundamental cultural shift described by Polanyi that turned the attention of Europeans to commodities and their exchange for profit.[22] But what brought this culture to life when it did? As I suggested earlier, materialism developed as an artifact of expanding trade when the meanings and value of goods became problematic with the arrival of new goods in European markets. Making these objects an understandable and useful part of material culture required the production of new meanings, new symbolism for the objects themselves and to describe their value. Once Europeans started to make pictorial prints, for instance, they created pictures that combined image qualities of medieval pictures with elements of Renaissance art, forging a new kind of imagery with its own distinctive aesthetics, an aesthetic that simultaneously made the prints popular with less affluent members of the public and gave European culture a new look.

The rise of fashion provides more evidence about this pattern. As trade brought new materials and styles to people, allowing them to make new kinds of clothing, and as they found their system of social stratification being undermined by this same trade, they developed new systems of taste that could be used to indicate more precisely their social station. They culled some ideas about the social meanings of dress from traditional medieval culture, identifying aspects of new cloth and clothing with the medieval hierarchy of fabrics and dress, but at the same time, they destroyed the medieval system of dress by social rank, making differences in dress more expressive of social class and cosmopolitanism than traditional social rank. In both the case of fashion and the development of commercial pictorial prints, Europeans created new symbolism *in* material culture and fashioned new meaning systems to explain the value of new goods.

The spread of printed books had a similar history. As Ong and Gouldner point out, printing fostered the development of new forms of writing as well as systems of thought based on these forms.[23] And, as the argument in chapter 5 suggests, these patterns of writing and thinking evolved from and with the new meanings and uses given books as they became more widely available items of trade.

The result of the proliferation of new meanings both in and about objects was increased demand for both consumer and capital goods, for those objects that could give people equipment for making social claims and for facilitating new varieties of economic action. People could use clothes for presenting achieved rather than ascribed social statuses; they could use maps and engineering drawings to create new patterns of production and distribution of goods. Because these new objects were specifically *designed* for uses that were being made meaningful just in this period, they shaped new kinds and levels of demand.

It is quite easy to trace the growth of consumerism in Europe during the early modern period, to see how new trade in and markets for goods created both new patterns of material culture and forces for social change. During the fifteenth and sixteenth century Europeans began to change the organization of production, moving away from the traditional guild system and providing goods for international markets as well as local ones. Under these circumstances, not only were traditional goods brought to new markets, but altogether new forms of material culture were made to suit the needs and interests of new consumers.

One result of this trade was increased affluence for some parts of the social order. Affluence reached some people as the bit of surplus they could use to become new consumers; it also gave merchants new power in the economy. That this wealth fell disproportionately in the hands of merchants is particularly noteworthy for this analysis because it helped to disrupt the traditional social order with its reigning forms of social expression. The resulting freedom of expression helped to encourage the development of a cosmopolitan culture that was independent of the traditional order and closely tied to the emerging international economy.

Once international patterns of taste developed, consumerism became a force in international trade, affecting trade balances in all the regions involved in the international capitalist economy. Where disparities existed between the goods traditionally produced in an area and the demand for goods, growth in manufacturing was made more difficult, threatening that area with economic dependence on the other countries that could supply desired commodities. Where nations developed techniques for producing the goods desired in the international market, they could enjoy both prosperity and increasing autonomy. Thus, in the seventeenth century India enjoyed economic growth because it could provide goods desired internationally, but once its cotton trade was usurped by the British, India's economy became more dependent on British trade.

The theories of economic development used to establish economic policies in early modern Europe were also part of this cultural system. Mercantilist and free trade theories were alike in defining the welfare of states in materialist terms. Both acted as international ideational systems that shifted in potency with changes in economic fashion, in just the way that tastes in clothing changed. Like other fashions, economic ones appeared (with some variations) in most of the European core states, creating consistency in the policies debated in (if not always adopted by) different states for promoting economic development.

While mercantilist and free trade theories were similar in equating the well-being of a country with economic development, mercantilist policies were generally less effective in reaching their goals because they could neither control demand nor insure that local manufacturers could provide the goods that were in demand; at most they could temporarily remove from national markets those goods whose consumption seemed to threaten local manufacture. But, as the history of the fashion for calicoes shows, mercantilist policies were of limited value in creating long-term growth. That is why innovators, who used their skills to alter international patterns of trade by developing new equipment for manufacturing the goods most desired on the world market, were able to create large fortunes for themselves and a new model for increasing national economic growth. A play of cultural meanings made them think that innovation for the specific purpose of manufacturing goods to meet international demand was a reasonable way to shape their fortune. Innovations in capital goods were tied to shifts of public taste, and therefore were not independent causes of expanding economic development.

The histories reviewed here suggest how modern materialism developed in the early modern period and how it acted as a social force, providing the cultural system legitimating, spurring and guiding the industrialization of European nations. The point of the analysis is to suggest that production and trade have a Janus face, that as patterned uses of material culture, they necessarily have both economic and cultural meaning. One virtue of looking to the early modern period to understand materialism is that the objects produced in that era are different enough to stand out from contemporary artifacts, making it easier to see in them the continuity of culture and economy, the ways that attempts to produce economic value depend on systems of meaning. This makes it easier to understand why a growing preoccupation with objects would accompany increased abilities to find or manufacture them. The purpose of this analysis is not, however, simply to point this out. It is also to help us see similar patterns in contemporary forms of manufacture and trade.[24]

Many of us, when we open our windows in the summer, hear less the stirring of leaves and sound of birds than sirens, traffic noise and the rock-and-roll music emanating from a neighbor's stereo. Many of us see nature only in parks designed and built by other people, in the hills cut through by roads, or in the fields and suburban tracts planted by other members of our enterprising species. Whole communities are built on land recovered from the sea or protected (at least in part) from the erratic rampages of wild rivers. As a result, even the things of nature we see in our daily lives are often not in their natural state. The trees and rocks in Central Park in New York may not have been literally created by human beings, but many have been arranged or vandalized by us, presumably to reflect and suit our needs and interests. But these ways of shaping nature are nothing compared to the forces of production that have been used to transform trees and oil into homes and furniture and that have employed stones (gravel, shale, and ores) to make roads and airplanes. These more profound attempts to make nature useful have made the environment in which most people live almost entirely a reflection of human will.

This world, seen as such a problem to environmentalists and romantics of all sorts who have imputed enormous significance to nature and the natural, expresses the sense of dominion over nature felt as early as the seventeenth century. The materialist culture that we have inherited from that period has produced this environment, not in some accidental fashion but as the systematic outcome of the interaction of capitalism and materialism. As the transformation of wild rivers into tame ones has been defined as culturally valuable, the construction and use of dams has been exploited as a source of revenue. As central heating has come to be defined as a necessity, the production of furnaces has been made a viable industry. In these ways and others, the identification of cultural values has been used to pursue economic interests, creating a dialectic that has been played out in nature.

Natural resources, cultural meanings, and economic interests have been played off against each other, straining each other's capacities and creating new sources of change. This pattern has become even more apparent in recent days because many strains on the environment and on some members of the population have come to light, making materialism seem a social problem. But this culture is not the kind of temporary social form that can be called a problem and easily "corrected." It is a fundamental part of what has made "the West" a self-consciously distinctive part of the world for many centuries. The roots of this culture reach back before industrialization, where materialism helped to shape patterns of capitalist development, including the industrial revolution itself. And its growth has continued to create new patterns of material culture and to exert new pressures on the economy. Drawing attention to this culture is a good antidote both to the impulse to define modern social life entirely in economic terms and to locate its cultural underpinnings only in the entrepreneurial spirit. The heart of capitalism and materialism alike lies in the shape of objects—in pens, books, chairs, and tables, cities and fields, warships and satellites—the theories and dreams we have embedded in matter perhaps less for the glory of God and tomorrow's profits than for the advancement of states and today's pleasures.

Notes

1. PATTERNS OF MODERN MATERIALISM

1. John Evelyn, *Navigation and Commerce, Their Original and Progress* (London: Benjamin Tooke, 1674), p. 9.

2. Eric Kerridge, *Farmers of Old England* (Totowa, N.J.: Rowman and Littlefield, 1973), pp. 136–37; Carlo Cipolla, *Before the Industrial Revolution* (New York: Norton, 1976), pp. 35–36; B. Sprague Allen, *Tides of English Taste* (New York: Pageant, 1958), chs. 1–7; Joan Thirsk, *Economic Policy and Projects* (Oxford: Clarendon Press, 1978), pp. 7–8; Lawrence Stone, *Family and Fortune* (Oxford: Clarendon Press, 1973), part 1, ch. 1; Maurice Tomlin, *English Furniture* (London: Farber and Farber, 1972), ch. 2; L. G. Ramsey, *Antique English Furniture* (London: The Connoisseur, 1961), pp. 41–42; W. G. Hoskins, *Provincial England* (London: Macmillan, 1963), ch. 7; Peter Thornton, *Seventeenth Century Interior Decoration in England, France, and Holland* (New Haven: Yale University Press, 1978); Agnes Arber, *Herbals* (Cambridge: Cambridge University Press, 1953), p. 89.

3. Joan Thirsk has commented on this association of mass consumption with the industrial revolution. See Thirsk, *Economic Policy*, p. 125. For theories that make this assumption, see Herbert Marcuse, *One-Dimensional Man* (Boston: Beacon Press, 1964); Stewart Ewen, *Captains of Consciousness* (New York: McGraw-Hill, 1976). See also Walter Benjamin, "The Work of Art in the Age of Mechanical Reproduction," in H. Arendt, *Illuminations* (New York: Schocken, 1968); Dwight MacDonald, "A Theory of Mass Culture" (1953), in Bernard Rosenberg and David Manning White, *Mass Culture* (New York: Free Press, 1957); Norman Cantor and M. Werthman, *The History of Popular Culture* (London: Collier-Macmillan, 1968); Max Horkheimer, "The End of Reason," *Studies in Philosophy and Social Science* (1941), vol. 9; Phillip Slater, *Earthwalk* (New York: Anchor, 1974); and Ann Douglas, *The Feminization of American Culture* (New York: Avon, 1977).

4. Max Weber, *The Protestant Ethic and the Spirit of Capitalism* (New York: Scribner's [1904–5], 1958).

5. Thirsk, *Economic Policy*.

6. Stone, *Family and Fortune*; Thirsk, *Economic Policy*; Michael Baxandall, *Painting and Experience in Fifteenth-Century Italy* (New York: Oxford University Press [1972], 1974); and Jacob Burckhardt, *Civilization of the Renaissance in Italy* (New York: Oxford University Press, n.d.). See also Jere Cohen, "Rational Capitalism in Renaissance Italy," *American Journal of Sociology* (1980), 85(6): 1340–55.

7. See for instance, R. S. Fitton and A. P. Wadsworth, *The Strutts and the*

Arkwrights (Manchester: Manchester University Press, 1958), pp. 90–92 and 169*n*.

8. Arnold Hauser, *Social History of Art* (New York: Vintage, 1951), vol. 2, pp. 207–25.

9. Stone, *Family and Fortune*, part 1, ch. 1.

10. Allen, chs. 6–7; Thirsk, *Economic Policy*; Alicia Amherst, *A History of Gardening in England* (Detroit: Singing Tree Books [1896], 1969), chs. 5–8; Richardson Wright, *The Story of Gardening* (New York: Dover, 1934), chs. 10–11, esp. pp. 190–93; Roy Strong, *The Renaissance Garden in England* (London: Thames and Hudson, 1979), pp. 75–80, 90–92, 130–32, 138–41, and 174–85.

11. Arthur Raistrick, *Dynasty of Iron Founders* (London: Longman, Green, 1953), chs. 10–11.

12. Robert Merton, *Science, Technology and Society in Seventeenth-Century England* (New York: Howard Fertig [1938], 1970); Lewis Feuer, *The Scientific Intellectual* (New York: Basic Books, 1963).

13. Hauser, vol. 2, pp. 207–25; Allen, vol. 1, ch. 1; F. Saxl and R. Wittrower, *British Art and the Mediterranean* (Oxford: Oxford University Press, 1948), pp. 37–60. There may have been less connection between Protestantism and the art of Holland and England than many people believe. The disruption of trade between Protestant and Catholic countries may have inhibited the flow of artwork and artists, and could have contributed to an isolation of Protestant artists that led to a different pattern of development for the arts in Protestant areas. But some art historians are not convinced that this disruption of trade was complete enough to have such an effect. See Seymour Slive, "Notes on the Relationship of Protestantism to Seventeenth-Century Dutch Painting" in James Ackerman, et al., *Seventeenth-Century Art in Flanders and Holland* (New York: Garland, 1976), pp. 23–26. Slive finds elements of "Catholic" art in Dutch art in this period. Similarly, one can see equivalents of genre paintings appearing in Catholic areas of Europe. See Julius Held and Donald Posner, *Seventeenth- and Eighteenth-Century Art* (New York: Harry N. Abrams, n.d.), ch. 5.

This kind of analysis echoes Pieter Geyle's thesis that the division of the northern provinces from the rest of the Netherlands was based on military factors rather than religious ones. He argues that because there were many Catholics in the north, what came to be known as Dutch culture was not, strictly speaking, Protestant. See Geyle, *The Revolt of the Netherlands, 1555–1609* (New York: Barnes and Noble, 1958).

Peter Burke argues that the elites of Catholic Italy and Protestant Holland had quite different structures which encouraged them to promote quite different cultural values and led to distinct patterns of culture in these two areas. His analysis concentrates on political structures and their effects on patterns of culture, but it accounts for political structures in part by examining the religious affiliations of the powerful. See Peter Burke, *Venice and Amsterdam* (London: Temple Smith, 1974).

14. Quentin Bell, *On Human Finery* (New York: Schocken, 1976).

15. Marcuse; Leo Lowenthal, "Historical Perspectives on Popular Culture," *American Journal of Sociology* (1950), 55:323–32.

16. Marshall Sahlins, *Culture and Practical Reason* (Chicago: University of Chicago Press, 1976); Karl Polanyi, *The Great Transformation* (Boston: Beacon Press [1944], 1957); Samuel Popkin, *The Rational Peasant* (Berkeley: University of California Press, 1979).

17. This idea comes from two seemingly contradictory theoretical sources, Sahlins and Karl Marx's *Capital* (New York: Modern Library, 1936). Sahlins argues that a distinctive type of culture developed in the modern West, utilitarianism, and that this culture was the basis for the dialectical materialism that Marx espoused. He makes this point to suggest that practical reasoning has not been the characteristic form of thought in all cultures and historical periods and that materialist interpretations of cultures, as a result, are frequently inappropriate. He suggests (quite convincingly) that the use value of an object is not a characteristic of the object itself but rather a symbolic product, the imposition of a meaning system on the object. He goes on to say that the growth of practical reason, which he associates with the rise of bourgeois society, constituted a cultural shift in the West, the creation of a new sensibility, which he calls materialism.

Sahlins is reacting against Marx (or more accurately Marxist anthropology) when he makes this argument, but his ideas show a debt to Marx and are frequently compatible with Marxist concepts. Marx argues, for instance, that with the development of capitalism there was a shift toward a concern for the market value of objects that had not existed previously. This shift is not unlike the one that Sahlins discusses as the rise of practical reasoning, if one takes the term "value" in the concept "market value" seriously. But there is one important difference. While Marx distinguishes carefully between use value and exchange value, Sahlins does not. Sahlins' concept of practical reason seems to include both, and it is, therefore, somewhat confusing and difficult to apply.

Ironically, Marx is the more careful chronicler of the culture of capitalism, since when Marx describes the transition from feudalism to capitalism he notes a shift from a concern for the use value of objects to an interest in exchange value. This transition is not illuminated by Sahlins' work because he does not consider the utilitarianism of feudal culture and its relationship to his term, "practical reason."

It should be noted here too, that there is empirical evidence as well as theoretical discussion of this cultural shift in the early modern period. Peter Burke, for instance, suggests that the rise of commercial capitalism generated new patterns of culture in Europe, but he is not clear *how* this was accomplished and what kind of culture was created. See Peter Burke, *Popular Culture in Early Modern Europe* (London: Temple Smith, 1978), *Venice and Amsterdam* (London: Temple Smith, 1974), and *Tradition and Innovation in Renaissance Italy* (London: Fontana, 1972). See also Thirsk, *Economic Policy.*

18. This is a complicated argument that will be elaborated later in the text,

but a few basic references can be cited here: Bell; Thorstein Veblen, *The Theory of the Leisure Class* (New York: Mentor [1899], 1953); Norbert Elias, *The Civilizing Process* (New York: Urizen [1939], 1978).

19. See Boies Penrose, *Travel and Discovery in the Renaissance* (Cambridge, Mass.: Harvard University Press, n.d.); Carlo Cipolla, *Guns, Sails, and Empires* (New York: Pantheon, 1965); J. H. Parry, *The Establishment of European Hegemony* (New York: Harper and Row, 1961); Carlo Cipolla, *Clocks and Culture* (London: Collins, 1967); Elizabeth Eisenstein, *The Printing Press as an Agent of Change* (New York: Cambridge University Press, 1979).

20. See Marcel Mauss, *The Gift* (New York: Norton, 1967); Sahlins; Polanyi; Mary Douglas and Baron Isherwood, *World of Goods* (New York: Basic Books, 1979).

21. Marshall McLuhan, *Gutenberg Galaxy* (Toronto: University of Toronto Press, 1962); Eisenstein.

22. Sahlins; Douglas and Isherwood.

23. See, for example, Nicholas Barbon, *A Discourse of Trade 1690* in Jacob Hollander, ed., *A Reprint of Economic Tracts* (Baltimore: Johns Hopkins Press, 1903). For reviews and analyses of this literature, see Joyce Appleby, *Economic Thought and Ideology in Seventeenth-Century England* (Princeton: Princeton University Press, 1978), and William Letwin, *The Origins of Scientific Economics* (Garden City, N. Y.: Doubleday, 1964).

24. Thirsk, *Economic Policy*; Appleby; Charles W. Cole, *French Mercantilism* (New York: Octagon, 1965); P. J. Thomas, *Mercantilism and the East India Trade* (London: Frank Cass [1926], 1963).

25. Cipolla, *Guns, Sails, and Empires.*

26. For a discussion of commercial iconography in Renaissance art, see Baxandall.

27. See for instance, Carlo Cipolla, *The Fontana Economic History of Europe* (London: Collins-Fontana, 1973), vol. 4, no. 1, ch. 3; Fernand Braudel, *The Mediterranean and the Mediterranean World in the Age of Phillip II* (New York: Harper [1949], 1966), vol. 1; Eli Heckscher, *Mercantilism* (New York: Macmillan [1931], 1962), vol. 1.

28. Immanuel Wallerstein, *The Modern World-System* (London: Academic Press, 1976).

29. J. H. Elliott, *The Old World and the New* (Cambridge: Cambridge University Press, 1970).

30. *Ibid.*

31. Stone, *Family and Fortune*; Lynn White, Jr., "The Iconography of *Temperantia* and the Virtuousness of Technology," in *Medieval Religion and Technology* (Berkeley: University of California Press [1969], 1978), pp. 181–204.

32. For an early articulation of this position, see Marc Bloch, *The Historian's Craft* (New York: Vintage Books, 1953), esp. ch. 2.

33. Erwin Panofsky, *Meaning in the Visual Arts* (Garden City, N.J.: Doubleday [1939], 1955), ch. 1.

34. Stone, *Family and Fortune*; Thirsk, *Economic Policy*; Braudel, *The Mediterranean*.

35. See for instance, Panofsky, *Meaning*; Ivins; Gombrich, *Art and Illusion* (Princeton: Princeton University Press [1960], 1972).

36. McLuhan; Lucien Febvre and Henri-Jean Martin, *The Coming of the Book*, trans. David Gerard (London: NLB [1958], 1976); Walter Ong, *Interfaces of the Word* (Ithaca: Cornell University Press, 1977); Alvin Gouldner, *The Dialectic of Ideology and Technology* (New York: Seabury Press, 1976); Eisenstein.

37. Polanyi; Sahlins; Marshall G. Hodgson, *The Venture of Islam* (Chicago: University of Chicago Press, 1974).

38. Polanyi, *The Great Transformation*.

39. Sahlins, *Culture and Practical Reason*.

40. Hodgson, book 5.

41. Veblen; Rosenberg and White; and McKendrick et al., *The Birth of a Consumer Society* (Bloomington: Indiana University Press, 1982).

42. Werner Sombart, *Luxury and Capitalism* (Ann Arbor: University of Michigan [1913], 1967); John Nef, *Cultural Foundations of Industrial Civilization* (New York: Harper, 1958).

43. Weber, *Protestant Ethic*; Emile Durkheim, *Suicide* (New York: Free Press [1930], 1951), and *Division of Labor in Society* (New York: Free Press [1893], 1933); Sombart; and Georg Simmel, *The Philosophy of Money* (London: Routledge and Kegan Paul [1900], 1978);

44. Marx; Sahlins; Simmel.

45. See for instance, Popkin.

2. PICTORIAL PRINTS AND THE GROWTH OF CONSUMERISM: CLASS AND COSMOPOLITANISM IN EARLY MODERN CULTURE

1. Jacob Burckhardt, *Civilization of the Renaissance in Italy* (New York: Oxford University Press, n.d.), p. 194.

2. Michael Baxandall, Frederick Antal and Peter Burke, among others, describe the character of this new materialist culture, focusing primarily on Italy, but also indicating that a similar culture was developing in the North (particularly Burgundy) around the same time. See Michael Baxandall, *Painting and Experience in Fifteenth-Century Italy* (New York: Oxford University Press [1972], 1974); Frederick Antal, *Florentine Painting and its Social Background* (London: Kegan Paul, 1947); Peter Burke, *Tradition and Innovation in Renaissance Italy* (London: Fontana, 1972). While recognizing the materialism in both regions, Burke also notes the differences in the cultures of northern and southern Europe in Peter Burke, *Venice and Amsterdam* (London: Temple Smith, 1974). Antal suggests that the tastes of the common people were not important to the material culture of this period (at least in Italy), but he said this long before the new research on early modern popular culture drew attention to popular artifacts. See Antal; For research on popular culture see Peter Burke, *Popular Culture in Early*

Modern Europe (London: Temple Smith, 1978); and Natalie Davis, *Society and Culture in Early Modern France* (Stanford: Stanford University Press, 1965).

3. It may be that there was greater internationalism in the elite culture of the period than in the popular culture, but there are too many variations in the patterns of culture to state this as a rule. Pins and prints were among the simple artifacts for common consumption that were traded internationally in this period. For other examples, see Joan Thirsk, *Economic Policy and Projects* (Oxford: Clarendon Press, 1978).

4. The significance of the growing consumerism in early modern Europe for explaining more noticed changes in European social life is a matter of some controversy. The authors who have contended that consumerism was a powerful source of change, namely, Werner Sombart, Frederick Antal, John Nef, Lawrence Stone, and Joan Thirsk, have not successfully attracted sustained attention to this idea. See Werner Sombart, *Luxury and Capitalism* (Ann Arbor: University of Michigan Press [1917], 1967); John Nef, *Cultural Foundations of Industrial Civilization* (New York: Harper, 1958); Lawrence Stone, *The Crisis of the Aristocracy* (London: Oxford University Press, 1965); Thirsk, *Economic Policy*; and Antal. Antal and Stone specifically note class conflicts and cultural innovation, but both focus exclusively on elite culture.

While the theorists listed above treat consumerism as a serious social force, many other scholars consider it simply too trivial to be potent. But, ironically, even scholars who would never agree that consumerism per se could act as a prime mover in large-scale patterns of social change, still often find themselves attracted to or persuaded by arguments that assume some variation on that position. Some take for granted that the introduction of some particular consumer good could have notable impact on social life. They are willing to entertain James Flink's ideas about the importance of the automobile to American culture or Elizabeth Eisenstein's arguments about the role of the printed book in the Renaissance or scientific revolution. See J. Flink, *The Car Culture* (Cambridge, Mass.: MIT Press, 1975), and Elizabeth Eisenstein, *The Printing Press as an Agent of Change* (New York: Cambridge University Press, 1979). Others are willing to believe that changes in aggregate consumption could affect the social order by affecting the economy. See William Barber, *History of Economic Thought* (Baltimore: Penguin, 1967), part 4. In early modern Europe, both specific and aggregate changes in consumption seem to have been powerful in shaping social change. The introduction of new kinds of goods made patterns of consumption qualitatively different than they had been in the past. And increased trade in goods stimulated new levels of consumption that fed the trading system and patterns of economic growth. For intuitive recognition of the importance of mass culture to economic growth in the early modern period, see W. G. Hoskins, *Provincial England* (London: Macmillan, 1963), esp. pp. 138–47; B. A. Holderness, *Pre-Industrial England* (London: J. M. Dent, 1976), pp. 83–85, 101; P. S. Crowson, *Tudor Foreign Policy* (New York: St. Martin's Press, 1973), part 3, ch. 4. And for arguments using consumer demand as an economic factor in the development of capitalism, see Phyllis Deane and W. A. Cole, *British Eco-*

nomic Growth, 1688–1959 (Cambridge: Cambridge University Press, 1967); Elizabeth Gilboy, "Demand as a Factor in the Industrial Revolution," in S. Lieberman, *Europe and the Industrial Revolution* (Cambridge: Schenckman, 1972); Dwight Robinson, "The Importance of Fashions in Taste to Business History," *Business History Review* (1963), 37:16–20; Lawrence Stone, *Family and Fortune* (Oxford: Clarendon Press, 1971); Stone, *Crisis of the Aristocracy*; Carlo Cipolla, *Before the Industrial Revolution* (New York: Norton, 1976); and McKendrick et al., *The Birth of a Consumer Society* (Bloomington: Indiana University Press, 1982).

5.   For the forms of these contracts see, Baxandall, part 1, esp. sects. 2, 3 and 4. Karl Marx, *Capital* (New York: Modern Library, 1936), part 1, sect. 4.

6.   Henry Peacham, *The Compleat Gentleman* (London: E. Tyler, 1661), p. 279.

7.   Marshall Sahlins, *Culture and Practical Reason* (Chicago: University of Chicago Press, 1976); Karl Polanyi, *The Great Transformation* (Boston: Beacon Press [1944], 1957).

8.   Burke, *Popular Culture*; J. Huizinga, *The Waning of the Middle Ages* (New York: Anchor, 1954), ch. 11 and pp. 64–66, 250, 252; Urban T. Holmes, *Daily Living in the Twelfth Century* (Madison: University of Wisconsin Press, 1952), pp. 112–13; Mark Girouard, *Life in the English Country House* (New Haven: Yale University Press, 1978), p. 10. Girouard describes the integration of the medieval household and contrasts it with the dual household of the early modern period.

9.   Henri Pirenne, *A History of Europe* (New York: University Books, 1936), pp. 60–64, 224–25; Max Weber, *General Economic History*, trans. F. Knight (New York: Collier [1920], 1961), esp. pp.110–14.

10.   J. Huizinga, *Men and Ideas* (New York: Meridian Books, 1959), p. 18; Burke, *Popular Culture*; Huizinga, *Waning of the Middle Ages*, pp.18–19.

11.   See for instance, Lynn White, Jr., *Medieval Technology and Social Change* (New York: Oxford University Press, 1962); Marc Bloch, *Land and Work in Medieval Europe* (Berkeley: University of California Press, 1967); Lucien Febvre and Henri-Jean Martin, *The Coming of the Book*, trans. David Gerard (London: NLB [1958], 1976). Compare with Huizinga, *Waning of the Middle Ages*, pp. 200–25.

12.   White, *Medieval Technology*, pp. 129–34.

13.   Burke, *Popular Culture*.

14.   Burke, *Popular Culture*; Pirenne; David Knowles, *The Evolution of Medieval Thought* (New York: Vintage, 1962); Carlo Cipolla, *Literacy and Development in the West* (London: Penguin, 1969), pp. 52–53.

15.   John Gloag, *Social History of Furniture Design* (New York: Crown, 1966), chs. 4 and 6; Maurice Tomlin, *English Furniture* (London: Faber and Faber), chs. 1, 5, 6, and 7; Holmes; Olive Cook, *The English Country House* (New York: Putnam, 1974), pp. 13–14, 162–63. Some historians might argue that the most elaborate meals were prepared in the Renaissance when medieval

norms of hospitality were strong but the material basis for conspicuous displays was much greater. This is the period that Lawrence Stone describes in *Crisis of the Aristocracy.* See also, Girouard, ch. 4. But Girouard also indicates the growing complexity of the architecture for entertainment in eighteenth-century homes (see ch. 7).

16. Ruth Pike, *Enterprise and Adventure* (New York: Cornell University Press, 1966); Cipolla, *Before the Industrial Revolution,* pp. 194–204. Burke, *Popular Culture,* ch. 9. Antal, ch. 2, esp. 48–53.

17. Because Mary Douglas and Baron Isherwood treat consumption as primarily a symbolic activity—a form of communication, a way of marking social location, and/or a means for controlling information—they have already drawn attention to the expressive meanings of goods to consumers. They have shown how consumption can be used as a symbolic resource to delineate and maintain social relations. Mary Douglas and Baron Isherwood, *The World of Goods* (New York: Basic Books, 1979). See also Mihaly Csikszentmihalyi and Eugene Rochberg-Halton, *The Meaning of Things* (New York: Cambridge University Press, 1981). Similarly, Marxist students of capitalist culture, such as Stewart Ewen and Herbert Marcuse, have also pointed to the expressive role of goods. See Stewart Ewen, *Captains of Consciousness* (New York: McGraw-Hill, 1976), and Herbert Marcuse, *One-Dimensional Man* (Boston: Beacon Press, 1964). Consumption, by their analyses, is driven by the dissatisfactions born of capitalist repression. As a result, while consumers may find amassing goods momentarily pleasurable, they cannot find it satisfying because it does not meet the need that inspired it. All it does is reinforce the pattern of *seeking* satisfaction in consumer goods and thereby ratify the values of the capitalist system.

In its fundamental structure, Douglas and Isherwood's model of consumer behavior is surprisingly similar to the Marxist one; it also describes consumption as a cultural pattern designed to support existing social relations. But their anthropological analysis differs from the Marxist one in other essential ways; Douglas and Isherwood say nothing about the value or legitimacy of the social systems they describe, and they seek as a theoretical goal some fundamental, or universal model of consumption rather than a theory relating consumption to given historical conditions. They are structuralists from the idealist rather than materialist school.

This does not mean that Douglas and Isherwood have no sense of history. On the contrary, they worry that historical differences in consumption may be too profound to justify their holding them constant (as they must to fashion a universal theory). They suggest, at least, that the differences between patterns of consumption in advanced industrialized societies and those in simpler societies and subcultures may be great enough to limit the usefulness of a theory, such as theirs, which is based on ethnographic evidence. In this way, they echo but do not consider in any depth the theoretical point that Sahlins makes in *Culture and Practical Reason*: that the importance and complexity of consumption increased enormously in the West with the shift to a materialist culture. But they may be correct in suggesting that the symbolic significance of consumption is essential to its manifestations in all societies. Their findings, along with the work by Marxists studying contemporary consumption, provide some support for this view.

Ironically, these theories, in spite of being most useful for dissecting the social dimensions of consumption, are also the ones least likely to explain the role of human agency in these economic activities. Because they must concentrate on the patterns of social *control* that shape the decisions of consumers and the producers of consumer goods, they tend to downplay human volition. They present an image of consumers as rather passive pawns in the hands of structural forces. They lack the sense of human agency that, for instance, Barber and others say Keynes sees in consumption. See Barber, part 4. This tendency is likely to be exacerbated in studies of stable social orders where the levels of compliance with social norms may be great enough and consistent enough to minimize the appearance of agency (or choice) in patterns of consumption. But attention to human agency is particularly important for describing consumption in periods of fundamental socioeconomic change, such as the early modern period. In periods of socioeconomic crisis (such as the depression, which was so central to Keynes's theoretical concerns), reality construction is less constrained by tradition, and therefore, can be potentially more consequential to social change. Since the early modern era was a similarly volatile period, attention to volition is important for any analysis of consumption.

18. Douglas McMurtrie, *The Book* (New York: Oxford University Press, 1943), ch. 8; N. F. Blake, *Caxton: England's First Publisher* (New York: Harper and Row, 1976), pp. 1–3; S. H. Steinberg, *Five Hundred Years of Printing* (New York: Criterion, 1959), pp. 114–15.

19. Carl Zigrosser, *The Book of Fine Prints* (New York: Crown, 1937), pp. 96–97. Some printed illustrations also underwent a transformation in meaning at about the same time. See for instance, Helen B. Mules, *Flowers in Books and Drawings* (New York: Morgan Library, 1980), introduction.

20. For prints and printing see Blake; McMurtrie; and for prints as art, see Zigrosser; Arnold Hauser, *Social History of Art* (New York: Vintage, 1951), vol. 2, ch. 10.

21. Burke, *Popular Culture*, p. 270.

22. Thirsk, *Economic Policy*, p. 3.

23. *Ibid.*, ch. 4.

24. *Ibid.*; Weber, *Protestant Ethic*; Blake, chs. 8 and 9.

25. Samuel Popkin, *The Rational Peasant* (Berkeley: University of California Press, 1979); Thirsk, *Economic Policy*, ch. 1.

26. For a discussion of the relationship between mass and popular culture, see Norman Cantor and M. Werthman, *The History of Popular Culture* (London: Collier-Macmillan, 1968); Bernard Rosenberg and David M. White, *Mass Culture* (New York: Free Press, 1957); George Lewis, *Side-Saddle on the Golden Calf* (Pacific Palisades: Goodyear Publishing, 1972); and Burke, *Popular Culture*, ch. 9. Prints were the first form of mass culture, developing before the machines for mass producing ribbons or stockings (see Hoskins, pp. 78–85; Thirsk, *Eco-*

nomic Policy, pp. 109–10). Coins were produced much earlier but were not intended to be used primarily for decoration or communication. In this sense, they do not seem to be a cultural form in the same way that prints are. Some lead "coins" were made as souvenirs for pilgrims during the Middle Ages. They seem closer to a form of mass culture because they were produced using stamps (i.e., were mass produced) and kept for their symbolic value. But they were not mass culture in the sense of being produced for wide distribution. They were made locally and sold in pilgrimage areas. Pilgrims took them to all parts of Europe, but did not set up a widespread market system for their sale. Thus, they seem more a precursor of mass culture than an early example.

Prints were distinctive in being designed and produced, by a mass production technique, for wide distribution. They were made to be sold throughout Europe, and made cheap enough to find buyers even among the less affluent. I have not been able to find prices for the most inexpensive woodblock prints to support this conjecture, but I have found other evidence. Dürer's journals indicate that he bought prints in the Netherlands that cost him about the same amount as a light meal. See Albrecht Dürer, *Records of the Journeys to Venice and the Low Countries*, ed. Roger Fry (Boston: Merrymount Press, 1913), esp. p. 40. But presumably he was in the market for the best rather than the cheapest prints so this does not tell us who could afford cheap prints. Natalie Davis in *Society and Culture*, p. 197, contends that sixteenth-century French almanacs designed for a mass audience were cheap enough that rural peasants could afford them. Sandra Hindman demonstrates that Dutch illustrated books of the same general period were also within reach of low-level artisans; see *Pen to Press* (Baltimore: Johns Hopkins University Press, 1977), p. 199. The much less expensive single-sheet woodblock prints, then, would be well within the budget of low-level urban artisans and rural peasants. This is also suggested by the fact that engravings sold in the seventeenth century in England could cost as little as two or three pence. See Leona Rostenberg, *English Publishers in the Graphic Arts, 1599–1700* (New York: Burt Franklin, 1963). Kunzle specifically argues that sixteenth-century pictorial prints were made for a popular audience. See David Kunzle, *The Early Comic Strip* (Berkeley: University of California Press, 1973), introduction.

27.   For a description of the development of the new draperies, see Barry Supple, *Commercial Crisis and Change in England, 1600–1642* (Cambridge: Cambridge University Press, 1964), pp. 155–57. For a description of the Dutch development of the new draperies, see Charles Wilson, *The Dutch Republic* (New York: McGraw-Hill, 1968), pp. 30–31. For comments on luxury goods and the rise of merchant/artisans, see Ralph Davis, *Rise of the Atlantic Economy* (Ithaca: Cornell University Press, 1973), p. 23; and for a description of the proliferation of material culture, see Burke, *Popular Culture*, ch. 9.

28.   Weber, *Protestant Ethic*, pp. 110–14.

29.   Hauser, vol. 2, ch. 3. Burke, *Tradition and Innovation*, pp. 108–23, 137–39, and 335–48; Baxandall, pp. 3–14. Elizabeth Eisenstein in *The Printing Press* associates the development of the artist as a social type in the Renaissance with the growth of the printed word. She reasons that printed gossip/biographical in-

formation made celebrity possible, stimulating an interest in individuality among culture producers because their individuality could be recorded and disseminated.

This analysis ignores the economic factors that permitted some culture producers to distinguish themselves from the bulk of artisans in the Renaissance and the dualism which was prerequisite to the definition of the artist as an intellectual/conceptual genius. Eisenstein's basic association of the growth of the artist with print could be enhanced by inclusion of these factors. My argument here shows how the development of the graphic arts participated in a Renaissance redefinition of culture production, again associating print with art. Although Eisenstein would deny it because she rejects cognitive analysis of print effects, it is also possible that the dualism mentioned above was, at least in part, stimulated by the further decontextualization of thought from talk that Alvin Gouldner identifies with print. See Gouldner, *The Dialectic of Ideology and Technology* (New York: Seabury Press, 1976), pp. 39–45; also Hauser, vol. 2, ch. 3; Alfred Von Martin, *Sociology of the Renaissance* (New York: Oxford University Press, 1944).

30.   A. Mumby and I. Norrie, *Publishing and Bookselling* (London: Jonathan Cape, 1930), ch. 2; Harold Innis, *Empire and Communications* (Toronto: University of Toronto Press [1950], 1972), pp. 141–42; David Pottinger, *The French Book Trade in the Ancien Regime, 1500–1791* (Cambridge, Mass.: Harvard University Press, 1958), ch. 15; Febvre and Martin, ch. 5; and Rudolf Hirsch, *Printing, Selling, and Reading, 1450–1550* (Wiesbaden: Otto Harrassowitz, 1967), pp. 27–28.

31.   Weber, *Protestant Ethic*; J. L. and B. Hammond, *The Rise of Modern Industry* (New York: Harcourt, Brace and World, 1926); Burke, *Tradition and Innovation*, pp. 61–62. Interestingly, you find the greatest flourishing of printing in Venice where the painter's guild was most restrictive. See Burke, *Venice and Amsterdam*, p. 77. Is it possible that guild policy there helped to make prospective painters more willing than most to work for printers under conditions that favored growth of the print business?

32.   Pottinger, ch. 12 and pp. 318–20; Marjorie Plant, *The English Book Trade* (London: Allen and Unwin [1939], 1974); Hirsch, pp. 27–29; Febvre and Martin, ch. 4; Leonardas Gerulaitis, *Printing and Publishing in Fifteenth-Century Venice* (Chicago: American Library Association, 1976), ch. 2; and Curt Bühler, *The Fifteenth-Century Book* (Philadelphia: University of Pennsylvania Press, 1960), pp. 56–57.

33.   For a discussion of regulation and control over projects, see Thirsk, *Economic Policy*, ch. 5.

34.   Colin Clair, *Christopher Plantin* (London: Cassell, 1960), pp. 8–9 and ch. 2.

35.   Hirsch, chs. 3 and 6; Pottinger, chs. 4 and 8 and p. 318; Gerulaitis, ch. 3; Febvre and Martin, pp. 239–47; George Putnam, *Books and Their Makers During the Middle Ages* (New York: Hillary House, 1962), part 3. For a discussion of censorship in France and the Netherlands, see Clair, ch. 2. Censorship in England under Charles I is described in Mumby and Norrie, pp. 96–99. And a case of the persecution of an engraver, Arnold Nicolai, is mentioned by Clair, p. 184.

36. William Ivins, *Prints and Visual Communication* (Cambridge, Mass.: MIT Press, 1953); Pottinger, chs. 4, 12 and 13; Hirsch, ch. 3. Some division of labor existed in medieval book production. Illustrations tended to be made in different shops than the ones where texts were copied. But there was greater breakdown of these processes when the printing press made the technical process of printing books quite different from preparing the text or picture to be put into book form. See Febvre and Martin, ch. 1. Farquhar also finds some division of labor within manuscript decoration/illustration but he is not clear whether this occurred before or after the development of print. See Hindman, ch. 1.

37. Hauser.

38. Baxandall, esp. pp. 86–94.

39. Max Friedländer, *Early Netherlandish Painting* (London: Phaidon, 1956); Detroit Institute of the Arts, *Flanders in the Fifteenth Century* (Detroit: Institute of the Arts, 1960); Harold Janson, *History of Art* (Englewood Cliffs, N.J.: Prentice-Hall, 1962), part 3, chs. 2, 3, 5; Hauser, vol. 2, chs. 1–4; and Von Martin, ch. 2; Erwin Panofsky, *Meaning in the Visual Arts* (Garden City, N.Y.: Doubleday, 1955), chs. 3 and 6. Antal attributes the rationality in fifteenth-century Florentine painting to commercial interests. See sect. 2, ch. 2. He even suggests that the interest in classical culture that developed in the Renaissance was a reflection of bouregois interests, based on the fact that Roman law was more supportive of trade than Church regulations. See pp. 45–46.

40. Ivins, chs. 1 and 2; Zigrosser, ch. 2.

41. Kunzle.

42. Antal, pp. 177–79.

43. Antal, p. 123.

44. Zigrosser, ch. 2; McMurtrie, ch. 16; H. O. Lehman-Haupt, *Gutenberg and the Master of the Playing Cards* (New Haven: Yale University Press, 1966); Clapham; Pottinger, pp. 37 and 313; Febvre and Martin, ch. 3, sect. 4; Bühler; Alfred Pollard, *Early Illustrated Books* (London: Kegan Paul [1893], 1917), ch. 8.

45. Lehman-Haupt; Kunzle, pp. 19–39; Zigrosser, ch. 2; Michael Clapham, "Printing," in Charles Singer, et al., *A History of Technology* (New York: Oxford University Press, 1957), vol. 3, ch. 15; McMurtrie, chs. 7 and 8; and Ivins, esp. pp. 19, 27–28, and 168–69.

46. Ivins, p. 28.

47. Blake, pp. 129–55 and 160; Richard Muther, *German Book Illustration of the Gothic Period and Early Renaissance*, trans. Ralph Shaw (Metuchen, N.J.: Scarecrow, 1972), pp. 1–57, esp. ch. 7; Svend Dahl, *History of the Book* (Metuchen, N.J.: Scarecrow, 1968), pp. 98–102. The importance of plants in decorating manuscripts and the frequent use of inaccurate representation in many early woodcuts of plants is demonstrated in Mules, nos. 1–50. See particularly no. 38 and plate no. 6 for a description of the mandrake in the *Herbarium*.

48. Hauser, vol. 2, pp. 52–84; Ivins, ch. 1.

49. Lehman-Haupt; Febvre and Martin, pp. 94–95, 100; McMurtrie, chs. 8 and 22; Bühler; Karen Reeds, "Renaissance Humanism and Botany," *Anals of Science* (1976), 33:519–42. Reeds shows how classical ideas about botany at first

inhibited this trend but did not win out over the need for more accurate pictures.

50.   Ivins, chs. 1, 2 and 8; Pottinger, p. 317; Febvre and Martin, ch. 8; McMurtrie, ch. 17; Bühler; G. R. Crone, *Maps and Their Makers* (London: Hutchinson Library, 1953), ch. 8; W. E. May and L. Holder, *A History of Marine Navigation* (New York: Norton, 1973), pp. 182–84; N. H. Thrower, *Maps and Man* (Englewood Cliffs, N.J.: Prentice-Hall, 1972), pp. 55–60; George Sarton, *Six Wings* (Bloomington: Indiana University Press, 1957), chs. 3, 4, and 5; Eisenstein, vol. 2, ch. 1.

51.   Gouldner, ch. 10; for discussions of utilitarianism, see also Sahlins, ch. 5; and for material on naturalism in prints, see Ivins and Reeds.

52.   Ivins, pp. 47 and 49.

53.   Febvre and Martin, pp. 100–1; Ivins, pp. 65–68.

54.   See Ivins, pp. 65–68 and ch. 8. A similar standardization in the form for presenting the printed word also developed in this period, according to Walter Ong, *Interfaces of the Word* (Ithaca: Cornell University Press, 1977) and McMurtrie, ch. 23. This standardization seemed to solve some early typographical problems faced by publishers in trying to make print easily readable.

55.   Ivins, chs. 3–4.

56.   George Putnam, *Books and Their Makers in the Middle Ages* (New York: Hillary House, 1962), ch. 7; H. T. Musper, *Albrecht ·Dürer* (New York: Abrams, 1966), pp. 9–10 and 33; Zigrosser, pp. 43–44; McMurtrie, p. 252; Erwin Panofsky, *Albrecht Dürer* (New York: Oxford University Press, 1948), vol. 1, pp. 4–5, 18–21; Muther, ch. 8.

57.   Musper, pp. 9–10; Zigrosser, pp. 43–44; Panofsky, *Dürer*, pp. 18–21.

58.   Musper, pp. 28 and 33; Panofsky, *Dürer*, vol. 1, pp. 5, 24–25.

59.   Musper, p. 10.

60.   Musper, pp. 10–14, 28; Zigrosser, p. 44; McMurtrie, p. 252; Panofsky, *Dürer*, vol. 1, p. 8 and chs. 2 and 3.

61.   Dürer, p. 40. Dürer also mentions on p. 40 that he paid 1 stiver for fruit and bread for a meal, and on p. 42 he says he exchanged 24 stivers for 2 florins. On p. 53 he records buying someone else's print for 1 stiver. These notes suggest something of the value of prints as commodities in general in this period and give us a sense of the value of his work in particular. The general point that he used his prints to finance his trips is made in other places as well. Musper, p. 13; Putnam, ch. 7.

62.   Musper, p. 29. Panofsky, *Dürer*, ch. 5.

63.   Musper, p. 57.

64.   Panofsky, *Dürer*.

65.   Ivins, chs. 2–3. The fifteenth and sixteenth centuries saw numerous attempts to codify practices for drawing the human form. The interest in developing formulas for representation was shared by fine artists and print designers alike. This is evidenced in Dürer's writings in Panofsky, *Dürer*, vol. 1, pp. 273–84. It represented what Gombrich refers to as the illusionism of Renaissance art in his *Art and Illusion* (Princeton: Princeton University Press [1960], 1972). This illusionism is certainly part of the technique that Dürer refers to when he is dis-

cussing what makes work attractive to uneducated audiences. But the technical virtuosity in his prints suggests that his concern about how one makes objects *seem* lifelike (illusionism) is only part of his project in making a print. The *technique* for using the medium was also an important element in the work. For the value of developing formulas for collective art-making, see Howard Becker, "Art as Collective Action," *American Sociological Review* (December 1974), 39:767–76.

66. Musper, p. 45.

67. For a description of this shift in the value of prints, see Ivins. For a discussion of the relative mobility of artisans and the relationship between the spread of print and the movement of artisans, see Cipolla, *Before the Industrial Revolution*, pp. 174–81. For a discussion of elite travel and the dissemination of styles that also provides some evidence of the role of print in encouraging this process, see J. Goag, *English Furniture*, 6th ed. (London: Adams and Black [1934], 1973), pp. 10–13, 52–53. Gardens were among the forms that became distinctively cosmopolitan in this period. See J. Hunt and P. Willis, *The Genius of Place* (London: Paul Elek, 1975), pp. 57–67; Richardson Wright, *The Story of Gardening* (New York: Dover, 1934), pp. 198–99.

68. Agnes Arber, *Herbals* (Cambridge: Cambridge University Press, 1953), ch. 4 and p.189; Mules.

69. See Rostenberg.

70. For reuse of German books see Muther, pp. 1–55; for similar activities by Caxton, see Blake, pp. 135–39; see also, Arber, pp. 26, 50, and 189–202; Pollard, p. 41; Rostenberg, p. 31; and Wilfrid Blunt, *The Art of Botanical Illustration* (London: Collins, 1950), pp. 70–74, 42, and 43; Sarton, pp. 135–41; Mules, esp. nos. 46–65.

71. Janson, p. 421.

72. Fernand Braudel, *The Mediterranean and the Mediterranean World in the Age of Phillip II* (New York: Harper [1949], 1966), part 2, pp. 760–61. Stone, *Family and Fortune*, part 1, chs. 1–2; see also Thirsk, *Economic Policy*, ch. 1.

73. See Ivins for a discussion of the international character of the Baroque and its regional variations; see also Victor Tapie, *The Age of Grandeur* (New York: Praeger, 1966). Tapie stresses regional variation but also concedes that there was a strong internationalism in the Baroque. See also John Martin, *Baroque* (New York: Harper and Row, 1977); and particularly Julius Held and Donald Posner, *Seventeenth- and Eighteenth-Century Art* (New York: Abrams, n. d.), introduction.

For discussions of Rubens and prints, see Ruth Magurn, ed., *The Letters of Peter Paul Rubens* (Cambridge: Harvard University Press, 1955), pp. 50–51, 87–88; Roger Avermaete, *Rubens and His Times* (London: Allen and Unwin, 1968), pp. 95–96 and 166–67; Zigrosser, ch. 4.

The fact that Rubens and other seventeenth-century artists used prints might suggest to some readers that prints were not so distinctively a form of mass culture in this period. After all, there were some fine artists who used prints as a major artistic medium (like Rembrandt). But prints of this sort did not get mass produced and sold; they were commercial failures. Most of the prints that had

art subjects and were commercially successful (like Rubens' prints) were reproductions rather than productions. Ivins calls them a genre of informational or
useful print rather than art prints (chs. 1 and 2).

This idea is underscored by the fact that prints were not collected as art until
the late seventeenth century and not collected routinely until the eighteenth century. Before that time art reproductions might be used for decoration as well as
information, but they were not taken as a serious form of elite culture. See
Hauser, vol. 2, ch. 10; and Zigrosser, pp. 97–98.

74.   For discussions of international influences on English furniture see, for
instance, Allen, vols. 1 and 2; Cook; A. F. Kendrick, *English Decorative Fabrics
of the Sixteenth to Eighteenth Centuries* (London: F. Lewis, 1934); Francis
Lenygon, *The Decoration and Furniture of English Mansions During the Seventeenth and Eighteenth Centuries* (London: T. Werner Laurie, 1909); and on costume see *Vecellio's Renaissance Costume Book* (New York: Dover [1598], 1977).

75.   Jan Van Gelder suggests that Dutch *humanists* showed a "peculiar ethno-
centrism" in this period. See Van Gelder, "Two Aspects of the Dutch Baroque,"
in James Ackerman et al., *Seventeenth-Century Art in Flanders, and Holland*
(London: Garland Publishing, 1976), p. 447. Thus, Dutch interest in the "little
tradition" may have been more a consequence of the growth of humanist ideas
than a rejection of them. The other and generally held view on Protestantism
and Dutch painting with some criticism of this perspective is presented by Seymour Slive in "Notes on the Relationship of Protestantism to Seventeenth-Century Dutch painting" in Ackerman et al., pp. 23–36; see also, Hauser, vol. 2, ch.
10.

76.   See Madlyn Kahr, *Dutch Painting in the Seventeenth Century* (New York:
Harper and Row, 1978), esp. pp. 198–203; Hauser, vol. 3; Friedländer.

77.   See Blunt, ch. 10, esp. pp. 117–18; Charles Mackay, *Extraordinary Popular Delusions and the Madness of Crowds* (New York: Harmony Books [1852],
1980), ch. 3.

78.   See Held and Posner, pp. 147–49, 187–89, 226, 320–21, and 368–69;
Burke, *Tradition and Innovation*, pp. 190–91; Slive also indicates the number of
Catholics who continued to live and paint in Holland in this period, showing the
lack of association of these "Dutch" styles with Protestantism.

79.   Whitney, p. 17. For more general background on emblem books, see
John Landwehr, *Dutch Emblem Books: A Bibliography* (Utrecht: Haentjens Deller
and Gurnbert, 1962), esp. p. viii, where he presents statistics on the production
of these books in different European countries from the sixteenth through the
eighteenth centuries.

80.   Steinberg, pp. 133–34.

81.   See F. Saxl and R. Witkower, *British Art and the Mediterranean* (Oxford:
Oxford University Press, 1948), pp. 34–44; Allen, vol. 1, ch. 1; Cook, chs. 3 and
4, esp. pp. 61, 66, 110, 112, 118, and 124 which discuss publications that influenced seventeenth-century British houses. She sees greater effects of publication
on architecture in the eighteenth century. See pp. 194 and 202. The lack of con-
gruence between religion and political lines at Dutch independence is described

by Pieter Geyle in *The Revolt of the Netherlands, 1555–1609* (New York: Barnes and Noble, 1958), ch. 5, sect. b. Geyle makes a point of showing that the culture in Holland was not entirely Protestant, but he also describes it as innovative. For a clearer picture of its distinctive character see Burke, *Venice and Amsterdam*, esp. ch. 2. There Burke indicates the role of the clergy in keeping Italy culturally more conservative than in the Netherlands. He suggests that the lack of power for the clergy in the Netherlands rather than an absence of Catholics may account for the cultural differences.

82.   For discussions of southern influences in Rembrandt's style, see Wilhelm Valentiner, "Rembrandt and the Latin School," and Fritz Saxl, "Rembrandt and Classical Antiquity" in Ackerman et al., pp. 119–43, 189–211; see also, Kahr, ch. 6.

83.   For the uses of herbals as sources of embroidery patterns, see Thomasina Beck, *Embroidered Gardens* (New York: Viking, 1978); For Evelyn's writings, see John Evelyn, *Sylva or Discourse on Forest Trees* (London: John Martyn, 1679). See also Gloag, *Social History*, pp. 27 and 40; W. C. Hazlitt, *Gleanings in Old Garden Literature* (London: Elliot Stock, 1904), pp. 37–38. For a discussion of the role of Alexandrian hydraulics on grottoes in mannerist gardens, see Roy Strong, *The Renaissance Garden in England* (London: Thames and Hudson, 1979), pp. 78–83.

84.   Michael Hechter, *Internal Colonialism* (Berkeley: University of California Press, 1975); Burke, *Popular Culture*, ch. 8, esp. 220–22.

85.   Steinberg, pp. 211–12; Gerulaitis, ch. 3, esp. pp. 36–37; Mumby and Norrie, pp. 88–89.

86.   Mumby and Norrie, pp. 48–50, 96–100. For a discussion of ficticious imprints as an economic and political opportunity for non-privileged printers in England, and particularly for a discussion of John Wolfe's career, see Denis B. Woodfield, *Surreptitious Printing in England 1550–1640* (New York: Bibliographic Society of America, 1973), chs. 3 and 4 and pp. 8–9.

3. A NEW WORLD-PICTURE: MAPS AS CAPITAL GOODS FOR THE MODERN WORLD SYSTEM

1.   W. E. May and L. Holder, *A History of Marine Navigation* (New York: Norton, 1973), p. 15.

2.   Fernand Braudel, *Afterthoughts on Material Civilization and Capitalism* (Baltimore: Johns Hopkins University Press, 1976).

3.   J. H. Perry suggests that chartmaking became commonplace in the thirteenth century, but was not useful for sailing out of sight of land until the fifteenth. See *The Establishment of European Hegemony, 1415–1715* (New York: Harper and Row, 1961), pp. 6–98. See also E. G. Taylor, *The Haven-Finding Art* (New York: Elsevier, 1971), pp. 98, 103–13. But D. W. Waters suggests that most medieval pilots used only their own notes (or rutters) along with experience

to guide their ships even in the fifteenth century. See *The Art of Navigation* (New Haven: Yale University Press, 1958), pp. 3–15. Waters also mentions that sailors had an active *distrust* of charts and thus limited their use. Braudel describes the "coasting" practices of navigators along traditional sea routes even in the sixteenth century; see Fernand Braudel, *The Mediterranean and the Mediterranean World in the Age of Phillip II* (New York: Harper [1949], 1966), vol. 1, pp. 105–8. Wilhelm Lang also described the existence of early road maps, but mentions their lack of general use until their publication. See "The Augsburg Travel Guide of 1563 and the Erlinger Road Map of 1524," *Imago Mundi* (1950), 7:85–88. For a description of the earliest road maps, see Herbert Krüger, "Erhard Etzlaub's *Ronweg* Map and its Dating in the Holy Year of 1500," *Imago Mundi* (1951), 8:17–26. See also Boies Penrose, *Travel and Discovery in the Renaissance* (Cambridge, Mass.: Harvard University Press, n.d.), ch. 16. Norman Thrower, *The Compleat Plattmaker* (Berkeley: University of California Press, 1979). See also Waters, p. 9, for British attempts to monopolize this information. D. B. Quinn, in *England and the Discovery of America* (New York: Knopf, 1974), p. 14, suggests that much information was kept secret by British fishermen in order to protect their livelihoods.

4. Most studies that evaluate the effects of printing in the sixteenth and seventeenth centuries refer only to the impact of printing on *culture*. Eisenstein, for instance, looks at the role of printing in the Reformation and the growth of modern science. While she notes the importance of print in disseminating information that had once been the monopoly of a small group, she emphasizes the cultural consequences of this pattern. Even when she discusses cartography during the sixteenth and seventeenth centuries, she is interested in its intellectual aspects and effects, i.e., how more accurate documents of the world's surface affected scientific thought. She seems less concerned that the widespread publication of geographical information contributed to *political and economic* changes in Europe that were of equal, if not greater, importance. See Elizabeth Eisenstein, *The Printing Press as an Agent of Change* (New York: Cambridge University Press, 1979), vols. 1 and 2, esp. vol. 2, pp. 514–18. See also Alvin Gouldner, *The Dialectic of Ideology and Technology* (New York: Seabury Press, 1976); F. A. Mumby and I. Norrie, *Publishing and Bookselling* (London: Jonathan Cape, 1930); Lucien Febvre and Henri-Jean Martin, *The Coming of the Book*, trans. David Gerard (London: NLB [1958], 1976); Walter Ong, *Interfaces of the Word* (Ithaca: Cornell University Press, 1977); Marshall McLuhan, *Gutenberg Galaxy* (Toronto: University of Toronto Press, 1962).

5. See Parry, *Establishment of Hegemony*, ch. 1; Penrose, pp. 268–74; Carlo Cipolla, *Guns, Sails, and Empires* (New York: Pantheon, 1965); David Quinn, *North America From Earliest Discovery to First Settlements* (New York: Harper and Row, 1975), ch. 4.

6. John Evelyn, *Navigation and Commerce* (London: Benjamin Tooke, 1674), pp. 9 and 15.

7. See Richard Hakluyt, *Principle Navigations* (London: George Bishop, 1598–

1600); John Huighen van Linschoten, *His Dicourse of Voyages into Ye Easte and West Indies* (London: John Wolfe, 1598).

8. Immanuel Wallerstein, *The Modern World-System* (London: Academic Press, 1974), ch. 4.

9. *Ibid.*; Braudel, *The Mediterranean*, part 2, pp. 657–61.

10. Wallerstein, ch. 4.

11. Parry, *Establishment of Hegemony*, pp. 7–12 and 27–32; Taylor, *Haven-Finding Art*, pp. 156–57; Frederico Marjay, *Dom Henrique the Navigator* (Lisbon: Quincentenary Commemorations, 1960), esp. ch. 7; Wallerstein, ch. 1, esp. pp. 38–60.

12. See Parry, *Establishment of Hegemony*, ch. 1; Penrose, ch. 3; Quinn, *North America*, ch. 4.

13. See Ralph Davis, *The Rise of the Atlantic Economy* (Ithaca: Cornell University Press, 1973), pp. 2–6; Penrose, pp. 268–73. See also Quinn, *England*, p. 84; Cipolla, pp. 74–81; Parry, *Establishment of Hegemony*, pp. 22–26.

14. Cipolla, *Guns, Sails, and Empires*, pp. 74–81; J. H. Parry, *European Reconnaisance* (New York: Walker, 1968), pp. 19–20; Braudel, *The Mediterranean*, pp. 224–29; Penrose, pp. 268–74.

15. Cipolla, *Guns, Sails, and Empires*. Quinn suggests that the British may have preceded the Spanish in reaching America by moving west from their northern fisheries. The British were able to take long voyages of discovery in the late fifteenth and early sixteenth centuries, as Cabot's first voyage suggests. But the British did not remain in the running for early expansion because Cabot's voyage made it clear that they had not found a route to Cathay. Thus, the information that the British had gathered during these early voyages was not as valuable as it had originally been thought to be. The timber and furs in the land they found were not so valuable or so easily transported as gold or spices. In addition, the British did not monpolize the information. Cabot was an Italian who had been in Spain prior to his arrival in England and seems to have made little effort to keep his knowledge out of the hands of the Spanish and Italians in England. As a result, the information gathered during his travels appears in Spanish sources, such as the early sixteenth-century map by Juan de la Cosa. See Quinn, *North America*, chs. 1–7 and Quinn, *England*, pp. 112–30. The French efforts to go around Africa were even more disastrous and undermined by a lack of geographical information.

16. Norman Thrower, *Maps and Man* (Englewood Cliffs, N.J.: Prentice-Hall, 1972), p. 47.

17. Penrose, pp. 18–19; G. R. Crone, *Maps and Their Makers* (London: Hutchinson Library, 1953), ch. 3; Raymond Lister, *Antique Maps and their Cartographers* (London: G. Bell, 1970), pp. 20–21.

18. See R. V. Tooley, *Maps and Map-Makers* (New York: Crown [1949], 1978), p. 12; Lister, pp. 16–17.

19. Penrose, pp. 274–75; Febvre and Martin, p. 259; J. H. Elliott, *The Old World and the New* (Cambridge: Cambridge University Press, 1970).

20. Quoted in Parry, *European Reconaissance*, pp. 54–55.

21. *Ibid.*, pp. 19–20; Taylor, *Haven-Finding Art*, pp. 140–41, 156–58.

22. Penrose, pp. 274–75; see also Gonzales de Reparaz Ruiz, "The Topographical Maps of Portugal and Spain in the Sixteenth Century," *Imago Mundi* (1950), 7:75–82; Febvre and Martin, pp. 278–79.

23. Penrose, chs. 16 and 17; Ruth Pike, *Enterprise and Adventure* (Ithaca: Cornell University Press, 1966).

24. Crone, pp. 77–78; Penrose, pp. 244–45.

25. Penrose, pp. 257, 277, 294, 305.

26. Parry, *European Reconaissance*, pp. 151–71; Penrose, p. 290.

27. Penrose, pp. 244, 257, 291–304; Ruiz, p. 70; Crone, pp. 82–83; Quinn, *England*, pp. 98–100.

28. Richard Hakluyt, *Divers Voyages*, ed. Irwin Blacker (New York: Viking [1582–1600], 1965), pp. 333–34.

29. Crone, pp. 93–95; Penrose, p. 250.

30. For information about the profitability of publishing maps, see Penrose, pp. 260, 304–6; Febvre and Martin, pp. 278–79.

31. See Febvre and Martin, ch. 4 and pp. 259, 278–82.

32. Febvre and Martin take this argument from Elliott, *The Old World and the New*, chs. 1 and 2.

33. Eisenstein, pp. 113–26, 512–18.

34. Penrose, chs. 16 and 17.

35. Tooley, *Maps and Map-Makers*, pp. 6–7, 19; Penrose, pp. 255–61; Febvre and Martin, pp. 248–52, 257–76; Robert M. Kingdon, "Patronage, Piety and Printing in Sixteenth-Century Europe," in David Pinkney and T. Ropp, *A Festschrift for Frederick B. Artz* (Durham, N. C.: Duke University Press, 1964), pp. 19–36.

36. Penrose, pp. 255–56; Crone, ch. 5.

37. Martin Lowry, *The World of Aldus Manutius* (Ithaca: Cornell University Press, 1979), pp. 127–29. David Pottinger, *The French Book Trade in the Ancien Regime, 1500–1791* (Cambridge, Mass.: Harvard University Press, 1958), pp. 23–32; Penrose, pp. 257–58, 277, and 291–92; Tooley, *Maps and Map-Makers*, p. 26.

38. Pottinger, pp. 23–32; Febvre and Martin, pp. 278–82.

39. For general works on the 1540–1550 expansion of printing, see Febvre and Martin, pp. 226–32; J. Thompson, *The Frankfort Book Fair* (New York: Burt Franklin [1911], 1968), pp. 226–32; pp. 29–31; for a discussion of inflation, see Wallerstein, pp. 67–80, 128–29; and for a discussion of economic fluctuation in the book trade, see Pottinger, pp. 23–39. For the figures quoted here see Febvre and Martin, p. 182.

40. Febvre and Martin, p. 186; Rudolf Hirsch, *Printing, Selling, and Reading, 1450–1550* (Wiesbaden: Otto Harrassowitz, 1967), pp. 66–67.

41. For sixteenth-century Italian publications, see Roberto Almagià, "On the Cartographic Work of Francesco Rosselli," *Imago Mundi* (1951), 8:17–26; Penrose, pp. 257–58 and 277; Tooley, *Maps and Map-Makers*, pp. 20–21; R. V.

Tooley, "Maps in Italian Atlases of the Sixteenth Century," *Imago Mundi* (1939), 3:12–14. For references to Spanish and Portuguese publications, see Penrose, pp. 291, 304; Crone, chs. 5 and 6; and Febvre and Martin, pp. 190–91.

42. S. H. Steinberg, *Five Hundred Years of Printing* (New York: Criterion, 1959), pp. 120–31; Douglas McMurtrie, *The Book* (New York: Oxford University Press [1943], 1960), ch. 24; Febvre and Martin, pp. 125–26; Colin Clair, *Christopher Plantin* (London: Cassell, 1960), pp. 9–13.

43. Cipolla, *Guns, Sails, and Empires*, pp. 48–66; Wallerstein, pp. 173–77; Steinberg, pp. 104, 129–31.

44. Crone, ch. 8; Penrose, pp. 260–63; Tooley, *Maps and Map-Makers*, p. 29; Lister, ch. 2; Thrower, *Maps and Man*, pp. 55–60.

45. Tooley, "Maps in Italian Atlases"; Penrose, p. 245; Clair, p. 200.

46. Crone, ch. 8; Penrose, pp. 260–61; Lister, ch. 2; Thrower, *Maps and Man*, pp. 55–60; Tooley, *Maps and Map-Makers*, p. 30; Clair, pp. 200–1.

47. Crone, ch. 8; Penrose, pp. 261–63; Lister, ch. 2; Thrower, *Maps and Man*, pp. 55–60; Johannes Kuening, "The History of an Atlas: Mercator-Hondius," *Imago Mundi* (1948), 4:37–62.

48. Penrose, p. 261; Crone, ch. 8; Kuening, "History of an Atlas"; E. J. S. Parsons and W. F. Morris, "Edward Wright and His Work," *Imago Mundi* (1939), 3:61–71; Pieter Geyle, *The Revolt of the Netherlands, 1555–1609* (Barnes and Noble, 1958), pp. 270–75; Charles Wilson, *The Dutch Republic* (New York: McGraw-Hill, 1968), pp. 110–17.

49. Crone, ch. 8; Penrose, pp. 261–63; Kuening, "History of an Atlas"; Febvre and Martin, pp. 194–95; Harold Innis, *Empire and Communications* (Toronto: University of Toronto Press [1950], 1972), pp. 146, 153.

50. Crone, p. 121; Kuening, "History of an Atlas." But it should be kept in mind that Mercator used a projection in his atlas that was *designed* to aid in navigation. Also when a follower of Mercator and Ortelius in the Dutch age of atlases, Petrus Plancius, was appointed as cosmographer to the Dutch East India Company, he displayed his geographical knowledge by producing an atlas which he said was also a sea chart. See Carl Enckell, "The Representation of the North of Europe in the World Map of Petrus Plancius of 1592," *Imago Mundi* (1951), 8:55–56. The design of many of the printed Dutch maps and atlases as both guides to navigators and goods for consumption by merchants and aristocrats is illustrated again in Anthonisz' "Caerte van Oostlant." See Johannes Kuening, "Cornelius Anthonisz," *Imago Mundi* (1950), 7:52–53. See also Lister, pp. 35–36.

51. Henry Peacham, *The Compleat Gentleman* (London: E. Tyler, 1661), p. 71.

52. Samuel Purchas, *Hakluytus Posthumus* (London: Henry Featherston, 1625), vol. 1, book 1, ch. 4.

53. Purchas, vol. 1, book 5, ch. 1.

54. Thomas Herbert, *Some Yeares Travels* (London: Jacob Blome and Richard Bishop, 1638), p. 8.

55. Herbert, p. 24.

56. Daniel Defoe, *A New Voyage Round the World by a Course that never failed before* (London: A. Bettesworth and Mears, 1725).

57. Hakluyt, *Voyages*, pp. 26 and 30.

58. Frobisher's accounts are presented in Waters, Appendices 10 B and C, pp. 530–31.

59. See Quinn, *England*, pp. 144–59.

60. Thomas Smith, "Manuscript and Printed Sea Charts in Seventeenth-Century London," in Thrower, *Compleat Plattmaker*, pp. 45–100; A. E. Stephens, "The Booke of the Sea Carte," *Imago Mundi* (1938), 2:55–59; Waters, pp. 12–13; Ralph Davis, *The Rise of the English Shipping Industry in the Seventeenth and Eighteenth Centuries* (London: Macmillan, 1962), p. 123; Helen M. Wallis, "Geographie is Better than Divinitie," in Thrower, *Compleat Plattmaker*, pp. 1–44; see also Coolie Verner, "John Seller and the Chart Trade in Seventeenth-Century England," in Thrower, *Compleat Plattmaker*, p. 203.

61. Hakluyt, *Voyages*; Linschoten.

62. Parry, *Establishment of Hegemony*, p. 99.

63. Linschoten, book 1, pp. 172–73.

64. Linschoten, book 2, introduction.

65. See Waters; G. J. Marcus, *Naval History of England*, vol. 1 (Boston: Little Brown, 1961), pp. 59–67; E. G. R. Taylor, *Late Tudor and Early Stuart Geography* (New York: Octagon [1934], 1968), chs. 2 and 3; Crone, p. 122–23; Penrose, p. 203.

66. Waters, pp. 232–36.

67. See John Smith, *A Sea Grammar* (London: John Haviland, 1627), p. 83 (apparently misnumbered for p. 73).

68. Michael Kammen, *Empire and Interest* (New York: Lippincott, 1970).

69. Febvre and Martin, ch. 8; Pottinger, pp. 33–35; Eisenstein; Hans Kohn, *The Idea of Nationalism* (New York: Collier, 1944), pp. 123–33; Reinhard Bendix, *Kings or People* (Berkeley: University of California Press, 1978), pp. 253–65.

70. See Charles Tilly, *The Formation of National States in Western Europe* (Princeton: Princeton University Press, 1975), p. 15.

71. Wallerstein, pp. 179–99; Michael Hechter, *Internal Colonialism* (Berkeley: University of California Press, 1975).

72. Tilly, pp. 17–28.

73. Penrose, p. 263; Taylor, *Late Tudor Geography*; R. A. Skelton, "Bishop Leslie's Maps of Scotland, 1578," *Imago Mundi* (1950), 7:103–6.

74. Thrower, *Maps and Man*, p. 73; Edward Lynam, *The Mapmaker's Art* (London: Batchworth Press, 1953), pp. 66–75, 79–90.

75. Tooley, *Maps and Map-Makers*, pp. 65–66; Sir Herbert George Fordham, *Some Notable Surveyors and Map-Makers of the Sixteenth, Seventeenth and Eighteenth Centuries and their Work* (Cambridge: Cambridge University Press, 1929), ch. 1, sect. 1.

76. Fordham, p. 7; Tooley, *Maps and Map-Makers*, p. 50; R. A. Skelton, *County Atlases of the British Isles, 1579–1850* (London: Carta, 1970), p. 235; Lawrence Stone, *Family and Fortune* (Oxford: Clarendon Press, 1973), pp. 3–4, 40–41.

77. Victor Morgan, "The Cartographic Image of 'The Country' in Early Modern England," in *Transactions of the Royal Historical Society* (1979), 5th ser. 29:129–54.

78. Compare John Norden, *Specvli Britanniae: The First Parte: An Historicall and Chorographicall Discription of Middlesex* (1593) with Christopher Saxton, *An Atlas of England and Wales* (1579) in the Huntington Library. See also Fordham, ch. 1, sect. 2; Tooley, *Maps and Map-Makers*, pp. 66–67.

79. John Norden, *Speculi Britanniae Pars, An Historicaland Chorographical Description of the County of Essex*, ed. Sir Henry Ellis (London: AMS Press for the Camden Society [1594], 1968), pp. 7–8.

80. Fordham, ch. 1.

81. Kuening, "Cornelius Anthonisz," pp. 51–57; Ruiz.

82. Karl Kůchar, "A Map of Bohemia of the Time of the Thirty Years War," *Imago Mundi* (1938), 2:75–77; W. V. Cannenberg, "An Unknown 'Pilot' by Hessel Gerritsz, Dating from 1612," *Imago Mundi* (1931), 1:49–51.

83. Rudolfo Gallo, "A Fifteenth Century Military Map of the Venetian Territory of Terraterma," *Imago Mundi* (1955), 12:55–57. See also R. A. Skelton, *Maps* (Chicago: University of Chicago Press, 1972), p. 7.

84. Tooley, *Maps and Map-Makers*, p. 54; Crone, ch. 9; Lang, pp. 85–88.

85. Eli Heckscher, *Mercantilism* (New York: Macmillan [1931], 1962), vol. 1, part 1, ch. 2.

86. "The King's Surveyor on the Improvements of the Forests, 1612" in Joan Thirsk and J. P. Cooper, *Seventeenth-Century Economic Documents* (Oxford: Clarendon Press, 1972), p. 119.

87. B. A. Holderness, *Pre-Industrial England* (London: J. M. Dent, 1976), pp. 56–59.

88. Stone, *Family and Fortune*, p. 134.

89. A. W. Richeson, *English Land Measuring to 1800* (Cambridge, Mass.: MIT Press, 1966), ch. 3.

90. Richeson, pp. 93–94.

91. Sir William Petty, *The History of the Survey of Ireland Commonly Called the Down Survey, 1655–1656* (New York: Augustus M. Kelley [1851], 1967), p. 8.

92. Petty, p. 9.

93. Parsons and Morris, pp. 61–71; Taylor, *The Haven-Finding Art*, chs. 10 and 11; May and Holder, pp. 187–94; Richeson, chs. 5 and 6; Tooley, *Maps and Map-Makers*, chs. 6 and 7.

94. See Vermeer's "Officer and Laughing Girl," "Young Woman with a Water Jug," and "Lady with a Lute." The popularity of wall maps is described in L. Bagrow, "A Page from the History of the Distribution of Maps," *Imago*

Mundi (1948), 5:62. For information on the sale of maps see Wilson, *The Dutch Republic*, pp. 110–17; Geyle, ch. 5; and Rostenberg.

4. SCIENTIFIC MATERIALISM: THE BOOK OF NATURE AND THE GROWTH OF RATIONAL CALCULATION

1. In Hugh Kearney, *Origins of the Scientific Revolution* (London: Longman's, 1964), p. 126, from Galileo, *The Assayer*, trans. Stillman Drake.

2. Douglas Kemsley, "Religious Influences in the Rise of Modern Science," *Annals of Science* (1968), 24:199–226. Elizabeth Eisenstein, *The Printing Press as an Agent of Change* (New York: Cambridge University Press, 1979), vol. 2, ch. 5.

3. Literature on the history of science tends not to consider printing as an important dynamic in patterns of scientific development. For instance, Merton's attempts to link rates of publication of scientific books to the rise of early modern science have been soundly criticized by Kemsley who finds no evidence of increased publication of scientific books in the seventeenth century. Kemsley's argument is supported by A. R. Hall, who finds evidence that the bulk of publishing in this period was of older texts, not new manuscripts (on science or other subjects). See A. R. Hall, *The Scientific Revolution, 1500–1800* (Boston: Beacon Press, 1954), Appendix C, pp. 375–77. These critics have dismissed any connection between seventeenth-century science and publishing because of their findings, but their dismissal is not convincing; they discuss only the *quantity* of books published and not the changes in the *qualities* of books and their use brought about by printing. It was the *qualities* of printed works and their uses that were important to science in the seventeenth century. See Eisenstein, vol. 2. Merton's attempts to link patterns of publication to science are most useful when he considers quality instead of quantity, for instance, when he points out that the first scientific journal began in the seventeenth century. See Robert Merton, *Science, Technology, and Society in Seventeenth Century England* (New York: Howard Fertig [1938], 1970), pp. 43–50, esp. p. 44. See also Lewis Feuer, *The Scientific Intellectual* (New York: Basic Books, 1963), pp. 66–68.

4. Max Weber, *The Protestant Ethic and the Spirit of Capitalism* (New York: Scribner's [1904–5], 1958).

5. *Ibid.*

6. The connection between science, technology, and capitalist development has been made by a number of authors, including Marshall Hodgson, *The Venture of Islam* (Chicago: University of Chicago Press, 1974); Richard Easterlin, "The Epoch of Modern Economic Growth," Colloquium, University of California, San Diego, November 25, 1980; W. W. Rostow, *How It All Began* (New York: McGraw-Hill, 1975); David Landes, *The Unbound Prometheus* (New York: Cambridge University Press, 1969). It might seem possible to argue that, if cultural materialism was essential to the scientific and technological thinking of the early modern period, then cultural materialism contributed to capitalist development *through* science and technology. Unfortunately, the historical situation

is not clear enough to allow this kind of simple interpretation. There has been a long-standing debate among specialists in the history of science about whether and to what extent innovations in science and technology were related in this period. See for instance, Peter Mathias, *Science and Society, 1600–1900* (Cambridge: Cambridge University Press, 1972); Landes; A. E. Musson and Eric Robinson, *Science and Technology in the Industrial Revolution* (Toronto: University of Toronto Press, 1979). If scientific and technological development were independent of each other, as some scholars suggest, then the literature that identifies the two as a single variable cannot be used in a straightforward manner. That is why I have not assumed this connection. The nature of this connection is explored in greater detail in chapter 7.

7. C. E. M. Joade, *A Guide to Philosophy* (New York: Random House, 1935), pp. 495–539. See also Barry Barnes, *Scientific Knowledge and Sociological Theory* (London: Routledge and Kegan Paul, 1974), pp. 1–3; Edwin Burtt, *The Metaphysical Foundations of Modern Physical Science* (London: Routledge and Kegan Paul [1924], 1959), pp. 96–127, 202–99.

8. Joade, pp. 495–539; Raymond Williams, *Keywords* (New York: Oxford University Press, 1976), pp. 163–67.

9. See Eisenstein, vol. 1, ch. 3 and vol. 2, ch. 5; and Stillman Drake and E. Drabkin, *Mechanics in Sixteenth-Century Italy* (Madison: University of Wisconsin Press, 1969), introduction.

10. This metaphor appeared in Kepler's work. See Gerald Holton, *Thematic Origins of Scientific Thought* (Cambridge: Harvard University Press, 1973), p. 72. For the importance of the image to scientific materialism, see Joade, p. 497.

11. Lynn White, Jr., "The Iconography of *Temperantia* and the Virtuousness of Technology," in *Medieval Religion and Technology* (Berkeley: University of California Press [1969], 1978), pp. 181–204.

12. One problem with trying to connect these two levels of early modern materialism through the metaphors is that the metaphors had medieval origins. The clockwork and the book certainly were bits of material culture with medieval heritages, but they also had specifically new referents in the early modern period. The clock existed in the medieval period, but the term "clockwork" was not used in the early modern period to refer to the clock per se but rather to the spring drive in clocks that was developed in the late fifteenth or early sixteenth century. The fact that writers frequently used the term "watch" interchangeably with clockwork in their metaphors makes their reference to spring-driven timepieces clearer. A similar argument holds for the book. The "book of nature" metaphor existed in the Middle Ages, but the book referred to in this period was a manuscript book, a book that could document information but could change in the hands of successive copyists. The book of nature metaphor in the seventeenth century referred to printed books, ones that were unchanged in reproduction and thus more self-contained and removed from influence by human hands and minds. Both the clockwork and the printed book, then, were new kinds of material culture in the early modern period that were more self-contained and self-sustaining than their medieval predecessors. They were bits of material culture

that were further removed from human thought and feeling. For a discussion of the clockwork in the development of the clock, see D. S. L. Cardwell, *Technology, Science, and History* (London: Heineman, 1972), p. 16. See also Maurice Daumas, *A History of Technology and Invention* (New York: Crown, 1964), p. 295, and Carlo Cipolla, *Clocks and Culture* (London: Collins, 1967), pp. 49–50. For a comparison of printed with manuscript books, see Alvin Gouldner, *The Dialectic of Ideology and Technology* (New York: Seabury Press, 1976), pp. 39–44; Lucien Febvre and Henri-Jean Martin, *The Coming of the Book*, trans. David Gerard (London: NLB [1958], 1976), pp. 15–28, 248–61; and Marshall McLuhan, *Gutenberg Galaxy* (Toronto: University of Toronto Press, 1962), pp. 186–93. For a description of the medieval "book of nature" metaphor, see Ernst Curtius, *European Literature and the Latin Middle Ages* (New York: Harper and Row [1953], 1963), pp. 319–26; McLuhan, pp. 183–93; and Eisenstein, vol. 2, ch. 5.

13. From Galileo's *The Assayer*, trans. Stillman Drake, in Kearney, p. 126.

14. Holton, *Thematic Origins*.

15. This approach provides an odd sort of support for Merton's contention that Protestantism was crucial to the development of modern science. But while Merton centers his case on the Protestant *ethic* and its effects on the *behavior* of seventeenth-century scientists, this chapter suggests that the *activities* of Protestants affected scientific *thought*. See Merton, *Science, Technology*. This argument similarly supports McLuhan's idea that the "book of nature" metaphor reveals something essential about the character of early modern science. But McLuhan mistakenly thinks this metaphor illustrates the medieval character of the seventeenth-century scientific thought because he does not see clearly how printing and Protestant uses of print transformed this image and made it useful as a guide to scientific research. See McLuhan, *Gutenberg Galaxy*.

16. Eisenstein, vol. 1, ch. 3 and vol. 2, ch. 5; Drake and Drabkin, introduction.

17. Eisenstein, *Printing Press*.

18. McLuhan; Gouldner; Eisenstein, vol. 2; William Ivins, *Prints and Visual Communications* (Cambrdige, Mass.: MIT Press, 1953); Walter Ong, *Interfaces of the Word* (Ithaca: Cornell University Press, 1977).

19. Ivins, *Prints and Visual Communication*.

20. Ivins. p. 15.

21. Ong, *Interfaces of the Word*; Gouldner, *Ideology and Technology*.

22. Ong, pp. 162–63.

23. Ong, pp. 162–64.

24. Ong, pp. 330–31.

25. Gouldner, *Ideology and Technology*.

26. Gouldner, p. 42.

27. See Douglas McMurtrie, *The Book* (New York: Oxford University Press, 1943), ch. 6, esp. pp. 84 and 99; Thomas Carter and L. Carrington Goodrich, *The Invention of Printing in China* (New York: Ronald Press, 1955), pp. 84–88; Robert Hegel, *The Novel in Seventeenth-Century China* (New York: Columbia University Press, 1981), pp. 10–22.

28. Carter and Goodrich, pp. 73 and 83–87.
29. Carter and Goodrich, pp. 84–85; Hegel, pp. 10–22.
30. N. F. Blake, *Caxton: England's First Publisher* (New York: Harper and Row, 1976); Martin Lowry, *The World of Aldus Manutius* (Ithaca, N.Y.: Cornell University Press, 1979), ch. 1; Gouldner, pp. 27–28.
31. Gouldner, pp. 27–28; Michael Walzer, *Revolution of the Saints* (Cambridge, Mass.: Harvard University Press, 1965).
32. Gouldner, pp. 27–28.
33. Geffrey Whitney, *A Choice of Emblemes and Other Devises* (Leyden: Plantyn, 1586).
34. See Eisenstein, vol. 1.
35. See Walzer; W. Clebsch, *England's Earliest Protestants* (New Haven: Yale University Press, 1964); A. G. Dickens, *The English Reformation* (New York: Schocken, 1964); Kenneth Lockridge, *Literacy in Colonial New England* (New York: Norton, 1974).
36. Eisenstein, vol. 1, pp. 329–67.
37. Lockridge; Cressey.
38. Lockridge.
39. Lockridge; see J. Tebbel, *The Media in America* (New York: New American Library, 1974), p. 10.
40. J. Thompson, *The Frankfort Book Fair* (New York: Burt Franklin [1911], 1968), ch. 3; A. E. Mumby and I. Norrie, *Publishing and Bookselling* (London: Jonathan Cape, 1930), p. 42. The following table from Thompson, pp. 89–90, showing the number of books printed in Germany and foreign countries listed in catalogues for the Frankfort and Leipzig book fairs, illustrates the early international character of these fairs:

German and Foreign Books at German Book Fairs

Year	Published Outside Germany	Published in Germany
1570	159	299
1580	141	339
1590	164	646
1600	263	791
1610	277	1233
1620	275	1102
1630	303	1041
1640	144	586
1650	218	725
1660	171	638
1670	82	615
1680	66	621
1690	30	871
1700	23	951

41. Thompson's, p. 88, figures on the numbers of Latin and German books handled by German book dealers provides another measure of the growing importance in the late seventeenth century of Protestant vernacular publishing in the German book trade.

Books Handled by German Book Dealers

Dates	Total	Latin	German	Other Vernacular
1571–1575	495	325	144	25
1596–1600	803	517	249	37
1621–1625	1216	783	381	49
1646–1650	1014	643	345	45
1671–1675	762	417	321	23
1696–1700	1103	461	620	22
1721–1725	1044	315	708	20

42. Thompson, p. 123.

43. John Calvin, *On the Christian Faith*. ed. J. McNeil (Indianapolis: Bobbs-Merrill [1559], 1957), pp. 105–10; Ong. Interestingly, Calvin seems to have used what Gouldner calls the form of modern rational discourse in his *Institutes*: "The reader is not allowed to escape from any serious point of doctrine into a realm of neutrality or indecision. In order to forestall our adverse vote, Calvin tried to deal with all actual and conceivable opposing arguments, and often with the motives of those who may favor them. He is an advocate in court, with adequate oratorical resources, making a case for God and his Word." Calvin, p. xvii.

That a Reformation leader would use such a style should not be surprising. Calvin's use of modern rational discourse only confirms that Reformation leaders helped develop the uses of print which have become directly associated with printing technology.

44. Calvin, pp. 33–35. The extent to which Protestants considered the words of the Bible as literally or symbolically "true," how closed a system of information they found the Bible, varied from sect to sect, but in contrast to the Catholic church, all Protestants treated the Bible as more or less a closed system.

45. Gouldner.

46. Ivins, pp. 51–63; Calvin, pp. 193–211; Martin Luther, *Three Treatises* (Philadelphia: Fortress Press [1520], 1960), pp. 40–41, 98–99, 169.

47. Calvin, pp. 19–26; Ivins, pp. 51–63; Luther, pp. 98–100; Eisenstein, p. 333; Ong; Gouldner.

48. Calvin, p. 19.

49. See for instance, Merton; Kemsley; Feuer; A. Rupert Hall, "Merton Revisited," *History of Science* (1963), 2:1–16; Margaret 'Espinasse, "The Decline and Fall of Restoration Science," in Charles Webster, *The Intellectual Revolution of the Seventeenth Century* (London: Routledge and Kegan Paul [1958], 1974),

pp. 347–68; Theodore Rabb, "Puritanism and the Rise of Experimental Science in England," *Cahiers d'Histoire Mondiale* (1962), 7:46–67; see esp. Barbara Shapiro, "Latitudianarianism and Science in Seventeenth Century England," in Webster, *Intellectual Revolution*, pp. 286–316.

50. For individualist histories, see Hall, "Merton Revisited" and Feuer. For connections between Protestantism and science, see Merton; Rabb; Christopher Hill, *The Intellectual Origins of the English Revolution* (New York: Oxford University Press, 1965); and Webster, *Intellectual Revolution*.

51. Eisenstein, vol. 1, pp. 648–60.

52. Eisenstein's argument is not adequate for explaining the appeal of science in the seventeenth century. She explains how science could become more complex and problematic in this period, but not why some scientists made it that way.

53. For example of the demand argument, see A. E. Musson, *Science, Technology, and Economic Growth* (London: Methuen, 1972); and Merton. For discussions of the arts and mathematics in science, see H. Butterfield, "Renaissance Art and Modern Science," in Kearney, pp. 3–17; J. Clagett, "Medieval Mechanics," in Kearney, pp. 40–44; M. Kline, "Painting and Perspective," in Kearney, pp. 18–30; David Lindberg and Nicholas Steneek, "The Sense of Vision and the Origins of Modern Science," in Allen Debus, *Science, Medicine, and Society in the Renaissance* (New York: Science History Publications, 1972). For politics and science, see Webster, *Intellectual Revolution*. For religion and science, see Merton; Shapiro in Webster. See also Musson.

54. See Merton.

55. Harold Innis, *Empire and Communications* (Toronto: University of Toronto Press, 1972); Shapiro in Webster and Wallerstein, pp. 151–57.

56. . Innis; Shapiro in Webster; see also, Frank Manuel, *The Age of Reason* (Ithaca: Cornell University Press, 1951), pp. 23–26. Boyle and others seemed to see the spread of natural philosophy as a way to create a new politicoeconomic order, one that would destroy the Catholic colonial empire. See J. R. Jacob, *Robert Boyle and the English Revolution* (New York: Burt Franklin, 1977), pp. 154–56.

57. Wallerstein, pp. 151–57. Antal also has interesting insights into why a Reformation occurred in the North and not commercial centers in Italy. He claims that the Church was a major economic power in Italian cities and therefore had developed an interest in abandoning Thomist economic philosophy there before the Reformation. The coincidence of interests between the Church and merchants reduced any class-based impetus for a revolt from the Church there. But in the less developed areas of the North, like England, France, and Germany, Church economic policy and philosophy remained more conservative. Hence economic development there required a religious revolt. See Frederick Antal, *Florentine Painting and its Social Background* (London: Kegan Paul, 1947), p. 42.

58. Merton, pp. 63–71; Feuer, pp. 1–182. Feuer describes these men as "hedonistic" but the behavior he describes could also be labeled rebellious.

59.   J. Newman, *The World of Mathematics* (New York: Simon and Schuster, 1956), vol. 1, p. 129.

60.   Hall, *Scientific Revolution*, pp. 161–68; Merton, pp. 116–19; Burtt, pp. 161–88.

61.   Ivins, pp. 51–63.

62.   Charles Webster states in his *The Great Instauration* (New York: Holmes and Meier, 1976), p. 15: "Thus the Puritans at the outset of the English Revolution were in a position analogous to that of the humanists of the Renaissance; they were totally disenchanted with their immediate intellectual inheritance and they looked back for inspiration to a distant unspoilt age. Just as much as the humanists, the Puritans sought justification in affiliation with an indisputable, ancient authority. But whereas the former could draw sustenance from the Golden Age of Greek antiquity, the Puritans were obliged to react against this pagan model. Their inspiration came from the Fathers of the early church or the patriarchs of Israel."

63.   William Gilbert, *De Magnete*, trans. P. F. Mottley (New York: Dover [1600:1893], 1958), pp. xliv–l.

64.   Robert Boyle, *Considerations* (c.1650), p. 29, quoted in Jacob, p. 116.

65.   Sprat quoted in Kemsley, pp. 224–25.

66.   See for instance, Frank Manuel, *A Portrait of Isaac Newton* (Cambridge: Harvard Univesity Press, 1968), pp. 122–24.

67.   Galileo quoted in Jacob Bronowski, *The Ascent of Man* (Boston: Little Brown, 1973), p. 209.

68.   Boyle quoted in Jacob, p. 116.

69.   Holton, p. 86.

70.   See Robert Hurlburtt, *Hume, Newton, and the Design Argument* (Lincoln: University of Nebraska Press, 1965), pp. 3–92; Frank Manuel, *Isaac Newton Historian* (Cambridge, Mass.: Harvard University Press, 1972), pp. 7–10; Burtt, pp. 282–99; Holton, p. 389; Merton, pp. 102–10.

71.   Webster, *Great Instauration.*

72.   Quoted in Webster, *Great Instauration*, p. 12.

73.   Francis Bacon, *Cogitata et Visa* in *Works*, iii, p. 584 quoted in Webster, *Great Instauration*, p. 24.

74.   William Letwin, *The Origins of Scientific Economics* (Garden City, N.Y.: Doubleday, 1964), pp. 131–38. Scientific economics developed in patterns similar to those in the natural sciences. It not only evolved from Protestant ideas about scholarship and the use of mechanistic imagery common to the natural sciences, but it also blossomed (like the physical sciences) in the seventeenth century, after numerous sixteenth-century attempts at systematic thinking. And just as the natural sciences were enhanced in the sixteenth century by both practical problems (in, for instance, ballistics) and theoretical questions (such as the movement of falling bodies), so scientific economics developed in response to a combination of practical problems such as recoinage and theoretical ones like the nature of inflation.

While the similarities between the beginnings of scientific economics and the natural sciences in early modern Europe were numerous enough to deserve careful attention, they were also limited. There was one major difference between these two areas of scholarship that had profound importance: there was no economics in classical scholarship. Aristotle's economics, in spite of its name, was a study of the domestic economy that was of no use in trying to understand patterns of international trade or the effects of changes in manufacture on a state's economy. This meant that economic thinkers in the early modern period were forced to rely more on experience rather than scholarship to address economic problems, and forced to do so without being given the academic legitimacy (however reluctant or circumscribed) given natural scientists in this period. These two problems may be sources for the other major difference between the natural sciences and scientific economics in the period: that economics reached its "classical" period in the eighteenth rather than seventeenth century, even though in the seventeenth century scientific economics first gained a distinctive form.

While the lack of Greek and Roman writing on economic theory was a hindrance to the development of scientific economics, there was a scholastic tradition of economic thinking that (Schumpeter claims) provided some useful ideas for early modern economic thinkers. See Joseph Schumpeter, *History of Economic Analysis* (New York: Oxford University Press [1954], 1966), part 1, ch. 1. The problem was that, because this intellectual tradition was being discarded in favor of either classical thought or millenarian Protestantism, its value for legitimating economic theorizing was limited. In addition, scholastic economics had been subsumed under theology in the Middle Ages, and therefore had not achieved for economics the independent status that would have helped to legitimate it later on. See Schumpeter, part 2, ch. 2. For these reasons, the scholastic tradition, while conceptually helpful, was not as useful as it might have been in establishing economic thinking as a distinctive and valuable area of research.

Given this lack of legitimacy, it may seem odd that scientific economics did, in fact, develop so rapidly in the early modern period, but there were a number of reasons. The most obvious one is that Europe was experiencing such profound economic changes that issues in economics were difficult to ignore. The other is that scientific thinking was gaining such strength that its application to practical economic problems was an obvious step.

75. Robert Boyle, *Aretology* (1646), quoted in Jacob, p. 69.

76. Francis Bacon, *De Augmentis*, quoted in Webster, *Great Instauration*, p. 424.

77. For mention of Copernicus's writings, see Schumpeter, p. 101; Newton's work is discussed more fully by Letwin, pp. 260–70. See also Webster, *Great Instauration*, p. 403 for the role of metallurgists; Letwin, p. 53 for the medical training of Barbon, Petty, and Locke.

78. Burtt, pp. 282–83, 330; Ivins, pp. 51–63.

79. Burtt, pp. 49–50, 159; Holton, pp. 76–78; Hall, *Scientific Revolution*, pp. 116–28, 143–48.

80.   Holton, p. 83.

81.   Ong, pp. 330–31. For Kepler's "great clockwork" metaphor, see Holton, p. 72. For Galileo's ideas, see Kearney, p. 126; Hall, *Scientific Revolution*, pp. 77–79; Burtt, pp. 64–73. For a description of Harvey's images of the movement of the blood, see Hall, *Scientific Revolution*, pp. 143–48.

82.   Gweneth Whitteridge, *William Harvey* (New York: Elsevier, 1971), p. 170.

83.   William Harvey, *De Generatione Animalum* (1651), p. 60 quoted in Whitteridge, p. 220.

84.   Whitteridge, pp. 151–59.

85.   Whitteridge, p. 43.

86.   For Newton's ideas, see Hurlburtt, ch. 1; Burtt, pp. 202–23; and Holton, pp. 457–58.

87.   Burtt, p. 80. For a discussion of motion in the theories of this period, see Hall, *Scientific Revolution*, ch. 3; Holton, pp. 437–41; Burtt.

88.   A. Rupert Hall, *From Galileo to Newton, 1630–1720* (New York: Harper and Row, 1963), p. 74.

89.   Leonardo expressed a similar idea 150 years before, but he was exceptional in the modernity of his thought and also not influential in his thinking because he hid rather than publicized his ideas.

90.   See Holton, pp. 7–85, 437–41; Hall, *From Galileo to Newton*, ch.3; Hurlburtt. Compare to Ong, pp. 160–66, and Gouldner, pp. 40–42; Burtt pp. 64–73, 202–23.

91.   Hall, *Scientific Revolution*, p. 122.

92.   See Holton, pp. 12–17; Hall, *From Galileo to Newton*, ch. 10; Burtt, pp. 44–46. Compare to Gouldner, p. 44.

93.   Samuel Hartlib, *Further Discovery*, quoted in Webster, *Great Instauration*, p. 423.

94.   Nicholas Barbon, *A Discourse of Trade* in J. Hollander ed., *A Reprint of Economic Tracts* (Johns Hopkins University Press [1690], 1903); and Whitteridge, p. 44.

95.   John Locke, *Law of Nature*, p. 117, quoted in Letwin, p. 189.

96.   Holton, pp. 440–41.

97.   Letwin, ch. 4; Ivins; Ong; Gouldner. For some discussion of the ideological character of economic writings that helped to stimulate skepticism in readers, see Joyce Appleby, *Economic Thought and Ideology in Seventeeth-Century England* (Princeton: Princeton Univesity Press, 1978), chs. 1 and 3. For an analysis of the rhetoric of science as subject for sociological analysis, see Joseph Gusfield, *The Culture of Public Problems* (Chicago: University of Chicago Press, 1981).

98.   See A. E. Musson and Eric Robinson, *Science and Technology in the Industrial Revolution* (Toronto: University of Toronto Press, 1969), ch. 1. An apt example of the possible relationship between scientists' uses of technology and their view of nature appears in the history of the clock. See Allan Lloyd, "Mechanical Timekeepers," in Charles Singer, et al., *History of Technology* (New York: Oxford University Press, 1957), vol. 3, pp. 648–75. And for an analysis of

writings and equipment as the material culture of science, see Bruno Latour and Stephen Woolgar, *Laboratory Life* (Los Angeles: Sage, 1979).

5. CULTURE AND INDUSTRIALIZATION, PART I: THE FASHION FOR CALICOES

1. Alfred Plummer, *The London Weaver's Company, 1600–1970* (London: Routledge and Kegan Paul, 1972), p. 297.
2. John Nef, *Cultural Foundations of Industrial Civilization* (New York: Harper, 1958).
3. See Nicholas Barbon, *A Discourse of Trade 1690*, pp. 14–16, in Jacob Hollander, ed., *A Reprint of Economic Tracts* (Johns Hopkins Press, 1903), pp. 13–14.
4. Quentin Bell, *On Human Finery* (New York: Schocken, 1976); Frances Baldwin, *Sumptuary Legislation and Personal Regulation in England* (Baltimore: Johns Hopkins University Press, 1926); Dwight Robinson, "The Importance of Fashions in Taste to Business History," *Business History Review* (1963), 37:16–20; Herman Freudenberger, "Fashion, Sumptuary Laws, and Business," *Business History Review* (1963) 37:38–39.
5. See for instance, W. W. Rostow, *Stages of Economic Growth* (Cambridge: Cambridge University Press, 1963); S. D. Chapman, *The Cotton Industry in the Industrial Revolution* (New York: Macmillan, 1972); Phyllis Deane, *The First Industrial Revolution* (Cambridge: Cambridge University Press, 1965); J. L. Hammond and B. Hammond, *The Rise of Modern Industry* (New York: Harcourt, Brace, and World, 1926); Neil Smelser, *Social Change in the Industrial Revolution* (Chicago: University of Chicago Press, 1959); A. P. Wadsworth and Julia Mann, *The Cotton Trade and Industrial Lancashire, 1600–1780* (Manchester: Manchester University Press [1931], 1965).
6. Rostow, *Stages of Economic Growth*; Chapman; Deane; Hammond and Hammond; Smelser; and Phyllis Dean and W. A. Cole, *British Economic Growth, 1688–1959* (Cambridge: Cambridge University Press, 1967).
7. D. Robinson; John Irwin and Katherine Brett, *Origins of Chintz* (London: Her Majesty's Stationery Office, 1970); Fernand Braudel, *Capitalism and Material Life, 1400–1800* (New York: Harper and Row, 1967).
8. R. S. Fitton and A. P. Wadsworth, *The Strutts and the Arkwrights, 1758–1830* (Manchester: Manchester University Press [1958], 1964); Charles Wilson, "The Entrepreneur," in S. Lieberman, *Europe and the Industrial Revolution* (Cambridge: Schenckman, 1972), pp. 377–95.
9. D. Robinson, p. 17; Bell, p. 202; Freudenberger, p. 39; Ladmila Kybalová, et al., *The Pictorial Encyclopedia of Fashion*, trans. C. Rosoux (New York: Crown, 1968), p. 101.
10. D. Robinson, p. 17, Freudenberger, p. 39; James Laver, *Costume* (New York: Hawthorne, 1963), pp. 21–31; Kybalová et al., pp. 101–19; Margot Hill and Peter Bucknell, *Evolution of Fashion* (London: Batsford, 1967), pp. 18–33.

11. Kybalová, et al., pp. 127–37; D. Robinson, p. 18; Michael Batterberry and Ariane Batterberry, *Mirror, Mirror* (New York: Holt, Rinehart, and Winston, 1977), pp. 86–88; Laver, p. 36; Michael Baxandall, *Painting and Experience in Fifteenth-Century Italy* (New York: Oxford University Press [1972], 1974), pp. 14–15; Detroit Institute of the Arts, *Flanders in the Fifteenth Century* (Detroit: Institute of the Arts, 1960), pp. 31–35.

12. Baxandall, p. 15; Batterberry and Batterberry, pp. 90–110.

13. Kybalová et al., pp. 163–75; Hill and Bucknell, pp. 62–73; Braudel *Capitalism*, p. 232; Batterberry and Batterberry, pp. 96–97; Laver, pp. 41–45.

14. D. Robinson, p. 19; Freudenberger, p. 39, places this pattern in the seventeenth century. He associates it with the rise of the French court as a center for fashion. Since his analysis focuses primarily on France, this period might seem a more important break in the history of fashion. But concern for fashion and keeping up to date seems to have started in the sixteenth century. See also Batterberry and Batterberry, pp. 90–106. Braudel, *Capitalism*, p. 231, declares that fashion became "sovereign" around 1700, but does not say when it began to be a force. Norbert Elias suggests that a new concern for outward appearance as a reflection of inner character developed in the sixteenth century. This notion fits with the idea of a new interest in fashion in this period. See Elias, *The Civilizing Process* (New York: Urizen Books [1939], 1978), pp. 55–59.

15. Henry Peacham, *The Compleat Gentleman* (London: E. Tyler, 1661), pp. 281–82. Peter Burke in *Venice and Amsterdam* (London: Temple Smith, 1974) may help explain why fashion could have been more powerful in Italy during the Italian period of fashion than in Holland during the Dutch period. He argues that there was greater desire in the Italian bourgeoisie to live like the nobility than there was in the Dutch bourgeoisie. The greater tension between the classes could have made fashion a more important and notable social force in Italy. But this analysis still leaves aside the question of why Peacham finds the Spanish less interested in fashion. The visibility of Spanish fashion throughout Europe and in the New World in the period of Spanish domination of dress makes Peacham's statement seem suspect. He may have mistaken the use of black cloth in both Spanish and Dutch fashions with a lack of interest in stylish dress. Certainly the greater use of decorated and colorful clothing by the English, French and Italians made their interest in fashion easier to identify. But that does not mean that they were the only ones taken by swings in fashion.

16. Freudenberger, p. 37, 41–45; Hammond and Hammond, pp. 16–23, 178–81; Elizabeth Gilboy, "Demand as a Factor in the Industrial Revolution," in S. Lieberman, *Europe and the Industrial Revolution* (Cambridge: Schenckman, 1972), pp. 267–68; Braudel, *Capitalism*, pp. 236–38; Batterberry and Batterberry, pp. 96–97.

17. D. Robinson, pp. 16–24; Batterberry and Batterberry, pp. 96–97; Braudel, *Capitalism*, pp. 231–43.

18. Bell, ch. 5. See also Gilboy; Freudenberger, p. 38; D. Robinson, pp. 14–20. Antal captures the tensions between the high bourgeoisie and nobility in fifteenth-century Florence, and indicates its importance to increased conspicuous

consumption there. See Frederick Antal, *Florentine Painting and its Social Background* (London: Kegan Paul, 1947), esp. p. 29.

19. Bell, ch. 6.

20. Freudenberger, p. 42; Kybalová et al., pp. 163–67; Batterberry and Batterberry, pp. 90–164; Braudel, *Capitalism*, p. 232; Bell, ch. 4. Compare this pattern to the world system described by Immanuel Wallerstein in *The Modern World-System* (London: Academic Press, 1976).

21. Joyce Appleby, *Economic Thought and Ideology in Seventeenth-Century England* (Princeton: Princeton University Press, 1978), ch. 9.

22. See Baldwin; Freudenberger; Bell; John M. Vincent, *Costume and Conduct in the Laws of Basel, Bern, and Zurich, 1370–1800* (Baltimore: Johns Hopkins University Press, 1935); Wilfred Hooper, "The Tudor Sumptuary Laws," *English Historical Review* (1915), 30:433–49.

23. Baldwin, pp. 46–47.

24. Baldwin, pp. 47–48.

25. Baldwin, pp. 48–51; see also, Hooper.

26. Phyllis Cunningham and Catherine Lucas, *Occupational Costume in England* (New York: Barnes and Noble, 1967).

27. Baldwin, pp. 248–49; Hooper, p. 449.

28. Barbon, pp. 65–66 (in reprint pp. 32–33).

29. Robert Boyle, *Considerations* [1655], in J. R. Jacob, *Robert Boyle and the English Revolution* (New York: Burt Franklin, 1977), p. 106.

30. P. J. Thomas, *Mercantilism and the East India Trade* (London: Frank Cass [1926], 1963), pp. 48–50; Eileen Power and M. M. Postan, *Studies in English Trade in the Fifteenth Century* (London: Routledge and Kegan Paul [1933], 1951), ch. 2 and pp. 139–55; Thomas Girtin, *The Golden Ram* (London: G. B. Company of Clothmakers, 1958), p. 27; George Unwin, *Studies in Economic History* (New York: Augustus M. Kelley [1927], 1966), part 2, ch. 5; Reinhard Bendix, *Kings or People* (Berkeley: University of California Press, 1978), pp. 278–79.

31. In the early part of the seventeenth century Basel passed a sumptuary law that restricted the use of English textiles. See Vincent, pp. 59–60. This law suggests the high respect these goods had on the international market.

32. Lewis Roberts, *The Merchants Map of Commerce*, 4th ed. (London: Thomas Horne, 1700), p. 44. John Locke also uses the success of the wool trade as a model for one of his economic arguments:

"Let us suppose *England* Peopled as it is now; and its Woollen Manufacture in the same State of Perfection, that it is at present; and that we, having no Money at all trade with this our Woollen Manufacture for the value of Two hundred Thousand pounds Yearly to *Spain*, whee ther actually is a Million in Money: Further let us suppose that we bring back from *Spain* Yearly in Oyl, Wine, and Fruit, to the value of One hundred Thousand pounds, and continue to do this Ten Years together: 'Tis plain we have had for our two Millions value in Woollen Manufacture carried thither, one Million returned in Wine, Oyl, and Fruit: But what is become of t'other Million? Will the Merchants be content to lose it? That you may be sure they would not, not have Trade on, if they had not every Year Returns made answering their Exportation. How then were the returns made? In Money it is evident."

Locke was using figures about the export of woolens and imports of wine, oil, fruit, and money for this analysis because it gave the example a sense of realism. This kind of exchange between Spain and England was not infrequent (even though the Spanish were wool producers) since English wools had such a fine reputation on the continent. See Locke, *Some Considerations of the Consequences of Lowering the Interest and Raising the Value of Money* (London: Awnsham and John Churchil, 1696) in *Several Papers Relating to Money, Interest & Trade & Etc. by John Locke* (reprint, New York: Augustus M. Kelley, 1968), p. 24.

33. Scoville summarizes this debate in Warren Scoville, *The Persecution of the Huguenots and French Economic Development, 1680–1720* (Berkeley: University of California Press, 1960), pp. 321–35.

34. Wadsworth and Mann, pp. 29–53; Cunningham and Lucas.

35. Joan Thirsk, *Economic Policy and Projects* (Oxford: Clarendon Press, 1978), pp. 30–33, 38–39.

36. Thomas, pp. 8–9, 36–37.

37. Thomas, pp. 36–37; Irwin and Brett, pp. 3–4; Charles Cole, *French Mercantilism* (New York: Octagon, 1965), pp. 37–39.

38. Bell, ch. 6; Hill and Bucknell, pp. 86–101; Kybalová et al., pp. 153–54; Laver, pp. 45–46.

39. F. J. Fisher, "The Development of London as a Centre of Conspicuous Consumption in the Sixteenth and Seventeenth Centuries." *Transactions of the Royal Historical Society* (1948), 30:37–50; Laver, pp. 55–59.

40. Thomas, pp. 25–26; T. Sprague Allen, *Tides of English Taste* (New York: Pageant Books, 1958), vol. 1, pp. 218, 220–22; Hill and Bucknell, pp. 102–9; Laver, p. 59.

41. Samuel Fortrey [1663], cited in Joan Thirsk, *The Restoration* (London: Longman, 1976), pp. 116–17.

42. Thomas, pp. 25–28; Alfred Plummer, *The London Weaver's Company* (London: Routledge and Kegan Paul, 1972), p. 292.

43. Baldwin, p. 219; Hooper. See also Thomas, pp. 31–36.

44. Cunningham and Lucas.

45. Allen, pp. 219–20; Hill and Bucknell, pp. 102–45; Plummer, pp. 292–93.

46. Roberts, p. 133.

47. Bell, p. 120; Irwin and Brett, p. 1.

48. Thomas, pp. 27, 132; Plummer, p. 292; Allen, pp. 221–22.

49. Pope quoted in Allen, vol. 1, p. 220.

50. Braudel, *Capitalism*, pp. 215–19; Irwin and Brett, p. 4 and ch. 5; Allen, p. 219; Thomas, pp. 27–28.

51. Irwin and Brett, p. 1; Geoffrey Turnbull, *A History of the Calico Printing Industry of Great Britain* (Altrincham, Eng.: John Sherrat, 1951), p. 17; Thomas, pp. 38–39; A. F. Kendrick, *English Decorative Fabrics of the Sixteenth to Eighteenth Centuries* (London: F. Lewis, 1934), pp. 66–69.

52. Turnbull, p. 17; Thomas, pp. 122–23; Wadsworth and Mann, pp. 177–83; Stuart Robinson, *A History of Printed Textiles* (Cambridge: MIT Press, 1969), pp. 12–15.

53. Thomas, pp. 128–31; L. C. A. Knowles, *The Industrial and Commercial Revolutions in Great Britain During the Nineteenth Century* (London: Routledge and Kegan Paul [1921], 1961), pp. 45–46; Wadsworth and Mann, pp. 174–76; Paul Mantoux, *The Industrial Revolution in the Eighteenth Century* (London: Methuen [1928], 1964), p. 202. See also L. Gopal, "The Textile Industry in Medieval India," *Journal of the Asiatic Society of Bombay* (1964), n.s., 39:100–2.

54. Joan Thirsk and J. P. Cooper, *Seventeenth-Century Economic Documents* (Oxford: Clarendon Press, 1972), sect. 1; Thomas, pp. 51–52; Barry Supple, *Commercial Crisis and Change in England, 1600–1642* (Cambridge: Cambridge University Press, 1964).

55. Thomas Mun, *England's Treasure by Forraign Trade* (New York: Macmillan [1664], 1895), p. 81.

56. Thomas, pp. 151–53.

57. Thomas, chs. 1 and 4; Heckscher, vol. 2, part 3, ch. 4; Plummer, pp. 293–95.

58. Thomas, p. 3; Heckscher, vol. 1, pp. 2–30; Wallerstein, pp. 192–93; Hechter, p. 91.

59. Jacob, pp. 154–56.

60. Wallerstein, ch. 4.

61. Wallerstein, chs. 2 and 4.

62. Malynes, p. 182.

63. Mun, p. 101.

64. See Heckscher, vol. 2, part 3, ch. 4; Wallerstein, pp. 276–79; and Michael Kammen, *Empire and Interest* (New York: Lippincott, 1970), pp. 4–8.

65. Thomas, pp. 8–16, 21–24; Heckscher.

66. Malynes, p. 93 H2

67. Mun, pp. 23, 29–30.

68. Thomas, ch. 1; Heckscher, vol. 1, part 1; Kammen, pp. 8–19. See also Robert Aston, "The Parliamentary Agitation for Free Trade in the Opening Years of the Reign of James I," *Past and Present* (1967), 38:40–55.

69. Philopatris, *A Treatise Concerning the East India Trade* (London: Robert Boulter, 1681), p. 1. This piece has been varyingly attributed to Sir Joshua Child and Benjamin Worsley. For a discussion of its authorship, see Letwin, pp. 19 and 253.

70. Wallerstein, pp. 276–79; Kammen, pp. 20–29; Heckscher, vol. 2, pp. 142–43; Girtin, ch. 5.

71. Heckscher, vol. 2, pp. 106–11; Thomas, pp. 22–23.

72. Deane and Cole, p. 34.

73. Henry Robinson, *Certaine Proposalls* [1652], p. 11, quoted in Webster, p. 457.

74. Webster, p. 463.

75. Hechter, pp. 84–85; Kammen, pp. 21–22; Heckscher, vol. 2, pp. 40–44.

76. Thomas, pp. 12–16; William Barber, *British Economic Thought about India* (Oxford: Clarendon Press, 1974), ch. 1.
77. Thomas, pp. 12–20 and ch. 4; Heckscher, vol. 2, p. 253; Barber, ch. 1.
78. Heckscher, vol. 2, p. 254; Thomas, pp. 16–20, 98–99; Ramkrishna Mukherjee, *The Rise and Fall of the East India Company* (New York: Monthly Review Press, 1974), pp. 66–68; Thirsk and Cooper, sect. 1, pp. 3, 14 and 22.
79. Thomas, pp. 57–66; Wadsworth and Mann, pp. 116–19; Plummer, p. 293.
80. Thomas, pp. 98–105; Plummer, pp. 293–94.
81. Thomas, p. 115; Plummer, p. 294. Berwick–On–Tweed was a contested area between England and Scotland.
82. Thomas, pp. 118–28; Wadsworth and Mann, pp. 119–44; Plummer, p. 295; Allen, pp. 222–24.
83. Thomas, pp. 140–41. See also Plummer, p. 296.
84. Plummer, pp. 296–305; Thomas, pp. 138–52. In making this argument the weavers were using what E. P. Thompson calls the "moral economy," in "The Moral Economy of the English Crowd in the Eighteenth Century," *Past and Present* (1971), 50:77–136. Thompson suggests that riots of this sort stemmed from the value differences between the growing market economy and the traditional tenets of paternalism that had been essential to prior economic arrangements.
85. Thomas, p. 160; Plummer, pp. 305–6. Calicoes dyed all blue were probably exempted because blue cloth was used by the working class and thus blue calicoes may not have seemed like an elite cloth. See Cunningham. This relationship between blue dyes and low status seems to have been partially the result of the success of woad-growing projects. See Thirsk, *Economic Policy*, ch. 1.
86. Thomas, pp. 161–65; Allen, pp. 228–32; Plummer, pp. 306–9.
87. Wadsworth and Mann, pp. 172–79; Hill and Bucknell pp. 94–95, 98–99, 110–13, 138–39.
88. Wadsworth and Mann, ch. 7.
89. Daniel Defore, *A Plan of English Commerce* (London: Charles Rivington, 1728), pp. 295–96.

6. CULTURE AND INDUSTRIALIZATION, PART II: THE BRITISH COTTON INDUSTRY

1. Carlo Cipolla, *The Fontana Economic History of Europe* (London: Collins/Fontana, 1973), pp. 63–64.
2. For a description of the steps in printing calicoes, see John Irwin and Katherine Brett, *Origins of Chintz* (London: Her Majesty's Stationery Office, 1970), esp. pp. 36–41. For a description of paper and printing, see Lucien Febvre and Henri–Jean Martin, *The Coming of the Book*, trans. David Gerard (London: NLB [1958], 1976) pp. 39–44. For a description of the problems in printing on fabric other than cotton, see A. P. Wadsworth and Julia Mann, *The Cotton Trade and Industrial Lancashire, 1600–1780* (Manchester: Manchester University

Press [1931], 1965), pp. 119–44; Geoffrey Turnbull, *A History of the Calico Printing Industry of Great Britain* (Altrincham, Eng.: John Sherrat, 1951), ch. 1.

3.   For a description of British dependence on Flemish fabric finishers, see Thomas Girtin, *The Golden Ram* (London: G. B. Company of Clothworkers, 1958), ch. 5; Eileen Powar and M. Postan, *Studies in English Trade in the Fifteenth Century* (London: Routledge and Kegan Paul [1933], 1951), ch. 2. The role of Huguenots in calico printing is described by Warren Scoville in *The Persecution of the Huguenots and French Economic Development, 1680–1720* (Berkeley: University of California Press, 1960), p. 327, and Wadsworth and Mann, pp. 129–30. The Indian role in the Asian textile trade appears in P. J. Thomas, *Mercantilism and the East India Trade* (London: Frank Cass [1926], 1963), pp. 31–34, and Indian protection of craft mysteries as caste secrets is illustrated in Thomas, p. 35. Irwin and Brett describe and in part reproduce the earliest known European description of Indian cotton printing and painting; see Beaulieu's 1784 account, pp. 36–41.

4.   See A. E. Musson and Eric Robinson, *Science and Technology in the Industrial Revolution* (Toronto: University of Toronto Press, 1969), ch. 8.

5.   The flexibility of beliefs that might have made this kind of behavior seem legitimate to artisans of the period is analyzed in Bennett Berger's *The Survival of a Counterculture* (Berkeley: University of California Press, 1981). For evidence of the behavior itself, see for instance, D. S. L. Cardwell, *Technology, Science, and History* (London: Heineman, 1972), pp. 100–1 and Peter Mathias, *Science and Society, 1600–1800* (Cambridge: Cambridge University Press, 1972), pp. 54–80.

6.   Some of the scholars who have studied Britain's industrial revolution claim that the putting-out system was the primary cause of and precursor to the factory system because it brought about a breakdown of traditional forms of independent craft manufacture and established the control of trading interests (or merchants) over production. By this logic, the change in the mode of production which is identified with the industrial revolution begins with the shift to the putting-out system. See David Landes, *The Unbound Prometheus* (Cambridge: Cambridge University Press, 1969), pp. 43–44; Maurice Dobb, *Studies in the Development of Capitalism* (New York: International Publishers [1947], 1976), ch. 4; Paul Mantoux, *The Industrial Revolution in the Eighteenth Century* (London: Methuen [1928], 1964), chs. 1 and 2. Other scholars have argued that technological innovation, the development of machines to do much of the work in textile manufacture, was of primary importance to the factory system because machines which required both sources of power and centralization of labor made forms of home labor—both craft production and putting-out—impossible. The only way to use machines was to put them into separate manufacturing facilities to which workers could go to do their work. See Elias Tuma, *European Economic History* (New York: Harper and Row, 1971), part 4; Carlo Cipolla, *The Fontana Economic History of Europe* (London: Collins–Fontana, 1973), vol. 4, no. 1, ch. 3; W. W. Rostow, *How it All Began* (New York: McGraw–Hill, 1975), ch. 4.

7.   Cressey Dymock, *An Invention of Engines of Motion*, in Henry Dircks, *A Biographical Memoir of Samuel Hartlib* (London: John Russel Smith, 1651), pp. 103–4.

8.   Dymock, p.104.

9.   E. P. Thompson, *The Making of the English Working Class* (New York: Vintage Books, 1963), pp. 251–58 and ch. 9. Landes, pp. 43–44. and Mantoux, pp. 62–96.

10.   See E. P. Thompson, *The Making of the Working Class*, pp. 291–92.

11.   See for instance, Charles Webster, *The Great Instauration* (New York: Holmes and Meier, 1976), esp. ch. 2; Musson and Robinson, ch. 1; E. G. R. Taylor, "Cartograhy, Survey, and Navigation, 1400–1750" in Singer, et al., *A History of Technology* (New York: Oxford University Press, 1957), vol. 3, pp. 530–57. Cyril Stanley Smith and R. J. Forbes, "Metallurgy and Assaying," in Singer, et al., vol. 3, pp. 27–71; A. Rupert Hall, *From Galileo to Newton, 1630–1720* (New York: Harper and Row, 1963), pp. 30–33; Jean Gimpel, *The Medieval Machine* (New York: Penguin, 1976).

12.   John Norden, *The Surveyors Dialogue* (London: Hugh Astley, 1607), Epistle to the Reader and book V, p. 188. See also, Lawrence Stone, *Family and Fortune* (Oxford: Clarendon Press, 1973), and B. A. Holderness, *Pre-Industrial England* (London: J. M. Dent, 1976).

13.   David Cressy, "Literacy in Pre-Industrial England," *Societas* (1974), 4:229–40; Carlo Cipolla, *Literacy and Development in the West* (London: Penguin, 1969); H. S. Bennett, *English Books and Readers, 1603–1640* (Cambridge: Cambridge University Press, 1970), ch. 6, esp. pp. 81–84.

14.   E. P. Thompson, *Making of the Working Class*, ch. 9.

15.   See Musson and Robinson, ch. 2, and A. E. Musson, *Science, Technology, and Economic Growth* (London: Methuen, 1972), introduction.

16.   E. J. Holmyard, "Chemical Industry: Developments in Chemical Theory and Practice," in Singer, et al., vol. 4, pp. 214–29; Wadsworth and Mann, ch. 21; English, ch. 1.

17.   Wadsworth and Mann, pp. 98–106; English, ch. 2.

18.   Musson and Robinson, ch. 1.

19.   E. P. Thompson, *Making of the Working Class*, ch. 9 and pp. 261–64 and 831.

20.   Phyllis Deane, *The First Industrial Revolution* (Cambridge: Cambridge University Press, 1965), pp. 85–86; Wadsworth and Mann, pp. 468–69; Maurice Daumas, *A History of Technology and Invention*, trans. E. Hennessy (New York: Crown, 1964), vol. 2, part 2, sect. 1; W. English, *The Textile Industry* (London: Longman's, 1969), p. 19; Richard Hills, *Power in the Industrial Revolution* (New York: Augustus M. Kelly, 1970), pp. 54–55.

21.   J. L. Hammond and B. Hammond, *The Rise of Modern Industry* (New York: Harcourt, Brace, and World, 1926), ch. 11; L. C. A. Knowles, *The Industrial and Commercial Revolutions in Great Britain During the Nineteenth Century* (London: Routledge and Kegan Paul [1921], 1961), pp. 30–57; Thomas, pp. 164–65.

22. Mantoux, pp. 204–9; Wadsworth and Mann, ch. 22; English, ch. 4.

23. Wadsworth and Mann, ch. 21; English, ch. 5; Mantoux, pp. 209–16.

24. English, ch. 6.

25. Wadsworth and Mann, pp. 468–69; Deane, pp. 85–86; R. S. Fitton and A. P. Wadsworth, *The Strutts and the Arkwrights, 1758–1830* (Manchester: Manchester University Press [1958], 1964), ch. 3.

26. For information on the demand for cotton cloth, see Wadsworth and Mann, pp. 126–28, and ch. 8. For the Mughal empire, see R. Mukherjee, *The Rise and Fall of the East India Company* (New York: Monthly Review Press, 1974), pp. 232–304; L. C. A. Knowles, p. 43.

27. Fitton and Wadsworth, pp. 81–90; Wadsworth and Mann, ch. 23; Turnbull, p. 25.

28. Fitton and Wadsworth, pp. 68–75; Wadsworth and Mann, pp. 482–85; Turnbull, p. 25.

29. For a discussion of the Mughal empire's collapse, see Mukherjee, pp. 232–304. The role of merchants in Parliament appears in Thomas, ch. 8. For a description of the rise of the fustian industry in England, see Wadsworth and Mann, pp. 173–78.

30. English, chs. 7 and 8; Hills, ch. 4; Fitton and Wadsworth, pp. 60–69; Mantoux, pp. 220–34; Cardwell, pp. 95–100; Wadsworth and Mann, ch. 23.

31. Deane, pp. 86–87; Wadsworth and Mann, ch. 23; English, ch. 7.

32. Deane, pp. 87–88; Wadsworth and Mann, ch. 23; English, ch. 8; Mantoux, pp. 220–23.

33. English, ch. 9; Hills, ch. 7; Cardwell, pp. 96–98; Mantoux, pp. 223–28.

34. Examples of these pressure prints are rare, but some are on public display in the textile collection of the Victoria and Albert Museum in London. They are also pictured and described by Isabelle Errara in the *Catalogue d'Étoffes Anciennes et Modernes* put out by the Museées Royaux du Cinquantenaire, Bruxelles, 1927 in the section entitled, "Étoffes Imprimées," esp. nos. 414–16, pp. 349–52.

35. Trenchard Cox for the Victoria and Albert Museum, *English Printed Textiles, 1720–1836* (London: Her Majesty's Stationery Office, 1960), pp. 5–7.

36. Cox, pp. 1–2.; Turnbull, pp. 25–97; Musson and Robinson, pp. 91–92, 240–245; A. E. Musson, *Science, Technology, and Economic Growth in the Eighteenth Century* (London: Methuen, 1972).

37. Geffrey Whitney, *A Choice of Emblemes and other Deuises* (Leyden: Plantyn, 1586), pp. 134–35.

38. A. R. Hall, "Science, Technology, and Utopia in the Seventeenth Century," in Peter Mathias, *Science and Society, 1600–1900* (Cambridge: Cambridge University Press, 1972), pp. 33–53; Landes, pp. 1–5; Cardwell, pp. 100–101.

39. Hall, "Science, Technology, and Utopia," pp. 33–53; Morris Berman, "Essay Review of Science, Technology, and the Industrial Revolution by Musson and Robinson," *Journal of Social History* (1972), 5:521–27; Cardwell, pp. 100–101; Mathias, pp. 54–80.

40. Musson and Robinson, pp. 240–45 and ch. 8.

41.   Musson and Robinson, ch. 7.
42.   Hall, *Galileo to Newton*, pp. 30–33; Musson and Robinson, ch. 1 and 2; Musson, introduction; and Robert Schofield, "The Industrial Orientation of Science in the Lunar Society of Birmingham," in Musson, ch. 5.
43.   R. Patterson, "Spinning and Weaving," in Singer, et al., vol. 3, p. 175.
44.   Irwin and Brett, p. 8.
45.   Archibald Clow and Nan Clow, "Vitriol in the Industrial Revolution," in Musson, p. 150.
46.   Archibald Clow and Nan Clow, "The Chemical Industry: Interaction with the Industrial Revolution," in Singer, et al., vol. 4, pp. 244–45.
47.   D. W. F. Hardie, "The Macintoshes and the Origins of the Chemical Industry," in Musson, ch. 7.
48.   Hardie.
49.   Michael Edwards, *The Growth of the British Cotton Trade, 1780–1815* (New York: Augustus M. Kelly, 1967), ch. 2; Arthur Gayer, W. W. Rostow, and Anna Schwartz, *The Growth and Fluctuation and the British Economy, 1790–1850* (Brighton: Harvester Press, 1975), ch. 1.
50.   Edwards, p. 149.
51.   Clow and Clow, "The Chemical Industry," pp. 230–57.
52.   Holmyard, pp. 214–29; Clow and Clow, "The Chemical Industry," pp. 230–57; Musson and Robinson, ch. 8.
53.   Clow and Clow, "The Chemical Industry," pp. 230–57.
54.   Hardie.
55.   Charles Wilson, "The Entrepreneur," in S. Lieberman, *Europe and the Industrial Revolution* (Cambridge: Schenckman, 1972), pp. 377–95.
56.   Edwards, pp. 147–63.
57.   Edwards, p. 154.
58.   Fitton and Wadsworth, pp. 47–50; Edwards, pp. 147–63.
59.   Edwards, pp. 30, 45–46. For a description of Peel's role as spokesman for calico printers, see Turnbull, pp. 73–77. For a description of this change in fashion, see James Laver, *The Concise History of Costume and Fashion* (New York: Scribner's, 1969), pp. 146–53.
60.   Edwards, pp. 45–46.
61.   Edwards, p. 51.
62.   Edwards, pp. 163–81.
63.   Edwards, pp. 177–81; Turnbull, pp. 133–35; Fitton and Wadsworth, pp. 297–98.
64.   S. D. Chapman, *The Cotton Industry in the Industrial Revolution* (New York: Macmillan, 1972), ch. 3; Edwards, ch. 5 and pp. 163–81.
65.   Chapman, ch. 4 and pp. 87–88; Fitton and Wadsworth; E. P. Thompson, *Making of the Working Class*, ch. 6; Wilson in Lieberman, pp. 377–95.
66.   Richard Sennett, *The Fall of Public Man* (New York: Vintage, 1978), compare pp. 66–72 to pp. 164–66.
67.   See for instance, Kurt and Gladys Lang, *Collective Dynamics* (New York:

Thomas Crowell, 1961), ch. 15; Robert Park, *Society* (Glencoe: Free Press, 1955), pp. 288–92; Bernard Barber and Lyle Lobel, " 'Fashion' in Women's Clothes and the American Social System," in Reinhard Bendix and Seymour Martin Lipset, *Class, Status, and Power* (Glencoe: Free Press, 1953).

7. MATERIALISM AND SOCIAL CHANGE

1. Pierre Bourdieu and Yvette Delsaut, "Le Couturier et sa Griffe" *Actes de la Recherche en Sciences Sociales* (January, 1975) 1:7–36; Pierre Bourdieu and Monique Saint Martin, "Anatomie du Goût" *Actes de la Recherche en Sciences Sociales* (October, 1976), vol. 5; and Jean Baudrillard, *Le Système des Objets* (Paris: Gallimard, 1968). But they find social class not the only factor. Other work on material culture under contemporary capitalism finds less association of objects with social class than with gender. See Mihaly Csikszentmihalyi and Eugene Rochberg-Halton, *The Meaning of Things* (New York: Cambridge University Press, 1981). Other dimensions of stratification and material culture deserve greater attention than I can give them here.

2. W. W. Rostow, *Stages of Economic Growth* (Cambridge: Cambridge University Press, 1963), pp. 13–14; W. W. Rostow, *How it All Began* (New York: McGraw–Hill, 1975); Neil Smelser, *Social Change in the Industrial Revolution* (Chicago: University of Chicago Press, 1959), p. 4; Paul Mantoux, *The Industrial Revolution in the Eighteenth Century* (London: Methuen [1928], 1964); Phyllis Deane and W. A. Cole, *British Economic Growth, 1688–1959* (Cambridge: Cambridge University Press, 1967), esp. pp. 163, 184 and 188.

3. Deane and Cole, pp. 182–92; and Michael Edwards, *The Growth of the British Cotton Trade, 1780–1815* (New York: Augustus M. Kelly, 1967), pp. 236–37. Deane and Cole do not present data on the role of the chemical industry in the eighteenth- or nineteenth-century economy. They do suggest that it only accounted for 1.1 percent of the national income in the early twentieth century. See p. 175.

4. Rostow, *How it All Began*, pp. 171–73; Deane and Cole, esp. pp. 62–97; see also S. Lieberman, *Europe and the Industrial Revolution* (Cambridge: Schenckman, 1972), part 5.

5. Deane and Cole, pp. 62–97 and conclusions. See also Elizabeth Gilboy, "Demand as a Factor in the Industrial Revolution," in Lieberman, pp. 193–208.

6. See Karl Marx, *Captial* (New York: Modern Library, 1936), pp. 81–96.

7. Gilboy; Harold Perkin, *The Origins of Modern English Society, 1780–1880* (Toronto: University of Toronto Press, 1969), pp. 85–97.

8. Perkin, *Origins*, pp. 95–97. Neil McKendrick et al., *The Birth of a Consumer Society* (Bloomington: Indiana University Press, 1982).

9. Perkin, p. 95, and N. McKendrick, "Josiah Wedgwood: An Eighteenth-Century Entrepreneur in Salesmanship and Marketing Techniques," *Economic History Review* (1960), ser. 2, 12:408–33. McKendrick et al., Part 1.

10. McKendrick et al.

11. John Nef, *The Rise of the British Coal Industry* (London: Anchor [1932], 1966), esp. conclusion; Rostow, *How it All Began*, pp. 162–64; Thomas Ashton, *Iron and Steel in the Industrial Revolution* (New York: Augustus M. Kelly, 1968). See also John Nef, *The Conquest of the Material World* (Chicago: University of Chicago Press, 1964); J. R. Harris, *Industry and Technology in the Eighteenth Century* (Birmingham: University of Birmingham Press, 1972).

12. See Ashton, chs. 1 and 2; Perkin, p. 96; Arthur Raistrick, *Dynasty of Iron Founders* (London: Longman, Green, 1953), chs. 2 and 3; Nef, *British Coal Industry*, vol. 1, pp. 196–200.

13. Raistrick, ch. 8; Perkin, p. 96; Ashton, ch. 3.

14. Perkin, p. 96; Raistrick, pp. 65–67; Ashton, ch. 6; Nef, *British Coal Industry*, vol. 1, pp. 224–25.

15. Ashton, pp. 14–15 and ch. 5.

16. Raistrick, chs. 2 and 3; Perkin, p. 96; Ashton, ch. 2.

17. Ashton, ch. 5. The politics of nonimportation in North America increased British anxiety about this trade. See Charles Andrews, *Boston Merchants and the Non-Importation Movement* (New York: Russell and Russell [1916], 1968), and Arthur Schlesinger, *The Colonial Merchants and American Revolution* (New York: Frederick Ungar [1918], 1957), chs. 3–5; Raistrick, ch. 4.

18. Daniel Defoe, *A Plan of the English Commerce* (London: Charles Rivington, 1728), p. 190.

19. John Tyler, "Technological Development: Agent of Change in Style and Form of Domestic Iron Castings," in Ian Quimby and Polly Earl, *Technological Innovation and the Decorative Arts* (Charlottesville: University Press of Virginia, 1974), pp. 141–65.

20. Karl Polanyi, *The Great Transformation* (Boston: Beacon Press, [1944], 1957); Marshall Sahlins, *Culture and Practical Reason* (Chicago: University of Chicago Press, 1976); Eli Heckscher, *Mercantilism* (New York: Macmillan [1931], 1962), vol. 2, ch. 3; Perkin, ch. 2; Lynn White, Jr., *Medieval Technology and Social Change* (New York: Oxford University Press, 1962), ch. 1.

21. This is one of the points made by Joan Thirsk in her *Economic Policy and Projects* (Oxford: Clarendon Press, 1978). See also, for a discussion of the ideological character of economic ideas, Joyce Appleby, *Economic Thought and Ideology in Seventeenth-Century England* (Princeton: Princeton University Press, 1978).

22. Polanyi.

23. Walter Ong, *Interfaces of the Word* (Ithaca: Cornell Univesity Press, 1977); Alvin Gouldner, *The Dialectic of Ideology and Technology* (New York: Seabury Press, 1976).

24. For some examples see Chandra Mukerji, "Artwork: Collection and examples, Contemporary Culture," *American Journal of Sociology* (September, 1978), 84:348–65; Baudrillard; McKendrick et al.; Csikszentmihalyi and Rochberg-Halton.

Bibliography

Ackerman, James, et al. *Seventeenth-Century Art in Flanders and Holland.* New York: Garland, 1976.

Allen, B. Sprague. *Tides of English Taste.* New York: Pageant, 1958.

Almagià, Roberto. "On the Cartographic Work of Francesco Rosselli." *Imago Mundi* (1951), 8:17–26.

Amherst, Alicia. *A History of Gardening in England.* Detroit: Singing Tree Books [1896], 1969.

Andrews, Charles. *Boston Merchants and the Non-Importation Movement.* New York: Russell and Russell [1916], 1968.

Antal, Frederick. *Florentine Painting and its Social Background.* London: Kegan Paul, 1947.

Appleby, Joyce. *Economic Thought and Ideology in Seventeenth-Century England.* Princeton: Princeton University Press, 1978.

Arber, Agnes. *Herbals.* Cambridge: Cambridge University Press, 1953.

Ashton, Thomas. *Iron and Steel in the Industrial Revolution.* New York: Augustus M. Kelly, 1968.

Aston, Robert. "The Parliamentary Agitation for Free Trade in the Opening Years of the Reign of James I." *Past and Present* (1967), 38:40–55.

Avermaete, Roger. *Rubens and His Times.* London: Allen and Unwin, 1968.

Bagrow, L. "A Page from the History of the Distribution of Maps." *Imago Mundi* (1948), 5:62.

Baldwin, Frances. *Sumptuary Legislation and Personal Regulation in England.* Baltimore: Johns Hopkins University Press, 1926.

Barber, Bernard, and Lyle Lobel. " 'Fashion' in Women's Clothes and the American Social System." In R. Bendix and S. Lipset, *Class, Status, and Power.* Glencoe: Free Press, 1953.

Barber, William. *British Economic Thought About India.* Oxford: Clarendon Press, 1974.

———— *History of Economic Thought.* Baltimore: Penguin, 1967.

Barbon, Nicholas. *A Discourse of Trade.* In J. Hollander, ed., *A Reprint of Economic Tracts.* Baltimore: Johns Hopkins University Press [1690], 1903, pp. 14–16.

Barnes, Barry. *Scientific Knowledge and Sociological Theory.* London: Routledge and Kegan Paul, 1974.

Batterberry, Michael, and Ariane Batterberry. *Mirror, Mirror.* New York: Holt, Rinehart, and Winston, 1977.

Baudrillard, Jean. *Le Système des Objets.* Paris: Gallimard, 1968.

Baxandall, Michael. *Painting and Experience in Fifteenth-Century Italy.* New York: Oxford University Press [1972], 1974.

Beck, Thomasina. *Embroidered Gardens.* New York: Viking, 1978.

Becker, Howard. "Art as Collective Action." *American Sociological Review* (1974), 39:767–76.

Bell, Quentin. *On Human Finery.* New York: Schocken, 1976.

Bendix, Reinhard. *Kings or People.* Berkeley: University of California Press, 1978.

Benjamin, Walter. "The Work of Art in the Age of Mechanical Reproduction." In H. Arendt, *Illuminations.* New York: Schocken, 1968.

Berger, Bennett. *The Survival of a Counterculture.* Berkeley: University of California Press, 1981.

Berman, Morris. "Essay Review of Science, Technology, and the Industrial Revolution by Musson and Robinson." *Journal of Social History* (1972), 5:521–27.

Blake, N. F. *Caxton: England's First Publisher.* New York: Harper and Row, 1976.

Bloch, Marc. *The Historian's Craft.* New York: Vintage, 1953.

—— *Land and Work in Medieval Europe.* Berkeley: University of California Press, 1967.

Blunt, Wilfrid. *The Art of Botanical Illustration.* London: Collins, 1950.

Bourdieu, Pierre, and Monique Saint Martin. "Anatomie du Goût." *Actes de la Recherche en Sciences Sociales* (1976), vol. 5.

Bourdieu, Pierre, and Yvette Delsaut. "Le Couturier et sa Griffe." *Actes de la Recherche en Sciences Sociales* (1975), 1:7–36.

Braudel, Fernand. *Afterthoughts on Material Civilization and Capitalism.* Baltimore: Johns Hopkins University Press, 1976.

—— *Capitalism and Material Life, 1400–1800.* New York: Harper and Row, 1967.

—— *The Mediterranean and the Mediterranean World in the Age of Phillip II.* New York: Harper [1949], 1966.

Bronowski, Jacob. *The Ascent of Man.* Boston: Little Brown, 1973.

Bühler, Curt. *The Fifteenth-Century Book.* Philadelphia: University of Pennsylvania Press, 1960.

Burckhardt, Jacob. *Civilization of the Renaissance in Italy.* New York: Oxford University Press, n.d.

Burke, Peter. *Popular Culture in Early Modern Europe.* London: Temple Smith, 1978.

—— *Venice and Amsterdam.* London: Temple Smith, 1974.

—— *Tradition and Innovation in Renaissance Italy.* London: Fontana, 1972.

Burtt, Edwin. *The Metaphysical Foundations of Modern Physical Science.* London: Routledge and Kegan Paul [1924], 1959.

Butterfield, H. "Renaissance Art and Modern Science." In H. Kearney, *Origins of the Scientific Revolution.* London: Longman's, 1964.

Calvin, John. *On the Christian Faith,* ed. J. McNeil. Indianapolis: Bobbs-Merrill [1559], 1957.

Cannenberg, W. V. "An Unknown 'Pilot' by Hessel Gerritsz, dating from 1612." *Imago Mundi* (1931), 1:49–51.

Cantor, Norman, and M. Werthman. *The History of Popular Culture.* London: Collier-Macmillan, 1968.

Cardwell, D. S. L. *Technology, Science, and History.* London: Heineman, 1972.

Carter, Thomas. *The Invention of Printing in China,* 2d ed. Revised by L. C. Goodrich. New York: Ronald Press [1925], 1955.

Chapman, S. D. *The Cotton Industry in the Industrial Revolution.* New York: Macmillan, 1972.

Cipolla, Carlo. *Before the Industrial Revolution.* New York: Norton, 1976.

────── *Clocks and Culture.* London: Collins, 1967.

────── *The Fontana Economic History of Europe.* London: Collins-Fontana, 1973.

────── *Guns, Sails, and Empires.* New York: Pantheon, 1965.

────── *Literacy and Development in the West.* London: Penguin, 1969.

Clagett, J. "Medieval Mechanics." In H. Kearney, *Origins of the Scientific Revolution.* London: Longman's, 1964.

Clapham, Michael. "Printing." In Charles Singer et al., *A History of Technology.* New York: Oxford University Press, 1957, vol. 3.

Clebsch, W. *England's Earliest Protestants.* New Haven: Yale University Press, 1964.

Clow, Archibald, and Nan Clow. "Vitriol in the Industrial Revolution." In A. E. Musson, *Science, Technology, and Economic Growth.* London: Methuen, 1972.

────── "The Chemical Industry: Interaction with the Industrial Revolution." In Charles Singer et al., *A History of Technology.* New York: Oxford University Press, 1957, vol. 4.

Cohen, Jere. "Rational Capitalism in Renaissance Italy." *American Journal of Sociology* (1980), 85:1340–55.

Cole, Charles W. *French Mercantilism.* New York: Octagon, 1965.

Cook, Olive. *The English Country House.* New York: Putnam, 1974.

Cox, Trenchard, for the Victoria and Albert Museum. *English Printed Textiles, 1720–1836.* London: Her Majesty's Stationery Office, 1960.

Cressy, David. "Literacy in Pre-Industrial England." *Societas* (1974), 4:229–40.

Crone, G. R. *Maps and Their Makers.* London: Hutchinson Library, 1953.

Crowson, P. S. *Tudor Foreign Policy.* New York: St. Martin's Press, 1973.

Csikszentmihalyi, Mihaly, and Eugene Rochberg-Halton. *The Meaning of Things.* New York: Cambridge University Press, 1981.

Cunningham, Phyllis, and Catherine Lucas. *Occupational Costume in England.* New York: Barnes and Noble, 1967.

Curtius, Ernst. *European Literature and the Latin Middle Ages.* New York: Harper and Row [1953], 1963.

Dahl, Svend. *History of the Book.* Metuchen, N. J.: Scarecrow, 1968.

Daumas, Maurice. *A History of Technology and Invention.* New York: Crown, 1964.

Davis, Natalie. *Society and Culture in Early Modern France.* Stanford: Stanford University Press, 1965.

Davis, Ralph. *Rise of the Atlantic Economy*. Ithaca: Cornell University Press, 1973.

―――― *The Rise of the English Shipping Industry in the Seventeenth and Eighteenth Centuries*. London: Macmillan, 1962.

Deane, Phyllis. *The First Industrial Revolution*. Cambridge: Cambridge University Press, 1965.

Deane, Phyllis, and W. A. Cole. *British Economic Growth, 1688–1959*. Cambridge: Cambridge University Press, 1967.

Debus, A. *Science, Medicine, and Society in the Renaissance*. New York: Science History Publications, 1972.

Defoe, Daniel. *A New Voyage Round the World by a Course that never failed before*. London: Bettesworth and Mears, 1725.

―――― *A Plan of English Commerce*. London: Charles Rivington, 1728.

Detroit Institute of the Arts. *Flanders in the Fifteenth Century*. Detroit: Institute of the Arts, 1960.

Dickens, A. G. *The English Reformation*. New York: Schocken, 1964.

Dobb, Maurice. *Studies in the Development of Capitalism*. New York: International Publishers [1947], 1976.

Douglas, Ann. *The Feminization of American Culture*. New York: Avon, 1977.

Douglas, Mary, and Baron Isherwood. *World of Goods*. New York: Basic Books, 1979.

Drake, Stillman, and E. Drabkin. *Mechanics in Sixteenth-Century Italy*. Madison: University of Wisconsin Press, 1969.

Dürer, Albrecht. *Records of the Journeys to Venice and the Low Countries*, ed. Roger Fry. Boston: Merrymount, 1913.

Durkheim, Emile. *Division of Labor in Society*. New York: Free Press [1893], 1933.

―――― *Suicide*. New York: Free Press [1930], 1951.

Dymock, Cressey. *An Invention of Engines of Motion*. In Henry Dircks, *A Biographical Memoir of Samuel Hartlib*. London: John R. Smith [1651], 1865.

Edwards, Michael. *The Growth of the British Cotton Trade, 1780–1815*. New York: Augustus M. Kelly, 1967.

Eisenstein, Elizabeth. *The Printing Press as an Agent of Change*. New York: Cambridge University Press, 1979.

Elias, Norbert. *The Civilizing Process*. New York: Urizen Books [1939], 1978.

Elliott, J. H. *The Old World and the New*. Cambridge: Cambridge University Press, 1970.

Enckell, Carl. "The Representation of the North of Europe in the World Map of Petrus Plancius of 1592." *Imago Mundi* (1951), 8:55–56.

English, W. *The Textile Industry*. London: Longman's, 1969.

Errara, Isabelle. *Catalogue d'Étoffes Anciennes et Modernes*. Brussels: Musées Royaux Quinquantenaire, 1927.

'Espinasse, Margaret. "The Decline and Fall of Restoration Science." In Charles Webster, *The Intellectual Revolution of the Seventeenth Century*. London: Routledge [1958], 1974, pp. 347–68.

Evelyn, John. *Navigation and Commerce, Their Original and Progress.* London: Benjamin Tooke, 1674.

———— *Sylva or Discourse on Forest Trees.* London: John Martyn, 1679.

Ewen, Stewart. *Captains of Consciousness.* New York: McGraw-Hill, 1976.

Febvre, Lucien, and Henri-Jean Martin. *The Coming of the Book*, trans. David Gerard. London: NLB [1958], 1976.

Feuer, Lewis. *The Scientific Intellectual.* New York: Basic Books, 1963.

Fisher, F. J. "The Development of London as a Centre of Conspicuous Consumption in the Sixteenth and Seventeenth Centuries." *Transactions of the Royal Historical Society* (1948), 30:37–50.

Fitton, R. S., and A. P. Wadsworth. *The Strutts and the Arkwrights, 1758–1830.* Manchester: Manchester University Press [1958], 1964.

Flink, James J. *The Car Culture.* Cambridge, Mass.: MIT Press, 1975.

Fordham, Sir Herbert George. *Some Notable Surveyors and Map-Makers of the Sixteenth, Seventeenth, and Eighteenth Centuries and their Work.* Cambridge: Cambridge University Press, 1929.

Freudenberger, Herman. "Fashion, Sumptuary Laws, and Business." *Business History Review* (1963), 37:38–39.

Friedländer, Max. *Early Netherlandish Painting.* London: Phaidon, 1956.

Gallo, Rudolfo. "A Fifteenth-Century Military Map of the Venetian Territory of Terraterma." *Imago Mundi* (1955), 12:55–57.

Gayer, Arthur, W. W. Rostow, and Anna Schwartz. *The Growth and Fluctuation and the British Economy, 1790–1850.* Brighton: Harvester Press, 1975.

Gerulaitis, Leonardas. *Printing and Publishing in Fifteenth-Century Venice.* Chicago: American Library Association, 1976.

Geyle, Pieter. *The Revolt of the Netherlands, 1555–1609.* New York: Barnes and Noble, 1958.

Gilbert, William. *De Magnete* [1600:1893], trans. P. F. Mottley. New York: Dover, 1958.

Gilboy, Elizabeth. "Demand as a Factor in the Industrial Revolution." In S. Lieberman, *Europe and the Industrial Revolution.* Cambridge: Schenckman, 1972.

Gimpel, Jean. *The Medieval Machine.* New York: Penguin, 1976.

Girouard, Mark. *Life in the English Country House.* New Haven: Yale University Press, 1978.

Girtin, Thomas. *The Golden Ram.* London: Company of Clothmakers, 1958.

Gloag, John. *English Furniture*, 6th ed. London: Adams and Charles Black [1934], 1973.

———— *Social History of Furniture Design.* New York: Crown, 1966.

Gombrich, E. H. *Art and Illusion.* Princeton: Princeton University Press [1960], 1972.

Gopal, L. "The Textile Industry in Medieval India." *Journal of the Asiatic Society of Bombay* (1964), n.s., 39:100–2.

Gouldner, Alvin. *The Dialectic of Ideology and Technology.* New York: Seabury Press, 1976.

Gusfield, Joseph. *The Culture of Public Problems*. Chicago: University of Chicago Press, 1981.

Hakluyt, Richard. *Divers Voyages*, ed. Irwin Blacker. New York: Viking [1582–1600], 1965.

_____ *Principle Navigations*. London: George Bishop, 1598–1600.

Hall, A. Rupert. "Merton Revisited." *History of Science* (1963), 2:1–16.

_____ *From Galileo to Newton, 1630–1720*. New York: Harper and Row, 1963.

_____ "Science, Technology, and Utopia in the Seventeenth Century." In Peter Mathias, *Science and Society, 1600–1900*. Cambridge: Cambridge University Press, 1972.

_____ *The Scientific Revolution, 1500–1800*. Boston: Beacon Press, 1954.

Hammond, J. L., and B. Hammond. *The Rise of Modern Industry*. New York: Harcourt, Brace, and World, 1926.

Hardie, D. W. F. "The Macintoshes and the Origins of the Chemical Industry." In A. E. Musson, *Science, Technology, and Economic Growth*. London: Methuen, 1972.

Harris, J. R. *Industry and Technology in the Eighteenth Century*. Birmingham: University of Birmingham Press, 1972.

Hauser, Arnold. *Social History of Art*. New York: Vintage, 1951.

Hazlitt, W. C. *Gleanings in Old Garden Literature*. London: Elliot Stock, 1904.

Hechter, Michael. *Internal Colonialism*. Berkeley: University of California Press, 1975.

Heckscher, Eli. *Mercantilism*. New York: Macmillan [1931], 1962.

Hegel, Robert. *The Novel in Seventeenth-Century China*. New York: Columbia University Press, 1981.

Held, Julius, and Donald Posner. *Seventeenth- and Eighteenth-Century Art*. New York: Harry N. Abrams, n.d.

Herbert, Thomas. *Some Yeares Travels*. London: Jacob Blome and Richard Bishop, 1638.

Hill, Christopher. *The Intellectual Origins of the English Revolution*. New York: Oxford University Press, 1965.

Hill, Margot, and Peter Bucknell. *Evolution of Fashion*. London: Batsford, 1967.

Hills, Richard. *Power in the Industrial Revolution*. New York: Augustus M. Kelly, 1970.

Hindman, Sandra. *Pen to Press*. Baltimore: Johns Hopkins University Press, 1977.

Hirsch, Rudolf. *Printing, Selling, and Reading, 1450–1550*. Wiesbaden: Otto Harrassowitz, 1967.

Hodgson, Marshall G. *The Venture of Islam*. Chicago: University of Chicago Press, 1974.

Holderness, B. A. *Pre-Industrial England*. London: J. M. Dent, 1976.

Holmes, Urban T. *Daily Living in the Twelfth Century*. Madison: University of Wisconsin Press, 1952.

Holmyard, E. J. "Chemical Industry: Developments in Chemical Theory and Practice." In Charles Singer et al., *A History of Technology*. New York: Oxford University Press, 1957, vol. 4.

Holton, Gerald. *Thematic Origins of Scientific Thought.* Cambridge, Mass.: Harvard University Press, 1973.

Hooper, Wilfred. "The Tudor Sumptuary Laws." *English Historical Review* (1915), 30:433–49.

Horkheimer, Max. "The End of Reason." *Studies in Philosophy and Social Science* (1941), vol. 9.

Hoskins, W. G. *Provincial England.* London: Macmillan, 1963.

Huizinga, J. *Men and Ideas.* New York: Meridian Books, 1959.

—— *The Waning of the Middle Ages.* New York: Anchor, 1954.

Hunt, J., and P. Willis. *The Genius of Place.* London: Paul Elek, 1975.

Hurlburtt, Robert. *Hume, Newton, and the Design Argument.* Lincoln: University of Nebraska Press, 1965.

Innis, Harold. *Empire and Communications.* Toronto: University of Toronto Press [1950], 1972.

Irwin, John, and Katherine Brett. *Origins of Chintz.* London: Her Majesty's Stationery Office, 1970.

Ivins, William. *Prints and Visual Communication.* Cambridge: MIT Press, 1953.

Jacob, J. R. *Robert Boyle and the English Revolution.* New York: Burt Franklin, 1977.

Janson, Harold. *History of Art.* Englewood Cliffs, N. J.: Prentice-Hall, 1962.

Joade, C. E. M. *A Guide to Philosophy.* New York: Random House, 1935.

Kahr, Madlyn. *Dutch Painting in the Seventeenth Century.* New York: Harper and Row, 1978.

Kammen, Michael. *Empire and Interest.* New York: J. B. Lippincott, 1970.

Kearney, Hugh. *Origins of the Scientific Revolution.* London: Longman's, 1964.

Kemsley, Douglas. "Religious Influences in the Rise of Modern Science." *Annals of Science* (1968), 24:199–226.

Kendrick, A. F. *English Decorative Fabrics of the Sixteenth to Eighteenth Centuries.* London: F. Lewis, 1934.

Kerridge, Eric. *Farmers of Old England.* Totowa, N. J.: Rowman and Littlefield, 1973.

Kingdon, Robert M. "Patronage, Piety, and Printing in Sixteenth-Century Europe." In David Pinkney and T. Ropp, *A Festschrift for Frederick B. Artz.* Durham: Duke University Press, 1964.

Kline, M. "Painting and Perspective." In H. Kearney, *Origins of the Scientific Revolution.* London: Longman's, 1964.

Knowles, David. *The Evolution of Medieval Thought.* New York: Vintage, 1962.

Knowles, L. C. A. *The Industrial and Commercial Revolutions in Great Britain During the Nineteenth Century.* London: Routledge and Kegan Paul [1921], 1961.

Kohn, Hans. *The Idea of Nationalism.* New York: Collier, 1944.

Krüger, Herbert. "Erhard Etzlaub's *Ronweg* Map and Its Dating in the Holy Year of 1500." *Imago Mundi* (1951), 8:17–26.

Kǔchar, Karl. "A Map of Bohemia of the Time of the Thirty Years' War." *Imago Mundi* (1938), 2:75–77.

Kuening, Johannes. "Cornelius Anthonisz." *Imago Mundi* (1950), 7:52–53.

_____ "The History of an Atlas: Mercator-Hondius." *Imago Mundi* (1948), 4:37 –62.

Kunzle, David. *The Early Comic Strip.* Berkeley: University of California Press, 1973.

Kybalová, Ladmila, et al. *The Pictorial Encyclopedia of Fashion*, trans. C. Rosoux. New York: Crown, 1968.

Landes, David. *The Unbound Prometheus.* New York: Cambridge University Press, 1969.

Landwehr, John. *Dutch Emblem Books: A Bibliography.* Utrecht: Haentjens Deller and Gurnbert, 1962.

Lang, Kurt, and Gladys Lang. *Collective Dynamics.* New York: Thomas Crowell, 1961.

Lang, Wilhelm. "The Augsburg Travel Guide of 1563 and the Erlinger Road Map of 1524." *Imago Mundi* (1950), 7:85–88.

Latour, Bruno, and Stephen Woolgar. *Laboratory Life.* Los Angeles: Sage, 1979.

Laver, James. *The Concise History of Costume and Fashion.* New York: Scribner's, 1969.

_____ *Costume.* New York: Hawthorne, 1963.

Lehman-Haupt, H. O. *Gutenberg and the Master of the Playing Cards.* New Haven: Yale University Press, 1966.

Lenygon, Francis. *The Decoration and Furniture of English Mansions.* London: T. Werner Laurie, 1909.

Letwin, William. *The Origins of Scientific Economics.* Garden City: Doubleday, 1964.

Lewis, George. *Side-Saddle on the Golden Calf.* Pacific Palisades: Goodyear Publishing, 1972.

Lieberman, Sandra. *Europe and the Industrial Revolution.* Cambridge: Schenckman, 1972.

Lindberg, David, and Nicholas Steneek. "The Sense of Vision and the Origins of Modern Science." In A. Debus, *Science, Medicine, and Society in the Renaissance.* New York: Science History Publications, 1972.

Linschoten, John Huighen van. *His Dicourse of Voyages into Ye Easte and West Indies.* London: John Wolfe, 1598.

Lister, Raymond. *Antique Maps and Their Cartographers.* London: G. Bell, 1970.

Lloyd, Allan. "Mechanical Timekeepers." In Charles Singer, et al., *History of Technology.* New York: Oxford University Press, 1957, vol. 4.

Locke, John. *Some Considerations of the Consequences of Lowering the Interest and Raising the Value of Money.* London: Awnsham and John Churchil, 1696. In *Several Papers Relating to Money, Interest and Trade & Etc. by John Locke.* Reprint, New York: Augustus M. Kelley, 1968.

Lockridge, Kenneth. *Literacy in Colonial New England.* New York: Norton, 1974.

Lowenthal, Leo. "Historical Perspectives on Popular Culture." *American Journal of Sociology* (1950), 55:323–32.

Lowry, Martin. *The World of Aldus Manutius.* Ithaca: Cornell University Press, 1979.

Luther, Martin. *Three Treatises.* Philadelphia: Fortress Press [1520], 1960.

Lynam, Edward. *The Mapmaker's Art.* London: Batchworth Press, 1953.

MacDonald, Dwight. "A Theory of Mass Culture." In Bernard Rosenberg and David Manning White, *Mass Culture.* New York: Free Press [1953], 1957.

Mackay, Charles. *Extraordinary Popular Delusions and the Madness of Crowds.* New York: Harmony Books [1852], 1980.

McKendrick, N. "Josiah Wedgwood: An Eighteenth-Century Entrepreneur in Salesmanship and Marketing Techniques." *Economic History Review* (1960), ser. 2, 12:408–33.

McKendrick, Neil, John Brewer, and J. H. Plumb. *The Birth of a Consumer Society.* Bloomington: Indiana University Press, 1982.

McLuhan, Marshall. *Gutenberg Galaxy.* Toronto: University of Toronto Press, 1962.

McMurtrie, Douglas. *The Book.* New York: Oxford University Press, 1943.

McQuail, Denis. *Sociology of Mass Communications.* Baltimore: Penguin, 1972.

Magurn, Ruth, ed. *The Letters of Peter Paul Rubens.* Cambridge, Mass.: Harvard University Press, 1955.

Mantoux, Paul. *The Industrial Revolution in the Eighteenth Century.* London: Methuen [1928], 1964.

Manuel, Frank. *A Portrait of Isaac Newton.* Cambridge, Mass.: Harvard Univesity Press, 1968.

———— *Isaac Newton Historian.* Cambridge, Mass.: Harvard University Press, 1972.

———— *The Age of Reason.* Ithaca: Cornell University Press, 1951.

Marcus, G. J. *Naval History of England.* Vol. 1. Boston: Little Brown, 1961.

Marcuse, Herbert. *One-Dimensional Man.* Boston: Beacon Press, 1964.

Marjay, Frederico. *Dom Henrique the Navigator.* Lisbon: Quincentenary Commemorations, 1960.

Martin, John. *Baroque.* New York: Harper and Row, 1977.

Marx, Karl. *Capital.* New York: Modern Library, 1936.

Mathias, Peter. *Science and Society, 1600–1900.* Cambridge: Cambridge University Press, 1972.

Mauss, Marcel. *The Gift.* New York: Norton, 1967.

May, W. E., and L. Holder. *A History of Marine Navigation.* New York: Norton, 1973.

Merton, Robert. *Science, Technology, and Society in Seventeenth-Century England.* New York: Howard Fertig [1938], 1970.

Morgan, Victor. "The Cartographic Image of 'The Country' in Early Modern England." *Transactions of the Royal Historical Society* (1979), 5th ser., 29:129–54.

Mukerji, Chandra. "Artwork: Collection and Contemporary Culture." *American Journal of Sociology* (1978), 84:348–365.

Mukherjee, Ramkrishna. *The Rise and Fall of the East India Company.* New York: Monthly Review Press, 1974.

Mules, Helen B. *Flowers in Books and Drawings.* New York: Morgan Library, 1980.

Mumby, A., and I. Norrie. *Publishing and Bookselling*. London: Jonathan Cape, 1930.

Mun, Thomas. *England's Treasure by Forraign Trade*. New York: Macmillan [1664], 1895.

Musper, H. T. *Albrecht Dürer*. New York: Harry M. Abrams, 1966.

Musson, A. E. *Science, Technology, and Economic Growth*. London: Methuen, 1972.

Musson, A. E., and Eric Robinson. *Science and Technology in the Industrial Revolution*. Toronto: University of Toronto Press, 1969.

Muther, Richard. *German Book Illustration of the Gothic Period and Early Renaissance*, trans. Ralph Shaw. Metuchen, N. J.: Scarecrow, 1972.

Nef, John. *Cultural Foundations of Industrial Civilization*. New York: Harper, 1958.

———— *The Conquest of the Material World*. Chicago: University of Chicago Press, 1964.

———— *The Rise of the British Coal Industry*. London: Anchor [1932], 1966.

Newman, J. *The World of Mathematics*. New York: Simon and Schuster, 1956.

Norden, John. *Specvli Britanniae: The First Parte: An Historicall and Chorographicall Discription of Middlesex*. London: John Norden, 1593.

———— *Speculi Britanniae Pars, An Historical and Chorographical Description of the County of Essex*, Sir Henry Ellis. ed. London: AMS Press for the Camden Society [1594], 1968.

———— *The Surveyors Dialogue*. London: Hugh Astley, 1607.

O'Brien, George. *An Essay on Medieval Economic Teaching*. New York: Augustus M. Kelley [1920], 1967.

Ong, Walter. *Interfaces of the Word*. Ithaca: Cornell University Press, 1977.

Panofsky, Erwin. *Albrecht Dürer*. New York: Oxford University Press, 1948.

———— *Meaning in the Visual Arts*. Garden City, N. J.: Doubleday [1939], 1955.

Park, Robert. *Society*. Glencoe: Free Press, 1955.

Parry, J. H. *The Establishment of European Hegemony*. New York: Harper and Row, 1961.

———— *European Reconnaisance*. New York: Walker, 1968.

Parsons, E. J. S., and W. F. Morris. "Edward Wright and His Work." *Imago Mundi* (1939), 3:61–71.

Patterson, R. "Spinning and Weaving." In Charles Singer et al., *A History of Technology*. New York: Oxford University Press, 1957, vol. 4.

Peacham, Henry. *The Compleat Gentleman*. London: E. Tyler, 1661.

Penrose, Boies. *Travel and Discovery in the Renaissance*. Cambridge, Mass.: Harvard University Press, n.d.

Perkin, Harold. *The Origins of Modern English Society, 1780–1880*. Toronto: University of Toronto Press, 1969.

Petty, Sir William. *The History of the Survey of Ireland Commonly Called the Down Survey, 1655–1656*. New York: Augustus M. Kelley [1851], 1967.

Philopatris. *A Treatise Concerning the East India Trade*. London: Robert Boulter, 1681.

Pike, Ruth. *Enterprise and Adventure.* New York: Cornell University Press, 1966.

Pinkney, David, and T. Ropp. *A Festschrift for Frederick B. Artz.* Durham: Duke University Press, 1964.

Pirenne, Henri. *A History of Europe.* New York: University Books, 1936.

Plant, Marjorie. *The English Book Trade.* London: Allen and Unwin [1939], 1974.

Plummer, Alfred. *The London Weaver's Company, 1600–1970.* London: Routledge and Kegan Paul, 1972.

Polanyi, Karl. *The Great Transformation.* Boston: Beacon Press [1944], 1957.

Pollard, Alfred. *Early Illustrated Books.* London: Kegan Paul, French [1893], 1917.

Popkin, Samuel. *The Rational Peasant.* Berkeley: University of California Press, 1979.

Pottinger, David. *The French Book Trade in the Ancien Regime, 1500–1791.* Cambridge, Mass.: Harvard University Press, 1958.

Power, Eileen, and M. M. Postan. *Studies in English Trade in the Fifteenth Century.* London: Routledge and Kegan Paul [1933], 1951.

Purchas, Samuel. *Hakluytus Posthumus.* London: Henry Featherston, 1625.

Putnam, George. *Books and Their Makers During the Middle Ages.* New York: Hillary House, 1962.

Quinn, David B. *England and the Discovery of America.* New York: Alfred A. Knopf, 1974.

—— *North America from Earliest Discovery to First Settlements.* New York: Harper and Row, 1975.

Rabb, Theodore. "Puritanism and the Rise of Experimental Science in England." *Cahiers d'Histoire Mondiale* (1962), 7:46–67.

Raistrick, Arthur. *Dynasty of Iron Founders.* London: Longman, Green, 1953.

Ramsey, L. G. *Antique English Furniture.* London: The Connoisseur, 1961.

Reeds, Karen. "Renaissance Humanism and Botany." *Anals of Science* (1976), 33:519–42.

Richeson, A. W. *English Land Measuring to 1800.* Cambridge, Mass.: MIT Press, 1966.

Roberts, Lewis. *The Merchants Map of Commerce,* 4th ed. London: Thomas Horne, 1700.

Robinson, Dwight. "The Importance of Fashions in Taste to Business History." *Business History Review* (1963), 37:16–20.

Robinson, Stuart. *A History of Printed Textiles.* Cambridge: MIT Press, 1969.

Rosenberg, Bernard, and David M. White. *Mass Culture.* New York: Free Press, 1957.

Rostenberg, Leona. *English Publishers in the Graphic Arts, 1599–1700.* New York: Burt Franklin, 1963.

Rostow, W. W. *How It All Began.* New York: McGraw-Hill, 1975.

—— *Stages of Economic Growth.* Cambridge: Cambridge University Press, 1963.

Ruiz, Gonzales de Reparaz. "The Topographical Maps of Portugal and Spain in the Sixteenth Century." *Imago Mundi* (1950), 77:75–82.

Sahlins, Marshall. *Culture and Practical Reason.* Chicago: University of Chicago Press, 1976.

Sarton, George. *Six Wings.* Bloomington: Indiana University Press, 1957.

Saxl, Fritz. "Rembrandt and Classical Antiquity." In James Ackerman et al., *Seventeenth-Century Art in Flanders and Holland.* New York: Garland, 1976.

Saxl, F., and R. Witkower. *British Art and the Mediterranean.* Oxford: Oxford University Press, 1948.

Saxton, Christopher. *An Atlas of England and Wales.* London: Christopher Saxton, 1579.

Schlesinger, Arthur. *The Colonial Merchants and American Revolution.* New York: Frederick Ungar [1918], 1957.

Schofield, Robert. "The Industrial Orientation of Science in the Lunar Society of Birmingham." In A. E. Musson, *Science, Technology, and Economic Growth.* London: Methuen, 1972.

Schumpeter, Joseph. *History of Economic Analysis.* New York: Oxford University Press [1954], 1966.

Scoville, Warren. *The Persecution of the Huguenots and French Economic Development, 1680–1720.* Berkeley: University of California Press, 1960.

Sennett, Richard. *The Fall of Public Man.* New York: Vintage, 1978.

Shapiro, Barbara. "Latitudinarianism and Science in Seventeenth-Century England." In C. Webster, *The Intellectual Revolution of the Seventeenth Century.* London: Routledge [1958], 1974.

Simmel, Georg. *The Philosophy of Money.* London: Routledge and Kegan Paul [1900], 1978.

Skelton, R. A. "Bishop Leslie's Maps of Scotland, 1578." *Imago Mundi* (1950), 7:103–6.

———. *County Atlases of the British Isles, 1579–1850.* London: Carta, 1970.

———. *Maps.* Chicago: University of Chicago Press, 1972.

Slater, Phillip. *Earthwalk.* New York: Anchor, 1974.

Slive, Seymour. "Notes on the Relationship of Protestantism to Seventeenth-Century Dutch Painting." In James Ackerman et al., *Seventeenth-Century Art in Flanders and Holland.* New York: Garland, 1976.

Smelser, Neil. *Social Change in the Industrial Revolution.* Chicago: University of Chicago Press, 1959.

Smith, Cyril Stanley, and R. J. Forbes. "Metallurgy and Assaying." In Charles Singer et al., *A History of Technology.* New York: Oxford University Press, 1957.

Smith, John. *A Sea Grammar.* London: John Haviland, 1627.

Smith, Thomas. "Manuscript and Printed Sea Charts in Seventeenth-Century London." In Norman Thrower, *The Compleat Plattmaker.* Berkeley: University of California Press, 1979.

Sombart, Werner. *Luxury and Capitalism.* Ann Arbor: University of Michigan [1913], 1967.

Stanley, Robert, and Charles Steinberg. *The Media Environment.* New York: Hastings House, 1976.

Steinberg, H. *Five Hundred Years of Printing.* New York: Criterion, 1959.

Stephens, A. E. "The Booke of the Sea Carte." *Imago Mundi* (1938), 2:55–59.

Stone, Lawrence. *Family and Fortune.* Oxford: Clarendon Press, 1973.

—— *The Crisis of the Aristocracy.* London: Oxford University Press, 1965.

Strong, Roy. *The Renaissance Garden in England.* London: Thames and Hudson, 1979.

Supple, Barry. *Commercial Crisis and Change in England, 1600–1642.* Cambridge: Cambridge University Press, 1964.

Tapie, Victor. *The Age of Grandeur.* New York: Praeger, 1966.

Taylor, E. G. R. "Cartography, Survey, and Navigation, 1400–1750." In Charles Singer et al., *A History of Technology.* New York: Oxford University Press, 1957.

—— *The Haven-Finding Art.* New York: Elsevier, 1971.

—— *Late Tudor and Early Stuart Geography.* New York: Octagon [1934], 1968.

Tebbel, J. *The Media in America.* New York: New American Library, 1974.

Thirsk, Joan. *Economic Policy and Projects.* Oxford: Clarendon Press, 1978.

—— *The Restoration.* London: Longman's, 1976.

Thirsk, Joan, and J. P. Cooper. *Seventeenth-Century Economic Documents.* Oxford: Clarendon Press, 1972.

Thomas, P. J. *Mercantilism and the East India Trade.* London: Frank Cass [1926], 1963.

Thompson, E. P. "The Moral Economy of the English Crowd in the Eighteenth Century." *Past and Present* (1971), 50:77–136.

—— *The Making of the English Working Class.* New York: Vintage, 1963.

Thompson, James W. *The Frankfort Book Fair.* New York: Burt Franklin [1911], 1968.

Thornton, Peter. *Seventeenth-Century Interior Decoration in England, France, and Holland.* New Haven: Yale University Press, 1978.

Thrower, Norman H. *The Compleat Plattmaker.* Berkeley: University of California Press, 1979.

—— *Maps and Man.* Englewood Cliffs, N. J.: Prentice-Hall, 1972.

Tilly, Charles. *The Formation of National States in Western Europe.* Princeton: Princeton University Press, 1975.

Tomlin, Maurice. *English Furniture.* London: Farber and Farber, 1972.

Tooley, R. V. "Maps in Italian Atlases of the Sixteenth Century." *Imago Mundi* (1939), 3:12–14.

—— *Maps and Map-Makers.* New York: Crown [1949], 1978.

Tuma, Elias. *European Economic History.* New York: Harper and Row, 1971.

Turnbull, Geoffrey. *A History of the Calico Printing Industry of Great Britain.* Altrincham, England: John Sherrat and Son, 1951.

Tyler, John. "Technological Development: Agent of Change in Style and Form of Domestic Iron Castings." In Ian Quimby and Polly Earl, *Technological In-*

novation and the Decorative Arts. Charlottesville: University Press of Virginia, 1974, pp. 141–65.

Unwin, George. *Studies in Economic History.* New York: Augustus M. Kelley [1927], 1966.

Valentiner, Wilhelm. "Rembrandt and the Latin School." In James Ackerman et al., *Seventeenth-Century Art in Flanders and Holland.* New York: Garland, 1976.

Van Gelder, Jan G. "Two Aspects of the Dutch Baroque." In James Ackerman et al., *Seventeenth-Century Art in Flanders and Holland.* New York: Garland, 1976.

Vasari, Giorgio. *Lives of Artists,* trans. George Bull. London: Penguin [1568], 1977.

Veblen, Thorstein. *The Theory of the Leisure Class.* New York: Mentor Books [1899], 1953.

Vecellio, Cesare. *Vecellio's Renaissance Costume Book.* New York: Dover [1598], 1977.

Verner, Coolie. "John Seller and the Chart Trade in Seventeenth-Century England." In N. Thrower, *The Compleat Plattmaker.* Berkeley: University of California Press, 1979.

Vincent, John M. *Costume and Conduct in the Laws of Basel, Bern, and Zurich, 1370–1800.* Baltimore: Johns Hopkins University Press, 1935.

Von Martin, Alfred. *Sociology of the Renaissance.* New York: Oxford University Press, 1944.

Wadsworth, A. P., and Julia Mann. *The Cotton Trade and Industrial Lancashire, 1600–1780.* Manchester: Manchester University Press [1931], 1965.

Wallerstein, Immanuel. *The Modern World-System.* London: Academic Press, 1976.

Wallis, Helen M. "Geography Is Better than Divinitie." In N. Thrower, *The Compleat Plattmaker.* Berkeley: University of California Press, 1979.

Walzer, Michael. *Revolution of the Saints.* Cambridge, Mass.: Harvard University Press, 1965.

Waters, D. W. *The Art of Navigation.* New Haven: Yale University Press, 1958.

Weber, Max. *The Protestant Ethic and the Spirit of Capitalism.* New York: Scribner's [1904–5], 1958.

———. *General Economic History,* trans. F. Knight. New York: Collier Books [1920], 1961.

Webster, Charles. *The Great Instauration.* New York: Holmes and Meier, 1976.

———. *The Intellectual Revolution of the Seventeenth Century.* London: Routledge and Kegan Paul [1958], 1974.

White, Lynn, Jr. "The Iconography of *Temperantia* and the Virtuousness of Technology." In White, *Medieval Religion and Technology.* Berkeley: University of California Press [1969], 1978.

———. *Medieval Technology and Social Change.* New York: Oxford University Press, 1962.

Whitney, Geffrey. *A Choice of Emblemes and Other Deuises.* Leiden: Plantyn, 1586.

Whitteridge, Gweneth. *William Harvey.* New York: Elsevier, 1971.

Williams, Raymond. *Keywords.* New York: Oxford University Press, 1976.

Wilson, Charles. *The Dutch Republic.* New York: McGraw-Hill, 1968.

——— "The Entrepreneur." In S. Lieberman, *Europe and the Industrial Revolution.* Cambridge: Schenckman, 1972.

Woodfield, Denis B. *Surreptitious Printing in England, 1550–1640.* New York: Bibliographic Society of America, 1973.

Wright, Richardson. *The Story of Gardening.* New York: Dover, 1934.

Zigrosser, Carl. *The Book of Fine Prints.* New York: Crown, 1937.

Index

English, 111
portolan, 86–87, 89, 91, 103, 123, 277–78n3
Portuguese, 86, 91–92, 98–99, 106, 112
printed, 83–84, 94, 97, 104–5
Spanish, 96, 98–99, 106
see also Geography
Checks, 208, 221; see also Cloth
Chiavez, Alonso de, 95
Chinese printing, 141–42
Chlorine, 231
Chronicles, 21, 83, 90–91, 95, 97–98, 108–9, 112, 119
Cipolla, Carlo, 14, 86, 206
Civil war, English, 125
Class, 12, 19, 30–31, 47, 53, 60, 118, 144, 177–78, 12, 185, 192, 196, 207, 227, 235, 238, 241, 244, 250, 257
Classical heritage, 7, 17, 27, 55, 67–70, 99, 101, 149, 151, 156, 161, 179; see also Great Tradition
Cleve, Duke of, 106
Clock, 11, 31, 35, 213, 252
Clockwork, 134, 156, 163, 285–86n12
Closed system, 136, 139–40, 146, 156, 163, 197, 244
Cloth:
fashion, see Fashion, and cloth
finishing, 169, 209, 212, 218, 223–38, 231–33
imitations, 208–9
printing on, 20, 28, 194–96, 206, 211–12, 224–25, 229
production, 42, 196, 209–12, 217–18, 223–25, 235, 238
smuggling, 207
sumptuary legislation, 180–81
see also Broadcloth; Checks; Cotton; Fustian; Linen; Muslin; Silk; Stripes; Wool
Clothing, see Dress
Cloth trade:
London, 184, 188, 206, 234–38, 241
Manchester, 237–38, 242
Collectors, 31, 38, 43, 47, 50, 68, 132
Columbus, Christopher:
journal, 94, 98
letter, 94, 99, 101, 103
voyages, 92, 94–95
Commodity fetishism, 27, 247; see also Consumption, consumerism

Communication:
forms of, 66, 137, 139, 146
goods as media of, 11
revolution, 11–12, 142
Consumption:
conspicuous display, 3–7, 22, 24, 26, 31–37, 47, 68–69, 71, 167, 180, 182, 196, 241
consumer goods, 2–4, 6, 13–14, 16–17, 22, 31, 33, 37, 39–40, 67, 79–80, 107, 128, 130, 166, 219, 240, 242–43, 246, 254, 256
consumerism, 2–4, 22, 24, 26–9, 31, 37–40, 47, 65, 78, 167, 169, 243, 250, 257–58, 267n4, 269–70n17
hedonist, 4–6
increases in, 16, 33, 42, 165
mass, 1–2, 4, 32–33, 38–42, 50–60, 262n3, 267n4, 270–71n26
as a social form, x, 1–8, 18, 20–26, 30–31, 47, 77, 132, 166, 176, 182–83, 207, 248, 254–55, 259, 269–70n17
Copernicus, 107, 155
Cosa, Juan de la, 95
Cosmopolitanism, 30–31, 38–39, 66–70, 73, 75–77, 172, 178–79, 182, 186, 188, 243, 247–48, 257–58
Costume, see Dress
Cotton:
fabrics, 185, 192, 194, 206–8, 210, 212, 222–23, 225
fashion for, see Fashion, for cotton
finishing, 169, 212, 223, 230–33
industry, 17, 19, 169–70, 209, 218, 221, 227, 230, 236, 238, 240–41, 245–49, 253
printed, 19–20, 169, 194, 206, 209
production, 212, 218, 220
technology, 20, 211, 218, 221, 227, 233, 238
thread, 196, 206, 208–9, 221–22
trade, 211, 218, 235–238, 253, 258
Council of Trent, 75
Crafts, see Projects; Skills, Craft
Creation:
revelation of, 19, 131, 133, 153, 156, 160
text of, 19, 131, 133, 153, 156, 160
Cresques, Abraham, 87
Crompton, Samuel, 223
Cromwell, Oliver, 127
Cunningham, William, 110

Febvre, Lucien, 25, 97–98, 102
Ferrera, Duke of, 92
Feuer, Lewis, 6–7, 150
Flanders:
 art, *see* Art, Flemish
 cartography, 99, 103–6, 122
 fabrics, 183–84, 205, 212, 225
 fashion, *see* Fashion, Flemish
 see also Burgundy
Flink, James, 267n4
Florence, 31–32
Fortrey, Samuel, 188
France:
 art, *see* Art, French
 censorship, 45, 143
 fashion, *see* Fashion, French
 mercantilism, 199
 metallurgy, 252
 power, 85, 249, 253
 printing, 44, 102–3, 110, 124
 Revolution, 235
 silk, 184, 188–90
 trade, 33, 170, 194, 203
Frankfurt, 8, 45, 102, 145, 287–88n40, 41
Frederick the Wise, 62
Free trade, 179, 199–200, 256, 258–59
Frobisher, Martin, 110
Fustian, 185, 207–8, 221–23; *see also* Linen

Galileo, 134–35, 153, 156, 159
Garcie, Pierre, 111
Gardens, 1, 5–6, 23, 74–75
Genre painting, 7, 58, 70–72
Geography:
 economic value of, 81–82, 84, 91, 97,
  101, 130, 254
 European, 81, 117–28, 277–78n3
 expansion and, 81–92, 94–101, 104–14,
  116, 130
 printing, 611, 82, 85, 96, 102–3, 123,
  145, 224
 publication of, 18, 81–83, 85, 89, 92, 97–
  99, 101–8, 111–12, 114, 116, 130
 secrecy, 94–97
Geyle, Pieter, 263n, 276–77n81
Gilbert, William, 164
Gilboy, Elizabeth, 247
God's word, 134, 146–47, 153, 161, 163

God's works, 147, 149, 153–54, 158–59,
 161
Goos, Pieter, 111
Gouldner, Alvin, 137, 139–40, 142, 147,
 163, 257
Great Tradition, 23–25, 36, 47, 50, 67–68,
 179; *see also* Classical heritage,
Grinville, Richard, 95
Guilds 34, 39–46, 60–1, 213, 216, 257; *see
 also* Artisans,
Gutenberg, Johann, 145

Habsburg empire, 71–72, 83, 85, 96, 107,
 116, 119, 122, 171
Hakluyt, Richard, 83, 109, 111
Halley, Edmund, 86, 116
Hargreaves, James, 221
Hartlib, Samuel, 154, 160
Harvey, William, 156, 158–59
Hechter, Michael, 118
Hedonism, 1–4, 6–7, 150, 166
Henry the Navigator, 86–87, 89–92, 98
Henry VIII England, 109, 175
Henry, Thomas, 228
Herbert, Thomas, 108
Hindman, Sandra, 271n26
Hoarding:
 information, 99, 254
 wealth, 3–4, 78, 254, 256
Hodgson, Marshall, 25–26
Hollar, Wenceslaus, 120
Holton, Gerald, 134–35, 153, 156, 162
Home, Francis, 230
Hondius, Jodocus, 106–7
Houses, x, 1, 3–6, 31, 36–37, 71, 73, 130,
 154, 189, 194, 208–9, 222, 236, 241,
 243, 250–51, 260
Humanists, 47–48, 57, 64, 76, 99, 133, 135,
 151, 276n75
Iberians, 18, 81–82, 85, 87, 91, 97, 100–7,
 112, 122; *see also* Portugal; Spain
Ideology, 2–3, 7, 15, 21, 75, 79, 89–90, 117,
 128, 135, 150, 179, 204
Illustration, 28, 38–39, 45, 50, 54–58, 61,
 66–67, 74, 101, 108, 112, 137, 142
Imagery:
 geographical, 89, 97, 100–1, 117, 119,
  122, 128

Marx, Karl, 27, 32, 247, 264*n*17
Marxists, 247
Mary, II (England), 194
Mary Queen of Scots, 119
Mass culture, 8, 17, 38–41, 46–47, 51, 57–
    58, 60, 65, 242, 262*n*3, 270–71*n*26
Master of the Power of Women, 50
Materialism:
    cultural, x, xi, 7–9, 14–17, 19–22, 24–28,
        37, 39, 131–36, 143, 152, 163–64,
        167, 169, 241–45, 247–48, 251, 254–
        56, 259–61, 262*n*3
    economic, 132, 176, 198, 209–10
    scientific, 19, 22, 132–34, 136, 152, 156,
        160, 163, 165, 214
    technical, 19, 22, 97, 210–11
    see also Calculation; Consumersim; Inno-
        vation
Measurement, 15, 48, 108, 124, 126–28,
    132, 163
Medici, Lorenzo de', 101
Medieval culture; *see* Middle Ages
Mercantilism, 19, 164, 169, 196–205, 208,
    210, 251–53, 258–59
Mercator, Gerhard, 104–7, 110
Merton, Robert, 6–7, 150, 286*n*15
Middle Ages, 16, 26–27, 30, 33
    clothing, 170, 176–77, 179–82, 211, 257
    culture, 26, 33–39, 44, 47, 61, 70, 75, 78,
        82, 91, 139, 148, 162, 164, 170, 189,
        213, 216–17, 219, 254–55, 257
    geography, 87, 89, 103, 123
    imagery, 33–34, 43, 50, 53, 57–58, 64,
        256; *see also* Art Gothic
Monopoly:
    information, 18, 82, 85, 87, 91, 97–98,
        217
    trade, 41, 43, 71, 76, 201, 205, 254
Mordants, 195, 212, 229–30, 232–33
Morveau, Guyston de, 231
Moxon, Joseph, 111
Mughal empire, 50, 221, 223
Mun, Thomas, 196, 199–201
Muslin, 207, 223–26, 238
Musper, H. T., 62
Musson, A. E., 228

Naturalism, 47–48, 50, 57–58, 64, 158
Navigation, 82–83, 91, 95, 105, 107–12,
    114, 116, 127–28, 213–14, 217

Navigation Acts, 202, 204
Navigators, 82–83, 96, 105, 108, 111–12,
    116, 164
Nef, John, 26, 166–67
Netherlands:
    art, *see* Art, Dutch
    economy, 199–204, 249–52
    expansion, 112–16
    fashion, *see* Fashion, Dutch
    geographical publishing, 111–12, 114,
        116
    independence, 85, 200
    and the Inquisition, 45
    manufactures, 20, 111, 202, 205, 217,
        232, 251–52
    publishing, 72–73, 82, 102, 107, 111–12,
        114, 116, 148
    revolt of, 85, 106
    seat of Habsburg empire, 62, 85, 96,
        103–4
    tulips from, 71
Newton, Sir Isaac, 139, 153, 155, 158–60
New World, 20–21, 85, 96, 103–4
Norden, John, 119–23, 126, 215
Nuremberg, 61–62

Observation, 89, 95, 133, 135–37, 140, 146,
    151, 156, 160, 215
Ong, Walter, 25, 137, 139–40, 146–47, 257
Ortelius, Abraham, 104–7
Owen, George, 120

Padron Real, 96
Paesi collection, 94–95, 99, 101, 103
Panofsky, Irwin, 23
Parry, J. H., 112
Patterson, R., 229
Paul, Lewis, 220, 222
Peacham, Henry, 32, 107, 176
Peel, Robert, 235–36
Perkin, Harold, 247–49
Petty, Sir William, 127–28, 155, 161, 163
Phillip the Bold, 170
Phillip II (Spain), 85, 122
"Philopatris," 202, 205
Plancius, Petrus, 107
Plantin, Christopher, 45, 73, 103–4
Pliny the Elder, 137
Polanyi, Karl, 8, 25, 33, 211, 256
Polo, Marco, 87, 90

328   Index

Pope, Alexander, 194
Popkin, Samuel, 8, 41
Portolans, see Charts, portolan
Portugal:
   expansion, 84–87, 107, 109, 112, 114, 117
   geographical information, 86–87, 89, 91–
      97, 99, 103, 106, 112, 114, 116, 122–
      23, 130, 203, 255
Pottery, 1, 248–50
Prester, John, 90–91
Printing:
   and culture, 12, 16–17, 20, 25, 28–29, 38,
      41, 44–45, 50, 53, 57, 76–77, 94, 96–
      99, 101–3, 123, 135–45, 149, 245,
      249, 254, 257, 273n36, 278n4; see
      also Publishing
   fabric printing, 195, 208–9, 211–12, 224–
      25, 229, 232–33, 236
   pressure printing, 225
Prints, 16–18, 28, 30–31, 37–39, 46, 48, 50–
   51, 53–55, 57–60, 62, 64–68, 70, 73,
   75, 136, 146, 190, 219, 255–57, 270–71
   n65, 275n67, 275–76n73, 276–77n81
Privileges, 41, 76–77, 147
Projects, 40–41, 44, 46, 66, 69, 86, 117–8,
   128, 166, 185
Protestants:
   consumption, 3, 4, 7
   culture, 7, 19, 70–71, 73, 134
   entrepreneurialism, 3, 7, 131–32, 261
   ethic, 2, 7, 13, 40, 79, 131–34
   and print, 142–48
   scholarship, 19, 131–33, 135, 143–44,
      147–52, 161, 163, 197, 290n62
Ptolemy, 89, 92, 99, 100–101, 103–4, 134
   Geographica, 99–100
Publishing, 42, 44–45, 67, 72, 76–77, 99–
   103, 106–8, 111, 132, 141–42, 144–45,
   148, 278n4, 284n3; see also Printing
Publishing houses, 67, 101–3

Rational calculation, see Calculation, rational
Reformation, 3, 45, 70, 73, 75–76, 125, 132,
   134–35, 142–43, 146, 148, 150, 152,
   214
Regional culture, 11–12, 18, 31, 35–36, 66–
   71, 75–76, 170, 178–79, 241, 244, 248,
   266n2

Regional maps, 81, 117–18, 210–21, 123–24
Regional trade, 167, 199, 241
Rembrandt, 73
Renaissance, 1, 3, 30, 33, 40, 48, 50, 53, 57,
   62, 64, 68, 78, 132–33, 139, 166, 179,
   256; see also Art
Ribbons, 5, 31, 41, 217, 243
Ribeiro, Diogo, 96
Roads, 11, 16, 40, 65, 67, 70, 76, 121, 123–
   24, 260
Roberts Lewis, 192
Robinson, Eric, 228
Robinson, Henry, 203
Roebuck, John, 230
Roselli maps, 103
Rostow, W. W., 246–47
Rubens, Peter Paul, 67–68, 275–76n73

Sahlins, Marshall, x, 8, 11–2, 25–7, 33,
   264n17, 269–70n17
Saxton, Christopher, 119–23
Scheele, Carl, 231
Schongauer, Martin, 48, 50, 61
Schumpeter, Joseph, 291n74
Scientific societies, 152, 215, 228
Seckford, Thomas, 119
Secrecy, 82, 91–92, 94–96, 99, 116, 123,
   212, 217, 228, 255
Seller, John, 116
Shapiro, Barbara, 149
Silks, 1, 19, 166, 171, 180–81, 184–85, 188–
   90, 192, 194, 197, 199, 205–8, 212,
   216, 218, 220, 225
Simmel, Georg, xi, 27–28
Skills, craft, 1, 42, 44, 46, 48, 51, 59, 61,
   64, 70, 91, 104, 118, 122, 114, 185,
   206, 209–11, 213, 215–16, 224–25, 227,
   233–34, 259
Smelser, Neil, 245
Smith, Joseph, 236
Soda, 231
Sombart, Werner, 26–27
Spain
   fashion, see Fashion, Spanish
   and geography, 84–85, 92, 94–97, 99,
      103, 106–7, 110, 114, 122–23
   power, 85, 92, 94–97, 103, 106–7, 110,
      114, 117

DATE DUE